RENEWALS 458-457

DATE DUE

GAYLORD			PRINTED IN U.S.A.

THE MUSIC OF HUGH WOOD

To Lois

The Music of Hugh Wood

EDWARD VENN
Lancaster University, UK

ASHGATE

Published by
Ashgate Publishing Limited
Gower House
Croft Road
Aldershot
Hampshire GU11 3HR
England

Ashgate Publishing Company
Suite 420
101 Cherry Street
Burlington, VT 05401-4405
USA

Ashgate website: http://www.ashgate.com

British Library Cataloguing in Publication Data
Venn, Edward
   The music of Hugh Wood
   1. Wood, Hugh – Criticism and interpretation
   I. Title
   780.9'2

Library of Congress Cataloging-in-Publication Data
Venn, Edward, 1974–
   The music of Hugh Wood / Edward Venn.
      p. cm.
   Includes bibliographical references (p.   ), discography (p.   ), and index.
   ISBN 978-0-7546-5029-4 (alk. paper)
   1. Wood, Hugh—Criticism and interpretation. 2. Music—20th century—History and criticism. I. Title.
   ML410.W855V46 2007
   780.92—dc22

2007029824

ISBN 978-0-7546-5029-4

Bach musicological font developed by © Yo Tomita.

Printed and bound in Great Britain by TJ International Ltd, Padstow, Cornwall.

Contents

List of Tables

List of Music Examples

All music examples are in C. Editorial accidentals are in square brackets [♭]; all other accidentals are original. Superscript numbers after rehearsal marks refer to the number of bars before or after the rehearsal mark: 40^{+4} means 'four bars after rehearsal mark 40'; 42^{-3} means 'three bars before rehearsal mark 42'.

Preface

The story goes that upon Andrew Davis's appointment as Chief Conductor of the BBC Symphony Orchestra in 1989, he stated that one of his aims would be 'to do something about Hugh Wood'.[1] At that time, Wood had some thirty scores to his name, with a reputation for composing music that is lyrical, passionate, densely argued and expressively intense. In 1977, he was appointed lecturer in music at Cambridge University, and was (and remains) well known as a broadcaster and writer. What, then, did Andrew Davis feel was to be done? A long-time admirer of Wood's music, Davis was doubtless referring to the scarcity of that music in orchestral programmes throughout the country during the late 1970s and 1980s. Quite simply, for a composer of Wood's stature, the neglect of his music was inexplicable.

The first half of the 1990s saw an upturn in Wood's fortunes. In January 1990, Wood was one of the featured composers in the Park Lane Group's Young Artist series; later that year Andrew Davis and the BBC Symphony Orchestra revived *Scenes from Comus*, the work with which Wood made his name at the 1965 Proms. The following year, Davis conducted what was only the third performance of Wood's magisterial Symphony (1974–82), and then gave with Joanna MacGregor the premiere of Wood's Piano Concerto Op. 32, one of the highlights of the 1991 Proms season. In 1993 Tasmin Little and the BBC Philharmonic gave the first performance in twenty years of Wood's Violin Concerto (1970–72), and Collins Classics released a recording of the Piano Concerto. 1993 also saw the Chilingirian Quartet give the first performance of Wood's Fourth String Quartet Op. 34; two years later, the Chilingirians released a recording of all four of Wood's numbered quartets, reflecting his major contribution to this genre. But by the middle of the decade, there was a steady drop in momentum; the European premiere at the Last Night of the Proms of Wood's *Variations* Op. 39 notwithstanding, the frequency of performances of Wood's music was steadily decreasing.

Few contemporary composers can lay claim to continued success; the story of Wood's music in the 1990s is by no means exceptional in this respect. But the growth and decline of Wood's representation in concert programmes in these years took place against a background of consistently favourable press notices. By the end of the decade, Wood's status was such that reviewers could confidently draw on a limited repertoire of positive descriptions without fear of contradiction. Thus we find phrases such as 'this most thoughtful of composers',[2] 'one of our most craftsmanly composers',[3] and 'one of our most distinguished composers'[4] appearing with predictable regularity. The adjectives are well meant, but ultimately their blandness – forced, no doubt, by the pressures of deadlines and word limits – show a refusal to

---

[1]   Michael White, 'In from the cold', *The Independent* (8 September 1991).
[2]   Geoff Brown, 'Thorns on the Lark', *The Times* (10 February 1999).
[3]   Paul Driver, 'Uncool, Britannia', *Sunday Times* (20 September 1998).
[4]   Paul Driver, 'On Record', *Sunday Times* (21 October 2001).

engage with Wood's music; it is regarded as self-evident that he is a composer that demands our respect. In this light one could interpret Stephen Pettitt's description of Wood as a 'grossly underrated composer' – written at a time when Wood's music was enjoying a comparatively high profile in concert halls – as a comment that is aimed less at the general opinion of Wood's music (which was mostly positive), but rather the uncritical manner in which this opinion was formed.[5]

We are coming to the nub of what I term the 'Hugh Wood problem'. It is true that Wood's music has never been modish. When his peers in the 1960s were exploring serial modality, transformation techniques and ritual drama, Wood was honing his lyrical expressiveness and frankly Romantic impulses in works such as *Scenes from Comus* and the Cello Concerto. When the pendulum of musical fashion swung back to the simplistic and the overtly tonal, Wood continued to challenge his audiences with densely wrought counterpoint knitted together with rigorous motivic, and sometimes twelve-note, working. Nevertheless, Wood's music has enjoyed a certain amount of success over the last four decades, but it remains 'grossly underrated' – that is, it suffers from a lack of critical engagement.

Writing in 1993 of music by Wood and his Cambridge colleague Alexander Goehr, David Fanning touched on this problem, noting

> how historical they now seem, how distant in their earnest complexities from the values of today's musical scene, which may of course be precisely their strength, if you take the view that most recent contemporary music has sold its soul to commercialism. And I wouldn't for a moment deny that there is beauty and deep feeling in them. Still, I do wonder if such works aren't destined to be more respected than loved.[6]

The respect that Fanning mentions looms large in the reviews cited above, and suddenly we might wonder if 'thoughtful', 'craftsmanly' and 'distinguished' are euphemisms for 'distant from the values of today's musical scene'. Returning to the reviews, our suspicions are confirmed: Wood's music uses 'old-fashioned 12-tone technique with incandescent sincerity';[7] it is written in a 'lean, post 12-tone, conservative idiom';[8] and, elsewhere, we find its 'post-Schoenbergian idiom ... seems particularly old-fashioned'.[9] Despite favourable reviews, Wood's output is considered well-meaning but irrelevant to the concerns of our time. What these concerns are, and why this should be, have never been stated clearly: critics seem unable to see the Wood for the trees.

The Hugh Wood problem, then, is how one is to engage critically with a substantial body of music that, for all its passion and conviction, remains on the margins of the contemporary canon for largely political reasons. Thus when describing Wood as 'one of the most unjustly neglected of contemporary British composers', Michael Kennedy ventured that this was 'perhaps because he has remained loyal

---

5   Stephen Pettitt, 'Thrills from the Punch and Judy man', *The Times* (26 June 1993).
6   David Fanning, 'Such Distant Memories', *The Independent* (6 March 1993).
7   Driver, 'On Record'.
8   Driver, 'Uncool Britannia'.
9   Gerald Larner, 'Reviews', *The Times* (20 July 1999).

to Schoenbergian precepts'.[10] That is, Wood's neglect stems not from low quality, but rather his adherence to 'old-fashioned' values. But one should be wary also of special pleading on behalf of the Unjustly Neglected, a sizeable body of composers that surely by now outnumbers the Justly Acknowledged (along with the Bafflingly Popular) by a large factor. In speaking of Frank Bridge, Wood noted that a neglected composer

> may well be rehabilitated for the wrong reasons. The tendency is for his virtues to be overpraised since they were lacking in those who neglected him; the reasons for neglect to be extrapolated to form a critique of the musical society. The composer himself becomes a symbol. But that doesn't necessarily mean he's a very good composer.[11]

I believe that there is more than a grain of truth in the suggestion that Wood's neglect is in part due to the musical values he espouses. And I also believe that a musical society in which these values are marginalized is somewhat the poorer as a result. But there is space within any society for different belief and value systems to co-exist, and it should become clear from the content of this book that Wood's music, and the values it embodies, is of a vitality that is deserving of a more central position in our understanding of contemporary music. And by this, I mean to say that he is to be considered at the very least a good composer; it is my hope that what follows will suffice as an introduction to a body of work that for too long has remained in the shadows.

EDWARD VENN
Crag Bank, Lancashire
January 2007

---

[10] Michael Kennedy, 'Classical CDs', *Sunday Telegraph* (28 October 2001).
[11] Hugh Wood, 'Frank Bridge and the Land Without Music', *Tempo* 121 (1977): 7–11 (p. 8).

Acknowledgements

The distant origin of this book can be traced to 1993, to a performance of Wood's Violin Concerto that I attended whilst studying for my A-levels. My teacher at that time, William Moss, was a constant source of inspiration and encouragement, fuelling my enthusiasm for contemporary music; our shared positive reaction to the concerto lodged both Wood's name and the memory of his music into my mind. Some years later, when discussing with Stephen Banfield potential topics for an MA dissertation at the University of Birmingham, Wood's name cropped up, and a research project was born. This gave rise initially to a survey of Wood's first four string quartets; the following year I began a Ph.D. on Wood's entire output (2001), which was subsequently re-written completely to form the present work.

My initial research into Wood's music was aided greatly by a grant awarded by the Bishop Laney's Trust to purchase scores in 1997; this was followed by bursaries from the University of Birmingham and a grant from what was then the Arts and Humanities Research Board (AHRB). I owe a debt of gratitude to Stephen Banfield, the Supervisor of both by MA and Ph.D., for all of his support and advice during these years.

I offer my sincere thanks to the staff at Ashgate, and in particular Heidi May and Anne Keirby, who have waited patiently through successive delays for me to submit the manuscript. The eventual completion of the book was aided greatly by two four-month sabbaticals granted to me by Lancaster University and a small grant from Practice and Theory: Research in Composition Research Centre (PATRIC); I am grateful too for the continued support and understanding of my colleagues. To my wife Lois, who read through multiple drafts of the book offering insightful criticism, and who supported me with superhuman reserves of tolerance, patience and love, I owe an immense debt.

Some of the material in Chapters 2, 8 and 9 first appeared in *Tempo* magazine, Vol. 59 no. 231 (January 2005) and Vol. 59 no. 233 (July 2005); I am grateful for the editorial advice offered to me by Malcolm MacDonald.

Finally, I must express my gratitude to Hugh Wood, who over the years has generously shared with me his time, scores and sketches. Most recently, he has read meticulously numerous drafts of my chapters, correcting factual errors and offering countless valuable, if at times painfully direct, suggestions as to how the expression might be clarified; his advice has improved this book greatly. Wood deliberately refrained from commenting on the content, however; this remains my own, for better or worse.

I acknowledge with gratitude the permission given by publishers for the reproduction of extracts from the following works:

Chamber Concerto Op. 15: Music by Hugh Wood © Copyright 1981 Chester Music Limited. All Rights Reserved. International Copyright Secured. Reprinted by Permission.

Violin Concerto Op. 17: Music by Hugh Wood © Copyright 1975 Chester Music Limited. All Rights Reserved. International Copyright Secured. Reprinted by Permission.

Robert Graves Songs Set I Op. 18: Music by Hugh Wood © Copyright 1987 Chester Music Limited. All Rights Reserved. International Copyright Secured. Reprinted by Permission. Words by Robert Graves taken from *Complete Poems in One Volume*, reproduced by kind permission of Carcanet Press, Manchester.

Song Cycle to Poems by Pablo Neruda Op. 19: Music by Hugh Wood © Copyright 1974 Chester Music Limited. All Rights Reserved. International Copyright Secured. Reprinted by Permission. Words by Christopher Logue taken from *Wand and Quadrant* (1953), reproduced by kind permission of David Godwin Associates.

String Quartet No. 3 Op. 20: Music by Hugh Wood © Copyright 1980 Chester Music Limited. All Rights Reserved. International Copyright Secured. Reprinted by Permission.

Symphony Op. 21: Music by Hugh Wood © Copyright 1991 Chester Music Limited. All Rights Reserved. International Copyright Secured. Reprinted by Permission.

Robert Graves Songs Set II Op. 22: Music by Hugh Wood © Copyright 1986 Chester Music Limited. All Rights Reserved. International Copyright Secured. Reprinted by Permission. Words by Robert Graves taken from *Complete Poems in One Volume*, reproduced by kind permission of Carcanet Press, Manchester.

Piano Trio Op. 24: Music by Hugh Wood © Copyright 1984 Chester Music Limited. All Rights Reserved. International Copyright Secured. Reprinted by Permission.

Horn Trio Op. 29: Music by Hugh Wood © Copyright 1992 Chester Music Limited. All Rights Reserved. International Copyright Secured. Reprinted by Permission.

Cantata Op. 30: Music by Hugh Wood, Words by D.H. Lawrence © Copyright 1995 Chester Music Limited. All Rights Reserved. International Copyright Secured. Reprinted by Permission.

Marina Op. 31: Music by Hugh Wood © Copyright 1994 Chester Music Limited. All Rights Reserved. International Copyright Secured. Reprinted by Permission. Excerpts from "Marina" from *Collected Poems* 1909–1962 by T.S. Eliot, copyright 1936 by Harcourt, Inc., and renewed 1964 by T.S. Eliot, reprinted by permission of the publisher (USA). Words by T.S. Eliot taken from *Selected Poems* (1961), reproduced by kind permission of Faber and Faber (rest of world).

List of Abbreviations

anon.	anonymous
ARCM	Associate of the Royal College of Music
b.	born
BBC	British Broadcasting Corporation
B.Mus.	Batchelor of Music
c	*circa*, about
CD	compact disc
cf.	*confer*, 'compare'
d.	doubling
ed., eds	editor, editors
edn	edition
ff.	following pages
ibid.	*ibidem*, 'in the same place'
mins	minutes
ms.	manuscript
n.	footnote
no., nos.	number, numbers
Op., Opp.,	opus, opera
Op. 21/iv	Opus 21, fourth movement
p., pp.	page, pages
Proms	BBC Promenade Concerts
RCM	Royal College of Music
SPNM	Society for the Promotion of New Music
rev.	revised
trans.	translator, translated by
vol.	volume
WoO	without Opus
orch.	orchestra
str.	strings
d.b.	double bass
hp	harp
pizz.	pizzicato
sord.	sordini
vla	viola
vlc.	violoncello
vln	violin
wind	woodwind
a.fl.	alto flute

b.cl.	bass clarinet
bn	bassoon
cbn	contrabassoon
cl.	clarinet
cor ang.	cor anglais
fl.	flute
ob.	oboe
picc.	piccolo
br.	brass
hn	horn
tba	tuba
tbn	trombone
tpt	trumpet
perc.	percussion
ant.cymb.	antique cymbals
b.dr.	bass drum
bong.	bongo
cast.	castanets
cel.	celesta
cl.cymb.	clashed cymbals
crot.	crotales
cymb.	crash cymbals
glsp.	glockenspiel
mar.	marimba
pno	piano
s.dr.	snare drum
susp.cymb.	suspended cymbals
t.bl.	temple block
t.dr.	tenor drum
timb.	timbales
timp.	timpani
tr.	triangle
t.t.	tom-tom
w.bl.	wood block
xyl.	xylophone
sop.	soprano
ten.	tenor

Chapter 1

Early Years

No history of twentieth-century British music is complete without an account of the group of musicians based in Manchester that came to maturity in the latter half of the 1950s. The most prominent composers of this group, Alexander Goehr (b. 1932), Peter Maxwell Davies (b. 1934) and Harrison Birtwistle (b. 1934), were unusual in their interest in both modern European trends (including Schoenberg) and an awareness of pre-Classical methods of composition. The group was centred on Richard Hall's composition class at the Royal Manchester College of Music, and guided by Goehr's first-hand knowledge of contemporary continental music.[1] Concerts organized by the Manchester group caused ripples in the national press: the emergence of a group of young composers who could be said to form an avant-garde, who were acquainted with the latest developments on the continent, and who composed music with a decidedly internationalist flavour, was definitely newsworthy.

To identify the Royal Manchester College with 'the renewal of British music in the 1950s and beyond, and in particular with its harbouring of a generation of composers and performers who excitedly embraced modernism and the avant-garde' carries with it the danger of suppressing complementary histories and methods of musical renewal.[2] We should remain sensitive to the fact that the Manchester group were not alone in their explorations, for other composers of that generation were tentatively, if not blindly, feeling their way along similar routes. One such composer is Hugh Wood, who, at the age of twenty-three, was in the audience at the Manchester group's final London concert on 9 January 1956. Like Davies and Birtwistle, he was from the northwest of England; he too was familiar with, and responsive to, contemporary European trends.

The receptivity to, and more pertinently the musical conclusions that Wood draws from eclectic sources, prompted Michael Kennedy to write that '[t]he music of Hugh Wood exemplifies the finest and most fruitful aspects of the new British cosmopolitanism'.[3] But Wood's cosmopolitanism has always been significantly different to that of the composers of the Manchester group. In July 1959, *The Times* reported that in a post-concert discussion at the Cheltenham Festival, Maxwell Davies had come 'near to decrying the only really good work in the programme, a string quartet by Hugh Wood, merely because it was intelligible – it did not repudiate the past, nor protest, nor be perverse for perversity's sake. In fact, it was in the direct line

---

[1]   An account of the activities of the Royal Manchester School and Goehr's influence upon it can be found in 'The Manchester Years', in Alexander Goehr, *Finding the Key: Selected Writings of Alexander Goehr*, ed. D. Puffett (London and Boston, 1998), pp. 27–41.

[2]   Jonathan Cross, *Harrison Birtwistle: Man, Mind, Music* (London, 2000), p. 11.

[3]   Michael Kennedy, [Hugh Wood: Chester Music promotional brochure], 1991.

from Beethoven's Rasoumovsky quartets.'[4] The work in question was Wood's String Quartet in B♭, which shared a programme with the first performance of Harrison Birtwistle's *Refrains and Choruses* at a concert organized by the Society for the Promotion of New Music (SPNM). The context of the *Times* article suggests that Wood's particular blend of modernism with traditionalism may have been the cause of Maxwell Davies's criticism. Wood's quartet, whilst drawing on influences from recent national and international trends (Tippett, Bush, Bartók, Berg), did so in order to enrich and build upon Classical and Romantic traditions. Similar compositional instincts can be found in Wood's Variations for Viola, which had been premiered two days before in another SPNM concert, the first public performance of Wood's music. In the Variations, which had been composed after the B♭ quartet, the influence of the Second Viennese School (Schoenberg, Berg, and Webern) is keenly felt; indeed, the combination of this stimulus with Wood's existing thematicist instincts enabled Wood to develop his own compositional voice.

An overview of the musical experiences and education that culminated in Wood's Variations for Viola forms the basis of this chapter, shedding light on how a composer who studied neither at a music college nor in a university music department was by the end of the 1950s composing works that belonged to the vanguard of contemporary British music. This overview serves two purposes, the most important of which is to provide a background and context to the survey of Wood's music in the remaining chapters of this book. A study at the end of this chapter of Wood's writings about music fleshes out this background further. The second function is to provide a much-needed corrective to accounts of British music in the 1950s that focus primarily on the Manchester group. Wood's musical biography points to the richness and diversity of opportunities facing an aspiring composer in this period, and that the path trodden by the Manchester group was by no means the only way.

Formative Musical Experiences

Wood was born into a northern middle-class family on 27 June 1932 at Parbold, a village northwest of Wigan, Lancashire. Wood's mother had trained professionally as a pianist with Frank Merrick, but chose marriage and family life over a musical career. His father was a solicitor: he too played the piano, albeit domestically, and enjoyed a wide range of music.[5] Both were regular concertgoers. Wood's elder brother John, eight years his senior, played piano and trombone, and later the French horn; he continued to play the latter as an enthusiastic amateur during a successful career in economics.

---

[4]   *The Times* (13 July 1959). Many years later, Maxwell Davies was to identify Wood as a composer 'whom I've always admired tremendously'; see Roderic Dunnett, 'Sir Peter Maxwell Davies: On Her Majesty's Service', *The Independent* (15 March 2004).

[5]   Wood's father had a liking for melancholic music, including Brahms's *Alto Rhapsody*. This work also holds some significance for Hugh Wood: see his comments in 'A Photograph of Brahms', in Michael Musgrave (ed.), *The Cambridge Companion to Brahms* (Cambridge, 1999), pp. 268–87.

Wood was taught the piano, and later the violin, by local teachers. He took up the viola and also had organ lessons. There was family music-making: even an attempt at the Brahms Horn Trio with Wood's mother on piano, his brother on horn, and Wood himself on violin. Piano duets were often played: sometimes arrangements of Haydn symphonies with his father. An ample collection of gramophone records provided a further valuable source of musical experience, and expeditions were made to hear the Liverpool Philharmonic and Hallé orchestras. The family were all Gilbert and Sullivan lovers, *Iolanthe* remaining a particular favourite for Wood, and the popular music of the day was another enthusiasm. This was a fairly typical music-loving family of the time.

In the summer of 1940, Wood started boarding at the Huyton Hill Preparatory School, which had been evacuated from Liverpool to the Lake District. The arrival of a new teacher, C.V. Hales, who had been a member of the Dolmetsch circle, encouraged Wood's burgeoning interest in the music of J.S. Bach. Together with a school friend, Wood founded a Society for the Appreciation of Bach's Music, apparently innocent of such enthusiasm existing elsewhere. Bach's music also proved a creative catalyst, for it was during this time that Wood began to compose. These early efforts were no more ambitious than to experience the pleasure of putting notes down on a page, often in imitations of Bach's style.

Wood's elder brother led the way in wider musical exploration. Having discovered the music of William Walton, he introduced *Portsmouth Point* to his brother: together they collected the records of the Finale of Walton's First Symphony. There was equal enthusiasm for Hindemith's *Mathis der Maler* Symphony, and an interest in English music such as Delius, Vaughan Williams and Holst.

In 1945, Wood began boarding at Oundle School, a school already distinguished by its pioneering all-school performances of Bach's B minor Mass, and one which offered many other musical opportunities. With a school friend, Wood organized and participated in concerts given mainly by pupils; the last of these consisted of music by English composers from Purcell to Vaughan Williams. These endeavours are symptomatic of Wood's continued whole-hearted enthusiasm for music and music making. Nevertheless, his pursuit of varied interests as an active member of several school societies, and the necessity to concentrate on preparing for a scholarship exam that was to take him to New College, Oxford, to read history, distracted him from his musical efforts. Indeed, Wood wrote as much poetry during these years as music. Such diversions and distractions, doubtless necessary for Wood the man, with his myriad intellectual curiosities, were nevertheless unwelcome for Wood the musician; one senses, however, that the one cannot exist without the other.[6]

---

[6] Take, for example, Nicholas Kenyon's description of Wood, written in 1991. 'Wood stands in the middle of the road, waiting to let the electricity man into a neighbour's house, looking forward to exploring the newly available 1891 census. Whether he's into local secrets, or drawing up intricate maps of the Kappelmeisters before Bach in northern Germany for his teaching at Cambridge, it will take his mind off the next pressing compositional deadline – something, one senses, that he fears rather deeply' ('Scourge of the Nigel Tendency', *The Observer*, 8 September 1991).

Bryanston Summer School – Egypt – Oxford

In the summer holidays of 1948, Wood attended the first year of the Summer School of Music, then at Bryanston School in Dorset, and later relocated to Dartington Hall in Devon. The musical world he found there was a revelation. He decided that he must try to make a career in music during a recital of French piano music given by the pianist Monique Haas. Wood attended the composition classes of Alan Bush, of whose music he was to become a lifelong admirer. Bush offered friendly advice and support, not just regarding the composition that Wood had shown him, but also concerning Wood's ambitions in general.

William Glock directed the Summer School and presented a wider range of music old and new than was then customary for English audiences. Not without controversy, Glock brought in distinguished international musicians to teach some of the courses, and, as far as contemporary music went, 'the main accent both in lectures and concerts lay in reviewing some of the fundamental figures in the first half of the century, as they then appeared'.[7] These figures included Bartók, Hindemith and Stravinsky, but, two lectures from Erwin Stein apart, the Second Viennese School was not represented – it would be some years before Wood was to become acquainted with this repertoire.

National Service in 1950–51 relegated Wood's musical activities to second place. The chances of keeping up piano and violin practice were naturally very limited, as were the opportunities available for listening to music. One such occasion, a broadcast of the Brahms Violin Concerto listened to in a barrack room, remains a vivid memory.[8] He was eventually stationed at Suez in Egypt, in the final era of British occupation of the Canal Zone. Despite the outbreak of the Korean War, the possession of a University Release made it possible for Wood to return to England in autumn 1951, in time to take up his place at Oxford.

At Oxford, Wood spent much of his time making music in one way or another: he played viola in a very amateur string quartet, and in equally amateur student orchestras. He sang in the chorus for the Music Club operatic concert performances, and composed for various student ventures. In addition to his Modern History classes, Wood attended classes given by Thomas Armstrong and Egon Wellesz in the Music Faculty; he also sat in on classes in Modern Greek, his interest having been stimulated by his time in Egypt. Wood sought, and received, help from two musicians: Bernard Rose of Magdalen and H.K. Andrews, the organist of New College. Rose made useful comments and gave some general guidance: Andrews went much further by providing lessons in harmony, freely given. Despite this assistance, both men emphasized that Wood should continue with his History degree.

Just before Wood's final exams in May 1954, H.K. Andrews suggested that he should try for the Royal College of Music (RCM): an interview with Herbert Howells was duly arranged. This took place in October 1954, and was for Wood a complete disaster. Wood's compositional weaknesses were (quite fairly) laid bare, and his already uncertain self-confidence destroyed. Subsequent help was to come through

---

[7]　　William Glock, *Notes in Advance – an Autobiography in Music* (Oxford, 1991), p. 55.

[8]　　Wood, 'A Photograph of Brahms', p. 286.

a friend of his brother, the composer Joseph Horovitz, who arranged a meeting with William Lloyd Webber, a colleague of Howells at the RCM. It was a question of starting from the beginning: from Autumn 1954 to the New Year of 1956 Wood studied privately with Lloyd Webber, doing an enormous amount of elementary academic harmony and counterpoint, and passing the ARCM exam in December 1955.

Widening Horizons

Wood's attendance at the Dartington Summer School continued for many years; he believes that Dartington formed the single most important part of his musical education. At first working in the office, Wood later started to assist some of the teachers there, including Thea Musgrave and Lutosławski: later still he lectured on Berg's *Lyric Suite* and Messiaen's *Vingt Regards sur l'enfant Jesus*. It was at Dartington in 1955 that Wood heard Webern's music for the first time, when the Julliard Quartet performed Webern's Op. 5. But this was not quite Wood's first encounter with the Viennese composers: Leo Black, a friend from Oxford with whom he had kept in touch, introduced him not only to Bruckner and Mahler, but also to some of Schoenberg's earlier piano music: Op. 11 and Op. 19. The music of these composers increasingly interested Wood.

Wood began regular composition lessons with Iain Hamilton in April 1956. Writing after Hamilton's death in July 2000, Wood recalled that '[a]s a private teacher, he was conscientious and encouraging, patient and wise, always eager to install professional standards of behaviour in his pupils'.[9] Hamilton's lessons were concerned for the most part with practical details such as learning how to sketch a piece, how to lay it out before working on it in detail, and problems of notation. Questions of style and philosophical reflection were not raised during these lessons. Also absent was discussion about the dramatic *volte-face* that Hamilton's own music was undergoing, from his earlier tonal harmonic language towards the type of serialism fashionable at that time.

Between 1957 and 1959, Wood attended the Darmstadt summer schools. The first such venture was with James Dalton, a friend from Oxford who became organist of Queen's College.[10] Darmstadt presented Wood with the opportunities to study in greater depth the music of the Second Viennese School. On his return to England, he began his Variations for Viola, his first work to draw significantly on the language and techniques of the Second Viennese School (see below).

Study with Iain Hamilton ended in early 1958, though not before a great deal of the Variations had been written (Hamilton is the work's dedicatee). Lessons with Anthony Milner followed, preparing Wood for a B.Mus. (London), which he failed. Wood also gradually took over Milner's three-year course in Harmony at Morley College, a post Wood held for nearly a decade. Wood also went on to teach Harmony at the Royal Academy of Music from 1962 to 1966, and in later years it formed the backbone of his teaching at Cambridge University. Teaching the nuts and bolts of music suited ideally the traditionalist in Wood: like the Schoenberg revealed in

---

9   Hugh Wood, 'Obituary: Iain Hamilton', *The Guardian* (3 August 2000).

10   Wood wrote his *Capriccio* for organ for Dalton, to whom it is dedicated.

his *Harmonielehre*, Wood holds that there can be no understanding of modern art without having a firm conception of the tradition which gave rise to it.

Keller – Seiber – Goehr

Besides the continuing quest for a good compositional technique, Wood's musical development led to his eager discovery of what was for him a new modern repertoire: not only the Viennese, but Stravinsky, Bartók and, later, Messiaen. Three individuals were particularly important to Wood: Hans Keller, Mátyás Seiber and Alexander Goehr. Their links with continental culture were close: two were émigrés, the other the son of an émigré. Wood, whose own attentions were focused on the continent at this time,[11] was interested in what they had to offer musically.

Wood first met Hans Keller at Dartington; Keller had begun teaching there in 1958. Keller became and remained for Wood a musical and intellectual standard. Wood's tribute to Keller reflects the esteem in which he was held:

> he taught a whole generation of us. Only a lucky few of us, formally, the rest by this process of friendly, undogmatic osmosis of a remarkable personality into one's own: by personal example, in fact. On first encounter, I remember a certain brusque aggressiveness, provocative in intention. He was trying you out, saying something impossible to see if you had the guts to stand up for yourself and contradict him. As often as not, the apparently impossible turned out to be the purest commonsense truth, wrapped in a paradox. Once you had argued back, though, however foolishly, then friendship began; and never thereafter wavered. There was no pulling of rank on grounds of superior intelligence, experience or age, all of which he undeniably, indeed formidably, possessed.[12]

One can readily detect Wood's affinities with Keller in his own staunch upholding of those musical values associated with the traditional repertory, including that of the Second Viennese School.

In February 1959, Wood had his first lesson with the teacher with whom he would most often be associated, Mátyás Seiber. Wood took with him the Variations for Viola; Seiber suggested certain changes to the Finale in order to provide a more convincing conclusion. This proved to be the most specific contribution that Seiber made to one of Wood's pieces, but it was the manner and substance of his teaching, and the influence it had upon Wood, that was ultimately more significant. As Wood later recalled, Seiber

> gave quite wonderful lessons, which I still try to pass on in my own teaching. He had a phenomenally agile mind – he'd switch from Bach Inventions to twentieth-century music with no sense of incongruity – together with the kind of discipline which is unfashionable today.[13]

---

[11] See Hugh Wood, 'English Contemporary Music', in Howard Hartog (ed.), *European Music in the Twentieth Century*, rev. edn (London, 1961), pp. 145–70.

[12] Hugh Wood, [Contribution to Hans Keller Memorial Symposium], *Music Analysis* vol. 5/2–3 (1986): 397–401 (p. 398).

[13] Cited in Richard Wigmore, 'Hugh Wood', *Cambridge Alumni Magazine* (Lent Term 1999): 40–41 (p. 40).

These qualities, which Wood had already found exemplified in Hans Keller, were doubtless already guiding principles of Wood's life and art. As with so many of Wood's teachers, Seiber seemed to provide specific examples of conduct – musical, behavioural and intellectual – which intensified and enriched Wood's existing practices. The broad historical sweep of Seiber's tuition was in order to show musical solutions for particular musical problems; that is, the emphasis was on analysing compositional practice rather than applying philosophical or music-theoretic models. And it is this practical basis that informs Seiber's creative processes, which Seiber has described in terms that strongly resemble those of Hugh Wood in later years:

> [W]hat so many of my younger colleagues seem to be able to do successfully, namely, to plan out the whole work on the basis of […] mathematical or architectonic calculations. For me the art of composing is still a journey of discovery: I discover all these possibilities inherent in the material as the piece begins to grow and unfold, and then I draw the consequences from them. It means often changing and re-composing many things until everything begins to fall into place. I know that this is a much more painful and time-consuming procedure, yet I still cannot bring myself to do otherwise.[14]

Here one finds the 'discipline' of which Wood speaks: Seiber demanded that his pupils were able to provide a musical rationale for every phrase, note and chord. One rather suspects that this is exactly the training that Wood had hoped for.

Wood had first encountered Alexander Goehr at the Bryanston Summer School in 1948; many years later, he recalled 'feeling impressed, fascinated and rather intimidated'.[15] The first performance of Goehr's *The Deluge* in February 1959, for which Wood attended both rehearsals and concert, marked the starting point of their lifelong friendship. The two lived near one another in London in the 1960s, their families becoming close, and for over two decades Wood worked in the Music Faculty at Cambridge where Goehr was Professor. Alongside Keller, Goehr ranks as the most significant influence on Wood's thinking about music. Having studied with Messiaen, and possessing knowledge of his father's studies with Schoenberg, Goehr was able to provide Wood with insights into both of these composers, and helped to shape Wood's musical tastes. Affinities between Wood and Goehr's compositional practices can be found in their shared respect for tradition, although this respect is realized in different ways in their music.

Early Works (1942–1957)

Wood's first record of his compositions consists of two pieces, a Tune in E♭ (1942) and a March in the same key, written the following year. 1944 proved a more productive year, with work carried out on the first movement of a (presumably aborted) Piano Concerto in B♭, as well as on a Cantata to words by Walter de la Mare. The Cantata

---

[14] Cited in Hans Keller, 'Mátyás Seiber 1905–1960', in *Hans Keller: Essays on Music* ed. Christopher Wintle (Cambridge, 1994), p. 87.

[15] This event, and many others, is recalled movingly in Wood's 'On Music of Conviction … and an Enduring Friendship', in Alison Latham (ed.), *Sing, Ariel: Essays and Thoughts for Alexander Goehr's Seventieth Birthday* (Aldershot, 2003), pp. 327–30 (p. 327).

was one of the first compositional fruits of Wood's enduring passion for Bach, but, just as significantly, it is his earliest work for the voice.

Whilst at Oundle School (1945–50), Wood's compositions were mostly settings of poetry that he had been reading. Cecil Day Lewis was a particular favourite, occupying for the adolescent Wood the role that Robert Graves was to in later years. A setting of Lewis's 'Now the Full-throated Daffodils' was sung on 20 February 1949 by a schoolmaster in one of the concerts Wood organized; Wood accompanied on piano.[16] Also of this era were settings of John Donne's 'Busie Olde Foole', a song from the *Tempest*, Housman's 'With Seed the Sowers Scatter', and Yeats's 'Sailing to Byzantium'. This latter song was the one shown to Bush at Bryanston.

Much of this music composed at Oxford was for specific events, such as incidental music for college plays, including *The Merchant of Venice* and *Two Gentlemen of Verona*, and a contribution to an entertainment, *Flagrant Flowers*, planned by Jeremy Sandford, who was later to find fame through his television drama *Cathy Come Home*. There are also records of instrumental works: a piece for four horns (now lost) and fragments of a Piano Duet sonata. Pages of a violin sonata were shown to Bernard Rose, along with an *Overture Alla Toccata*. An arrangement of this Overture for two pianos, *Concertino*, was performed in November 1953, one of two works of the period to receive short notices in *The Isis*, the undergraduate student magazine. Of this piece, the reviewer noted that 'the acoustics tended to cover the delicate rhythms and texture, but that did not obscure the rare skill in developing rhythms as well as melodic material shown in the work'.[17] This tantalizingly suggests that something of the rhythmic and melodic suppleness that distinguishes Wood's mature music (to be described in Chapters 2 and 3) can be found, at least in nascent form, in the *Concertino*.

Judging by the second *Isis* review, evidence of other characteristics of Wood's later music can also be found in his *Songs for Springtime* for choir and piano. The reviewer, Leo Black, draws attention to the 'rather wide intervals' of Wood's melodic style, as well as the 'truly vernal quality of freshness and joy-of-living',[18] both of which, to differing degrees, are to be found throughout Wood's career. The work is in five movements, drawing on texts from Housman, Auden, Donne and Day Lewis. Three of the movements are new; the third and fifth movements return to poems set by Wood in the late 1940s: Donne's 'Busie Olde Foole' and Day Lewis's 'Now the Full-throated Daffodils'. The final incarnation of this latter song came in 1958, when Wood orchestrated it, along with the Housman and Auden settings.

A setting of Donne's 'The Good Morrow' from the summer of 1955 was considered by Wood at the time to be his best work to date; it was apparently a mixture of Britten (of the *Michelangelo Sonnets*) and romantic harmony after Wagner. It was

---

[16]   A faintly condescending but generally positive review by another (anonymous) master in the April 1949 issue of *The Laxtonian*, the Oundle School magazine, noted that the 'song showed some quite original promise', although on occasion Wood was advised to reconsider the accentuation of words. Lest the boys of the school be disturbed by 'certain influences of present-century composers' that could be detected in the song, the master added that such tendencies 'are both natural and healthy'.

[17]   *The Isis* (25 November 1953).

[18]   *The Isis* (3 March 1954).

followed in early 1956 by a Suite for Piano, dedicated to Lloyd Webber; the titles of the movements (Prelude, Gavotte, Sarabande, Gigue) and an abundance of fourths suggest a Hindemithian influence. A choral setting of Gerard Manley Hopkins's 'At the Wedding March' was written for, but not performed at, a friend's wedding; more successful was the setting in April 1956 of Laurie Lee's 'April Rise'.

Wood's first year of study with Iain Hamilton saw completion of the first movement of a String Quartet in B♭, as well as the start of a projected song cycle for voice and string orchestra (only the first movement, a setting of Dylan Thomas's 'Why East Wind Chills' was completed). The neo-classical influence remained strong in works written in the autumn and winter of 1956: a one-movement Cantilena for viola and piano (forces which Wood was to return to for his Op. 1) and a Concertante Movement for piano and orchestra – Stravinsky's *Danses Concertantes* of 1941–42 was the immediate influence here. A choral setting of 'Rise up, my Love' (Song of Solomon) was written in 1957 for Jeremy Sandford's wedding, as was a Hindemithian chorale prelude for organ. In terms of Wood's development, the chorale prelude is of interest, for it contains his first twelve-note melody, appearing in an overall (if extended) G major context.

The End of the Apprenticeship

The works from 1957 demonstrate Wood's continuing evolution towards a post-tonal and highly chromatic harmonic vocabulary. Two movements were added to complete the B♭ string quartet: the language of what became the slow middle movement in particular reflects this development. Whilst at Darmstadt, Wood wrote three miniatures for clarinet and piano, as well as a short piano piece intended as a prelude. More significant was Wood's first post-Darmstadt composition, the Variations for Viola. Of this piece, Wood has written:

> In 1957 I knew I had newly discovered the music of Schoenberg and his pupils and I knew at once that they were to show me the way forward for my music; as, indeed, they have ever since. The revelation was primarily an emotional experience for me, and however imperfectly their influence was received, it was obviously reflected in the all-out chromaticism (new for me then), in the many chains of twelve notes, or lesser chromatic formations (which do not here amount to serial working, and have only rarely done so since), in the characteristic harmonic and rhythmic formations, the wide and sometimes angular intervals of the melodies and in general the introverted romanticism.[19]

The first version of the Variations for Viola was completed in July 1958, the final version in 1959 after suggestions from Seiber. Wood also completed during his studies with Seiber four more songs to poems by Laurie Lee, to go with the 1956 setting of 'April Rise'. Against the hitherto uncharted expressive regions that Wood explored in the Variations, the Laurie Lee songs appear conservative, closer in language to the first movement of the B♭ String Quartet. Together, these three works – the quartet, the songs and the Variations, reveal how rapidly his musical language and sensibilities developed in the late 1950s.

---

[19] Composer's note to the score of the Variations for Viola Op. 1.

Example 1.1a   String Quartet in B♭/i, bars 1–8

Wood has described the String Quartet in B♭ (1956–57) as 'a quite serviceable student work in which new-found enthusiasm for the music of Tippett, of Bartók and Alan Bush contends with some dim proto-Schoenbergian aspirations'.[20] Each of the three movements of the quartet reflects these influences to different degrees. The ebullient opening allegro in B♭, the first to be composed, owes most to Tippett. The first subject (Example 1.1a) is based on material reminiscent of an idea from the second Ritual Dance of Tippett's *The Midsummer Marriage* (rehearsal mark 201 ff.), which Wood had heard during its first Covent Garden run in 1955. Tippett's Concerto for Double String Orchestra and Second String Quartet are also an influence on Wood's quartet, not least in the examples they provide for texture and rhythmic vitality.

The first subject group consists of inventive reworkings, combinations, and juxtapositions of material derived from the opening theme. Although the ensuing

---

[20]   Composer's note to the score of String Quartet No. 5 Op. 45.

second subject group is in the dominant, the tonal argument of the first subject, oscillating between the tritone poles of B♭ and E, suggests that traditional tonal functions co-exist with alternative methods of organizing the material. For instance, harmonic motion by major thirds, as between the chords of A♭ and C in bars 5–7 of Example 1.1a provides an alternative to tonic-dominant relationships; note too the presence of the sharpened fourth above both of these chords, which is characteristic of Wood's tonal music. This harmonic progression can also be found leading into the second subject, the recapitulation, and at the final cadence of the movement.

The developmental processes unleashed in the exposition continue in the development (for instance, in Example 1.1b). The recapitulation of the first subject group closely adheres to the model of the exposition. The most obvious deviations are made in order to change the character of the material. Thus the recapitulation opens with *piano* arpeggios rather than *forte*; the texture is thinned and reworked to lighten the effect. The first subject group is also intensified through the transposition of certain passages up by a tone. The second subject group is re-worked more extensively: the simple lyricism of the exposition (derived from the second half of Example 1.1a) flowers into close imitation that extends and intensifies the argument. A coda over a tonic pedal offers an early example of Wood using the material with which he opens a movement to close it.

Example 1.1b   String Quartet in B♭/i, bars 88–95

Composed the following year, the chromatic language and motivic working of the D minor slow movement looks towards Berg and Schoenberg. One can also detect numerous traits of Wood's later melodic style. The displacement of what could be regular semitone steps into angular and highly expressive major sevenths is one such trait; the frequent use of appoggiaturas that resolve only briefly another. The emphasis on counterpoint and the intensity of expression serve to position this movement at the start of a line of weighty Adagios in Wood's output, to which the slow movements of the first and fourth quartets also belong.

The driving rondo Finale, also in B♭, is informed by the music of Bartók and Bush. Despite drawing on different influences to both the first and second movements, it nevertheless manages to act as a fitting conclusion to both, by bringing together some of the ideas in each of these movements. Thus, the melodic contour of the principal theme of the Adagio recurs in the rondo theme; the characteristic major sevenths of the slow movement can be heard in the harmonies that open the Finale. The fluid harmonic motion, led principally by linear motion, recalls some of the first movement too, not least in the final cadence in which there is a prominent motion by major third in the bass.

Similar tonal arguments can be found in the Laurie Lee songs of 1958–59. For instance, although all the songs establish tonal centres at the outset which are then returned to at the close, few of the intervening harmonic progressions can be described as functional. Harmonies are often colouristic, and although recognizably triadic sonorities tend to mark phrase endings, they are often embellished by the use of added notes or bitonal elements. Certainly, some of the chordal constructs found in the set reflect a growing awareness of Schoenberg's atonal music, with chords in fourths, particularly the combination of an augmented and perfect fourth, making regular appearances.[21] Musical direction is supplied, as in Wood's later music, primarily by means of linear progressions, and through rhetorical gestures, such as the manipulation of textural densities or degrees of otherwise non-functional dissonance.

The collection of songs is more akin to a suite than a cycle; a common nature theme runs through them all. The vocal writing is characteristic for Wood, marked by a wide range and frequent wide leaps. The hovering tonality of Example 1.2, taken from the close of 'April Rise', the last of the set, demonstrates the degree to which the final close, here in D major/minor, can be implied without recourse to traditional cadential gestures. Bass motion is largely by step (occasionally displaced by an octave): after the initial phrase which gives prominence to F in the bass (bars 36–9), the bass-line descends to B♭ for the climax of the phrase (bar 42), before gently rising back to D for the close. This cadential formula of a rising third (B♭–D) mirrors the equivalent motion D♭–F in the previous phrase (bars 38–9). However, it is the interval of the second (both major and minor), not the third, which is most prominent melodically and harmonically. Other melodic fingerprints within the example include the leaps of sevenths and ninths (displaced seconds), and the use of the tritone within the melodic line. But what is most significant for Wood's mature compositions is the very late return to the nominal key centre, not just here, but in each song of the set. In every case, the return to the tonic occurs only at the very end of the song, providing a potent symbol of closure, rather than a traditional (functional) tonal release.

---

[21]   In Chapter 2, I define these as 0,1,6 trichords: see p. 43.

Example 1.2   Laurie Lee Songs, 'April Rise', bars 36–46

The musical language Wood developed for the String Quartet in B♭ and the Laurie Lee songs might erroneously be considered, developmentally speaking, a dead end in his development as a composer. Although Wood was to abandon with few exceptions such clear tonal centres in his mature music, these early works provided compositional methods that were not language-specific. In particular, the motivic writing and the ability to fashion a language in which symmetrical structures and linear motion were more crucial to the harmonic logic than the hierarchical structures of traditional tonality provided Wood with a model of working that could be applied to a more chromatic idiom.

As reported above, it was through the encounter of the music of the Second Viennese School that Wood was able to find his own voice. This discovery, and the technical and expressive breakthroughs that it stimulated, is demonstrated in the Variations for Viola Op. 1 (1957–58). Although almost contemporaneous with the String Quartet, the harmonic language of the Variations, and in particular the tendency towards chromatic saturation, represents a significant moment in Wood's career, and his own recognition of this led him to assign it his first opus number. Significantly, and characteristically, Wood appropriated for his Op. 1 only those aspects of the music of the Second Viennese School that he needed. In particular, despite the melodic use of twelve-note material, there are no serial workings. Nor should it be overlooked that, towards the end of the work, the Viennese composer that Wood quotes is Beethoven, and not Schoenberg.

The Variations is formally orthodox. It opens with an Introduction saturated with the motif consisting of a rising minor third followed by a major seventh (motif x in Example 1.3) and is followed by a slow theme which begins with a twelve-note idea. Note how the continuation of the theme is not twelve-note, but that characteristic intervals and motifs from the first half of the theme inform both the continuation and accompaniment. The melodic rhetoric recalls that of the Adagio of the B♭ String Quartet, but the absence of an unambiguous tonal centre renders the melodic figures unable to discharge fully their emotional affect: the traditional associations of the figures are intensified by the avoidance of their expected fulfilment.

The variations that follow are highly contrasted. The first, *Giocoso*, is almost double the tempo of the theme, transforming the languid rhythms of the latter into quirky syncopations. The theme passes into the piano for the second variation, *Inquieto*; the viola's scurrying figures at the outset are related to the piano accompaniment of bars 17 and 20 of the theme (Example 1.3, motif y). Everything is thus subject to development; nothing is 'merely' accompanimental, but rather part of a dense motivic argument.

The extended third variation, *Furioso*, begins with a flurry of semiquavers, before the texture thins out into a severe three-part invention on the theme between viola, piano right hand and piano left hand. Immediately following the violence of the *Furioso* is an elegant *Appassionato* variation. Here, the intervallic content of much of the sinewy piano accompaniment of the theme is reworked into sonorous chords rich in sevenths and ninths, that hint at a tonal background. Above these chords floats a passionate and lyrical reworking of the theme given to the viola, spanning a full three octaves. If the third variation demonstrates Wood at his most terse and violent, the fourth is indicative of his equally important romantic leanings. The fifth and sixth variations are also contrasted. The fifth, *Capriccioso*, plays with semiquaver groupings of twos and threes; the sixth, *Mediazione*, belongs to the same emotional world as the instrumental recitatives in late Beethoven.

Example 1.3   Variations Op. 1, bars 12–23

It is in the Finale that firstly the theme, and then the harmonic progression, of Beethoven's 32 Variations in C minor WoO 80 emerge. This conclusion raised the eyebrows of reviewers such as Peter Evans, who wrote that 'Hugh Wood's variations are [...] tenuous in their tonal links, yet contrive to reach their final cadence in a last statement of the theme above a pointedly orthodox progression to C minor – and still more dangerous, an orthodox chromatic progression'.[22] More emphatically, John Weissman found 'the stylistic incongruity manifested in the last page's explicit C minor a disturbance rather than the intended release of tension'.[23]

But it seems that Evans and Weissman missed at least some of the point. The motif of a rising minor third and major seventh that can be found throughout the Variations (motif *x*), is but an intensification of the rising minor third and falling semitone with which Beethoven's Variations begin. Thus Beethoven's theme has been prepared for, melodically at least, from the outset. I have already noted how Wood's melodic and harmonic formulations hint at a tonal background, and gain expressive force by evading direct tonal reference. The conclusion to the Variations provides both an affective and effective resolution for the pent-up energy that these allusions create, harmonizing Wood's theme with the harmonic progression drawn from Beethoven. It is not that C minor has been a goal that has been prepared for from the outset, as Evans and Weissman appear to suggest, but that the quotations from Beethoven provide a particular emotional outlet. In other words, whilst the quotation can be shown to 'fit' technically, its primary function is expressive.

The works of the late 1950s demonstrate Wood's assimilation of a melodic, harmonic and rhythmic syntax that was influenced by the music of the Second Viennese School. However, although the surface details of the B♭ Quartet and Variations for Viola clearly differ, the methods by which the materials are developed are strikingly similar. When Jim Samson describes Wood as 'Schoenbergian in his commitment to thematic organization of a traditional kind and in his reliance on classical genres and formal types', he is referring to such developmental methods, and to a particular mode of musical thought that is not determined solely by the material.[24] This mode of thinking came about partly through Wood's studies with Lloyd Webber, Hamilton, Milner and Seiber, and through his contact with Keller and (later) Goehr, but above all through his own immersion in a wide variety of music. I shall return to Wood's musical thinking again in Chapters 2 and 3.

Writings about Music

In the early 1960s, Wood supplemented his income by writing for *The Musical Times*. Since then, he has regularly written or spoken about music in reviews, articles, programme notes, symposia and on the radio. The impression one gets is that Wood

---

[22]   Peter Evans, [Wood's Variations for Viola], *Music and Letters* 42 (1961): 190–91 (p. 191).

[23]   John Weissman, [Wood's Variations for Viola], *The Music Review* vol. XXIII (1962): 337.

[24]   Jim Samson, 'Instrumental Music II', in Stephen Banfield (ed.), *The Blackwell History of Music in Britain vol. 6: The Twentieth Century* (Oxford, 1995), pp. 278–342 (p. 297).

would play down the significance of his writings. In a 1970 article about his Cello Concerto and Second String Quartet, Wood joked:

'The composer speaks' – as great a moment as 'Groucho sings.' Similar, too, in other ways: you hope that this is not what he does best. I've always said no to writing about my music before: what's that proverb about not selling the skin until you've shot the bear? I suspect some composers are happier selling the skin than going out bear-shooting: why else does the bear so often turn out to be a rabbit?[25]

Like all good jokes, there is an underlying seriousness: our attention should be on the music first, and only then should we see what Wood says about it. But what might we make of his writings about other composers? When reviewing the composer Thomas Adès's contribution to a book about Janáček, Wood noted that 'Adès deals in curiously precise detail with the piano music, in a way which tells you a certain amount about himself as a composer (always the most interesting aspect of analytical articles, which should always be written by composers)'.[26] Correspondingly, Wood's writings, although occasional pieces which certainly do not outline any theoretical manifesto, tell us 'a certain amount' about *him* as a composer. For this reason, they form an interesting and important adjunct to Wood's music, and are worthy of our attention.

As with his compositions, Wood's writings concerning the criticism and appreciation of music belong firmly to the Schoenbergian tradition. The methods and aims of this tradition can be understood with reference to Berg's essay 'Why is Schoenberg's Music so Difficult to Understand?'.[27] Setting out to describe 'what happens musically in Schoenberg's works', Berg achieves his aim by demonstrating how the musical techniques employed in Schoenberg's First String Quartet are to be considered as developments or derivations of methods employed in German music over the previous 150 years or so.[28] In one sense, Schoenberg's quartet emerges not as a self-contained work, but rather as a nexus of interrelated musical methods that provide links to a much wider repertory. At the same time, through Schoenberg's particular arrangement and deployment of these methods for expressive purpose, the quartet exists as a unique entity that ultimately has to be understood on its own terms. Berg's account is based on a number of principles axiomatic to the Schoenbergian tradition. The two that have the most bearing on Wood's writings (and by extension his compositions) are (a) a formalist approach to musical understanding, and (b) the recognition of a body of works against which individual compositions can be compared.

Formalism The first of these axioms, formalism, understands and interprets music by means of comparison with a background of established musical procedures. In Berg's words: 'I am concerned solely with what happens musically in Schoenberg's works; the compositional mode of expression which, like the language of any work of

---

[25]   Hugh Wood, 'Hugh Wood on his own Work', *The Listener* (29 October 1970): 605.

[26]   Hugh Wood, 'Intimate Letters, Overgrown Paths', *The Times Literary Supplement* (19 November 1999).

[27]   A translation of this article appears in Willi Reich, *The Life and Work of Alban Berg*, trans. Cornelius Cardew (London, 1965).

[28]   Berg, 'Why is Schoenberg's Music so Difficult?', p. 189.

art [...], must be considered the only one adequate to the object to be represented'.[29] Extramusical modes of enquiry, '[i]n other words, to do what is frequently done: [to] get to grips with music by means of philosophical, literary or other arguments',[30] may provide an insight into why the composer may have chosen or rejected certain ideas, or it may explain a work's reception, but it says nothing about the music as music.

The focus of this particular brand of formalist analysis is therefore on the technical details of the music. But the purpose of the analysis is not how a work is put together, but what the interrelationship of the constituent elements might mean. When Hans Keller states that '[i]ntellectual music is only emotional music before it is understood',[31] an aphorism Wood is fond of quoting, he is referring to just this: the way in which musical techniques can lead to musical expression. A letter of 14 January 1913 from Schoenberg to Berg about the latter's *Altenberg Lieder* makes clear this link: 'There is one thing, though, that I find disconcerting: the rather too overt striving to employ new techniques. Perhaps I will learn to understand better how these techniques connect organically with expressive necessity. But right now, they bother me.'[32] To understand 'new' techniques in terms of the historical precedents from which they are derived – that is, to understand a work in relation to the tradition from which it springs – is to understand the emotional and expressive force of the work.

Wood's writings, as with Berg's essay, attend to the quality and nature of the musical argument in question. As Stephen Walsh notes, he is 'brilliantly effective especially as a polemicist against hack criticism, and a superb apologist for music that he happens to admire'.[33] One can find both of these tendencies exemplified in a short 1977 article on the music of Frank Bridge.[34] After an opening discussion regarding the uncritical appraisal of British music (including a retraction of unguarded comments of his own),[35] Wood turns to the reception of Frank Bridge. The critic Frank Howes is soundly taken to task for his dismissal of Bridge's music in terms that say nothing about the way in which musical ideas are presented or developed. In Howes's submission, Bridge 'served his generation', but 'suffered from being awkwardly placed by the Time Spirit'. Continuing, Howes notes that in the 1920s Bridge 'began to uglify his music in order to keep it up to date', and his 1937 String Quartet No. 4, 'was roundly condemned (at any rate by me [Frank Howes] in *The Times*) as straining after something so unnatural as to be not even well written for

---

[29]   Ibid.

[30]   Ibid.

[31]   Wood, [Keller memoriam]: 398.

[32]   Cited in Mark DeVoto, 'Berg the Composer of Songs', in Douglas Jarman (ed.), *The Berg Companion* (Basingstoke and London, 1989), pp. 35–66, (p. 49).

[33]   Stephen Walsh, [Sleeve notes to Collins Classics 20072] (1993).

[34]   Wood, 'Frank Bridge and the Land Without Music'.

[35]   From the perspective of 1977, Wood felt that his 1961 chapter 'English Contemporary Music' (see n. 11) was too negative in its assessment of the achievements of English music. However, the chapter tells us a great deal about the continental influences on Wood's music at the time.

strings'.[36] Wood's summary is characteristically forthright: within this small sample we find a 'vacuous cliché', a remark that is 'extraordinarily crude for a journalist to make about even the most nugatory of composers', and 'a more specific, boastfully putting-down judgement'.

Wood then turns to critics who by contrast deal directly with the music and its influences. Most tellingly, Wood concludes with the most important critical tool, that of the actual aural experience of the music. And it is in this discussion that Wood's critical priorities mark him as a true Schoenbergian, for he exalts above all the craftsmanship of the music:

> The results of further listening are startling [...] First of all, Bridge's music sounds professional to a degree that all too many of his contemporaries simply were not. His music really *works*, and you don't find yourself having to make allowances [...]. Secondly (and I think it has to be *secondly*) Bridge does have his own tone of voice, which is easier to experience than to describe. [...] [I]t is a serious, quiet voice, that of an inner life intensely lived. And in that last sentence, don't you have one of the essential qualities of 'Englishness'?[37]

The emphasis on craftsmanship in Wood's writings about music reflects the careful working-out of material in his own compositions. His art is conceived and worked out against the background of examples set by music of the past, and these are the principles against which he assesses others' music.

Wood's attention to the sound of a work, and his appraisal of its musical procedures, provides a refreshing antidote to the (sometimes inadvertent) ideological prejudices one finds in much criticism. In an otherwise positive review of Charles Rosen's study of Schoenberg,[38] Wood took to task Rosen's 'austere limitations of twentieth-century music' which served to emphasize a select group of composers at the expense of the achievements of composers such as Britten, Milhaud, Poulenc, Rachmaninoff, Pfitzner, Fauré, Honegger, Strauss, Sibelius, Bartók, Prokofiev and Hindemith.[39] Wood's defence of these composers, many of whose reputations have suffered at the hands of musical fashion, can be summed up in a single sentence: 'In the end, only the music matters: if we did not believe that, we should all have given up long ago'.[40]

Tradition   At this point, we might ask what we mean by 'music' and 'musical procedures'. These are generally treated as transparent concepts, or as Keller-like 'purest common-sense truth'.[41] But on what basis are these truths grounded? This brings us to the second of the axioms of the Schoenbergian tradition that I mentioned above. Put crudely, there exists a repertory of pieces that manifest those musical

---

[36]   Frank Howes, *The English Musical Renaissance* (London, 1966), pp. 160–62; cited in Wood, 'Frank Bridge and the Land Without Music': 9.

[37]   Wood, 'Frank Bridge and the Land Without Music': 10–11 (original emphasis).

[38]   Charles Rosen, *Schoenberg* (London, 1976).

[39]   Hugh Wood, 'Following the Row', *Times Literary Supplement* (10 June 1977).

[40]   Wood, 'On Music of Conviction', p. 327.

[41]   Wood, [Keller memoriam]: 398.

techniques and procedures that serve to justify and explain the appearance and development of such techniques and procedures in subsequent music.

An example of this can be found in Schoenberg's 1931 defence against Nazi accusations about the relationship of his music to German art. Schoenberg stated that his teachers 'were primarily Bach and Mozart, and secondarily Beethoven, Brahms and Wagner'.[42] Whilst Schoenberg may have been primarily interested in self-preservation, his comments were grounded in truth, for his art was rooted in the examples set by the past:

> My originality comes from this: I immediately imitated everything I saw that was good, even when I had not first seen it in someone else's work. And I may say: often enough I saw it first in myself. For if I saw something I did not leave it at that; I acquired it, in order to possess it; I worked on it and extended it, and it led me to something new.[43]

A repertory of works from the past (and present) does more than provide a model for imitation and development. As discussed with Berg's analysis of Schoenberg, it provides criteria and standards against which other works can be assessed.

In Wood's writings, the corpus of works that provide positive examples for imitation is equated quite simply with 'tradition'. More specifically, his musical thinking belongs to the dialectical Germanic tradition that Schoenberg described in the quote above, in which succeeding generations build upon, rather than replicate or replace, the achievements of their forebears. In this way, Wood has argued, composers can find their own voice:

> Maybe our respect and love for the past is best, indeed can only be, demonstrated by *trying to do something different*. Of course you build on your immediate predecessors, you imitate them through love for them; but thus you hope eventually to find your own voice without striving for it. The real struggle, the real search, goes on deep inside ourselves. Outwardly, our energies are best turned to the new – however we may choose to define it.[44]

The engagement with tradition runs deeper than finding one's own compositional voice, for, as we have seen, Wood esteems artistry above originality for the sake of it: indeed, for him, meaningful originality can only come from artistry. The examples set by music of the past and present provide models that are familiar to both composer and listener: tradition offers methods of working and means of communication. This forms the basis of Hans Keller's 'two-dimensional' theory, in which art

> consists of the meaningful contradiction of well built-up expectations, so that the true composer prepares your expectations, stimulates them, and then proceeds *meaningfully* to contradict them. It's got to have meaning, that contradiction – there has to be a strong link between that which you expect and that which contradicts it. There has to be unity between the two. Otherwise – if the contradiction is meaningless – that important tension

---

[42]   Arnold Schoenberg, *Style and Idea: Selected Writings*, ed. Leonard Stein and trans. Leo Black (London and Boston, 1975), p. 174.

[43]   Ibid.

[44]   Hugh Wood, 'Thoughts on a Modern Quartet', *Tempo* 111 (1974): 23–6, (p. 26).

between what I call the 'background' (that is, the sum total of your expectations) and what I call the 'foreground' (that is, their meaningful contradiction) is not established.[45]

In my submission, Wood's music clearly and consistently manifests the artistic tensions between expectation and realization: the use of the quotation of Beethoven in his Variations for Viola is an example of how this can be used for expressive purpose.

The background of expectations resulting from Wood's relationship to tradition is generated in a number of ways in his music. On the most basic level, the use of quotations from, or allusions to, particular works provides examples of composers with whom Wood closely identifies. In some cases, quotations or allusions are chosen for specific programmatic or emotional purposes; in others, the reasons for inclusion may be circumstantial or an act of personal homage.[46] Wood's writings make it clear that such moments are deeply felt, describing 'the way in which the past can – for artistic or private reasons, or, best of all, an inextricable mixture of both – suddenly mean so much to you that you wish to invoke it, to summon it all up in one moment of intense quotation'.[47] The result is that we can treat such quotations as symbols of the tradition to which Wood's music belongs (or as tokens of the canon which 'means so much' to Wood, and with which he identifies). A roll-call of names suffices to identify this tradition: Beethoven, Elgar, Gerhard, Kurtág, Pfitzner, Wolf, Schubert and Mozart have all been quoted directly; to this list one might add the Second Viennese School, Stravinsky, Messiaen, Mahler, Janáček and Tippett for near-quotations and appropriations of gestures and textures. Many of these names recur in Wood's writings and reviews: to these we must also add the central figures of Bach, Brahms and Seiber, as well as Dallapiccola and Bridge.

What strikes the listener about Wood's use of quotation is the degree to which it is integrated into his music. Although the quotation may cause stylistic jolts, it nevertheless possesses strong thematic links with the material that surrounds it, as with the Beethoven quotation in the Variations for Viola. The use of thematicism is another of Wood's debts to tradition; allied to this is Wood's use of genres and forms associated with the Viennese Classical tradition, with a particular emphasis on chamber music. As with Wood's use of quotation, the use of traditional forms and methods of constructing a musical argument are intensely felt: Wood has written how he has 'always believed, and still do[es], that the old forms can be made to glow with renewed life'.[48]

---

[45] Mark Doran (ed.), 'Hans Keller in Interview with Anton Weinberg', *Tempo* 195 (1996): 6–13, (pp. 10–11; original emphasis).

[46] This is apparently the case with the Beethoven quotation in the Variations for Viola, which has a great deal more to do with Wood's biographical context than, for example, the historical or generic associations that the quotation creates.

[47] Wood, 'Thoughts on a Modern Quartet': 26. Though the topic of Wood's remarks was ostensibly George Rochberg's Third Quartet, one is inclined to believe that he was thinking equally of his own Symphony which he had begun a few months earlier. See Chapter 6, pp. 136–7.

[48] Wood, 'Hugh Wood on his own Work': 605.

Towards an Appreciation

With an awareness of Wood's formative influences, his conception of musical thinking, and his relationship with tradition, one can begin to appreciate why he has never aligned himself with any particular school or artistic movement. It also makes clear why commentators have demonstrated a steadfast inability to pigeon-hole Wood's music: 'he has at different times been dubbed "an unrepentant serialist" and "an English romantic"'.[49] What the commentators have missed, in their rush to classify, is that the Schoenbergian tradition does not presuppose any particular musical language, and nor does it preclude the integration of different styles. (Witness the variety of the music Schoenberg composed after his emigration to the United States, or the varied modes of expression in Berg's Violin Concerto, all of which manifest similar qualities of musical thought.) It may also explain why Wood's music has never occupied a more prominent position within British musical life, for in an age of marketing and spin, such a resistance to categorization and easy sound-bites, let alone a commitment to traditional values, often serve to isolate and marginalize.

But knowing the intellectual and musical ideas that have influenced Wood's compositional craft is at most a stepping-stone towards an appreciation of his music. Rather, these influences recede into the background (in Keller's sense of the word), allowing us to understand why particular musical techniques have been chosen over others in individual musical works. But it does not validate these individual pieces of music, nor does it explain their musical logic: that can only be achieved through study of the notes (or better still, repeated close listening). To this end, I offer the remainder of this book.

---

[49]   Cited in Wigmore, 'Hugh Wood': 40

Chapter 2

Style (I): Melody and Harmony

Over the last half-century or more one has become accustomed to composers ruminating on questions of musical identity and language, to the extent that stylistic development is often felt to be influenced by the dictates of fashion rather than creative necessity. Against such a background, Wood's continued adherence to the technical and expressive devices that were first given voice in his Variations for Viola speaks of an artist impelled to create regardless of the whims of fashion. Jeremy Thurlow, in his excellent *New Grove* article, summarized Wood's style thus:

> Like the previous *Scenes from Comus*, the [Cello Concerto] was acclaimed at its Proms première; the two works brought to the attention of a sizeable audience not only Wood's ability to shape dynamic forms on the largest scale, but also his characteristically intense, yearning lyricism, in which cantabile lines are stretched over angular contours defined by wide dissonant intervals. Together with warm, sonorous harmonies based on 7th chords and moving by semitones or 5ths, such melodies reflect his love of Berg, the composer he is perhaps closest to in spirit. But there are also moments of reticence which give the music an oft-noted English quality, for all its European credentials.[1]

Not even the lure of a 'late style' – that musicological trope which composers such as Tippett and Carter have been influenced by – holds any sway over Wood. In an article in which Alexander Goehr pondered on adopting a late style of his own, he noted Wood's pragmatic approach to the matter. Goehr asked: 'What then remains for the old artist to do? Recently, in a series of Cambridge lectures, Hugh Wood proposed quite simply that one should go on as before, and that seems modest and sensible'.[2] 'Going on as before' does not, however, mean artistic stagnation. Wood's musical sensibilities demand of him a constant self-critical engagement with external influences, which prompts expansions and refinements of his musical language without sudden or arbitrary changes.[3]

---

[1]   Jeremy Thurlow, 'Hugh Wood', in Stanley Sadie (ed.), *The New Grove Dictionary of Music and Musicians II* (London, 2001) vol. 27, pp. 548–50 (p. 549).

[2]   Alexander Goehr, 'What's Left to be Done?', *Musical Times* Vol. 40, no. 1867 (1999): 19–28 (p. 24).

[3]   Compare this with Robert Graves's self assessment that 'I always aimed at writing more or less as I still do' (Robert Graves, *Collected Poems 1965* (London, 1965) p. i; in his expansion on this point, Martin Seymour Smith notes that Graves's 'development has been less a matter of a series of fresh inventions, or successions of changed attitudes, than of a continuously expanding awareness of his purposes as a poet' (Martin Seymour Smith, 'Robert Graves', in James Vinson and D. L. Kirkpatrick (eds), *Contemporary Poets*, 4th edn (London and Chicago, 1985), pp. 317–21 (p. 320). Further parallels between Wood and Graves are made in Chapter 7, pp. 153–4.

For Hans Keller, it is a composer's 'character of invention' that enables one to instantly recognize their music: that is, to recognize their 'personal style'.[4] The emphasis in Keller's account is that character need not be equated with 'purity of method',[5] but rather the ways in which diverse materials and techniques are brought together in a single composition (or body of works). The way in which Wood gradually absorbs influences into his language reveals a consistent character of invention ('going on as before') even if the nature of the material differs from piece to piece. A stylistic overview of Wood's compositional output would accordingly focus on the recurring technical and expressive devices that enable us to recognize Wood's personal idiom.

Thurlow's description of Wood's music can only be a starting point for such an overview: despite the classification of certain features, such as 'wide dissonant intervals', there is no sense of how such traits combine in order to 'shape dynamic forms' or produce 'moments of reticence'. To study a composer's style, then, is to analyse the ways in which the classifiable components of an oeuvre combine to create characteristic musical statements, and the ways in which a composer manipulates such stylistic norms to create new expressive meanings.

In this chapter and the next, I will survey those elements of Wood's music that might be considered stylistic in the above terms. The focus of this inquiry will be on the interrelationships between the various features of Wood's music, such as melody, harmony, rhythm, and form. Each of these will be taken in turn, and though it is impossible to treat them as completely independent, the shifting of the spotlight from one feature to the next results in fresh observations. The resulting stylistic analysis forms part of the shared background (in Keller's terms) of all of Wood's pieces, providing 'terms of reference which the composer and his recipients have in common before the composition starts'.[6] Coupled with Chapter 1, which provided a historical context for Wood's stylistic development, these chapters form a prolegomenon to the study of specific works; a broad background against which to compare and understand individual foregrounds.

Melody

Wood's music is characterized by its all-pervasive thematicism: for him, this represents 'the surest, most human means of communication'.[7] This fundamental

---

[4]   Hans Keller, 'Principles of Composition' in *Essays on Music*, pp. 212–32 (p. 216). When talking of 'personal style', Keller refers to 'character', thus reserving 'style' for technical usage such as homophonic or polyphonic style. 'Character of invention' is analogous to what Leonard B. Meyer calls 'compositional strategies'. See Meyer's, *Style and Music: Theory, History, and Ideology* (Chicago and London, 1989), pp. 20ff. My own approach to style is indebted to Meyer's work, and particularly that of Robert S. Hatten: see Hatten's *Musical Meaning in Beethoven: Markedness, Correlation, and Interpretation* (Bloomington, 1994) and *Interpreting Musical Gestures, Topics, and Tropes: Mozart, Beethoven, Schubert* (Bloomington, 2004).

[5]   Keller, 'Principles of Composition', p. 216.

[6]   Hans Keller, 'Towards a Theory of Music' in *Essays on Music*, pp. 121–5 (p. 124).

[7]   Wood, 'Hugh Wood on his own work': 605.

tenet conditions the nature of his musical material. Wood's melodies may leap and swoop over many octaves, making great demands on performer and listener alike, but all of his melodies have a carefully wrought and distinctive shape that enables their recognition on their return and through their transformations. Crucial, too, is the sharply defined motivic content of Wood's melodies, which enables the development of related ideas from a single source. But for musical communication to be humanly meaningful as well as logical, there has to be expressive content. In Wood's music, technique and expression are fused: there cannot be one without the other, as the following close readings will demonstrate.

The opening horn melody of *Scenes from Comus* (Example 2.1) provides a succinct example of Wood's lyrical, romantic vein. Within it, one can readily identify the characteristics that Jeremy Thurlow listed for Wood's melodies: it is lyrical, angular and 'defined by wide dissonant intervals'. Coupled with the romantic and natural associations of the French horn (the outdoors, hunting), the melody enables Wood to conjure up the sense of mystery and magic that pervades Milton's masque from which Wood drew his *Scenes*.

Example 2.1   *Scenes from Comus* Op. 6, bars 1–7

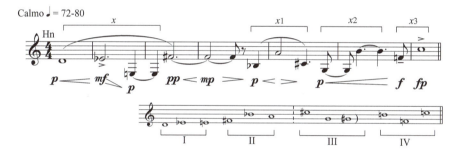

Nevertheless, as with Comus (the sorcerer central to the masque), the magic in Wood's music is in part the result of artifice and technical mastery. The highly chromatic language – eleven different notes are used – is given direction through a series of ascending peaks (D–E♭–F♯–A–B–C). These peaks in turn suggest a distant, if unstable, tonal background of D major/minor – note how both the 'tonic' D and 'dominant' A are given prominent positions within the melody. Alternatively, one might interpret these peaks as belonging to a composed-out diminished seventh chord (E♭–F♯–A–C) to which chromatic auxiliary notes (D and B) have been added. This diminished seventh belongs to the octatonic collection D–E♭–F–F♯–(G♯)–A–B–C, the notes of which all occupy the register above the opening D. The stratification of the musical surface into an octatonic collection (the G♯ follows shortly after) and its complement (the notes lying beneath the opening D) suggests that octatonicism is important in determining the harmonic character of the extract. But one might also draw attention to the latter half of the melody, in which the group A–C♯–G–B–F suggests yet another collection, that of a whole-tone set. The chromatic foreground is thus able to allude on a variety of levels to tonal, octatonic or whole-tone backgrounds without ever unambiguously settling in any single one. Such richness of allusion provides the means for the music later in the work to draw 'magically' (that is, poetically and expressively) on a wide variety of harmonic material without incongruity.

The strong sense of melodic motion and harmonic richness is complemented by taut motivic construction. The first half of the melody consists of a four-note motif (x), followed by three varied repetitions. Because each motivic unit is shorter in duration than the one preceding it, we have also the aural impression of an accelerando culminating in the final semibreve C, at which point the perceived durations stretch out once again. This reflects the tendency in tonal music, for example, for harmonic rhythm to accelerate to a cadence. Finally, the dynamic profiling of the motifs also serve to place emphasis on the closing C, for while the gentle dynamic climaxes of motifs x and x_1 occur *within* the motif, during the final dissolution the climax occurs at the very end with a dramatic *fp*. The combination of rhythmic and dynamic factors thus reinforce the ending implied by the motivic development, allowing us to perceive the passage as a coherent whole.

Against the lyricism of the opening to *Comus*, such technical narratives can seem overly dry and cumbersome. However, analysing the finer details of the musical thought within such passages reminds us that the best 'Emotional music is also Intellectual music'.[8]

Whereas the text set in *Comus* is drawn from the seventeenth century, Wood's preference has been for twentieth-century English verse. This he has described as 'a treasure-house, and our poets continue to produce good lyric poetry to this day: it's a waste of being English not to draw on these riches; and the composer has a particular duty to the poets of his own time'.[9] More recently, Jeremy Thurlow has drawn attention to Wood's 'idiomatic and refined response to English verse: his songs for voice and piano form a considerable part of his oeuvre and must be considered the most distinctive and substantial contribution to British song writing since Britten and Tippett'.[10] In fact, about half of Wood's compositional output is vocal: most of it consists of songs for voice and piano. In these, Wood's expressive musical language is frequently paired with a poetic language of similar concentration. Besides four sets of songs to poems by Robert Graves (Opp. 18, 22, 23, and 36) and also the song cycle *Wild Cyclamen* (Op. 49), he has set on more than one occasion poems by, amongst others, Ted Hughes, Edwin Muir, D.H. Lawrence, Laurie Lee and Christopher Logue.

Example 2.2 gives the opening of 'A Last Poem', drawn from Wood's first set of songs to poems by Robert Graves. The vocal writing, characterized by terse and wide expressionistic contours and leaps, differs markedly from the gentle lyrical curves of Example 2.1. The motivic repetitions nested within the extract provide a vivid musical analogy to the poet's inability to produce a 'last poem': there is always one further musical repetition on its way, just as there is always another poem to write. The difficulties involved in performing such a line reflect the angst

---

8   See Chapter 1, p. 18.

9   Composer's note to the recording of *The Horses* Op. 10 (Argo ZRG 750).

10   Thurlow, 'Hugh Wood': 549.

of the narrator, heightened by the inexorable grind of the chromatic line traced out by the melodic peaks (F–F♯–G). The varied sequence that underpins this ascent is a typical characteristic of Wood's melodies; here, the technique mirrors the expressive content of a poet writing repeated variants of a poem.

Example 2.2   Robert Graves Songs Set I Op. 18/v, 'A Last Poem', bars 1–5

The structural significance of the preparation for each of the melodic peaks is also of note. The leap of a minor ninth that opens the first phrase is repeated as an augmented ninth in the second and third phrases, filled out by rapid arpeggiations in thirds. Such figuration in Wood's music generally has an upbeat role, giving emphasis to the final note of each arpeggio. It is important to recognize that such figures are not just passagework, but an integral component of the sound world of each piece: the intervallic properties of such figures are reflected in the language of the work as a whole. With the fourth phrase, the original leap of a minor ninth (A–B♭) is repeated to reach the melodic climax of the theme; the recollection at the end of a section of an interval from the start functions cadentially. It is characteristic that the audible struggle to reach this climax (in a phrase spanning some fifteen crotchets) is followed by a rapid dissolution: the collapse from B♭ down to middle C (the lowest point of the phrase) occurs within a third of the time (five crotchets). The relative ease with which the achievements of the melodic struggle are undone is a typical expressive gesture in Wood's music: unambiguous apotheoses are rare and all the more powerful as a result. Here, the poet struggles, but the struggle is in vain: he will never 'give over'.

The recollection of the opening melodic interval at the start of the final phrase is representative of a more general compositional habit of Wood's, that of reprising material from the start of a section at the end. A particularly compressed instance of this can be found in Example 2.2: the first four notes in the vocal part (labelled *x*) are repeated at the close of the extract in the bass of the piano accompaniment in bar 5. The strained intervals of motif *x* are crucial in defining the character of the first phrase; similarly, an augmented triad F♯–B♭–D (*y*) shapes the second. It is first heard in the vocal line in bar 2, repeated immediately in the bass of the piano. The augmented triad is heard again in bar 5, again in the piano left hand, in figuration derived from the combination of both *x* and *y*. Within Wood's music, repetition of pitch material has a particularly important structural role: here it is used to signify the end of the first section by drawing together its two most prominent motifs.

An increased emphasis on D in the bass throughout the extract is also of importance, not least because the bass motion E♭–A–D over the five bars of the example suggests D as a distant tonal background. Against this background, the melodic ascent in the voice takes on a new significance: it can be understood as a rise from the flattened third of the scale to the dominant (F–A), in which the climactic B♭ is understood an appoggiatura. The expressive force of this ascent is not that it mirrors traditional tonal melodic structures, but rather that the tension created by the distance between the chromatic foreground and the implied tonal background renders such structures ambiguous. One can sense that the ascent is striving for an goal, but one is not always sure of what this goal is, or if indeed it can be reached: 'when can I give over?'

A similar density of musical argument is put to contrasting expressive ends in Example 2.3, the noble Passacaglia theme from Wood's Symphony Op. 21 (1974–82). The motivic derivations from the opening gesture are labelled in the example. The repetitions of the motifs suggest that a two-part melodic form lurks in the background, signalled by the return of motif *x* in free rhythmic diminution in bars 6–7. In comparison to the first half of the theme, the second half is somewhat compressed, distilling the statement and continuation of the former into four notes, recalling the asymmetries of Example 2.1.

So strongly etched is the motivic content of the theme, one barely notices that it is twelve-note in origin. These twelve notes are organized into two whole-tone sets that, freely permuted, provide the bass to one another in a very loose invertible counterpoint. But it is important to note that phrase structure cuts across this twelve-note background: the upper line of the first phrase (bars 1–6), for instance contains eight notes, consisting of one whole-tone hexachord plus an extra two notes. The strained interaction between twelve-note and motivic structural processes is a key characteristic of Wood's music: the importance of his twelve-note ideas is to be found in their role as a source of motivic material, rather than as twelve-note series.

Example 2.3   Symphony Op. 21/iv, bars 1–9 (Brass only)

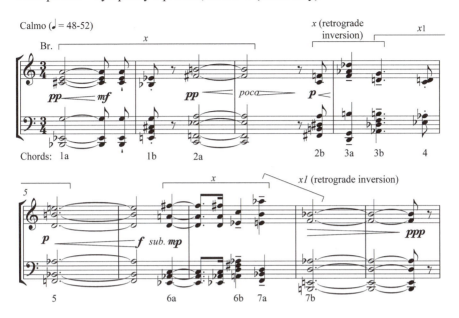

The melodic sweep of Example 2.4, from Wood's Piano Trio Op. 24 (1983–84), is achieved through strikingly simple means. The opening bar of the violin line, for example, is based a descending chromatic fragment, expanded to encompass a range of nearly three octaves. The use of the chromatic scale to generate this intensely lyrical line is by no means arbitrary. On the one hand, it belongs to the family of chromatic lines that underpin some of Wood's melodies.[11] But on the other hand, within the local context of the Piano Trio, it is related to a chromatic figure that appears in various guises throughout the work. The characteristic motivic shape and rhythm of this idea, which can be found in bar 24 of Example 2.4 (motif *y* in the piano accompaniment), is as cramped as the violin melody is expansive: the resulting contrast of character and melodic shape is heightened by the unifying force of the chromatic figure.

Motif *y* in inversion forms the basis of the melodic continuation in bars 27–39. Beginning with the C♯ upbeat to bar 27, the continuation is more or less a descending chromatic scale, albeit with octave displacements, slight kinks and embellishments, covering all twelve notes so as to end in bar 29 on the C♯ with which it started. Wood's characteristic method of indicating the end of a formal unit through the repetition of material is achieved in bars 30–31, in which a short figure (motif *z*) recapitulates the pitches of motif *x*. Overall, this repetition suggests that a ternary structure forms the background to this melody.

---

[11]   For instance, the linear ascent of Example 2.2 is based on a rising chromatic fragment. By way of contrast, the opening theme of the Violin Concerto (Example 6.2, p. 129) is built around a descending chromatic line embellished by small intervals.

Example 2.4   Piano Trio Op. 24/i, bars 24–32

The importance of counterpoint in the affirmation and refinement of the expressive and structural content of Wood's material can be discerned from bars 26–30 of the Piano Trio. A short homophonic piano interlude (bar 26; motif *w*) serves to link the first phrase of the violin melody with the chromatic descent through an octave in bars 27–9. This in turn motivates a brief three-part invention in which the violin combines with the piano right hand (bar 27, beat 2) and then left (bar 27, beat 5). In this invention, the chromatic descent implicit in the violin melody recurs in the two countermelodies; the expressive character of the violin line is thus reinforced and intensified by its contrapuntal companions. A spikier piano figure accompanies the final part of the melody (bars 29–30): one finds that the shifting textures of the accompaniment are used to articulate the form of the extract. Furthermore, the textural alterations – and particularly the contrapuntal textures – encourage mobility: to varying degrees, the music is kept in a constant state of activity. The 'early' entry of the cello, overlapping with the close of the violin idea, further encourages continuity and serves to evade too pronounced a formal division.

The use of a chromatic scale as the basis of a melody is not unique to the Piano Trio: examples can be found from throughout Wood's career. Evaluated against the tenets of high modernism, the repeated use of an *objet trouvé* in a non-ironic manner would probably fall foul of demands for originality. But it is fruitless to evaluate Wood's music against an aesthetic that is alien to him, just as it would be to criticize Mozart when he uses stock accompaniment figures such as the Alberti bass. Far more relevant would be to ask why Wood makes use of melodies consisting of chromatic scales, and how they relate to the material around them. In doing so, we can observe that such melodies mostly appear as secondary ideas, or even second subjects (as is the case for the Piano Trio), which build upon the chromatic tendencies in the primary material. In these cases, there is a clear distinction of character between primary and secondary ideas, with the latter tending to be lyrical and expansive: in a word, romantic. Thus the use of the chromatic scale as the basis of melodic ideas serves a direct expressive purpose, one that can readily be perceived even if the large leaps obscure the semitonal voice leading.

The opening melody of Wood's 1988–89 Op. 31 setting of T.S. Eliot's *Marina* exemplifies many of the characteristics discussed so far (Example 2.5). Note the gradual unfolding of a line from E up through a minor ninth to F (an appoggiatura to the E an octave above the starting point), often guided subcutaneously by chromatic voice leading. The underlying chromaticism is also reflected on the musical surface by means of composed-out chromatic clusters (for instance, the first four notes; motif *x*). The pervasive motion by semitones suggests yearning appoggiaturas, as in bars 7–8. Divorced from a clear tonal context, these would-be appoggiaturas are unable to resolve fully: they employ the rhetoric of tonal conventions, but cannot convey quite the same meaning. In the context of the text – a father's meditation over a lost daughter – they are invested with an unspeakable poignancy. Just as the chromatic foreground remains suspended at an irresolvable distance from its implied tonal background, the father is forever separated from his child.

As the text turns from nautical imagery to that of the dry land, the musical material alters accordingly. The use of alternating ascending major thirds and falling semitones at the words 'And scent of pine' (motif *y*) is a characteristic lyrical motif in Wood's music, particularly in his later works. In the context of *Marina* it offers both contrast and, by virtue of the falling semitone, coherence, with the material based on *x*. A recollection of *x*, which implies a ternary structure, occurs with the words 'What images return'. Here we get the characteristic semitones and minor thirds of motif *x* but not the contour; only with the final words do we get the first three notes of motif *x* itself, transposed up by a semitone. Within Wood's style, the return of this material suggests the end of a section; the fact that it is not at the original pitch suggests it is only a temporary port of call.

Example 2.5   *Marina* Op. 31, bars 2–16 (accompaniment omitted)

The vocal writing found in 'A Last Poem' and *Marina*, though strongly contrasted in character, is nevertheless typical of the composer. The syllabic settings, making use of heightened speech-rhythms, can be found in all of his songs. Of greater importance is the use of inflections in the vocal line to convey the meaning of the text. Note, for example, how the use of triplets in Example 2.5 alludes to the gentle swaying of the barcarolle or the berceuse (both genres appropriate to the textual subject), not least at the words 'water lapping the bow'. The crescendo through the extract, combined with the rise in tessitura, mirror the growing intensity of the images conjured up by the father. At the pivotal moment in which his thoughts turn to his daughter, the whirlwind of sensations cease: the dynamic drops to *piano* and the vocal line returns to its original register, conveying a sense of loss with a minimum of means and a maximum of impact. The opening of *Marina* is thus an effortless blend of lyricism, motivic rigour, a heightened sensitivity to the text and the capabilities of the human voice, and a deep awareness of how technique fuses with expression. These qualities can be found throughout Wood's vocal output, and infuse too his instrumental writing.

Melodic Characteristics

The above examples are all instances of themes in Wood's music: sources of material to be developed later in the work. Each begins with a clearly defined motivic unit or phrase, labelled *x*. The function of such motifs relates to the Schoenbergian concept of the 'basic idea'.[12] Erwin Stein, a pupil of Schoenberg, described the basic idea as follows:

> The basic shape [the basic idea] consists of several notes whose melodic structure (i.e. the relation between whose intervals) is binding upon the entire piece. The rhythm, however, is free. […] Three typical mirror forms of the melodic motif [the basic idea] play a fundamental role: inversion, retrograde motion, and retrograde inversion. They greatly change the physiognomy of the motif but retain its structure.[13]

The distance between Stein's definition and Wood's practice is instructive. Whilst Wood's motifs are subjected to strict inversion, retrograde motion and retrograde inversion, Wood also freely alters the intervallic structure of his motifs, though the contour will usually remain recognizable. Wood's approach is in fact not far removed from the way Bartók composed: a method of motivic working with which Seiber would have inculcated Wood.[14] In other words, the 'basic idea' in Wood's music consists of a musical gesture (comprising one or more distinct motifs) from which further material can be generated, without rigid adherence to the intervals of the original shape.

But Schoenberg's notion of the basic idea was far from static, for eventually it became synonymous with the series upon which a piece was based.[15] Schoenberg's initial impulse was always melodic, from which he abstracted a twelve-note row.[16] Similarly, Wood's themes, and not just their opening motivic shape, are made to function as 'basic ideas' within his music, albeit in a manner far freer than 'classical' twelve-note writing. I will return to Wood's use of twelve-note material, and the ways in which it differs from Schoenbergian precedent, below.

---

[12] Although Schoenberg did not furnish us with a detailed explanation of what the 'basic idea' might be, his pupils did venture definitions. The publication in 1995 of Carpenter and Neff's translation of Schoenberg's *Gedanke* manuscripts as *The Musical Idea* (New York, 1995) contains Schoenberg's incomplete thoughts on the subject, corroborating the arguments advanced by his pupils on his behalf.

[13] Erwin Stein, 'Neue Formprinzipen', *Musikblätter des Andruch* 6/8–9 (1924), translated by the author as 'New Formal Principles' in Stein's *Orpheus in New Guises* (London, 1953), pp. 57–77; cited in Bryan R. Simms, *The Atonal Music of Arnold Schoenberg 1908–1923* (Oxford and New York, 2000), p. 181 (the ellipsis is Simms's).

[14] 'Seiber taught a sophisticated blend of modern thinking, with particular emphasis on Bartók and Kodály and the techniques of motivic composition ... Hugh Wood retains links with the Bartók-Seiber type of motivic thinking, though he later became much more involved with the Schoenbergian world too.' Alexander Goehr in conversation with Julian Anderson, 'The Way to the New', in Alison Latham (ed.), *Sing, Ariel: Essays and Thoughts for Alexander Goehr's Seventieth Birthday* (Aldershot, 2003), pp. 33–41 (p. 34).

[15] See Simms, *The Atonal Music of Arnold Schoenberg*, pp. 200–201.

[16] See Keller, 'Principles of Composition', p. 214.

The content of Wood's basic ideas, be they motifs or extended melodies, is crucial in determining the manner of their continuation. Often, particular intervals are used to characterize a passage, such as the pervasive use of thirds in Example 2.2 or the combination of minor sixths and tritones in Example 2.3. Linear patterns that create a sense of direction are similarly derived from intervallic properties of the basic idea. For instance, the ascending motion of x in Example 2.1 is continued through the subsequent motivic variations; the underlying line that guides this motion affirms and intensifies the latent octatonic properties of x.[17] The combination of motivic working with directed linear motion lends itself to the use of varied sequential repetition that one finds throughout Wood's output.[18]

The chromatic surface of Wood's music is frequently inflected by material that is octatonic or whole-tone in origin, suggesting modal, if not tonal, coherence.[19] Although this tonal background makes certain emotional references and allusions possible, it does not function traditionally. Instead, it is coloured by the symmetrical properties of the octatonic and whole-tone material, not least in the way that symmetrical organizations tend to privilege those intervals that divide the octave equally (semitones, tones, major and minor thirds, and tritones) rather than the perfect fourth and fifth that are of pivotal importance in defining tonal relationships. The use of symmetric material in this way provides an instance of Wood's musical modernism: examples of similar interactions between tonal, symmetric and chromatic modes of organization can be found in the music of Stravinsky, Debussy, Bartók and Webern, to name but four composers.[20] For Wood, the relationship between different types of material is guided solely by the dictates of his ear: he does not think in terms of abstract 'sets' and their manipulation, but empirically, in terms of thematic properties and musical character and how they relate to a specific piece of music.

Wood regularly employs rhetorical devices derived from tonal models for cadential purposes. For instance, returning to Example 2.1, the symmetries created by the use of an octatonic line to govern the melodic motion means that no particular pitch necessarily has the magnetic attraction of a tonic: the theme could end on any note of the octatonic scale, or continue indefinitely. It is only through particular dynamic and rhythmic emphasis that the potentially infinite development is suppressed, cadencing on the final semibreve C. Commonly, passages that are important formally – those that are climactic or cadential in character – are reinforced structurally with the return of pitch material from the basic idea. Where such a reprise is divorced from the contours and rhythmic shapes of the basic idea,[21] it is highly unlikely that the average listener will be able to perceive a relationship. When allied to a distinct shape,[22]

---

[17]   Similarly, Examples 2.2 and 2.4 develop the chromatic arguments advanced in their respective basic ideas.

[18]   See, for instance, Example 2.2.

[19]   As discussed in relation to the opening of *Scenes from Comus*, Example 2.1.

[20]   See, for example, Pieter van den Toorn, *The Music of Igor Stravinsky* (New Haven, 1983); Richard S. Parks, *The Music of Claude Debussy* (New Haven, 1989) and Allen Forte, *The Atonal Music of Anton Webern* (New Haven, 1998).

[21]   As in Example 2.2.

[22]   As in Example 2.5.

the musical character and motivic connections enable the listener to recognize the formal and expressive importance of the recollection.

Counterpoint

The exploration of the contrapuntal possibilities inherent in his ideas as a vital source of energy and power is central to Wood's art. In this, he follows in the footsteps of his musical mentors Bach, Beethoven, Brahms and Schoenberg, as well as Tippett and the Messiaen of the *Vingt Regards sur l'enfant Jésus*. Drawing attention to the form-building qualities of counterpoint in Wood's music, the composer Anthony Payne notes how the 'judicious deployment of points of contrapuntal engagement' are a means by which Wood maintains the 'pace and impetus' of his music.[23] Even more tellingly Wood, writing of Bach and Brahms (but by implication all of the above composers, including himself), states that 'counterpoint is the child of passion not calculation [...] there is no conflict between technique and expressiveness, but rather that one feeds the other, and that both are mutually dependent'.[24]

Hints of this mutual dependence can be found in the discussion about Wood's Piano Trio (Example 2.4), above. A more extended contrapuntal passage, demonstrating similar form-building qualities and control of energy, can be found in Example 2.6, from Wood's First String Quartet. The various contrapuntal combinations of the material give rise to a range of melodic and harmonic shapes that are carefully organized in order to give the passage as a whole a coherent structure. This economy of means contributes to the intensity of the passage, which progresses from relative calm to a striking lyrical climax characterized by impassioned leaps. Note the careful organization by which simultaneous attacks are avoided wherever possible: there is a palpable ebb-and-flow of energy that result from lines 'coming together'. This is particularly salient in the first half of the extract, in which simultaneous events occur on the downbeat in spans that are progressively halved in length (spans of 16 crotchets, then 8, then 4; see the annotations to the example). Subtle touches such as this help structure the rhythmic flow of the extract, and provide a sense of momentum. Common sense suggests, in part, that this avoidance is to ensure maximum comprehensibility of the contrapuntal lines. Certainly, towards the end of the extract, harmonic concerns seem to be given prominence over linear; this is reflected in part by an increase of simultaneous events. Note, however, that even within a texture of relative complexity, one can still detect linear motion, particularly in the F–G–A–B whole-tone ascent that directs the first violin line in bars 53–7. Note too that this occurs in the second half of the extract; the first half gains its momentum not from linear motion, but by employing progressively shorter phrases. Although the different structural processes are separated, overlapping phrases serve to conceal the join.

---

[23]   Anthony Payne, 'Hugh Wood', in Stanley Sadie (ed.), *The New Grove Dictionary of Music and Musicians* (London, 1980) vol. 20, pp. 518–19 (p. 518).

[24]   Wood, 'A Photograph of Brahms', p. 286.

Example 2.6   String Quartet No. 1 Op. 4/i, bars 46–57

General Characteristics of Wood's Twelve-Note Practice

Wood only sporadically treats twelve-note themes in a serial manner. Of the 'classical' serial operations, he most commonly utilizes transposition and inversion: the use of retrograde forms of the row are particularly rare in Wood's output. It is important to note that the horizontal and vertical in Wood's music are rarely treated as equivalent, as in Schoenberg. For instance, the harmonization of the twelve-note theme on which the Passacaglia of the Symphony is based (Example 2.3) is not serial in origin.[25] Subsequent variations of the theme tend to preserve its linear status, with only the occasional verticalization of melodic dyads providing a serial relationship between horizontal and vertical. In variation fourteen, this relationship is altered: the theme is divided into four trichords, which form the basis of the harmony; in variation seventeen, it is divided into hexachords. In these variations, the serial harmony is used to harmonize melodic ideas which are not derived from the series, thus reversing the situation that is found in the theme itself.

The frequent repetition of the twelve-note row demanded by the Passacaglia is unusual in Wood's music. More commonly, the use of twelve-note ideas is reserved for formally significant moments.[26] Connecting these ideas is a musical fabric derived from the motivic content of the twelve-note material. It is crucial for the understanding of Wood's music to observe that he treats twelve-note ideas as sources from which motivic material can be generated, and not as rows to be manipulated. Thus when, for example, Jim Samson states that Wood's orchestral works 'are among the most intensively "thought-through" serial compositions written in Britain in recent decades', the emphasis is firmly on the 'thought-through' rather than 'serial'.[27]

When Wood (re)uses material at important formal junctures, it is sometimes only the pitch sequence that recurs; details such as rhythm, dynamics and contour can be different. This evidently relates to serial thinking, in that pitch can be separated from other musical parameters. The practice of the Second Viennese School provides an important compositional model for this, in which the original pitches are used structurally in an analogous way to the tonic in tonal music.[28]

The division of a twelve-note row into a series of mutually exclusive cells, which can then be used melodically, harmonically, or both, is one of Wood's most characteristic methods of manipulating his material. Neither the ordering of these cells within a work, nor the ordering of pitches within the cell is fixed: they can appear in any order, with any frequency, although Wood commonly tries to keep all the cells 'in play' so as to ensure chromatic saturation (the use of all twelve chromatic pitches within a given span). Typically, Wood restricts the number of pitches in these cells to three or four; these can then be combined to create larger melodic and harmonic units. This technique, which amounts to a re-ordering of the twelve-note row according to certain fixed constraints, can be found in Schoenberg's late music (String Trio, *Ode to Napoleon*) and, more commonly, in Berg's output. In the writings of the Viennese theorist Josef Hauer, a twelve-note row divided into

---

[25] The relationship between the melody and harmony of this theme is discussed below.

[26] This is the case, for instance, with the repetition of the themes of Examples 2.1 and 2.3.

[27] Samson, 'Instrumental Music II', p. 298.

[28] See, for example, Anton Webern's *The Path to the New Music* ed. Willi Reich, trans. Leo Black (Bryn Mawr, 1963): 'The original form and pitch of the row occupy a position akin to that of the "main key" in earlier music; the recapitulation will naturally return to it. We end "in the same key!". This analogy with earlier formal construction is quite consciously fostered; here we find the path that will lead us again to extended forms' (p. 54).

such cells and its transpositions is called a *trope*.[29] As Wood does not, in practice, transpose such a row, I will adopt Hauer's term to indicate a twelve-note row that has been segmented into unordered cells of three or four notes.

A concentrated example of Wood's use of twelve-note tropes can be found in Example 2.6, above. The twelve-note basis of the passage is maintained through the (almost) equal distribution of the four cells both horizontally and vertically. Thus the outer voices consist of twelve-note lines constructed from the permutation of the four cells: the first violin in the order I–III–IV–II–(I), the cello IV–III–III–I. Taking all four voices together, bars 48–51 introduce the cells in the order II–III–IV–I, bars 51–3 in the order IV–II–III–I. It is important to note that the cells of a trope are not bound to any particular motivic shape. For instance, cell IV [F–F♯–G] first appears (cello, bars 47–8) with a typical allusion to a rising appoggiatura (F–F♯) followed by a fall of a major seventh. The same figure can be found in the second violin part, bars 51–2. However, in bars 49–50, the cell appears at the end of a six-note fragment in the viola, with a dotted rhythm imitating a figure in the cello, bar 49. The cell also appears vertically, in bar 56. The method of troping can thus be related to Wood's motivic working, but it can work independently from it too.

In addition to the use of twelve-note ideas as a source of motivic material and structural articulation, we must also observe its expressive significance. One senses the same forces impelling Wood that Webern described at the start of the century. Of these forces, Webern stated:

> About 1911 I wrote the Bagatelles for String Quartet (Op. 9), all very short pieces, lasting a couple of minutes – perhaps the shortest music so far. Here I had the feeling, 'When all twelve notes have gone by, the piece is over.' Much later I discovered that all this was a part of the necessary development. In my sketch-book I wrote out the chromatic scale and crossed off the individual notes. [...] The inner ear decided quite rightly that the man who wrote out the chromatic scale and crossed off individual notes *was no fool*. [...] The most important thing is that each 'run' of twelve notes marked a division within the piece, idea or theme.[30]

The sense of unity to be felt within a twelve-note idea is thus a direct consequence of all twelve notes being employed; it is of a different order to the unity felt by a tonal phrase.

The expressive world to which a twelve-note idea alludes is significant. When Wood wrote of his initial engagement with the music of the Second Viennese School, both serial and non-serial, he drew attention not to the technical procedures he encountered, but to the resulting 'emotional experience'.[31] It is reasonable to assert that Wood's use of twelve-note ideas alludes in part to the expressive world of introverted romanticism that he found in the music of the Second Viennese School. To describe Wood as a twelve-note composer, as plenty have, makes most sense when understood in these expressive and emotional terms; otherwise, without further explanation, it becomes so general as to be meaningless.

---

[29]   Paul Lansky and George Perle, 'Twelve-note composition', in Stanley Sadie (ed.), *The New Grove Dictionary of Music and Musicians II* (London, 2001) vol. 26, pp. 1–11 (p. 1).

[30]   Webern, *Path to the New Music*, p. 51.

[31]   See Chapter 1, p. 9.

To summarize, Wood's melodies are designed to create coherent, comprehensible, and deeply expressive lines that serve as a source for both form-building and further motivic development. In particular, this is often realized using contrapuntal combinations of material, which is a prime means of creating or sustaining energy within Wood's musical language. Whilst the linear and contrapuntal aspects of his music can sometimes be related by twelve-note practice to the harmonic (vertical) aspect, such as when Wood uses twelve-note troping methods, this need not always be the case. In order to understand better the relationship between these musical dimensions, we must now turn to Wood's harmonic characteristics.

Harmony

As with his melodic writing, Wood's harmonic language is characterized by its eclecticism and allusiveness. Whilst acknowledging this diversity, many commentators, and, indeed, Wood himself, have drawn attention to the highly chromatic nature of much of his music.[32] The pervasive chromaticism of Wood's harmonic language is only occasionally organized according to serial principles, and even more rarely is it tonal in origin. What is of importance is what the varied components of this music are, and how they are made to interact. The harmonic pluralism of Wood's music, one of the defining features of his modernism, is thus balanced by an opposing classicizing tendency that seeks the fruitful coexistence, if not integration, of contrasting material.

Tonal Implications

Although Wood's music is not tonal in the traditional sense, it frequently alludes to tonal practices. I have already demonstrated how melodic formulations reminiscent of those in traditional tonal music gain expressive force from the presence of a tonal background, no matter how distantly it is felt. Many of Wood's harmonic formulations are similarly evocative of those to be found in tonal music, yet ambiguous in terms of direct tonal reference. This is achieved through the use of material that challenges traditional tonal hierarchies by implying, or having the potential to imply, more than one key simultaneously. For instance, the augmented triad is often to be found both melodically and harmonically in Wood's music. Schoenberg noted that such

---

[32] For instance, Leo Black: 'Wood's harmonies are gaunt, astringent or purposefully harsh; at other times, of a complexity more clearly linked to that of the sensuously chromatic models provided by late-romantic music' ('Hugh Wood', in Lewis Foreman (ed.), *British Music Now: A Guide to the Work of Younger Composers* (London, 1975), pp. 53–9 (p. 55)). Or Wood, speaking of the influence on his music of the Second Viennese School: 'it was obviously reflected in the all-out chromaticism, in the many chains of twelve notes, or lesser chromatic formations, in the characteristic harmonic and rhythmic formations' (Composer's note to the score of the Variations for Viola Op. 1). The characteristic harmonic formations of which Wood speaks are clearly to be understood in relation to the 'all-out chromaticism' and 'chromatic formations' that he also mentions.

a chord 'belongs to at least three minor keys',[33] and 'it can be introduced, because of its ambiguity, after almost any chord'.[34] It is this potential for the augmented triad to be used in a large number of contexts that allows it, and other similarly 'vagrant' chords,[35] to weaken the tonal definition of a phrase. The more widespread the use of vagrant chords in a piece, the greater the potential there is of creating a fluctuating (*schwebend*) or even suspended (*aufgehoben*) tonality;[36] in other words, of undermining tonal hierarchies.

In addition to discussing vagrant chords, the latter chapters of Schoenberg's *Harmonielehre* also theorize about non-triadic harmonies. These include sonorities that contain 'non-harmonic tones': in other words, chords which in tonal music would be classified as unresolved dissonances that have been elevated to harmonic units in their own right. Other non-triadic harmonies discussed by Schoenberg include those built in fourths or fifths, harmonies derived from the whole-tone scale, and chords built from six or more notes. Wood's music, like the post-tonal music of Schoenberg,[37] makes use of many of vagrant and non-triadic chords. Depending on context, these can gain expressive force by virtue of unconventional or omitted resolutions,[38] but they can also be treated as stable harmonic constructs in their own right.

I have already observed how the use of material derived from symmetrical constructs such as the augmented triad or the octatonic scale is a common means by which many twentieth-century composers have sought to create forms of stability that differ from the hierarchies of traditional tonality. For instance, the way in which the material in the opening of *Scenes from Comus* gravitates to a single transposition of the octatonic scale (Example 2.1) can be considered 'stable' in that there is no definitive motion away from this point of reference. More commonly, however, Wood's music focuses on the juxtaposition of, and sometimes the deliberate contrast between, materials derived from a number of different sources. This is analogous to Wood's general twelve-note practice in which numerous intervallically related twelve-note sets are preferred to a single series in which one intervallic pattern reigns supreme.

Example 2.3 demonstrates how different transpositions of symmetrical material are used to generate momentum in a non-tonal context. All of the chords can be understood as the superimposition of two major triads a tritone apart: the pitch content of chords 1a and 1b, for example, comes from the combination of A major and E♭ major triads.[39] Such chords are used frequently in Wood's music, particularly in later years. Part of their richness stems from the fact that they can be organized to emphasize either one triad or the other, or even a dominant seventh built on one root or

---

[33]   Arnold Schoenberg, *Harmonielehre* 3rd edn (Vienna, 1923); English translation *Theory of Harmony* trans. Roy E. Carter (London, 1978) p. 241.

[34]   Ibid., p. 243. For Wood, the augmented triad is also the most characteristic chord of the whole-tone collection.

[35]   Ibid., p. 134.

[36]   Ibid., pp. 383ff.

[37]   See Simms, *The Atonal Music of Arnold Schoenberg*, p. 16.

[38]   Schoenberg, *Theory of Harmony*, p. 418.

[39]   Chord 4, whilst not containing six notes, can nevertheless be understood in this context as a superimposition of an A♭ major and D major triad, even though the F♯ and A♮ are missing from the latter.

the other. Thus the bottom four notes of chord 1a in Example 2.3 enharmonically spell out the dominant seventh of A♭ major – the whole chord can be heard as a dominant seventh with flattened ninth and sharpened eleventh; chord 1b similarly implies the dominant of D major.[40] (The fourth in the bass, suggesting a second inversion, is also characteristic of Wood's chords based on common triads.) The combination of major triads in this manner has a distinguished pedigree: for instance, Musorgsky uses it (in the form of two dominant sevenths) in the coronation scene of his *Boris Godunov*, as does Stravinsky in *Petrushka* (C and F♯ major). The chord is thus both syntactically and, by virtue of such intertextual references, semantically rich.

More relevant to Wood's music in general is the fact that the chord is a subset of the octatonic collection. Many of Wood's dominant-type harmonies are octatonic in origin, and thus their continuation (or 'resolution') employs a different logic to that of traditional tonality. In the case of Example 2.3, the progression from one chord to the next is determined by the retention of a tritone between pairs of chords; the tritone A–E♭ is common to chords 1a, 1b, 2a and 2b; F–B links chords 2a, 2b, 3a and 3b, and so on. Moreover, as each chord is derived from a different transposition of the octatonic collection (see Table 2.1), the progression is from one transposition to another, rather than motion *within* a single collection, as in Example 2.1. The shared tritones between adjacent chords provide one means of linking the chords; further coherence comes from the shared intervallic properties between chords (a trivial fact, in this case, as each chord contains the same intervallic content).

Table 2.1   Octatonic relationships between chords in the Symphony Op. 21/iv, bars 1– 9 (see Example 2.3) [41]

				Pitch Content				
Octatonic set CI	C♯	D	E	F	G	A♭	B♭	B
Chords 3a and 3b	D♭	D		F	G	A♭		B
Chords 5, 7a, and 7b		D	E	F		A♭/G♯	B♭	B
Octatonic set CII	D	E♭	F	F♯	G♯	A	B	C
Chords 2a and 2b		E♭/D♯	F	F♯		A	B	C
Chords 4, 6a, and 6b	D	E♭		F♯	A♭	A		C
Octatonic set CIII	E♭	E	F♯	G	A	B♭	C	C♯
Chords 1a and 1b	E♭	E		G	A	B♭		C♯
'Chord 8'		E	F♯	G		A♯	C	C♯

[40] The possibilities of such a chord to be considered as a 'vagrant' should be clear: each chord implies at least four tonics (taking the roots of each triad to be a tonic or dominant); if we consider that a dominant chord could also appear as a secondary dominant (Schoenberg, *Theory of Harmony*, p. 385) then the chord in principle could appear in any key.

[41] The three different transpositions of the octatonic set are often classified as CI, CII and CIII. Although the sequence of alternate semitones and tones can begin on any pitch, these transpositions conventionally begin on C♯, D and E♭.

Because of the whole-tone emphasis within the theme (see above), the roots of the first three pairs of chords all belong to one whole-tone collection, and the roots of the remaining chords all belong to the other. The crucial change from chords rooted in one whole-tone scale to the other comes at the melodic climax (Example 2.3, bars 4–5, chords 4 and 5). Note, however, that the harmonic content of the second half of the theme consists of only two different octatonic chords: a third, based on roots of C and F♯ major ('chord 8'), is not used. It may be significant that the chord built on C and F♯ is drawn from the same octatonic set as the first chord of the example (A and E♭); to return to this set would be to return to a form of the 'tonic' (octatonic set CIII; see Table 2.1). This would be at odds with the general harmonic thrust of the passage, which leads towards the 'dominant' sonority of E and B♭ major (octatonic set CI). Thus the harmonic profile of the passage creates its own tonal logic, moving from 'tonic' to 'dominant' and preparing, eventually, the triumphant return to A major at the end of the Symphony.[42]

The interaction in Example 2.3 between whole-tone and octatonic material as part of a twelve-note theme is representative of Wood's harmonic language, in which shared intervallic properties *between* contrasting materials can be made to yield coherent and expressive musical results. In the case of Example 2.3, the aurally perceptible harmonic unity between melody and harmony results in part from the presence of a trichord that belongs to both the octatonic and whole-tone collections. This trichord consists of a tritone divided into a major second and a major third, as can be found in the opening three melodic pitches. The intervallic relationship can be seen more readily if we re-order the pitches to read A–B–E♭, which in set-theoretical notation can be represented as an 0,2,6 trichord.[43] (The use of such notation as an analytic shorthand should not be taken to imply that Wood thinks in, or uses, sets.) The same trichord is also present in the harmonies: the opening chord, for instance, contains the seventh, root and third of a 'dominant' on A (G–A–C♯) and a similar, overlapping, 'dominant' on E♭ (D♭–E♭–G). Indeed, the extract is saturated in such trichords, both melodically and harmonically. Moreover, because the 0,2,6 trichord can be found in both the whole-tone and octatonic collections, it allows Wood to draw on, or allude to, material from either collection without having to remain bound to it for any significant length of time, thus encouraging harmonic mobility without tonal or modal obligation.

One can find the 'dominant' 0,2,6 trichord in much of Wood's music, either in the ascending form (as here), or in inversion. The second and third trichord cells of the twelve-note trope in Example 2.6 are two such 'dominant' trichords in inversion (for instance, E♭–D♭–A), used to great effect in order to create allusions to sevenths at the close of the extract. Used in isolation or as a building block in larger (octatonic) dominant chords, the 'dominant' trichord frequently contributes to the

---

[42]   See Chapter 6, pp. 149–52.

[43]   The integer notation of set theory represents the number of semitones between the notes of the set. Thus if A is 0, B is two semitones higher (2) and E♭ six semitones higher (6). Equally, if we count downwards from A, G is two semitones lower (2) and E♭ six semitones lower (6). Thus, at least as far as set theory is concerned, the second trichord is inversionally equivalent to the first.

more sonorous passages in Wood's music, often alluding to traditional diatonic tonal practices and materials. Similarly, his tonal music can allude to octatonic material. The characteristic sharpened fourth in Wood's tonal music suggests an octatonic inflection as well as the Lydian mode (see Chapter 1, pp. 10–11), and both octatonic and tonal elements can be found in Example 1.2 (p. 13; the melody in bar 38 is entirely octatonic).

Another characteristic chord in Wood's music, used both on its own and as the basis for more complex sonorities, is the 0,1,6 trichord. Just as the 'dominant' 0,2,6 trichord enables interactions between whole-tone, octatonic and diatonic materials, the 0,1,6 trichord can be found in overtly chromatic formulations, octatonic passages and, theoretically if not in practice in Wood's music, diatonic passages. It is most regularly to be found as a perfect fourth superimposed over a tritone, as in Example 2.4 (bar 27, beat 4; it is also the basis of the closing cadence). The 0,1,6 tritone is common in the music of the Second Viennese School, where it is frequently used without implying any particular continuation; Schoenberg's discussion of it in his *Harmonielehre* suggests that in a tonal context, it would have a dominant function.[44] This is also how Messiaen treats the trichord when it appears as the upper three notes of his 'chord on the dominant'.[45] The models of the Second Viennese School and Messiaen thus suggest that, according to context, the 0,1,6 trichord can be heard as astringent or sensuous, as stable or implying the need for resolution; this is certainly the case for its use in Wood's music.

The 0,1,6 trichord is also a particular instance of a chord built in fourths (or, if inverted, in fifths), albeit in fourths of different sizes. Wood also makes use of chords in perfect fourths (or fifths). Often, such chords imply points of stability: a particularly prominent case is the twelve-note chord in fifths that is used to close the Cantata Op. 30 (1989).

Although Wood's music is most characteristically chromatic, his later music has occasionally explored the expressive contrast provided by the inclusion of diatonic material. As is to be expected from a composer interested in exploring the 'manifoldness of symphonic movements' and the integrations of contrasts, one can find motivic and intervallic connections between chromatic and diatonic passages.[46] The relationship between diatonicism and tonality in Wood's music is similar to that between chromaticism and tonality: the degree to which tonal forces are felt to be present depends on the particular context in which the diatonicism occurs. To evoke a distinction made by Tovey, Wood's diatonic music can be 'in' a key, or 'on' a key, but it can also be delicately balanced between these two states, refusing to go one way or the other for more than a few bars at a time.

---

[44] See Schoenberg, *Theory of Harmony*, p. 368, Example 306a.

[45] Olivier Messiaen, *Technique of my Musical Language*, trans. John Satterfield (Paris, 1956), vol. 1, p. 50, and vol. 2, Example 201, p. 37.

[46] Black, 'Hugh Wood', p. 54.

Alternative Approaches to Harmony

A great deal of Wood's melodic writing employs twelve-note material: similarly, his harmonic language often tends towards chromatic saturation. The simplest means by which this is achieved is with twelve-note chords. Just as twelve-note melodies often occur at formally significant moments, twelve-note chords also frequently possess an articulatory role, most frequently appearing at the start or end of a section or work.

More commonly, chromatic saturation is achieved in Wood's music through a series of mutually exclusive chords that together exhaust the chromatic scale. The practice of twelve-note troping is the most obvious and systematic instance of this (see Example 2.6), but by no means the only one. One often finds chords followed by their complement, such as with two mutually exclusive hexachords. Sometimes Wood, like Berg and Bartók, juxtaposes chords that are built predominantly or totally from the black notes on the piano keyboard with those based on the white notes.

An example of chromatic saturation can be found in bar 26 of the Piano Trio (Example 2.4). Here, the expanded semitones B♭–A and C♯–C in the violin mark the end of one phrase and the beginning of another. Bridging this gap, the piano provides a short melodic gesture (*w*) that combines the contour of the violin figures into a single idea. This gesture is thickened into a series of trichords followed by a dyad, each of which contain at least one expanded semitone, thus reflecting the intervallic content of the violin line. At the same time, the trichords establish a harmonic language in which all twelve chromatic notes are in play. The opening violin B♭–A recurs as the final pair of notes in the piano, and the concluding violin C occurs in the first piano chord, thus avoiding any overemphasis of specific pitches within this short space of time. More importantly, the piano part contains eleven different notes: the twelfth, a C♯, is given to the violin. Just as nature abhors a vacuum, so too does the harmonic language here: the violin fulfils a harmonic 'need' established by the piano. Moving from one thing to something different thus creates a sense of motion; coherence is assured by ensuring the continued presence of all twelve notes.[47] Although the listener may be able to discern to a greater or lesser extent this motion, whether they can or not is ultimately irrelevant. Rather, chromatic saturation acts as a compositional constraint for Wood, one of the tools by which he chooses to organize his material. What guides the listener is what the composer does with the material once he has drawn on a particular technique.

For instance, in the case of Example 2.6, the uniformity of pitch resources (the four trichords of the twelve-note trope) does not translate into a uniform harmonic tension. Rather, manipulation of dynamics, texture and especially chord spacing serve to create a sense of progression throughout the phrase. The relationship between the bass and the upper voices is of particular relevance here. As the British composer George Benjamin has observed, if the upper parts relate to the bass 'in a way reminiscent of tonal thinking',[48] functional implications result. Benjamin continues:

---

[47]   Schoenberg describes such motion as being 'regulated by the tendency to include in the second chord tones that were missing in the first', *Theory of Harmony*, p. 420.

[48]   George Benjamin, 'Interview with Risto Nieminen', in *George Benjamin* (London: 1997), p. 16.

> To get away from the quasi-functionality of the bass line, you have to curtail the resonance by using more than one note. [...] Tritones, ninths, sevenths, the type of interval in which the frequency ratios are not so simple, help produce a harmonic texture where the higher registers are freer and the bass line does not resonate in a functional manner.[49]

Wood would have no interest in talk of resonance and frequency ratios, but his own harmonic practice, which is based fundamentally on aural impressions, makes telling use of the bass to manipulate harmonic tension in his music. Thus in Example 2.6, the increasing tendency to emphasize the minor seventh above the bass, particularly in the final bar, serves to shift attention from the linear to the vertical (by alluding to dominant sevenths), emphasizing the harmonic motion just prior to the cadence. Through the careful spacing of vertical events, Wood is therefore able to imply or deny harmonic motion without the listener being aware of other compositional constraints.

One of the consequences of freeing the texture from the demands of a functional bass is that vertical structures frequently become dependent on linear motion for direction. This is most obviously found in Wood's music when diverging lines that create a 'wedge shaped' pattern are thickened. In this way, entire sections or even complete movements can be given linear and harmonic direction. Perhaps the most extreme example of this can be found in the harmonic structure of the first movement of Wood's Chamber Concerto Op. 15 (1970–71; rev. 1978, Example 2.7a). The harmonies of the first half of the movement derive from a 'fanning' out of pitch materials from a central E (chords I–III). A reverse wedge shape can be found in Example 2.7b, from Wood's Fourth String Quartet Op. 34 (1993). Both the treble and bass voices travel through an octave in contrary motion, consistently thickened harmonically by minor sixths. The open noteheads represent chords sustained en route; examination of these reveals that the linear motion of the passage is governed by a diminished seventh (D–F–G♯–B) in both of the outer voices. The close of the extract is achieved not just by returning to the chord with which it began, but by reversing the opening chord pairing: in other words, by re-using material at an important formal juncture.

Example 2.7a   Harmonic structure of Chamber Concerto Op. 15/i

---

[49]   Benjamin, 'Interview with Risto Nieminen', pp. 16–18.

Example 2.7b   Harmonic structure of String Quartet No. 4 Op. 34/iv, bars 1–18

Linear motion in the outer voices need not be confined to wedge-shape motion. In Example 2.6, the bass in bars 52–7 can be understood as the slowly unfolding line C♯–D–E♭, rising to B♭ at the cadence, which complements and counterpoints the rising whole-tone line F–G–A–B in the treble.[50] But it can also occur alongside more traditional bass implications, as in Example 2.2. The basic idea (motif *x*) consists of two overlapping 0,1,6 trichords: E–F–B and F–B–F♯. The pitches present in the harmony (E♭–E–B♭–B–F) can also be segmented into overlapping 0,1,6 trichords: E–E♭–B♭, E–F–B♭ and F–E–B. On this evidence, it seems safe to suggest that the intervallic properties of the vocal motif recur in the piano accompaniment. But before one becomes too caught up in identifying intervallic patterns of this nature, it pays to consider how they contribute to the musical argument. The opening E♭ in the piano initiates chromatic motion in the voice and the upper notes of the piano part that shadows it. The texture is thickened further on the downbeat of bar 1 through the addition to the sustained E and F in the piano of tritones (B♭ and B). The opening of 'A Last Poem', then, hovers precariously between two states. On the one hand, the resonant low E♭ gives the illusion of the piano building up a chord (the implications of this as a functional bass were explored in the melodic analysis of this extract, above pp. 26–8). On the other hand, it can be thought of as part of a heterophonic thickening of the vocal line. Further evidence for this reading can be found in the 0,1,6 trichords that are used to harmonize the final three notes of the vocal line in bar 2. With motivically important intervals occurring in both the horizontal and vertical dimensions of the music, the aural properties of one infusing the other, one can speak of the extract creating a coherent and consistent sound world. In the sense that certain pitch successions (or vertical events) are more likely than others in any given piece (or section of a piece), Wood's music can be considered modal. Thus a set-theoretical demonstration of how the opening bars are saturated with 0,1,6 trichords enables one to appreciate both the rigour of Wood's motivic working and the acuity of his ear.

Expressive Functions

Wood's eclectic harmonic language, and the diverse means by which it is shaped, can be used as a means to articulate the musical structure. For example, adjacent sections can be fashioned from contrasting harmonic materials, which may or may

---

[50]   The bass line is embellished by falling sixths: thus A–C♯, B–D, C–(G)–E♭.

not be integrated at a later stage. But the use of seemingly unrelated material, along with thematic and textural juxtapositions, can also be used for expressive purpose. The jolt created by sudden contrasts is one means by which this is achieved. An equally powerful emotional effect is also created through the sudden welling-up or submergence of tonal allusions.

The technical means by which tonal materials or backgrounds can be alluded to in Wood's music have been discussed at length above. The sensation of dissonances that resolve only fleetingly, if at all; the sense of striving for a point of rest that remain tantalizingly out of reach; the hard-won tonal cadence over an second inversion triad: such struggles infuse Wood's music and inform his style.[51] What gives such allusions their expressive force is their sincerity. There is no sense of emotional detachment or ironic distance from this material, but rather its integration into a post-tonal environment serves to give it renewed meaning. Such sincerity can only be a result of an authentic musical experience, and one that emerges from the concentrated grappling with the musical material rather than as the result of an external or arbitrary imposition.

Sincerity also characterizes Wood's regular use of quotation. Whereas some composers introduce quoted material in order to alienate their listeners, Wood draws on borrowed material for expressive and emotional directness.[52] On many occasions, this material is seamlessly integrated into the musical flow by virtue of shared motivic or intervallic properties; at other times, it interrupts Wood's musical argument, in order to shape or be absorbed into what follows.

Wood's harmonic language contains all the materials available to the post-tonal composer, from twelve-note aggregates and dense chromatic clusters through to luminous major and minor chords. And, in common with all post-tonal composers, Wood has faced the compositional problem of how to integrate such material in order to contribute meaningfully to the musical flow. Solutions to these problems include the creation of a harmonic syntax that is demonstrably relatable to the motivic ideas of the work in which they appear. Wood is also predisposed towards creating a dynamic harmonic language for each work that has its own internal tensions, thereby generating a sense of momentum. The combination, juxtaposition, and synthesis of the various materials and techniques, along with the liberal use of quotations and tonal allusions, in Wood's music are used to create deeply expressive musical arguments, and project an artistic voice that is instantly recognizable as Wood's own.

---

[51] We might note here that Wood's frequent evasion of implied (tonal) cadences often give rise to the 'moments of reticence' in his music identified by Thurlow.

[52] In this, Wood clearly relates to the Schoenbergian tradition; consider Schoenberg's use of the folk song 'Ach! du lieber Augustin' in his Second String Quartet, or the quotations one can find in Berg's *Lyric Suite* and Violin Concerto. See also Chapter 1, p. 21.

Chapter 3

Style (II): Rhythm and Form

Rhythm

Given the importance of communication for Wood, it is not surprising that his material draws on a traditional rhythmic vocabulary that listeners and performers will recognize and respond to. The rhythmic figurations and motifs of the examples given in Chapter 2 are unexceptional in this respect: at the very least, one can readily detect basic upbeat and downbeat gestures. In this, as with his approaches to pitch, Wood's treatment of rhythm is best understood against the background of expectations that his music arouses.

The examples of the previous chapter are essentially Schoenbergian: within them, we can find the fluidity of phrase structure that one finds in Mozart, Brahms and Schoenberg, and a displacement of metric stress that one finds in Beethoven and Tippett.[1] In other words, it can be characterized as Central European. In Hans Keller's words,

> [t]he music of the central-European tradition flows. It is developmental music, and the square, metrical dance schemes against which its unfolding melodies are thrown into relief make sure that the supremacy of time, in both its psychological and its musico-technical sense, is never endangered, even though it may be questioned by sundry healthy opposition motions across bar-lines.[2]

The organization of time is a subject that Leo Black explores in his two articles on Wood's music. In these, Black contrasts two opposing attitudes. The first is that music 'is or can be a static [art], in which there is neither before nor after, no succession; music as architecture, or as a picture gallery, with the listener creating his own unity of perception'.[3] The other attitude, which Black identifies with Wood's music, is that '[t]ime does persist, things in music must by definition occur one after the other, and the impression of time's suspension comes about precisely because of the relationships, the unity, that a composer creates and the listener in turn senses

---

[1] See Schoenberg, *Style and Idea*, p. 174 and Ian Kemp, *Tippett: the Composer and his Music* (Oxford, 1987), 97–101. Note too Anthony Payne's description of Wood's first published works, claiming that they show 'the influence of Schoenberg's ... post-1920 rhythmic configurations' ('Hugh Wood', p. 518).

[2] Hans Keller, 'Rhythm: Gershwin and Stravinsky' in *Essays on Music*, pp. 201–11 (p. 207).

[3] Leo Black, 'The Music of Hugh Wood', *Musical Times* vol. cxv (1974): 115–17 (p. 115).

within a train of events whose principal dimension is clock-time'.[4] This attitude, which Black describes as firmly traditionalist, 'imposes obligations and offers opportunities, among these the manifold techniques of thematicism'.[5]

The relevance of this to Wood's music is that it draws our attention to Wood's articulation of musical time: his sense and control of the pacing of events, and how these relate to the unfolding thematic argument. Against a background of regular metrical schemes and symmetrical phrase structures, Wood's rhythms are supple and fluid, imparting buoyancy to the music. Moreover, the contrast between 'sundry healthy opposition motions across bar-lines' and rhythmic articulations that emphasize the downbeat serve to create in Wood's music long-breathed phrases which have a genuine sense of motion. Wood's music therefore possesses the dynamic qualities associated with extended upbeats, and is punctuated with occasional downbeats that articulate the rhythmic structure.

The greater the freedom taken on the foreground, the simpler the background model has to be to ensure that comprehensibility is not compromised. The opening of *Scenes from Comus* is instructive in this respect (see Example 2.1, p. 25). It was suggested in Chapter 2 that the decreasing duration given to each motivic unit generates rhythmic impetus, if not the sense of an accelerando.[6] This occurs against the background of a traditional two-part form. Yet where the classical model would consist of two four-bar units, the second half of Wood's melody is compressed into three bars.

It should be noted, of course, that, for the listener, the opening of *Comus* does not imply an underlying metre, less still a distortion of a typical eight-bar phrase structure. The dislocation between the metrically limber foreground and the implied regularity of the background is too great for the relationship between the two to be heard, particularly if the performer indulges in *rubato*. Where a clear relationship between the foreground and the notional background *does* exist is on the page of the score, and here the notation is crucial in allowing the performer to understand how one relates to the other. Oversimplifying, one can say that significant events on the foreground tend to gravitate towards (notated) downbeats. This can be understood with reference to Example 2.1, in which the climaxes of the first two melodic gestures (the E♭ and A♮) are metrically (and dynamically) emphasized. Conversely, the position of the B♮ in bar 6 away from the notated downbeat serves to inform the performer that the weight of the phrase should fall on the final C. All other rhythmic events occur within a fluid framework governed on the one hand by the rhythmic co-ordinates just described, and on the other by motivic demands. The result is that the phrase is neither aimlessly floating, nor straitjacketed by metrical stresses: the listener hears irregularly spaced downbeats towards which the other rhythmic events gravitate. The delicate balance between freedom and constraint that results gives the phrase its life and magical effect.

A similar fluidity can be found in Example 2.2 (p. 27), in which the rhythms of the vocal line are organized in order to place the weight of the phrase onto the climactic

---

4   Black, 'Hugh Wood', pp. 54–5.
5   Ibid., p. 55.
6   See Chapter 2, p. 26.

B♭. Note too how the most structurally salient pitches (those of the underlying 'line') are made prominent by virtue of their greater durations. These are 'framed' by notes of shorter durations: the rising semiquaver and quaver arpeggios in thirds, and falling quavers (in fourths) throw the longer notes into relief. However, the impact of the perceptible 'downbeats' in the vocal line is constrained by the rhythmic organization of the piano part, for the accompaniment's implied harmonic and motivic rhythm continually cuts across that of the vocal line. The mild cross-rhythmic effect, in which the two parts are – restlessly – in slight disagreement with one another, intensifies the poetic meaning of the extract: there will never be a final poem, a sense of closure. Yet the two parts are similar enough that the general rhythmic effect of the extract is immediately audible. If we understand the underlying harmonic progression to be governed by the low bass notes, then not only is there a hint of a traditional harmonic progression (♭II–V–I), but a decreasing rate of harmonic change (6 crotchets, 6 crotchets, 8 crotchets) that mirrors the general broadening of the vocal line. As with the monodic opening to *Comus*, there is enough allusion to traditional metric notions of regularity and symmetry to ensure the passage is comprehensible, but it is sufficiently distant to enable it to establish its own rhythmic identity.

The rhythmic characteristics described above result from Wood's engagement with, and development of, Central European traditions. Although they demonstrate considerable freedom, these are to be considered instances of 'multiplicative' or 'divisive' rhythms that, by being understood as the division of larger units (the spans separated by the audible metric downbeats) into smaller units, can be thought of as 'top-down' in organization.[7] For example, in a march, events are understood within the rhythmic framework provided by the regular stresses within a bar, and the regular phrasing of groups of bars.

Theorists often contrast divisive rhythms with 'additive' rhythms, which can be understood as being organized from the 'bottom-up', in which small units are grouped into larger units. Wood's use of additive rhythms derives from twentieth-century trends outside of the Central European tradition. The synthesis, or more commonly the co-existence, of different rhythmic traditions within Wood's music points to the way in which he learns from the example of diverse traditions in order to find his own voice (see Chapter 1). Although instances of additive rhythms can be found in numerous contexts in Wood's music, their most common use is in order to achieve a dancing effect quite unlike the dance rhythms of the Central European tradition, which are understood against the background of a regular metric scheme. Anthony Payne has observed that additive rhythms are 'a prime outlet for pent-up energy' in Wood's music.[8] In a similar vein, Leo Black has observed that 'Hugh Wood's music dances, and here it continues a distinguished British line – Vaughan Williams, Holst, Tippett – even though its way of achieving its aims by quite simple combinations of two and three, in compound metre, has as much in common with Bartók or Stravinsky'.[9] One

---

[7] See Justin London, 'Rhythm', in Stanley Sadie (ed.), *The New Grove Dictionary of Music and Musicians II* (London, 2001) vol. 21, pp. 277–309 (p. 286).

[8] Payne, 'Hugh Wood', p. 518.

[9] Black, 'Hugh Wood', p. 56.

might also add to this list the influence of Gerhard – a composer whose music Wood came to know very well in the late 1950s and early 1960s.[10]

The use of additive rhythms in Wood's music can lead to an irregular placing of stresses that owes nothing to a regular metrical scheme (unlike a march) but rather an accumulative logic. The rhythm of the first five bars of Example 3.1 is instructive: the two phrases are 15 and 20 quavers long respectively, the second phrase extended by the addition of two extra groups, one of three and the other of two quavers:

Quavers	2	2	2	3	3	3	3	2
Phrase 1	♪♪	♪♪	♪♪	♫♫	♫♫	♫♫		
Phrase 2	♪♪	♪♪	♪♪	♫♫	♫♫	♫♫	♫♫	♫

Similar qualities can be found in an early instance of additive rhythms in Wood's String Quartet in B♭ (Example 1.1a, p. 10). The first two bars, for instance, consist of groups of 3+3+2+3 quavers; in bar five, the pattern changes to 3+2+3. These irregular groupings of quavers cohere into regular phrases: four two-bar phrases that themselves fall into two groups of two. But the simplicity of this account is disarming, for it does not take into account how the rhythmic groupings interact with the character of the material. The first four bars are comparatively taut and dynamic, opening with the tonic, but rapidly spiralling away to more remote harmonic areas. At the start of the second group of four bars, the harmonic motion comes to rest on A♭ major: a moment of great poetic beauty. The rhythmic organization of these bars is based on a greater number of groups of quavers; the result is spacious, diffusing, but not dispelling, the energy generated by the opening.

The metrical patterns of this theme become part of the work's background, which generates expectations that Wood can later play with for expressive effect. Thus when the theme is developed (Example 1.1b, p. 11), pervasive use of additive rhythms in each part serves to suspend any perceptible metrical scheme until the downbeat of bar 95, disrupting the normative phrase lengths. The tension created between implied or suppressed divisive metrical backgrounds and additive foregrounds is fundamental to Wood's characteristic rhythmic fluidity.

The energetic and dance-like qualities of additive rhythms can be found frequently in Wood's scherzi, a form that 'he is convinced can most rewardingly be injected again and again with new life and meaning'.[11] In many of these, the refusal of the foreground rhythms to conform to the expected metrical background can be taken as an assertion of the injection of 'new life'. Such freedom can be found, for instance, in Example 3.1, drawn from the central dances of *Scenes from Comus*. Like many of the dances, a sustained note in the bass supports the more complicated material that is suspended above it. These notes provide a large-scale harmonic rhythm that

---

[10]   See Chapter 4, pp. 69–70.

[11]   Andrew Kurowski, 'Sea, Sun and Shadow', *The Listener* (16 August 1984): 30–31 (p. 30). Note again the topic of renewal through the use of traditional forms (cf. Chapter 1, pp. 20–21). That this renewal should occur with primarily rhythmic devices recalls Ian Kemp's analysis of rhythm in Tippett's music: 'If the twentieth century is to take heart from its creative artists it is ... a matter of importance that rhythmic energy should be reasserted' (Kemp, *Tippett*, p. 97).

Example 3.1   *Scenes from Comus* Op. 6, rehearsal marks 40⁺⁴-42⁻³

governs the dances, as well as more local orientation for the twelve-note harmonic material. On the surface, however, the play between rhythmic groupings in twos and threes determines the points of arrival and departure. In the opening six bars of the example, the beginnings of phrases are clearly characterized by the use of duple rhythms (bars 1 and 4) and their continuations by groups of three quavers (see above).

From rehearsal mark 41, there is a change in rhythmic organization. The horns capture our attention first, with a four-chord ostinato in which the durations of events contract and expand. The bassoons that accompany the ostinato follow the horns inexactly, providing an off-beat accompaniment to the notated metre, but placing the horn chords in continually shifting harmonic contexts (compare the first and fourth bars from rehearsal mark 41). The string accompaniment, on the other hand, cuts across the rhythmic emphasis in both the horn and bassoons; on their entry, the strings are grouped into a 3+3+2 (additive) quaver pattern against the (multiplicative) organization of material in the horns and bassoons. In the fifth bar, the wind is organized into a 2+3+3 pattern, the strings 3+2+3, and similar cross-rhythms can be found in the following bar. The result is that one hears a combination of buoyant, vital lines, whose contradicting accentuation patterns serve to delay a clear aural 'downbeat', thereby creating an extended paragraph of considerable energy. This is, of course, closely related to Wood's practice of creating extended paragraphs using multiplicative rhythms: the difference is that in additive passages, the result is frequently more dance-like and driving, rather than lyrical and floating.

Additive rhythms are also characteristic of Wood's fugal textures, which occur with increasing regularity in his later music. For Wood, fugues are 'a great source of energy': he has cited examples by Beethoven, Tippett and Messiaen to support his case.[12] The combination of counterpoint, itself a source of energy within Wood's music, with the drive of additive rhythms is central to his conception of the fugal texture. Some measure of this can be detected in Wood's fugue subjects, a sample of which can be found in Example 3.2.

The pitches of Example 3.2a are derived from the simple Bergian opposition of a hexachord of 'white notes' with its complement (the 'black notes' plus F). Whilst this opposition acts as a compositional constraint, determining pitch successions, it does not interfere with motivic, rhythmic or phrasing decisions. For instance, the first phrase of the theme consists of the whole of the first hexachord and half of the second: the hexachords do not impose artificial limits on phrase length. Rhythmically, one notes that the opening four crotchets contrast with the more limber material in groups of three quavers that follows, ensuring that the fugue theme is always audible when it recurs; the contour is also important in this respect. The additive rhythms that emerge from the regular crotchets at first have the character of syncopations against the notated metre, but in bars 31–2 these become genuinely additive rather than multiplicative. The descending fourths of the example are another means by which energy is created: see too the closing bars of Example 3.1.

---

[12] Hugh Wood in conversation with Sarah Walker, *Hear and Now*, BBC Radio 3, 19 December 1997.

Example 3.2 Fugal themes in Wood's music: (a) Horn Trio Op. 29/ii, bars 28–32;
             (b) Op. 29/ii, bars 68–71; (c) Op. 29/ii, bars 119–22; (d) Variations for
             Orchestra Op. 39, bars 284–8

The fugue subject of Example 3.2b is an inversion of 3.2a, embellished with trills
and grace notes. The theme also recurs in Example 3.2c, which initiates the third
fugue in the second movement of Wood's Horn Trio. This latter example makes use
of motion at a variety of speeds: the minims of the head-motif; their diminution into
crotchets in the following bar, and the hint of additive rhythms the bar after that.

The final example of Example 3.2 is the fugue from Wood's Variations for
Orchestra Op. 39. As with the earlier examples, the insistent crotchets of the opening
give way to an energetic additive rhythm organization. Here, the underlying pitch
organization is that of a twelve-note trope; in contrast to the close relationship
between pitch cells and motifs in Example 2.6 (p. 36), the cells in Example 3.2d are
independent from the unfolding motivic and rhythmic argument.

Whilst the manipulation of divisive and additive rhythms is a vital component of
Wood's style, two other approaches to organizing musical time deserve mention. The
first of these is through ostinati. 'Traditional' uses of ostinati to generate cumulative

rhythmic tension are comparatively rare: a few instances can be found in the central Scherzo of *Scenes from Comus*, in the context of sustaining particular harmonies (as with Example 3.1).

Ostinati that suspend metre are far more characteristic of Wood's music. One way in which this is achieved is through scurrying figures, often semiquavers, which are distributed amongst a number of parts. The figures are usually chromatic, and derived from motivic material, but the combination of a number of these figures serves to conceal this fact from the listener. What the listener perceives instead is a Ligeti-like static 'cloud' against which thematic material can unfold. Obviously, harmonic regions such as this can be established for any length of time. In these circumstances, such ostinati are harmonic and textural rather than rhythmic in purpose: any sense of momentum towards points of rhythmic or formal articulation comes from the melodic material superimposed above the clouds.[13]

The final approach to organizing musical time that will be considered here is related to additive techniques, in that it is based on 'bottom-up' manipulation of durations rather than the division of longer units. This technique consists of the systematic augmentation or diminution of chord lengths by a fixed amount.[14] This, as with Wood's use of ostinati, does not manifest the same developmental trends or form-building potential that inform his other compositional habits. Nor does it have the same fluidity and expressive range of the rhythmic practices described above. Consequently, the systematic manipulation of durations tends to attract attention to itself, disrupting the sense of momentum achieved elsewhere in the work. For this reason, this technique is most commonly used at climaxes. Such is the case in the first movement of the Chamber Concerto between rehearsal marks 9 and 10: each successive chord (the filled-in noteheads in Example 2.7a, p. 45) decreases by one quaver. Each chord is given to a different instrumental family, so that the sense of acceleration caused by the diminutions is married to a kaleidoscopic shifting of instrumental colour. Note, though, that there remains a clear logic to the passage: the top note of each group of four chords (including the climax of the movement at rehearsal mark 10) spells out a diminished seventh tetrachord; together these three diminished sevenths create a twelve-note line. In the Second Quartet and Cantata, chords that decrease in length on each repetition alternate with material that steadily *expands*, as if one idea is subsuming the other.[15]

Form

One of the most compelling features of Wood's music is his masterly control of form. Commentators often refer to the shapeliness and clearly felt direction of his music. Such teleological impulses relate to Black's comments about the organization

---

[13]   See, for instance, Example 8.3 (p. 191).

[14]   This technique seems to owe more to Messiaen's concept of *personages rythmiques* than the numerical manipulations of Berg; the rhythm of the horns in Example 3.1 belongs to a similar method of working. (See Robert Sherlaw Johnson, *Messiaen* (Berkeley and Los Angeles, 1975), pp. 35–6.)

[15]   See Chapter 5, p. 110, and Chapter 7, p. 172.

of musical time – one of Wood's characteristics is the sense of certainty about these designs; the listener is led through the musical argument. 'Formal problems', he has noted, 'are problems of continuity.'[16]

Regarding form, Schoenberg has observed that 'without organization music would be an amorphous mass':[17] it is therefore central to the comprehensibility of the music. Binary and ternary form, for instance, refer to the overall organization of a piece in terms of number of parts; sonata form, on the other hand, suggests the number, size and relationship between parts. Dance forms, in Schoenberg's submission, guide not only the number and relationship of parts, but also the metric, rhythmic and thematic substance of the movement. In all of these cases, prior knowledge of the formal archetypes – part of the background to a work – creates expectations that an individual piece can fulfil and frustrate. But Schoenberg was also talking about form in the aesthetic sense, referring to the thematic and motivic logic and coherence of a work, and the expectations that material, or a particular manner of working, will generate.

Wood's use of form is Schoenbergian. Coupled with his commitment to thematicism, Wood's formal plans are, in the vast majority of cases, determined by the decisions concerning the treatment and relationship between themes (exceptions include the first movement of the Chamber Concerto: see Example 2.7a). When discussing his music in programme notes, Wood's most common practice is thus to identify themes that clarify the formal outline. For instance, of the second movement of his Piano Trio Op. 24 (1982–84), he has written:

> The slow movement is simply ternary. The opening tune, with its falling sixth, is heard on the highest register of the violin: then solos for violin and cello soon turn into a sustained duet. The piano begins the middle sector, which should move along in a more easily lyrical character without changing tempo. Its climax is plunged into tremolando *sul ponticello* playing, which has a climax of its own, then dissolves back into the return – the piano has the tune this time. Cello then violin solo turn once more into a sustained duet. The piano apparently tries to start the middle section again, but after a brief passage for the strings alone, the music rises to the highest register in which it began.[18]

The programme note is characteristic in its avoidance of discussing anything other than musical details (compare this with the multitude of programme notes that discuss everything *apart* from the music). By picking out salient thematic events and musical characters, Wood's programme notes reinforce the audible formal structure: the notes, like the form itself, help establish a specific background within which closer listening and understanding can take place.

Many of Wood's formal schemes draw on traditional models. In such cases, the 'landmarks' of these models, the introduction of contrasting themes and thematic return, are defined clearly. Between these landmarks, though, one finds considerable formal fluidity and invention. Traditional models are thus not formulas that can be

---

[16]   Wood, 'Hugh Wood on his own work': 605.

[17]   Arnold Schoenberg, *Fundamentals of Music Composition*, ed. Gerald Strand (London, 1967), p. 1.

[18]   Composer's note to the score.

adopted uncritically, but rather guidelines to composer and listener alike that serve to orient and provide means of interpretation. One might suggest, therefore, that there are analogies between Wood's rhythmic and formal methods. Just as Wood's rhythmic structures suggest metric co-ordinates between which there is considerable freedom, so too do his formal schemes articulate, but not constrict, the unfolding musical argument.

This can be seen with reference to Wood's *Overture*, written in 2005. The programme notes for the first performance give little away about the form, but nevertheless contain enough information for expectations to be generated: 'The Overture for Piano Trio is a one-movement piece designed as a concert opener and cheerful in nature'.[19] An overview of the form can be found in Table 3.1. The first column provides the most elementary formal divisions, which can be characterized as statement – development – restatement – closure. The second column hints at the distribution of thematic material. As is to be expected, contrasts between materials often mask connections between them. Thus the vigorous counterpoint that closes section A begins with the same pitches and contour as the fanfares that open it. Similarly, the middle section of the piece develops the lyrical character of theme b, but with extensive use of whole-tone steps that relate more closely to theme a.

Table 3.1   Form of *Overture* Op. 48

Section	Basis of material	Bars	Description
A	a	1–11	Fanfare-type material in strings; rushing semiquavers in pianos
	b	12–23	Lyrical violin/cello duet; accompaniment in piano
	c (a)	24–9	Reworking of fanfare material; vigorous counterpoint in piano
B	b	30–40	Unaccompanied violin/ cello duet; lyrical
	b (a)	41–66	All three instruments: lyrical reworking of fanfare material
	b (a)	67–76	Piano solo (extension and development of previous section)
A$_1$	a	77–93	Spectral recapitulation of opening
	b	94–107	Transformed recapitulation of duet; melodic material now in piano
	c (a)	108–16	Extended and increasingly exultant version of closing counterpoint
Coda	a	117–37	Return of fanfares; review of material; emphatic close

---

[19]   Programme note to premiere of Op. 48.

From the table, it is clear to see that the Overture is in ternary form with a coda, in which the middle section is characterized by lyrical material. The outer sections are themselves ternary, in that more vigorous material based on the opening fanfare frames a lyrical central idea. These basic contrasts of character help articulate the formal organization. However, the developmental processes within the piece serve to continually vary the forms of expression within these basic contrasts. For instance, the fanfare material at the outset is loud and energetic, the strings for the most part in octaves and the piano introducing the basic harmonic material of the work as well as rippling semiquaver arpeggios. On its recapitulation, the dynamic has dropped to pianissimo, the violin playing the fanfares as a tremolando whisper, the piano adding light arpeggios ending in trills, the cello a new pizzicato counterpoint. In a similar vein, the recapitulation places the violin and cello duet from bars 12–23 into the piano part, with the original piano accompaniment suggested in the strings. Such reworkings of ideas, in conjunction with the extensions or contractions that one can find in Wood's recapitulations, serves to find new timbral and expressive potential within themes without necessarily altering the basic oppositional quality between them.

What the above discussion demonstrates is that there is an interaction between the static architecture of a formal plan (ABA$_1$ Coda) and the ongoing developmental musical narrative. Wood's music dramatizes the dialogue between these two approaches. For instance, moments of thematic recapitulation are frequently characterized by a reversal of dramatic fortune (such as in the Cello Concerto) or a re-orchestration that explores the effect different instrumental colours and associations can have on the material (Piano Trio, Clarinet Trio).

The sense of direction and shape that one observes in individual movements can also be found in Wood's multi-movement works. In works such as the First and Fourth String Quartets and the Symphony, the first movement functions as an extended introduction, thereby shifting the musical weight onto the Finale. Wood has suggested the nineteenth-century symphony as one model for such end-weighted designs; the influence of Beethoven's later string quartets is also important. Classical precedent informs too Wood's choice of middle movements: in all three of these works, there is both a Scherzo and an Adagio (positioned third in both the quartets). The significance of the scherzo in Wood's music has already been observed: the line of intense adagios that stem from the First Quartet form another important part of Wood's oeuvre. The integration of contrasting characters in this way, and the dynamic balance between diversity and coherence is central to his musical thinking.

The influence of the symphonic formal archetype can also be felt in vocal works. In the Four Logue Songs Op. 2, for example, the ordering and character of songs are similar to those to be found in instrumental music. Thus the first song, in ternary form, is marked allegro, approximating in function to a sonata-allegro. The second exhibits rhythmic devices characteristic of Wood's scherzi, especially in the use of additive rhythms; the third song is the slow movement of the set. Only the rhapsodic final song differs from the symphonic archetype, its predominantly slow tempo and valedictory character bringing the set to a wistful close. It does, however, possess the greatest depth of feeling of all the songs of the cycle, creating an emotional weight that balances the preceding songs. Similar formal patterns can be found in the Five Piano Pieces Op. 5, *The Horses* Op. 10, and the Clarinet Trio Op. 40.

Wood's music surfaces (and formal patterns) tend towards the juxtaposition of contrasting material, with little or no transitional material to connect them. The model here is late Beethoven, particularly the final string quartets, but a more far-reaching prototype is Stravinsky's *Symphonies of Wind Instruments*, which Wood has described as presenting a 'formidable challenge to all [his] formal preconceptions'.[20] The notion of contrasted sections that develop independently from one another, as exemplified in *Symphonies*, was tentatively explored in the first movement of Wood's Trio Op. 3. Greater refinement of this formal technique can be found in Wood's Second String Quartet, which consists of 39 short sections. Although the inspiration for this refinement was in part extramusical, Wood's description of the work makes it clear how non-musical metaphors are swiftly translated in his thinking into 'purely musical' procedures:

> I thought also of sculpture: you can walk round a statue, you can have as many differing perceptions of it as there are angles of vision. Music takes place in time. But suppose you kept each block of material quite integral, and relied for 'development' on ever-changing juxtaposition with other blocks, so destroying any kind of cause-and-effect continuity: would this not produce an allotropic effect, like one's perception of sculpture? And you could alter each block in a wholesale way or allow it to grow of shrink independently of its surroundings. Would this not be 'showing it in a different light' (visual metaphor again)?[21]

Shortly before the first performance of the Second Quartet, Wood wondered if his use of blocs in the work would 'be the first step on a new road',[22] presumably towards a more radical, less teleological, formal organization. Of all of Wood's music, it is the final movement of the Chamber Concerto, premiered a year later, that comes closest to realizing this ideal. However, the first movement of the same work, which consists of blocs that are defined by instrumentation and harmony, suggests a rapprochement between the fragmentary tendency of the bloc technique and the continuity created by many of Wood's compositional methods. The unifying force in this instance is the through-composed linear/harmonic structure (see Example 2.7a), which is articulated by the individual blocs. It is this creation of a new kind of continuity, rather than an 'allotropic effect' that is the enduring legacy on Wood's music of thinking in blocs.

For example, in works such as the Third String Quartet Op. 20 and the Horn Trio Op. 29, formal plans are created from the 'bottom up' through the use of blocs. Developmental processes both within and between blocs, plus the continued re-ordering and juxtaposition of material, are harnessed to Wood's strong teleological instincts to create original and compelling forms. The 'bottom up' approach thus relates to Wood's traditional use of form in the way that his additive rhythms relate

---

[20]   Composer's note to the score.

[21]   Wood, 'Hugh Wood on his own music': 605. In later years, Wood was to prefer the variant spelling 'bloc' when describing this formal process, which is the version that has been adopted in this book.

[22]   Ibid.

to his divisive rhythms: that is, it provides an alternative approach to musical organization that nevertheless produces a similarly dynamic sense of directed motion.

Extended Stylistic Analysis: Cello Concerto Op. 12, bars 1–31

The opening of Wood's Cello Concerto Op. 12 provides an extended example of the mutual dependence of technique and expression in Wood's music. It begins with a twelve-note theme (the 'basic idea', Example 3.3a) that is subsequently developed to create an extended line. Over a funereal march in the sparse, low-pitched accompaniment, the cello intones a lament. There are two motivically related phrases (bars 1–2 and 4–5) separated by the tritone E♭–A. This tritone is afforded particular expressive significance, in part a result of its characteristic rhythmic and intervallic profile, through which it becomes a motif that haunts the concerto. This significance is also due to its sparing use within the theme: the only other tritone occurs between the G and D♭ at the end of the theme (see Examples 3.3a and b). With the exception of the final interval (an inversion of the opening notes), these tritones are the largest melodic leaps: the highly chromatic (semitonal) writing that characterizes the majority of the melody emphasizes the mournful quality of the material. To this, the linear ascent from the opening D♭ to the C a major seventh above it adds a specifically yearning characteristic that shapes the expressive profile of the concerto as a whole.

Example 3.3a   Cello Concerto Op. 12, bars 1–6

For those sensitive to such matters, the E♭–A tritone divides the twelve notes of the theme into two chromatic hexachords a tritone apart: this is made clear in the re-ordering of the notes in Example 3.3b. The transpositional relationship between the two halves of the theme contributes to the compressed and chromatic nature of the material. The melodic and harmonic use of this chromaticism, allied to the motivic significance of the interval of the tritone, is of great expressive importance, for it informs the musical character of the concerto. For instance, the forward drive of the melodic ascent is tempered by the poised quasi-symmetrical construction of the theme about the central tritone. The opening semitone (D♭–C, bar 1) is repeated in inversion a tritone higher in bar 4 (F♯–G); the ♫♩ figure in bar 2 is also repeated a tritone higher. The tensions created by yoking the romantic impulses present in the theme – the striving melodic ascent – to a classicizing (symmetrical) framework of this nature give the theme an expressive quality of restraint, a quality that recurs frequently in Wood's music.

Example 3.3b–d   Analytical details of Op. 12, bars 1–6

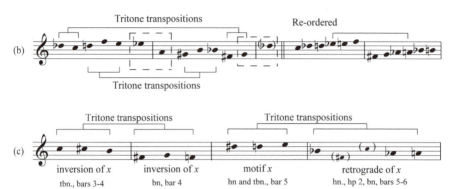

A highly chromatic counterpoint can be found in the accompaniment (Examples 3.3a and c; Example 3.3c omits the sustained tritone B♭–E in the harp and double bass, and the A–A♭–E fragment in the double basses in bar 4). The appearance of this counterpoint, beginning just before the second half of the cello theme, serves to articulate the phrase structure of the passage as a whole. Note, though, how the points of rhythmic articulation in the two lines do not converge: as with so much of Wood's counterpoint, the lack of rhythmic agreement is designed to promote mobility. As with the cello theme, the principles underlying the construction of the counterpoint are strongly dependent on tritone transpositions of individual motifs, although here the tritone transpositions occur from one motif to the next, rather than symmetrically arranged around a central pivot (see Example 3.2c). Although the individual motifs are given specific instrumental timbres, they combine to create a single line (a rare instance of *Klangfarbenmelodie* in Wood's music).

There is a strong degree of motivic similarity between theme and counterpoint: Example 3.3d notes those instances in which pitch shapes are shared either literally or in inversion between theme and accompaniment. The example gives compelling evidence for the evolution of the pitch material: the opening of both theme and counterpoint are strongly dependent on tight-knit chromatic figures which gradually open up across the extract to wider leaps in the fifth bar. What emerges is a dense web of motivic associations and allusions that is typical for Wood's music in its density of thought, yet lucid in its presentation. Moreover, it provides another demonstration of how a twelve-note idea is used to generate further material in a non-serial manner. Expressively, the echoes of motivic ideas in the accompaniment serve to intensify the mournful quality of the theme.

The metrical structure is unusually regular for Wood: even if the harp were not providing a steady crotchet tread, one can detect a regular duple pulse in the cello line. Nevertheless, Wood avoids placing a heavily accented note on the metrical strong beats by the use of short semiquaver 'upbeats' that shift the rhythmic emphasis onto the second quaver beat of bars 2 and 3. These 'upbeats' hint at more strident material that occurs later in the concerto; they also combine with the crotchet tread to suggest the expressive background of a funeral march. The dislocation between metrical and rhythmic accentuation continues until the start of bar 6, when the orchestral lines (Example 3.3a) close on the strong metrical downbeat. This encourages performers and listeners to hear the entire passage as a closed formal unit.

This leaves to be discussed the harmonic language of the theme. The notes of the theme that Wood has emphasized (those longer than a semiquaver), are all part of the octatonic scale CIII.[23] As with so many of the twelve-note themes discussed in Chapter 2, the opening of the Cello Concerto owes something of its harmonic character to the interaction between the surface chromaticism and an implied octatonicism. The vast majority of the 'harmonies' created by the intertwining lines in the opening five bars are derived from either the octatonic set CI or CIII. Those that are not have been marked in Example 3.3a with an asterisk. These are fleeting 'passing chords', with the exception of the harmony that arises on the second and third crotchet beats of bar 5. Even here, however, there is a strong octatonic connection: and the chord may be thought of as a chromatic intensification of the chord that precedes it (that is, the pitches B♭, C, E♭ and E are common to both, and are 'spiced up' with the addition of an extra semitone through the addition of a D). Note that this chord also marks the climax of the phrase: the most obvious deviation from the characteristic sonorities of the passage is also the most intrinsically dissonant.

The mournful yearning of bars 1–5 continues to be the dominant expressive topic of the extension in bars 6–31. However, a gradual accelerando throughout the

---

[23]   See Table 2.1, p. 41.

extension, a lengthy ascent in the cello line (thereby opening out the registral space) and an increased emphasis on the ♩♩♩ figure inflect the prevailing atmosphere with greater intensity and urgency. A thickening of texture culminates in the build-up of a eleven-note chord (bars 22–30); over this, the cello intones the E♭–A motto tritone. The tension is released in a climactic cadence in bar 31. The extension thus transforms the taut argument of the opening five bars into something expansive that communicates expressively with a rare directness.

The musicologist Jim Samson has discussed briefly these bars, stating:

> The truly impressive feature of the work is Wood's ability to build extended paragraphs where motivic working is incorporated within broader directional melodic and bass motions which give structural perspective to serial manipulation. The opening is such a paragraph [...] The magnificent melodic span of the cello line is built from a succession of the work's basic motifs and intervals while the bass line has the dual function of outlining these motifs and intervals in augmentation and at the same time providing a strong directional momentum towards the climax.[24]

Samson provides a graphic summary of these bars, which does indeed demonstrate how both the cello's melodic line and the bass line in bars 6–31 are saturated with motifs drawn from the opening theme. However, Samson's criteria for reduction appear to be based on the entirely laudable analytical premise of identifying the motivic features that appear to guide Wood's compositional decisions: harmonic, rhythmic and expressive aspects are omitted. Example 3.4 provides an alternative reduction of the first thirty-one bars around which a more comprehensive survey can be based. The chords in the reduction are those that are sustained by the strings (with woodwind and brass additions towards the end of the paragraph), rather than those created in passing by melodic motion. Notes in brackets are not sustained (such as notes in the harp), but still register aurally.

The first thing to be noted is that octatonicism continues to be crucial in defining the harmonic language of the concerto: all but one of the chords are octatonic in origin (in this case, the hexachord in bar 20, which is a whole-tone pentad, plus one adjacent semitone).[25] Although the harmonic language is far richer than in the comparatively austere introductory bars, the octatonic chords are once again drawn exclusively from octatonic sets CI and CIII. The outer voices of the chords are in predominantly contrary motion, moving outwards in a wedge shape that provides compensation for the absence of traditional tonal motion. Voice leading is generally by step, and frequently by semitone, recalling the mournful air of the opening bars.[26]

---

[24]   Samson, 'Instrumental Music II', p. 298.

[25]   Note that the chord in bar 22, initiating the motion towards the climax, is the *Petrushka*-type chord that Wood used in the Passacaglia theme to his Symphony (see Example 2.3, p. 29, and Table 2.1). Although the Symphony and Cello Concerto both make use of an octatonically inflected chromaticism, their harmonic language, whilst rich in dominant-type chords, is nevertheless realized differently.

[26]   One is reminded here of the idea of 'creeping chromaticism', introduced by Mark DeVoto in reference to Berg's harmony, with implications of both tonal and octatonic backgrounds. Mark DeVoto, 'Alban Berg and Creeping Chromaticism', in David Gable and

The wedge shape notwithstanding, the prominence of B♭ and E in the bass suggests that this tritone might be thought of as the harmonic basis of the passage – and in particular B♭, which frames the example.[27] There are parallels here to the first subject group of the String Quartet in B♭, which shows a similar equivalence between B♭ and E (see Chapter 1, p. 11).

Possibly the most striking aspect of the harmony in Example 3.4 is the manner in which Wood approaches the vertical ordering. The first chord, in bar 12, has a major sixth between bass and tenor. This expands to become a minor seventh in the next two chords, creating a strong allusion to dominant sevenths chords. Indeed, the lower three notes of the chords in bars 14 and 18 consist of the 0,2,6 'dominant' trichord, which in fact is common in some form to all of the chords in the passage. Whilst these sonorities do not create as strong a sense of forward motion as their equivalent in tonal music would inevitably do, any listener versed in late romanticism or jazz would undoubtedly hear them as some sort of altered dominant, and would thus expect some directed motion. This motion is provided by the linear motion in the outer voices, but I would argue all of these elements combine to create a stronger sense of direction than they would if heard in isolation from each other. The listener perceives therefore that motion of some sort is underway, and comes to expect an arrival; expressively, one is lead to expect some sort of resolution to the yearning created by the upward motion in the solo line.

In bar 20, the interval between the bass note and upper voices changes to a major tenth. This might imply some sense of resolution after the chain of dominant-type chords, and indeed, what follows is sufficiently different texturally to consider bars 20–21 as a significant harmonic co-ordinate within the opening paragraph. Significantly, the chord in these bars is the only one in the extension that is not octatonic in origin: it acts, perhaps, as a 'dominant' to the chord rooted on B♭ that is built up over bars 22–30.[28] Just prior to the cadence closing the passage, the bass interval becomes a less stable tritone (albeit underpinning chords that consist of piled-up thirds), leading to the final eleven-note chord of the passage, which is over a fourth. Like the 0,2,6 dominant trichord, the use of a fourth in the bass is another Wood fingerprint, often indicating a close at some level, in both tonal and post-tonal contexts.

The soloist, the orchestra, or both, melodically reinforce the harmonic changes shown in Example 3.4, either through fast-moving arpeggiations in thirds, or ascending demisemiquaver scales, which terminate on the metrical downbeat. Clearly, the changes of harmony are to be heard as points of arrival en route to the cadence. Melodically, both the soloist and woodwind frequently employ the motif *x* or its inversion (see Example 3.3d): an example of Samson's motivic 'saturation'. Similarly, the underlying melodic ascent D♭–C of the opening six bars provides the

---

Robert Morgan (eds), *Alban Berg: Historical and Analytical Perspectives* (Oxford, 1991), pp. 57–78.

[27]   The tritone B♭–E can be found in the octatonic sets CI and CIII, but not in CII.

[28]   Recall Wood's practice of creating motion by juxtaposing a chord with its complement (see Chapter 2, p. 44); here, the use of a non-octatonic chord in an octatonic context creates a similar effect.

Example 3.4   Cello Concerto Op. 12, bars 1–31 (reduction)

foundation for the linear motion across the entire opening paragraph, working its way up over four octaves to reach a C♯ in bar 22 (the start of the cadential preparation.) From here, the line ascends further, culminating with the E♭–A motto in bars 27–9. This tritone also occurs in the orchestra, echoing the soloist. The three pitches that are of vital importance in the build up to the cadence, D♭–E♭–A (another 0,2,6 dominant trichord), assume pivotal roles in the musical argument that unfolds in the remainder of the concerto.[29]

The motivic content of the accompaniment is equally densely argued. Every accompanying figure in the woodwind or brass can be related rhythmically and melodically to the opening five bars. As the line ascends, the instrumentation of the accompaniment accordingly adjusts in timbre. The woodwind are added one by one into the dialogue, beginning with the bassoons, then the clarinets, oboes, flutes and finally piccolo at the end of the paragraph. Likewise, the brass entries begin with trombones and horns in their lower registers, gradually ascending with the cello, before the trumpets are introduced, again at the end of the paragraph. The tuba is reserved also for the final climax. Obviously, many of the orchestration decisions are designed with balance in mind, but the increasingly bright sound of the orchestration combines with the dynamic pitch structures to create directed motion.

The opening of the Cello Concerto thus demonstrates many of the stylistic features described in the previous two chapters. This includes, but is not exhausted by, the following:

a) the use of recognizable generic and emotional states (for instance, funeral march, yearning) for expressive purpose;

b) attention to the intervallic properties of the basic material;

c) use of the basic material as a source of motivic material;

d) derivation of secondary material from the motivic and intervallic content of the basic material;

e) counterpoint as a means of textural and formal articulation;

f) a balance between external (formal) models and internal properties of the basic material;

g) a strongly defined linear motion in outer voices;

h) a melodic and harmonic language that balances octatonic, chromatic and twelve-note features;

i) sensitivity to vertical arrangements of chords to emphasize or deny functional (tonal) implications;

j) a rhythmic framework in which material gravitates towards certain events (downbeats) but is otherwise fluid; and

k) use of instrumental colour to articulate and define formal and expressive function.

These features, and those like them, cannot be taken in isolation. It is, rather, the unique interaction between such features that results in the effective and affective opening of the Concerto. And it is here that we can begin to appreciate fully Wood's

---

[29] See Chapter 5, pp. 101–8.

style, not in the abstracted habits of Chapters 2 and 3, but in their concrete realizations – the combinations, juxtapositions, affirmations and denials of methods, manners and techniques – in complete works. In doing so, we move from background to foreground, from categorization to interpretation, and understand Wood's compositions not as an accumulation of gestures, but as coherent works of art.

Chapter 4

From the Four Logue Songs to
Scenes from Comus, 1959–1965

Musical life in Britain, and particularly London, experienced a significant upheaval in the early 1960s. This time has been described as 'a period of radical thought at a time of public prosperity, as a strong reaction against the British musical status quo, characterized by a surge of interest in the alternatives offered by the avant-garde and historical repertories'.[1] The appointment of William Glock as Controller of Music of the BBC in 1959 was a significant factor in this 'surge of interest', not least in his innovative concert programming and choice of repertory. In this time, London's reputation as an international centre for contemporary music was confirmed.[2] For Wood, the buoyancy and the vitality of this rejuvenated culture, coupled with the opportunities it provided, formed a positive catalyst for his own compositions.

The two summer schools held at Wardour Castle in 1964 and 1965 encapsulated the adventurous spirit of the times. Conceived by the three Manchester composers, Goehr, Maxwell Davies and Birtwistle, the school offered what was for the time a broad and unconventional programme of concerts, lectures and teaching. Wood and Tippett were also on the teaching staff; Anthony Gilbert taught in 1964 only. Of his time at Wardour, Wood has written: 'The spectacles through which one views the past often become tinted with rose. Nevertheless (and I think anyone who was there would agree) this succession of frantic days amid idyllic surroundings provided an experience hard to come by anywhere today: its idealism and optimism were entirely typical of the 1960s and have vanished with them'.[3]

Wood's continued exploration of a wide variety of music and composers during the first half of the decade shaped his compositions of the period. Alexander Goehr, with whom he formed a close and lasting friendship, was a major influence on Wood's study of Schoenberg and Messiaen. William Glock's championship of Roberto Gerhard at Dartington provided another critical discovery for Wood. The figures of Debussy, Berg, Webern and Eisler were also important. Traces of these influences can be found in Wood's music composed between 1960 and 1963: the Four Logue Songs Op. 2, the Trio Op. 3, a String Quartet Op. 4 and Three Piano Pieces Op. 5. These works bear witness to an increasingly sophisticated treatment of a number of compositional techniques, such as Wood's use of the twelve-note trope. Rhythmically, Wood continued to nurture his rhythmic sensibilities learnt

---

[1]   David Wright, 'London (i): Musical Life since 1945', in Stanley Sadie (ed.), *The New Grove Dictionary of Music and Musicians II* (London, 2001) vol. 15, pp. 148–54, (p. 148).

[2]   See ibid., p. 154.

[3]   Wood, 'On Music of Conviction', p. 328.

from the Central European tradition whilst introducing a more propulsive kind of material into his language, as for example, in his scherzi. There were innovations and refinements too in Wood's use of form: the exploration of discontinuous forms in his Trio Op. 3 can be found alongside strategies devised to give a greater sense of continuity in multi-movement works.

Wood's major work of the period, *Scenes from Comus* Op. 6, was premiered at the 1965 Promenade Concert series at the Royal Albert Hall. At that time, *Comus* was Wood's largest work, in duration, forces and emotional range: for *The Times*, 'it seemed that the composer had shed inhibitions of a sort and allowed himself to grow outwards in a work of expansive melodic lines, orgiastic rhythms and spacious architecture'.[4] The advancements in style, technique and expression evident in *Comus* reflect the three years it took to compose, which was roughly the same duration as that taken to compose the four previous works: the achievements of these early years providing a solid foundation upon which to build *Comus*. Although composition had not necessarily become any easier for Wood, it had, combined with the congenial cultural context in which Wood was working, certainly become more probable.

Developing a Language (1959–1963)

Four Logue Songs Op. 2

The Four Logue Songs for contralto, clarinet, violin and cello, were composed between autumn 1959 and spring 1961, using texts from Christopher Logue's collection of love poems *Wand and Quadrant*. Wood's selection – 'The Image of Love', 'Bargain my Love', 'In the Beloved's Face' and 'Love, do not Believe' – outline a traditional narrative of love and loss. The energy and the nature imagery of the first two songs, recounting the early stages of a relationship, yield firstly to calm reflection (the third song), and then finally an elegy for lost love. Wood's settings intensify this narrative by drawing on a vestigial symphonic structure: the four songs are in turn an allegro, a Scherzo, a slow movement and then, as a Finale, a valediction which nevertheless possesses the greatest weight of the four songs: an early instance of Wood placing the weight at the end of a multi-movement work.

The lengthy gestation of the songs can be accounted for by the fact that Wood was exploring new musical terrain. This was Wood's first post-tonal vocal composition, and the first for which the accompaniment consisted of a mixed instrumental ensemble. Alongside the demands of good vocal writing and handling of texture, the score demonstrates that Wood was tentatively experimenting with the use of twelve-note tropes for the first time. Another significant technical feature was the return of pitch material presented initially in the opening (vocal) melodic statements at the end of the song. Indeed, the return of these pitches in the vocal line, either in part or full, occurs always with the final stanza (or even line). This is true even in ostensibly strophic settings such as 'Bargain my Love', in which the original pitches occur

---

4   'Climax let Down by the Dance', *The Times* (13 April 1967).

at the opening of the first and last stanzas, but not the middle ones. The practice is clearly analogous to the tonal return in the Laurie Lee Songs (see Chapter 1, p. 11).

Wood's settings are expressionistic, responding to the nuances of the text with frequent inflections of tempo, changes of texture and contrasting dynamics. The focus on the text also results in instrumental lines, particularly in the first two songs, that eschew the clear motivic writing of the Variations for Viola in favour of a more gestural syntax. These gestures, often taking the form of extended upbeats, punctuate the unfolding vocal line, commenting on, and responding to, the shifting emotional context. At times, the instrumental lines relate to the voice by means of shared segments of the twelve-note trope; at other times, choice of pitch appears to be determined by a desire to maintain a consistent harmonic language.

There is no place for dramatic gestures in the rapt opening of the third song, 'In the Beloved's Face', but the harmonic organization is representative of the set as a whole (Example 4.1). The vocal line is twelve-note, divided by the text into four three-note cells. A more important source of material for this song however is the twelve-note trope that initially appears in the first four notes of the vocal line (y), the clarinet (x) and cello (z). Yet the cells of this trope do not remain mutually exclusive, as in Wood's later practice: the return of first two notes of x in the cello at the end of the extract, along with the final two notes of z, form another cell (w) that also appears in the harmony. This suggests that groups of two or three notes could be drawn from the four-note cells and combined to create related material. Indeed, the opening harmony combines material from cells y and z, thereby forming part of the complement of cell x that it accompanies.

Operating alongside the nascent troping method of Example 4.1 is a harmonic language that preserves the character of both the opening chord and melodic line. More precisely, the opening chord can be thought of as an E♭ minor chord to which two chromatic notes have been added (D and A; it can also be thought of as a D major chord with added chromatic auxiliary notes). Similarly, cell x consists of an E major chord plus an F; cell y is an F♯ minor chord with a G. Cell z interprets this harmonic 'rule' more loosely: it can be thought of as a C minor seventh chord, with an added auxiliary note D and without a fifth. The chords that follow all belong to this broad harmonic family of altered triads: firstly an altered B♭ major chord, then two altered F major chords and finally an altered E♭ minor chord that, in recalling the opening sonority of the song, serves to end the phrase. The exact choice of harmony at any given point results from the interaction between this harmonic family, the twelve-note trope, and the independent twelve-note line given to the singer. Note how, for example, the melodic material tends to form intervals of semitones (or octave transpositions of a semitone) with notes within the accompanying chords. The harmonic language of the song is thus self-contained, logical, and, if we assume the harmonic 'roots' given above are plausible, provides a sense of progression.

Example 4.1   Four Logue Songs Op. 2/iii, 'In the Beloved's Face', bars 1–8

Trio Op. 3

Some measure of the cultural climate in London in the early 1960s can be gauged from the fact that Wood's Trio for flute, viola and piano Op. 3 (1961), was commisioned by the John Lewis Partnership and premiered in their Oxford Street store. The unusual combination of instruments may have been stipulated in the commission (Wood can no longer remember); at its premiere, it was coupled with an early eighteenth-century work by Leclair employing the same forces. Wood treats the three instruments as equal partners: their different timbres help clarify the contrapuntal material, as does the typically careful rhythmic organization, in which simultaneous attacks are avoided where possible.

The first movement consists of the alternation of contrasting blocs of material: Wood's first attempt at an agglutinative 'mosaic' form of construction (see Table 4.1). The first bloc, *Vivace*, opens with an explosive burst of contrapuntal energy from flute and viola; this dissolves into a trill for viola under which the piano, rising from its low bass register, supplies an extended upbeat into the second bloc. This is marked *Pochissimo meno mosso*; glacial minor ninths in the piano are sustained under an expressive melody in the flute's bottom octave.

Table 4.1   Form of Trio Op. 3/i

Section	Bars	Tempo ($\downarrow$ per minute)	Number of $\downarrow$ beats	Approximate duration (in seconds)
A	1–5	120	15	7.5
B	6–14	104	26	15
A$_1$	15–28	120	43	21.5
B$_1$	29–38	56	36	38.6
A$_2$	39–88	132–8	155	67.4–70.5
	89–100	88	40	27.3
B$_2$	101–15	52–4	56	62.2–64.6
A$_3$	116–23	52–4	21	23.3–24.2
B$_3$	124–9	104	16	9.2
A$_4$	130–31	120	5	2.5

Subsequent developments of the two blocs result in increasingly divergent expressive characters, even though they draw on the same motivic material for coherence. For instance, the flute line at the start of the work begins with successive falls of a minor sixth, outlining the pitches of an augmented triad D♭–F–A; the final note of this is followed by a short chromatic descent in which the second note is displaced by an octave A–A♭–G. These two elements – the augmented triad and chromatic slide – with or without octave displacements form the basis of much of the material of the movement, and are given variety through the expressive contexts in which they are placed. The second section, for instance, begins with a semitone fall followed by a re-ordering of the original augmented triad. The material now appears in the lowest register of the flute, creating a softer 'impressionistic' character; a more lyrical quality is achieved by rhythmic and dynamic changes that serve to further differentiate the second section from the first. One might also note that the flute part in the second section suggests a compound melody, chromatically slithering in a variety of tessituras, rather than the more aggressive mono-linear writing of the first section.

It can be seen in Table 4.1 that in subsequent developments of each bloc there is an expansion of material (in duration, at least), up until the second presentation of that idea, followed by a corresponding contraction (the crotchet beats are given to give an idea of length, because of the regularly changing metre). The two lengthiest sections – sections A_2 and B_2 – form respectively the dramatic and expressive foci of the movement. The first of these, a series of grand upbeat gestures leading to increasingly emphatic downbeats (bars 89–100), is prepared for by an extended and rhythmically vital contrapuntal passage (bars 39–88). By way of contrast, the languid rhythms and meditative lyricism of section B_2 explores a radically different emotional world, eschewing the blood-and-thunder of the dramatic climax for a deeply affective restraint. A similar introspection characterizes the modified reprise of the opening sections in A_3 and B_3, the music fading to a whisper. The movement ends with a dramatic reversal of fortune. A sudden recall of the opening section, compressed into six crotchets (A_4), draws on a characteristic recollection of pitch material to establish the close. The effect is similar to the Coda of the second movement of Beethoven's Ninth Symphony, in which fragments of contrasting material jostle with one another, to be concluded by emphatic octave leaps. In Wood's Trio, the gesture achieves a similar purpose, ending the movement with a gruff smile.

The second movement consists of a theme followed by eight variations and a finale. The opening belongs to the hushed sound world of the latter sections of the first movement, as if the concluding rhetorical outburst had not happened. The first half of the theme consists of two three-note melodic gestures, each beginning with a chromatic dyad in the flute that is completed by the upper note of a trichord in the piano. To this, the viola adds solitary notes underneath the flute line, creating in total four three-note cells: two in the flute/viola, and the two piano trichords. The flute also plays an important role in defining the material of the second half of the theme. Having shared with the piano the six melodic notes of the first half, the melody in the flute completes a twelve-note set. The first three of these notes give rise to a fragment of imitative counterpoint, the viola and piano contributing overlapping melodic figures in a momentary burst of energy that hints at later variations. The final three notes occur over chromatic rustlings in the viola and piano that dispel the momentum generated by the counterpoint, the last of which serves as the first note of variation one.

The theme therefore offers two principal types of material available for development. The first of these is the most traditional: the contours and phrasing of the twelve-note line in the flute and piano provide a source for motifs and a formal model. That the opening five pitch-classes of this theme are a transposition of the opening of section B in the first movement is not without significance. The relationship between the movements that this creates enables thematic material from the first movement to be recalled at the close of the second: a technique to which Wood frequently returns in order to bind together multi-movement forms. The second source of material is the four trichords of the first half of the theme, which together make a twelve-note trope. Throughout the subsequent variations, the two types of material – the melodic line and the trope – interact with one another, sometimes favouring one mode of organization, sometimes the other.

Whereas the variations of Wood's Op. 1 tended to be marked by increasing diversity, much like the blocs in the first movement of the Trio, the second movement of the Trio places greater emphasis on continuity between variations in order to create larger sections. For instance, variations one to four for the most part effect a steady increase in energy and momentum (though not always tempo); this leads to a return to the *Tempo del'Tema* in the extended variation five which closes the group. In addition to the momentum that binds together the first five variations there is also a high degree of textural continuity: only variation three, which makes use of a nervous semiquaver figuration that belongs to Wood's repertory of scherzo gestures, significantly deviates from the textural norms established by the theme.

Textural variety is established in the next group of variations (six to eight), a series of cadenzas for, respectively, the piano, the flute, and the flute and viola. The greater rhythmic freedom the cadenzas provide is neither new nor arbitrary: the second half of the theme consists of a slight accelerando and decelerando, and tempo fluctuations can be found in the variations that follow. The cadenzas can be regarded as a logical conclusion to these fluctuations, and by virtue of a number of references to the first movement, they prepare for the Finale of both the second movement and the Trio as a whole.

The two-part writing of variation eight continues into the Finale, the flute in its upper register, softly intoning the theme. Upon its completion, the theme is repeated in the bass register of the piano. To this is added a counterpoint in the viola, whilst the flute recapitulates the opening theme of the first movement. The slow tempo and soft dynamics transform the latter so that its energy is dissipated: what remains is a tender farewell. This brief coupling of themes dissolves into gentle figuration in the piano: fragmentary gestures suggesting downbeats that never arrive. Hints of melodic figures in the flute and viola are followed by chords based on the twelve-note trope, and the work fades into silence, ending as gently as the first movement ended robustly.

No matter how rooted in tradition Wood's working is, the sound world he conjured in the Trio was far from staple fare for an Oxford Street store; there were letters of complaint to the John Lewis Partnership's magazine. A performance in February 1963 at the Institute of Contemporary Arts in London was to a more appreciative audience. In its review of the concert, *The Times* drew attention to the 'peculiarly mature and sagacious' quality of the Trio, one of three 'striking and enjoyable works' singled out for particular attention.[5]

The *Times* reviewer would not have been aware just how 'mature and sagacious' the compositional techniques used in the Trio are in the wider context of Wood's later career. Wood's formal experimentation and the refinement of the twelve-note troping method in the work provide models that are explored in greater depth in his subsequent music. Although the Trio demonstrated advancements in working practice, the musical results were not always completely successful. The juxtaposition of contrasting material in the first movement of the Trio lacks the intensity of his later uses of this technique. Similarly, the choice and manipulation of cells in the trope restricts harmonic contrast in the second movement. Despite such criticisms, one should not overlook the many attractive features of the music, nor the fact that the Trio remains a significant milestone in Wood's early development.

---

[5]   'Lively young composers', *The Times* (27 February 1963).

String Quartet Op. 4

The Op. 4 String Quartet, written in the first half of 1962, was Wood's first BBC commission. Like the String Quartet in B♭ before it, the Op. 4 Quartet was premiered at the Cheltenham Festival, the performers being the work's dedicatees, the Dartington Quartet.[6] Further comparison between the two quartets is instructive. The most obvious difference is the musical language employed: whereas the earlier piece is tonal, the First String Quartet is post-tonal and highly chromatic, making use of angular melodies and dissonant harmonies. But this difference is somewhat superficial, for the underlying compositional habits, such as an emphasis on motivic working, are similar in both works. Where the two works differ most strongly is in terms of the relative weighting of the movements. The first movement of the String Quartet in B♭ is the weightiest of the three, being a fully worked out sonata allegro with an extended development. The following Adagio runs a close second, with the Finale, for all of its vigour, the most lightweight. For the String Quartet Op. 4, Wood adopts the formal strategy that was to become the norm in all of his subsequent multi-movement works: the placing of the main weight of the work in the Finale. As its name implies, the first movement, *Introduzione*, functions as an extended introduction, presenting material to be developed in the subsequent movements. At times, this development recalls nineteenth-century cyclic models: the Trio of the second movement (a Scherzo) contains themes from the *Introduzione*, and thematic material from the first three movements is recalled in the Finale.

The *Introduzione* is cast in ternary form. The first section is a broad paragraph consisting of three melodic ideas, presented in turn by the viola, the first violin and the cello; these provide a repertory of motivic shapes for subsequent development. The melodic ideas are accompanied by four sustained trichords held in the other instruments: together these form a twelve-note trope. Once all the melodic material and trichords have been introduced, the section closes with a cadential gesture in which denser chord formations are made by superimposing two or more of the trichords.

The melodic material is constructed from sharply defined motivic ideas that are susceptible to development later in the quartet. In contrast, the trichords of the twelve-note trope are motivically neutral and treated as malleable cells, frequently inflected by the rhythms, intervals and contours of the opening thematic material. This can be found in the contrasting middle section, in which the texture of melody plus accompaniment of the outer sections is replaced by a contrapuntal working-out of the trichords, first as two sub-sections characterized by duets and then as four-part counterpoint. Each of these sub-sections begins quietly, growing towards a climax: only on the third occasion do we actually get a release, with the restatement of the opening material in the recapitulation (see Example 2.6, p. 36). But where the opening of the quartet was hushed, the viola contributing an almost lamenting tone,

---

6   The Dartington Quartet also gave the premiere of Wood's Second Quartet Op. 13. They recorded both works for Argo Records (Argo ZRG 750, 1973). The First Quartet has also been recorded by the Aeolian Quartet (Argo ZRG 575, 1968) and the Chilingirian Quartet (Conifer 75605 51239-2, 1994).

the recapitulation is strident and forceful: the melodic material returns in the first violin and cello, two octaves apart. From here, the intensity is sustained throughout the final paragraph, only to dissipate mysteriously after the cadential gesture, an eight-note chord followed by its complement. Out of the ghostly remainder emerges a sustained B for second violin, which leads initiates the Scherzo.[7]

The second movement results, Wood has suggested, from 'liking Mendelssohn, and liking Roberto Gerhard, and perhaps making some unholy compôte'.[8] Although scherzo elements can be found in 'Bargain my Love' (Op. 2/ii) and in some of the variations of Op. 3/ii, this is Wood's first published essay in the genre. It is also somewhat macabre: muted throughout the outer sections and rarely rising above *mezzoforte*, it provides contrast with the dramatic outbursts of the *Introduzione*. The movement opens with a sustained B♮ in the second violin; against this, the viola and then the first violin introduce material derived from the viola melody in the first movement. Developments of this material alternate with a secondary idea based on oscillating semitones in quavers: there is witty play between groups of two and three quavers. The secondary material of the movement, often characterized by ostinati, is frequently interrupted by recollections of the cadential build-up in the first movement.

Further allusions to the first movement occur in the Trio, which is roughly the same speed as the *Introduzione* (♩ = 84 in the *Introduzione* and 84–8 in the Trio); the texture at times recalls the contrapuntal working-out of the development in the first movement, interspersed with arpeggios derived from the Scherzo. In the transition back to the Scherzo, a brief snatch of melody given to the cello in bars 11–12 of the *Introduzione* is re-used, looking ahead to the Finale, when it becomes more prominent.

An Adagietto makes for a brief yet profound third movement. As with the first two movements, the initial melodic motion is a rising minor third, here preceded by a semitone. The resulting motif G–A♭–B is a re-ordering of the pitches of the opening of the second movement of the Trio Op. 3, and has the same rhythm; indeed, the Adagietto shares something of its nocturnal character. Whereas the theme of Op. 3/ii is presented as a relatively straightforward melody and accompaniment, the string quartet soon flowers into more complex contrapuntal texture. The combination of genre, texture and thematic character creates considerable depth of expression with minimal resources: the influence of the late Beethoven quartets is keenly felt here.

What follows is an alternation of the melody with more lyrical variations of the tune, a bloc-like construction that is also suggestive of Op. 3. The simple elegance of the closing four bars – a sighing first violin melody over a rocking accompaniment in the viola – says more in eight notes than many of Wood's peers say in an entire movement.

The Finale opens with a review and reworking of material from the first three movements; the main body that follows is in ternary form, like the *Introduzione* and the Scherzo and Trio. In common with much of Wood's music, there is a basic contrast between the lyric and dynamic: the outer flanks of the ternary form are in a

7   The link between the *Introduzione* and Scherzo was Wood's first idea for the work.
8   Black, 'The Music of Hugh Wood', p. 117.

vigorous allegro character, set against a lyrical middle section. Reminiscences of the previous movements penetrate the substance of the Finale. The main melodic idea is derived from the cello figure that occurs in the *Introduzione* (bars 11–12) and again in the Trio of the second movement; the transition to the recapitulation of the allegro material draws on the Adagietto and the Scherzo; and the reworked cadence figure of the *Introduzione* permeates and articulates the entire movement.

The transformations of the material of the *Introduzione* in the middle movements serve to create clearly defined emotional states and musical characters. Reference to such states in the Finale draws together the disparate trends of the preceding movements, and reinforces the work's end-weighted narrative. If we can talk of the integration of these contrasting emotions and characters, it is not in terms of the resolution of the tensions between them. Rather, through their continued juxtaposition and interrelation in the final movement, new ways of manipulating the tensions between them are discovered, yielding further expressive resources. Unlike the Trio Op. 3, the introduction of material from earlier movements does not therefore serve a climactic function in the Op. 4 Quartet, but rather it forms part of the continual and delicate balance between coherence and contrast that is central to Wood's compositional strategies and sensibilities.

Three Piano Pieces Op. 5

The Three Piano Pieces of 1960–63, written for Wood's wife Susan McGaw, was premiered at Cheltenham, the year after the first performance of the String Quartet Op. 4.[9] That the set is conceived as a whole is beyond question, given the numerous thematic interrelationships that exist; the motivic coherence is matched by a concern for pacing and overall architecture. Within Wood's output, the slow-fast-slow arrangement of movements is relatively uncommon: here, the weight falls in the central movement, *Energico*, a rondo with a pronounced scherzo character. The first movement, *Lento*, begins with a slow introduction, before unfolding gradually an increasingly impassioned songlike melody. The final movement, *Calmo*, is the slightest of the three, reminiscing on the material present in the first two movements.

The first movement was also the first to be written, dating from 1960. Although hints of the twelve-note troping method (along the lines of the Four Logue Songs) can be found in its organization (see Example 4.2a), it owes as much to the freely chromatic writing of the Variations for Viola. The piano writing calls for extreme sensitivity: intertwined melodic lines need subtle dynamic shading in order to avoid obscuring their motivic and intervallic shapes, and the delicate figurations that articulate the movement evoke Chopin. The illusory Romantic world is dispelled, however, in the build-up to the climax (bars 39–43): a series of fragmentary gestures, often involving cross-rhythms between parts, disrupt the evolving melodic line. A restoration of the original twilight romanticism in the closing bars fails to heal the rupture caused by the climax: the opening melodic dyad of the piece returns at the very end, darkened by a thicker, more dissonant accompanying chord.

---

[9]   McGaw recorded the Three Piano Pieces for HMV (ASD 2333, 1967).

Example 4.2a   Three Piano Pieces Op. 5/i, bars 13–16

Example 4.2b   Op. 5/ii, bars 1–4

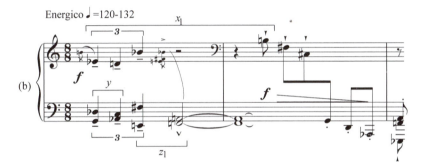

The middle movement, the centrepiece of the set, is 'best thought of as a Rondo'.[10] In the best tradition of a Wood scherzo, it is replete with pounding quavers grouped additively. The opening choral-like idea is rhythmically at odds with the quaver pulse established soon after, consisting of crotchet triplets (Example 4.2b). In the context of the whole set, it has the dual function of initiating the second movement, but also to continue and ultimately absorb the gestural language that caused the first movement to fracture at its climax. Structural support for this reading comes from the reworking of the material of the first movement into four three-note cells in the second (the three triplet chords and the combination of the concluding F–A dyad with the melodic B that follows it). As with the Trio and String Quartet, the resulting twelve-note trope provides a harmonic background that interacts with the motivic and melodic foreground.

Table 4.2 presents a summary of the form: the varied presentations of the refrain are characteristic of a composer for whom formal repetition functions as an opportunity for extensive reworking.[11] In fact, the formal divisions indicated in the Table serve more to convey textural, dynamic and expressive contrasts than thematic regions,

---

[10]   Composer's note to the score.

[11]   See Chapter 3, pp. 56–61.

for the Rondo teems with all manner of melodic and contrapuntal inventions that refuse to be contained by textbook conventions. To take one example from many, the first appearance of the refrain (bar 20) transposes the first four pitches of Example 4.2b down a tone, combining it contrapuntally with its own retrograde (using the original pitches). The transposition of the opening melodic figure (to D♭–C–A♭–G) serves to highlight its family resemblance to Example 4.2a (compare with cell *y*). The inventiveness and formal freedom that characterize the movement looks ahead to the dances from *Scenes from Comus*.

The final autumnal movement, *Calmo*, returns to the lyricism of the opening *Lento*; its exclusive use of the twelve-note trope of the Rondo, coupled with a soft quotation of the opening chords and descending fifths of Example 4.2b, reveals its debt to the second movement. Two expressive crescendi to *forte* and *mezzoforte* respectively provide warmth, not force: the movement is otherwise subdued in dynamics.

Table 4.2   Form of Three Piano Pieces Op. 5/ii

Section	Bars	Description
Introduction	1–19	Alternation of derivations of chordal motif (Example 4.2b) with driving quaver figures
Refrain	20–44	Refrain derived from *x*; mainly in the bass register; concludes with chordal idea
Episode I	45–61	Characterized by trills underpinning development of material from the introduction
Refrain	62–97	Variation and extension of refrain, ending again with the chordal idea (bars 84–88); bars 89–97 recall close of episode I
Episode II	98–115	*Calmo*: lyrical development of *x*
Refrain	116–40	Strongly varied repetition of Refrain material, concentrated in treble register
Coda	141–80	Based on introductory material

Scenes From Comus Op. 6 (1962–1965)

William Glock commissioned *Scenes from Comus* for the BBC: its 25 August 1965 performance was the first of a number of Wood's works to be premiered at the annual Promenade concerts. Wood began the composition on 1 September 1962. The first year saw little committed to paper: work began in earnest in 1963, and it was completed on 25 June 1965. During this time, Wood received 'many hours of patient help and encouragement' from Tony Wright, an employee of Universal Edition, to whom the work is dedicated.[12] Wright's support ensured that Wood was able to complete what was at the time his largest work to date. It was also

---

[12]   Composer's note to the score.

his most ambitious: Wood having hitherto composed in traditional genres, *Comus* was defiantly *sui generis*, containing elements of a cantata, a dramatic scena and a tone poem, but resisting easy categorization. Scoring for soprano, tenor and full symphony orchestra, Wood's treatment of a conventional story (indeed, something of a morality play) imbues it with an almost licentious *joie de vivre*. The same sense of freedom can be heard in the music, in which the influence of the Second Viennese School is enriched by the sensuousness of Gerhard and Messiaen: the resulting language fluidly moves between hard-hitting modernism and affirming romanticism with no sense of incongruity.

Milton's *Comus*, or to give it its proper title, *A Masque Presented at Ludlow Castle, 1634 Before the Earl of Bridgewater Then President of Wales*, was written for an intimate family occasion, evinced by the allocation of the principal roles to the three children of the family – an elder daughter and two young sons. The masque opens with a prologue in which an Attendant Spirit, who was despatched for the 'defence and guard' of the children, sets the scene with reference to the Bridgewaters and the innocence of the children, and of the peril of Comus's wood in which the children find themselves lost.[13] On his departure from the stage, the sorcerer Comus and his entourage appear, 'making a riotous and unruly sound'. Proclaiming the setting of the sun, Comus exhorts his followers to 'knit hands, and beat the ground/ In a light fantastic round'. 'The Measure', denoting both dance and music, follows. The orgy is halted as Comus senses the approach of the Lady, who is wandering alone in the woods, having been separated from her brothers. The revellers hide themselves, just as the Lady, enticed by the sound of the 'ill-managed merriment', enters. Believing that she is alone, she sings a song to the nymph Echo, hoping to discern the location of her brothers, but, as with all petitions to Echo, the Lady remains unanswered. At this point Comus reveals himself and, posing as a shepherd, offers to escort the Lady to a safe haven to await her siblings. In the next scene, the two brothers are searching for their sister, and are approached by the Attendant Spirit, 'habited like a shepherd'. He leads them to Comus and the Lady, who is trapped in an enchanted chair. Despite having foolishly gone off with a stranger, she has by now realized that all is not well, and is refusing to drink from Comus's enchanted cup. This is just as well, for doing so would cause her to transform into a half-human, half-animal. At the moment when it appears that Comus will force her to drink, the brothers appear and drive the villain and his helpers away. However, because the enchanter's wand has not been captured, the Lady remains bound to the chair. The Attendant Spirit sings therefore an invocation to the water spirit Sabrina (associated with the river Severn and thus the setting of the original performance), who eventually rises, also singing, and releases the Lady. In a final epilogue, the Spirit sings a series of songs that end the work.

Wood's selection of scenes and texts re-orders Milton's narrative slightly. After a prologue representing the Attendant Spirit, the Lady enters with her invocation to Echo, sung by the solo Soprano. A short musical interlude encapsulates the mystery and menace of the wood in which the Lady finds herself. Only then does Comus

---

[13] Henry Lawes, the children's music-master, composed music for the original performance, also playing the Attendant Spirit.

enter with his call to dance: here Wood sets most of Comus's opening monologue, sung by the Tenor, and follows it with a Scherzo to represent the 'light fantastic round'. During this riotous orchestral interlude, the opening bars of the Lady's song intrude, representing her arrival upon the scene. There then follows a duet for Soprano and Tenor, who sing first the Attendant Spirit's song that summons Sabrina, and then Sabrina's response. Finally, the music of the opening returns, symbolizing the withdrawal of the Attendant Spirit whence he came. The most telling difference between Milton and Wood's presentation of the tale, however, is with Wood's omission of the two brothers, whose role in the original masque was to rescue the Lady and thus preserve her virtue. Wood's setting presents a far less prim and proper Lady, who doesn't appear to want or need saving: on her appearance in the Scherzo, 'she appears to be enjoying herself'.[14] Indeed, one can detect throughout the work sympathy for the party-loving Comus and his cohort, for whom life and love are things to be savoured; the theme of love as something to be experienced in all its highs and lows runs throughout Wood's career.

Wood's changes to the order of events serve a musical purpose, as can be seen in Table 4.3. Without compromising the essential details of the plot, Wood's ordering of material results in a musical organization that consists of readily comprehensible alternations between instrumental and vocal sections. The recollection of the opening material at the end of the work serves neatly to frame the narrative. It is also, of course, a typical compositional device in Wood's music, signifying the close of a large-scale formal unit, and is one of many such interlocking gestures to be found within the work. Other important musical features, such as allusions to a slow movement and scherzo, serve also to remind us of the symphonic thinking that can be found in much of Wood's music.

Table 4.3   Narrative and musical designs in *Scenes from Comus* Op. 6

Rehearsal mark	Narrative content	Musical section
Start–5	The Attendant Spirit	Prelude (for orchestra)
5–9	The Lady	Soprano Solo
9–19	The Wood/Comus approaches	Interlude/Slow movement (for orchestra)
19–34	Comus	Tenor Solo
34–63	'The Measure'	Scherzo (orchestral dances)
63–8	Sabrina	Soprano and Tenor duet
68–end	The Attendant Spirit	Coda (for orchestra)

The Prelude consists of the alternation of contrasting ideas: one based on lyrical material (Example 2.1), the other more urgent, primarily harmonic, and based on a trope of the opening (see the trope beneath Example 2.1, p. 25). To the subsequent presentations of the lyrical material, Wood adds a second melodic line to create

---

[14]   Composer's note to the score.

brief two-part inventions that in later years become an important source of energy in his compositions. The harmonic material becomes increasingly inflected by the contours and rhythms of fanfares. Eventually, the two ideas are superimposed: a trumpet presenting the tune (a major seventh higher than in Example 2.1) against an accumulation of fanfares in the accompaniment. The end of the melody is delayed through repetitions of the penultimate tritone in a written-out accelerando; the eventual release to the final note of the theme coincides with the climax of the Prelude, and a rapid dissolve into the Soprano solo.

Comparison between the Prelude of *Scenes of Comus* and the works that preceded it demonstrates the development of Wood's musical language in the two years since the completion of the Three Piano Pieces. The alternation between the lyric and the dynamic is common in Wood's music: indeed, it formed the basis of the first movement of the Trio Op. 3. Yet where the earlier work does not seem to strike a fruitful balance between form and content, nor a clear enough distinction between contrasting ideas, *Comus* succeeds admirably. The use of the twelve-note trope to derive the harmonic material from the lyrical satisfies Wood's demands for aural and logical coherence whilst simultaneously maintaining diversity. A firm control of the length of ideas and the pacing of events within them prevents the energy of the ideas from dissipating, and yokes them into a larger structure that only releases its grip at the climax. The sense of dramatic pacing of the Prelude is not entirely new in Wood's music: see, for instance, the String Quartet Op. 4, or the Rondo of Op. 5. What is new is the assuredness with which it is handled: here one feels that the local manipulation of material is now the equal of the composer's natural feeling for large-scale structure.

The magic of the Prelude has been discussed with reference to the allusive qualities of the opening horn solo (see Example 2.1 and discussion, pp. 25–6). This is a magic shrouded in mystery: for all of the warmth of the orchestral colours, the harmonic language is rich in semitones and their octave expansions. The 0,1,6 trichord is the most characteristic sonority of the opening pages of the score. Only with the move to the climax, and the superimposition of the lyric and dynamic, does the harmonic palette begin to warm, exploring further the octatonic and whole-tone implications of the opening melody.

With the entry of the Soprano solo at rehearsal mark 5, the harmonic language flowers into Wood's most romantic form of expression (see Example 4.3).[15] If the opening chordal progression, with implied plagal motion in the bass ('Amen'), might be said to reflect the Lady's virtue, the sensuous chords above hint at a barely suppressed eroticism. The first of these chords is a dominant ninth: to this, chattering woodwind and harp complete the entire whole-tone set. It is followed by a Messiaen-like dominant thirteenth chord on C, drawn from the octatonic set CIII; the Soprano's C♯ also belongs to this set. The richness of the chords, and the sets from which they are drawn, suggest the opulence of late-Romantic harmonic practices. Such allusions co-exist with practices that are more constructivist in nature. The harmonic continuation in the third and fourth bars of Example 4.3 contrives to avoid

---

[15]   There is a strong allusion here to the passage preceding the entry of the Soprano in the first of Berg's *Altenberg* Lieder Op. 5.

Example 4.3   *Scenes from Comus* Op. 6, rehearsal marks 5–6⁻³

B♮, presumably due to its prominence at the Soprano's entry; equally, the Soprano's melody avoids touching on F and C until all the other chromatic pitches have been used. Whilst the Prelude owes much to the troping method adumbrated in Opp. 2–5, the Soprano section has more in common with Wood's songs for voice and piano of the period (which were published later). The bringing together of two contrasting modes of organization in this way demonstrates the pluralism in Wood's musical language that characterizes his mature output.

The Soprano solo ends with reference to the motivic shapes of its opening. The fact that this close avoids the pitches of the opening material, however, strongly indicates that, as with the Prelude, the material has a further role to play within the work as a whole. Some of this play occurs in the Interlude that follows. Here, the motif originally sung to 'Sweet Echo' echoes in the orchestra (just as it does in the horn in Example 4.3, bar 3). Spectres of other sounds haunt the woods in which the Lady finds herself, including fragments of the Prelude, passages of two-part counterpoint, and hints of the revelries of Comus to come. The momentum generated by the juxtapositions of thematic fragments is held in check by warm impressionistic sonorities that reveal Wood's deft hand at orchestration. The balance between static chords and developmental motivic working generates considerable latent energy that is only released in the central dances.

One of the significant melodic differences between *Comus* and the works that preceded it is the greater sense of direction to be found in the melodic and harmonic material, contributing to the dynamism of the work as a whole (for instance, the opening horn solo, Example 2.1). The rising line of the tenor solo (Example 4.4) functions as a refrain throughout Comus's speech, and contrasts with the less driving soprano solo (Example 4.3). Moreover, the scalic motion underpinning Example 4.4 permeates the fabric of the accompaniment: varied sequences, melodic and harmonic, combine with propulsive rhythms to generate the rising excitement of Comus's band of revellers. This is true even in more reflective passages, such as at the lines 'Rigor now is gon to bed' (rehearsal mark 24). Comus's final exhortation ('Come, knit hands, and beat the ground/ in a light fantastic round') reprises material from Example 4.4, thereby signalling the end of the section.

Comus's solo is punctuated by hints of the Scherzo to come; the urge to dance is barely suppressed. The most characteristic way in which this is achieved is through the 'orgiastic use of rhythm and texture'.[16] The latter half of Example 3.1 (p. 53) is particularly instructive in this respect. Over what is usually a static harmony, layers of conflicting rhythmic material and ostinati combine to create a tumult of sound that in the Scherzo frequently builds up to a climactic release (the sexual metaphor is somewhat appropriate). A series of descending major thirds in the brass (reminiscent of the 'statue theme' from Messiaen's *Turangalîla*) which appears first in the middle of Comus's song – and which recurs at key moments within the dances – has a slightly different function. Its characteristic texture, timbre and gestural shape isolate it from the other Scherzo material, resulting in it functioning as an interruption, thereby intensifying the dances it disrupts.

---

[16]   Payne, 'Hugh Wood', p. 518. Although specifically referring to the Three Piano Pieces Op. 5, Payne's comments are equally applicable to *Scenes from Comus*.

Example 4.4   *Scenes from Comus* Op. 6, rehearsal marks 19–20

A variation of Example 4.3, given first to solo oboe and later to cellos, announces the arrival of the Lady into the dances. The end of the Lady's song (from one bar before rehearsal mark 7 to four bars after rehearsal mark 9) is not recapitulated instrumentally. The omission of material that originally set lines devoted to the discovery of the Lady's siblings implies that the Lady has abandoned her search for her family, and given herself over to the dance. The appearance of the Lady creates at first a comparatively still centre to the dances. From here, though, the revels begin afresh, culminating in a climax in which brazen trumpets outline Comus's refrain. Suddenly the music dissolves: an extended presentation of the 'statue theme' draws the proceedings to a halt, balancing an equivalent use of the descending thirds that initiated them.

The Attendant Spirit's invocation to Sabrina that follows the dances introduces yet another idea, one which returns to the lyricism of the Lady's song rather than the strident rhythmic vitality of Comus's exhortations and the Scherzo. The words are given to both soprano and tenor in a close-knit duet. Much of the harmonic organization is based on imitation between parts, often at octave transpositions of the semitone. The strict contrapuntal practice of this section is an extension and development of the numerous fragments of two-part counterpoint throughout the work. But where earlier uses of counterpoint created energy, the use of the same technique here serves a different purpose. Now, the gentle intertwining of lines creates a meditative atmosphere recalling the spiritual detachment of the Prelude, against a lightly scored background that emphasizes increasingly important major thirds. This atmosphere continues in Sabrina's brief response, first given to solo Soprano and then duet.

In both the invocation and response, hints of material from earlier in the work give a retrospective air to the music. Scalic fragments (recalling Example 4.4), lyrical alternations of rising major thirds and falling semitones (from the Lady's solo), and short-long rhythms in both voices and accompaniment (recalling the material of the Prelude) suggest a calm gathering-up of motifs. The character of these closing gestures is reinforced structurally by the recollection of the material (at the original pitch) and spacious and airy orchestration of the Prelude. The work closes with a solo violin in its upper register, intoning the last six notes of the opening horn theme a semitone lower than the original pitches. Against the last note (a high B♮) are a series of major third dyads in the harp and piano, recalling and finally dissipating the thirds of the 'statue theme', and linking to the harmonic material of much of the work. But above all, this still, transparent ending embodies the magic that infuses the score, revealing expressive worlds that were barely hinted at in Wood's earlier music.

Scenes From Comus is a masterpiece, prompting William Glock to state in his autobiography:

> I think that one can look back on a few of the Prom commissions with […] satisfaction. They have weathered the ten-year limit laid down in Cyril Connolly's *Enemies of Promise*, and well beyond. Three outstanding examples are Harrison Birtwistle's *Nomos* (1968), Nicholas Maw's *Scenes and Arias* (1962) and Hugh Wood's *Scenes from Comus*.[17]

For all that *Comus* readily fits the contemporary usage of the word 'masterpiece', it also very much relates to the original term: that of a 'piece' presented by an apprentice to demonstrate his ability to be admitted to the rank of master. *Comus* does indeed represent a compositional rite of passage, drawing on the multifarious technical and formal strategies employed by Wood in his earlier works, combining them with a hitherto unsurpassed inventiveness, in order to create one of his most compelling works.

---

[17]   Glock, *Notes in Advance*, p. 117.

Chapter 5

More than One Homage
1966–1971

Scenes from Comus proved a pivotal moment in Wood's career, and the period after its premiere bore witness to Wood's growing reputation. In 1966, Wood was made the first Cramb Research Fellow in Composition at Glasgow University. He remained based in London, though, until the end of 1970. Commissions came from a variety of sources: the Music Group of London (Quintet Op. 9), Dartington (*The Horses* Op. 10) and the London Sinfonietta (Chamber Concerto, Op. 15). The Glock regime at the BBC commissioned two further works: the Cello Concerto Op. 12 for the 1969 Proms, and the Second String Quartet Op. 13. Recordings of the Three Piano Pieces and the First String Quartet were released in 1967 and 1968 respectively. Wood was also increasingly in demand as a broadcaster: his 1970 talk on Beethoven, later printed in *The Listener*, is an excellent example of the deeply personal and stimulating responses Wood brings to his topics.[1]

The first ideas for the Cello Concerto came three weeks after the premiere of *Scenes from Comus*, whilst Wood was teaching at the Wardour Castle Summer School. Composition began in earnest in the latter half of the year, and again – after a break to compose the Three Choruses Op. 7 in early 1966 – in the following summer. Other interruptions followed: a *Capriccio* Op. 8 for organ, the Quintet, two sets of songs (*The Horses* Op. 10 and *The Rider Victory* Op. 11) and the Second String Quartet.

With the exception, perhaps, of the Second Quartet, one can detect strongly in these works certain influences of *Comus* – in the treatment of the voices in the vocal works, or in the ebullient rhythms of the *Capriccio* and Quintet. However, Wood explores other ideas as well, most notably how an entire piece can be spun out from a bare minimum of material. Wood was ever an economical composer – consider the First Quartet, for example – but in the Concerto, and particularly in the instrumental works of this period, the approach is taken to extremes. As Leo Black says of the concerto:

> He works his basic material very hard indeed: like Rimsky-Korsakov rather than Schumann. Mahler took some such risk in the slow movement of his Sixth Symphony. The resulting obsessed quality is moving, and unenviable: one would not care to see those one admires forced into such risk-taking too often.[2]

---

[1]   See Hugh Wood, 'Beethoven', in *The Listener* (10 September 1970): 325–8.
[2]   Black, 'The Music of Hugh Wood': 116.

The Cello Concerto embodies the kind of logic and coherence that Wood has attributed to twelve-note composition, 'which springs from the wish to make your artistic results very exact and logical, 'watertight', even 'foolproof', every note claiming a function and therefore a significance'.[3] The influence of Seiber can be detected in these remarks (see Chapter 1, pp. 6–7). Whether the paring down of thematic resources in the Concerto inspired similar efforts in the smaller works or vice versa is open to conjecture, but it is evident that it was a concern close to Wood's heart at this time.

By the end of the 1960s Wood had come to find such an approach limiting: when technique is so intimately related to expression, restrictions imposed on the former lead to a narrowness of range of the latter. For all of the grandeur and sweep of the Cello Concerto, Wood evidently felt the artistic necessity of exploring new technical resources and approaches, thereby opening up new areas of expression. The first fruits of this exploration were the String Quartet No. 2 and the Chamber Concerto. Perhaps the most experimental works of Wood's oeuvre, these pieces result from a rethinking and enrichment of the resources at his disposal; some of the consequences of these experiments were to be played out over the following decade.

Towards the Cello Concerto (1966–1969)

Three Choruses Op. 7

John Alldis trained the choir at the Wardour Castle Summer School in 1965; his own choir gave the first performance of Wood's Three Choruses the following year.[4] The challenging vocal demands of Wood's settings, along with the dissonant harmonies, the intricate textures, and rapid changes of mood and sonority, take full advantage of the choir's gifts: no other of Wood's choral music requires so much from the performers.

The basic contrast between the perspectives of the poet and the hawk in Ted Hughes's poem 'The Hawk in the Rain' is reflected in similar contrasts of material and texture in Wood's setting. Dense tutti writing, often in close imitative counterpoint, represents the narrator grounded 'in the drumming plough-land'. The description of the hawk hovering 'effortlessly at height' makes use of solo voices and lighter textures. Both types of material represent the immobility of the protagonists through focal pitches: a recurrent A♮ in the bass for the tutti sections, and a high F♯ for solo soprano (often with an appoggiatura G) for the hawk. With the conclusion of the poem – the hawk's fatal fall to the earth – the voices polarize, the sopranos spiralling to a top B♭ whilst the basses remain fixed to the low A of the ground. The death of the hawk is deeply affective: the word 'smashed' to be performed 'almost toneless, but consonants articulated with great force in a low register',[5] the change of vocal production as startling as it is fitting.

---

[3]   Wood, 'Hugh Wood on his Own Work': 605.

[4]   In 'On Music of Conviction', Wood describes the John Alldis Choir as 'a virtuoso group that did so much for us all in the 1960s' (p. 328).

[5]   Composer's note to the score.

For the text of the second chorus, Wood set part of the 'Sirens' chapter from James Joyce's *Ulysses*. Wood's arrangement of the text draws certain pivotal ideas from the original – in particular, the increasingly elaborate variations of the phrase 'Bronze by Gold' that open the passage in question. Between these variations, Wood intersperses fragments of textual material drawn from throughout the chapter. In doing so, he draws a paean to music from Joyce's intricate narrative, climaxing with the phrase 'sorrow from each of them seemed to depart'. The complexity of Joyce's text is reflected in Wood's setting, in which the full choir is often needed to render a line sensible: the bulk of a phrase might be present in one or two voices, but certain salient words might be restricted to the other voices. Only in combination can the full effect be registered. Some of the wordplay remains strictly visual – the pun on 'blew/ Blue/ Bloom' (bars 6–9) is not aurally perceptible. Nevertheless, it is the musical aspects of the text, particularly the onomatopoeia, which stands out, and is reflected, in the musical surface. Words such as 'ringing' and 'throbbing' have both textual and musical resonance, recalling the impressionistic sonorities of the Interlude in *Scenes from Comus* and presaging Wood's experiments with texture in the 1970s. But the choice of text also predicates (or was predicated by) the musical techniques of the setting. The recurrent 'Bronze by Gold' idea motivates a series of varied and extended repetitions that contrast with sonorous *Calmo* passages, recalling the bloc construction of the Trio Op. 3. Elsewhere, contrapuntal devices such as canonic imitation serve to integrate the sonorous with the dynamic, providing a source of energy that mirrors the singsong in the pub depicted in the text.

The final chorus sets Edwin Muir's brief poem 'All We'. The first half of the poem is a rumination on the 'Pleasure in ev'rything/ And the maker's solicitude'. Gentle imitative writing permeates the setting of this meditation, contrasting with the strictly homophonic setting of the second half (from bar 17 to the end) in which the focus is on the specific rather than the general. Whilst the musical surface makes use of melodic motion by tritones and expanded semitones, and canons at these intervals (for instance, bars 5–8), the harmonic structure is that of an expanded G major. The first half of the chorus is characterized by a large-scale bass movement in fifths beginning on G, reaching E by bars 12–15. At the climax, the bass returns to a G via an E♭, a cadential motion by a major third that is common to many of Wood's tonal settings (see Chapter 1, p. 11). The return to the tonic coincides with the return of the opening material, which is abbreviated and reworked to end with a dissonant and embellished perfect cadence.

Instrumental Music: Capriccio *Op. 8 and Quintet Op. 9*

The *Capriccio* Op. 8 (1966–67, revised 1968) and Quintet Op. 9 (1967) share a number of technical and formal features that were later to be expanded in the Cello Concerto. The former work was written with vivid colours and precise articulation of the Frobenius organ that had recently been installed at Queen's College, Oxford, in mind.[6] Similar virtues can be found in the contrasting timbres of clarinet, horn,

---

[6]   See the composer's note to the score. The work's dedicatee, James Dalton, was the organist of Queen's College. The premiere was given not in Oxford, but at Westminster Cathedral by Gillian Weir.

violin, cello and piano called for in the Quintet, which allow both precision and lyricism. The scoring of both of these works recalls Messiaen: the Quintet adds a horn to the forces of Messiaen's *Quatuor pour la fin du temps*, the organ of the *Capriccio* recalls Messiaen's significant contribution to the organ repertory. These superficial similarities to Messiaen are intensified by the treatment of the musical material, in particular the vital additive rhythms of both works, the ebullience of which surpasses that of the dances of *Comus*.

The timbral clarity and rhythmic virtuosity of the *Capriccio* and Quintet are wedded to a formal sophistication and developmental urge characteristic of Wood's earlier music. Both works incorporate aspects of a multi-movement design into a single movement – an approach to form that one would expect a Schoenbergian such as Wood to tackle. A similar integration of formal designs can be found in the Cello Concerto, but the *Capriccio* and Quintet are no mere preparatory studies: the unique response to the thematic material results in significant variations of form and expression from one work to the next.

Table 5.1 gives a formal overview of the *Capriccio*. The ternary form of the work (fast-slow-fast) corresponds to a traditional three-movement design. The outer sections are also ternary, thus mirroring the overall architecture of the work. The middle Adagio section corresponds to a development section. The final section, however, is no simple recapitulation, for the nature and order of events are substantially altered and developed. This contrasts with Wood's earlier uses of such a formal model such as the first movement of the First String Quartet, in which the exposition and recapitulation were highly similar. The *Capriccio* recalls instead the recapitulatory procedures of the Three Choruses, in which the material is substantially reworked in order to reflect better the continuous development of material throughout the work.

Table 5.1   Form of *Capriccio* Op. 8

Section	Sub-Section	Bars	Details
A *(Molto Vivace)*	a	1–20	Toccata-like theme
		21–8	Chorale-like theme
	b	29–58	*Leggiero* secondary theme
	a$_1$	59–88	Altered reprise of toccata material
		89–91	Codetta based on chorale theme
B *(Adagio)*		92–112	Slow movement/Development
A$_1$ *(Tempo Primo)*	a$_1$	113–40	Contrapuntal development of primary material
	b	141–68	Development of secondary material
	a	169–94	Reprise of opening
		195–205	Coda based on chorale theme

The Capriccio opens with a toccata-like flurry of semiquavers in each hand, *fortissimo*. There is no notated metre: bar lines serve to clarify the additive rhythmic construction. A more sustained theme appears in the pedals in the third bar, which consists of three progressively shorter gestures, each of which sinks lower in pitch. On reaching the final note, the toccata figuration in the manuals fragments and the dynamics steadily decrease. Transpositions of the opening semiquavers in the right hand coalesce into irregularly and increasingly distantly placed chords between which the left hand adds brief semiquaver gestures. A calm chorale-like idea emerges in the manuals (bar 21); the pedals interject with an inversion of the chorale theme. There are numerous motivic and pitch correspondences between the chorale theme and the theme presented in the pedals in bar 3, which has significant implications for the close of the work.

The right-hand semiquavers that open the work trace out a twelve-note line (x), repeated immediately a tone lower. Indeed, much of the first twenty bars can be serially derived (inversion, retrograde, transposition) from portions or all of x, as is the case for the right-hand chords that lead into the chorale section. The chorale melody (bar 21) transposes the pitches of x down a major third, the leisurely presentation of the material contrasting with the quick-fire opening of the work. (There is a parallel here with the G–E♭ shift in the chorus 'All We'; see above.) The harmonization of the chorale is non-serial, although there are shared intervallic properties with the serially derived chords that precede it. The music thus moves between serially, motivically and intervallically related material; the caprice suggested by the title can be understood in terms of technical fluidity as well as musical character.

The lighter second subject combines the semiquavers of the toccata theme with their inversion, harmonized by a slower series of chords: these build to a climax in bars 53–8. The reprise of the toccata material from bar 59 reverses the dynamic shape of the first 30 bars, building quickly from quiet to loud. The final bars of the section refer back briefly to the chorale theme.

The middle section of the *Capriccio* (corresponding to a slow movement) begins with lyrical melodic fragments; the use of solo stops emphasizes the colours of the organ. The fragments are based on further reworkings of x, beginning first with the original pitches, and then their transposition *up* by a major third (reversing and balancing the motion *down* a major third in the first section). As with the development of the First String Quartet, the emphasis is soon on the contrapuntal possibilities inherent in the material. Following the lyrical fragments, a further idea is introduced; these then combine with the chorale theme to create a three-part counterpoint that gently dissolves at the end of the section.

The final section reworks and re-orders the material of the exposition. The reprise of the toccata material midway through the section (bar 169) places a rhythmically augmented version of x in the pedals; the right and left hands provide a continuous accompaniment in semiquavers. The material once again fragments (bar 186), out of which comes a final swirl of semiquavers, *alla cadenza*. This leads to a final cadential presentation of the chorale theme, the material once again derived from transposing x down by a major third. This is the final statement of the work: unusually for Wood's music, this does not involve the opening pitches (x). However, the close relationship between the chorale theme and the theme introduced in the pedals in bar 3 suggests that the use of one is sufficient to stand for the other, enabling the thematic close that is an important aspect of Wood's style.

The use in the *Capriccio* of lyrical passages to punctuate a generally scherzo character is also characteristic of the Quintet (see Table 5.2). Such is the motivic and formal density of the Quintet that one is surprised that it is only six minutes long. The scale of the thematic development and allusions to a multi-movement plan suggest a work of at least twice the length. The illusion of expansiveness is in part a result of the masterly control of dynamic and lyrical material and the manipulation of musical characters that this requires. Like the *Capriccio*, a slower interlude in the middle of the work functions as a contrapuntal development separating two faster sections. The latter of these, however, divides into two: a second development (or perhaps a compressed recapitulation of the entire first section), followed by a more extended recapitulation. This second recapitulation excludes the slower material, enabling a concentrated thrust towards the thrilling conclusion of the work.

Table 5.2   Form of Quintet Op. 9

Section	Sub-section	Bars	Details
A (*Molto vivace*)	a	1–14	Opening theme (see Example 5.1)
		15–24	Closing figure
	b	25–43	Lyrical fragments; bars 33–7 clarinet solo; bars 38–43 reference to opening fanfare material
		44–55	*Cantabile* duet between violin and cello
	a_1	56–69	Reworking of bars 1–14
		70–90	Reworking of bars 15–24
B (*Poco meno mosso*)		91–125	Contrapuntal episodes recalling bars 25–55; climax at bars 105–12; Piano solo bars 113–19; duet between cello and piano bars 120–25
A (*Tempo Primo, ma scherzando*)		126–55	Opens with reference to bars 1–5; bars 149–155 refer back to bars 44–55 and 91–125
A_1	a	156–78	Development of opening material: unison passage bars 167–178
		179–204	Reworking of bars 15–24
	a_1	205–19	Development of bars 70–88
		220–31	Coda (based on opening fanfare)

The vigorous fanfare that opens the Quintet is given in Example 5.1. The upper line is twelve-note, both it and the opening and closing chords of the extract are fourths, fifths and tritones. These intervals permeate the score, contributing to the driving and open qualities of the melodic and harmonic material respectively. The ways in which the lyrical material contrasts with the fanfare material reveals the simple yet effective means by which Wood was able to tease out constantly fresh ideas from a single source. The manipulation of texture, juxtaposing the busy textures of the fanfare material with lyrical solos and duets (see Table 5.2) is one way, as is the octave displacements of notes which transform the bristling energy of the fanfare into arching and yearning melodies. Above all though, rhythmic changes most tellingly differentiate the dynamic from the lyrical in the Quintet. Whereas the fanfare predominantly uses additive rhythms in compound metres, the lyrical material is multiplicative and duple (in sound, if not in notation). The effect is startling: when the solo clarinet emerges from fanfare material in bar 33, the sudden change of rhythmic organization threatens to destabilize the considerable forward momentum that had been building up. A further outburst of fanfares interrupts the solo, only to be cut off once again by an extended duet between violin and cello (bars 44–55).

Example 5.1   Quintet Op. 9, bars 1–5

Once the duet reaches its gentle conclusion, Example 5.1 returns, now scored for clarinet and piano: the other instruments gradually join them. In bar 70, there is a burst of contrapuntal energy, with tightly constructed duets between violin and cello, clarinet and horn (and later piano). This makes possible the close of the first section, a reworking of the extended cadence of bars 15–25, complete with jubilant trills. Contrapuntal energy of a different kind characterizes the second section, a 'slow movement' that draws upon and extends the lyrical material of the first section. The ensemble is repeatedly broken up into smaller groupings, frequently involving imitative writing and overlapping lines. The section ends with first a piano solo, and then a solo for cello accompanied by piano, mirroring and reworking the solo and duet that close the first section.

The first of the two reprises of the opening material intensifies the scherzo character of the opening fanfare. Part of this character comes from the play of rhythmic organization: the additive (and largely compound) fanfare material and lyrical (and duple) material are here juxtaposed and intertwined. Out of this, the violin emerges, *appassionato*, initiating a final statement of the lyrical material.

The second reprise opens with *scherzando* variations of the fanfare passed between instruments that twice build into pregnant chords that are abruptly curtailed. On the third appearance of the *scherzando* variations, the line is extended into a lengthy unison. The unison – a series of ascending waves that grow in dynamic and intensity – leads to a dramatic and extended series of chords and fanfares based on Example 5.1. Towards the end of the section, the texture becomes increasingly intricate, with tightly argued contrapuntal passages joining the chords – now embellished with trills – and fanfares. The 'almost Brahmsian sense of cumulative complexity' finds its release in the coda,[7] in a final burst of fanfares and chords that makes room for a brief allusion to the lyrical material in the horn before reaching an exhilarating close.

The Quintet was commissioned by the Music Group of London, and premiered by them on 11 July 1967 at the Cheltenham Festival. The shifting colours and textures of the score allow the group to demonstrate its virtuosity as individuals and as an ensemble. The ways in which the Quintet integrates soloistic and tutti passages into a compelling and dynamic musical argument embodies the concertante writing to be explored in greater depth in the Chamber Concerto Op. 15 and Variations for Orchestra Op. 39. At one point, Wood had considered adding additional movements to the Quintet,[8] but such are the delights of this warm, pithy and witty work, one can scarcely conceive what could possibly remain to be said in it.

Songs for Voice and Piano: The Horses Op. 10 and The Rider Victory Op. 11

The two song collections published in the late 1960s, *The Horses* and *The Rider Victory*, like the earlier Three Choruses, draw, respectively, on texts by Ted Hughes and Edwin Muir.[9] The somewhat convoluted composition history for *The Horses* is by no means atypical for Wood, who has frequently turned and returned to different poets, poems and settings: numerous songs to texts by Robert Graves and D.H. Lawrence (amongst others) were first conceived in the 1960s, only to be completed in later decades.

---

[7]   'Quintet is Brief but Vital', *The Times* (12 July 1967).

[8]   From a talk given by the composer in Oxford, 5 November 1997.

[9]   Both song sets were recorded for Argo Records in 1973, by the soprano April Cantelo and pianist Paul Hamburger (Argo ZRG 750).

The Horses was commissioned by the Dartington Summer School; Jane Manning and Susan Bradshaw performed two of the set there in August 1967. A note of the score of the first of these, 'The Horses' suggests that it was finished shortly before this concert ('midnight 1 Aug 67 Dartington'); the second, 'September', was 'mostly written Aug 63' and revised 'July 66'). A third, 'Pennines in April', completed in Glasgow on 7 November 1967 became the middle song of the set, and all three were performed, again by Manning and Bradshaw, in the Wigmore Hall on 13 November. In April and May 1968, Wood revised the songs, offering them to William Glock for his sixtieth birthday on 3 May that year.

The three songs of *The Horses* reveal a concern for overall architecture; there is a similarity with the Three Piano Pieces in the ordering slow-fast-slow. The weight, however, is on the first song of the set, 'The Horses'. The nature imagery in the text inspires from Wood a richly varied and evocative setting (see below). Rolling arpeggios and murmuring quaver oscillations characterize 'Pennines in April', which functions as a scherzo. The final song, 'September' sets an autumnal romantic lyric as a remembrance of summer and the memories of love.

The composition of *The Rider Victory* was by contrast straightforward, occupying Wood for the first four months of 1968. Of all of Wood's music the collection is most directly related to his position as Cramb Research Fellow at Glasgow University. Setting poems by the Scottish Edwin Muir, whose early career was based in Glasgow, the collection was dedicated to 'Professor F. Rimmer and the Cramb Trustees' and first performed in Glasgow in November 1968.

Like the Logue Songs before it, *The Rider Victory* consists of four songs that draw on instrumental multi-movement characters. The first song ('The Rider Victory') is a lively *Vivace* characterized by whole-tone fanfares in the piano. The middle pair of songs are respectively a slow movement ('Sorrow') and scherzo ('The Bird'). The last is a rapt and passionate love song ('The Confirmation'); as with the Logue Songs and *The Horses*, the set ends with a quiet intensity.

The vocal writing in the two song sets is characteristic: much of it syllabic, reflecting Wood's straightforward approach to word setting. There are only three instances of melismatic writing in the seven songs: once in 'The Bird' ('airy', bars 30–31) and twice in 'The Confirmation' ('blowing' in bar 23 and 'wandering' in bar 25). All of these words lend themselves to word-painting, but it is Wood's sparing use of this technique that makes it so emphatic when it occurs. Wood demands much from his vocalists: the musical response to nuances of meaning in the text requires a wide variety of vocal techniques, from *molto cantabile* lyricism to *recitando* declamation. Take, for example, the opening of 'Sorrow' from *The Rider Victory*. Each line is coloured differently. The first, 'I do not want it so / But since things so are made', is based on alternately rising and falling augmented triads. Marked *molto semplice*, the line demands a manner of delivery that reflects a calm acceptance of sorrow. This is followed by a pair of descending major thirds to the word 'sorrow' that the singer is instructed to sing *piangendo* (in a tearful manner). The contrast between the mannered opening and its expressive continuation highlights the difference between the emotional state of the protagonist and that of the emotion he/she is describing, even though the musical material (major thirds) is the same. A third phrase, 'Be you my second trade', *sostenuto ma con moto* offers a different perspective: the melodic material is more chromatic and characterized by large expressive leaps. Underneath, the piano echoes the descending thirds of 'sorrow'; no matter how positive the protagonist is, sorrow cannot be avoided.

The first three lines of 'Sorrow' are placed in the lower register of the singer's voice, yet still span an octave and a fourth; as the passions rise, this range is extended by a further fifth to cover two octaves. Most of the songs in the two sets have a similar range; the smallest can be found in the introspective 'September', which spans a minor thirteenth. The exploration of vocal extremes is an important expressive resource in Wood's writing, particularly in the songs of the 1960s and 1970s. In Opp. 10 and 11, it is most frequently used to signal emotional intensity, as in the opening declamation of 'The Confirmation': 'Yes, yours, my love, is the right human face'. Within the first seven notes the setting of these words covers a major thirteenth, falling first through a minor tenth (from G to E) and then an eleventh (E♭ to B♭). Elsewhere, similar means are used for depictive purposes: the representation of the enormous masses of the Pennines ('Pennines in April') and the alternately staccato and soaring motions of a bird ('The Bird') both employ vocal extremes and wide leaps to achieve their end.

The piano accompaniment frequently draws on material first presented by the voice. In some instances, such as 'Pennines in April', and 'The Bird', the opening vocal line suggests a motivic figure that saturates the movement; elsewhere, such as 'Sorrow', it is the intervallic content of the opening that informs the piano part (although here, the traffic is not just one way: the opening piano motif becomes the closing motif for the voice). These all happen to be the middle songs of their respective collections; 'Pennines in April' and 'The Bird' are scherzo-type movements, and demonstrate a similar economy of means to that of the *Capriccio* and Quintet. The range of gesture in the accompaniments to these songs is narrower than that for the outer movements (see below), but sufficiently varied to respond to the poetic situation. That for 'The Bird', for example, consists of rapid alterations of airy arpeggios, short chorale-like passages and staccato chords. These capture the dynamic motions and nervous energy of a small bird; 'pictorial' accompanimental figures, such as stylized birdsong are avoided. A short passage at the end – a moment's reflection – introduces a further textural idea, an oscillating quaver cluster marked *murmurando* – an instruction (and figuration) that occurs in several of Wood's songs (for instance, 'Pennines in April'; the triplet figuration of Example 4.1 is also related to this). Such figures tend to be used for their restraint, and often accompany moments of reflection or intensity in the text.

The texts of the outer songs of the two collections offer greater opportunity for more complex relationships between voice, accompaniment and text. The simplest of these is where the piano offers a primarily supportive role, doubling important melodic notes, if not whole lines; fragments of the vocal part may be echoed in the accompaniment. Such an accompaniment places the expressive focus on the voice. The converse of this can be found in 'The Rider Victory', in which, save for one apt echo of the phrase 'ghostly ridge' in the piano, and the occasional doubled note, the parts are otherwise independent. The material given to the accompaniment, a whole-tone trumpet call and a driving ostinato quaver figure, are ironic references to the horse and rider depicted in the poem, for they are ultimately revealed to be a statue.

More direct forms of expression can also be found in the piano accompaniments that relate to the romantic vein found in *Comus*. In 'The Confirmation', for example, warm emotional climaxes are underpinned by chromatically sliding dominant chords and rich arpeggio upbeats. Linear motion in the outer voices creates a sense of motion, balancing and controlling the individual sonorous qualities of the chords. Elsewhere, the textures are thinner, sometimes no more than voice and repeated resonant quavers in the bass moving by step. These quavers recur in later songs by Wood, always connected with emotional intensity. In the context of 'The Confirmation', the romantic climaxes are heightened by the sparser surroundings; both contribute to the overriding expression of love.

The longest song of the two collections, 'The Horses' is also the finest, both poetically and musically. The scene described in the poem is set just before dawn as the narrator ascends through a wood on a frosty hill; the world is still. Leaving the wood, the poet encounters the horses of the title, their mythic qualities exaggerated by the text ('megalith still'). The silence is broken by a curlew's cry in the distance. Dawn breaks; on the return down the hill, the narrator passes the horses again, still immobile. The vividness of the encounter endures in his or her memory long after the event.

The shifting relationship between voice and piano in Wood's setting, and the variety of textures and musical styles invoked matches closely the narrative of the poem. Recurring ideas in the poem, such as the horses and the curlew, are given their own thematic ideas, low sonorous chords in the piano evoking the massiveness of the horses, high trills and clusters the curlew. These ideas function as pillars around which the setting revolves (much as in the poem), rather than as malleable themes to be developed according to Wood's standard practice.

Elsewhere, Wood's setting avoids specific details such as these, following instead the general mood of the text. At the opening, for example, the stillness of the frost-covered hill at night motivates an accompaniment of quiet, sparse chords that follow the rhythms and shapes of the voice. The opening and closing chords of the phrase are static 0,1,6 trichords, the second a minor third higher than the first; the transposition perhaps representing the ascent through the wood. These chords both belong to the same octatonic set – CIII – to which the vocal line and intervening harmonies also gravitate: the immobility of the harmonic language reflects that of the text.

Upon leaving the woods, the narrator glimpses first the darkness in the valleys below, the emptiness conjured up by the piano doubling the voice in unison and a further three octaves beneath that. The change of poetic scene is thus realized through an alteration of texture and timbre; this is also achieved harmonically, as the centre of gravity shifts to octatonic set CII. The third significant change occurs with the sighting of the horses and their associated low chords (two superimposed 'dominant' trichords; CI is now the harmonic centre). After the encounter, there is a return to the opening textures and sonorities; the implication is that the horses share the same frozen qualities as the landscape they inhabit. Only the cry of the curlew (trills and high-placed clusters) disturbs the scene.

Then, in one of the most affecting moments of the two sets, dawn breaks (Example 5.2). Against a slow harmonic rhythm suggested by the bass motion of E♭–F, the increasingly impassioned melody has something of the character of an

Example 5.2   *The Horses* Op. 10/i, 'The Horses', bars 49–57

alleluia celebrating the sunrise. A slow linear ascent of a fourth traced out by the vocal line (D–G) is balanced by driving descending fourths in the accompaniment. The growing intensity of the passage reaches its climax in bars 55–6, in which vocal extremes are once again explored for emotional impact. The bars open with the largest leap of the extract, a descending diminished twelfth to the lowest note of the phrase (F♯–C), that instigates a broadening of the tempo in the approach to the final G (the highest note). Nevertheless, the prevalence of diminished fifths and (expanded) semitones in both melody and harmony tempers the jubilation of the passage: this is a particularly frosty dawn.

From this emotional climax, the music follows the poem back to the horses, with their associated chords, through to the epilogue. The materials of the opening are reworked here, with the memory of the horses prompting a final *appassionato* declamation. The texture suddenly thins again, the curlew crying once more, and the song fades to nothing.

Cello Concerto Op. 12

Towards the close of the Cello Concerto, there is a brief quotation of Elgar's Cello Concerto, which Wood suggests is present 'in order to pay more than one homage'.[10] One such homage is undoubtedly to Jacqueline du Pré, whose cello playing Wood admired greatly. (Wood had heard her give a performance of the Elgar Concerto in April 1965, a few months before he started work on his Op. 12.) Wood had du Pré in mind when writing the concerto, and her full-blooded interpretations helped inspire a sustained intensity of feeling and directness of expression rarely matched elsewhere in Wood's output. Du Pré never performed Wood's concerto: the premiere was given by Zara Nelsova with Colin Davis and the BBC Symphony Orchestra in the 1969 Promenade concerts.[11] It was subsequently toured through Europe under Pierre Boulez's baton, and later conducted in the USA by William Steinberg and Colin Davis.[12]

It is doubtful that Boulez was sympathetic towards the concerto's overt romanticism nor its use of traditional form, both far removed from Boulez's aesthetic position. Wood has suggested that the form of the concerto is 'best understood as a large-scale sonata movement' (see Table 5.3).[13] The inherent drama of sonata form, with its implication of integrating contrasts, is used as a vehicle to combine and contrast extremes of texture (solo and tutti) as well as emotion. As with similar forms employed in Opp. 8 and 9, there is also the potential to hear hints of a multi-movement form in operation as well. Such a reading would place the 'slow

---

[10] Composer's note to the score.

[11] In her biography of the cellist, Elizabeth Wilson reveals that although du Pré was unable to give the premiere of the Cello Concerto, the possibility of a performance was tantalizingly close. In 1971, Robert Ponsenby, then the manager of the Scottish National Orchestra, asked if du Pré would open the orchestra's season with Wood's Cello Concerto, to which du Pré 'agreed without hestitation'. The dates were subsequently put forward to March 1972, then postponed again; in the end, du Pré was unable to perform the work. See Wilson, *Jacqueline du Pré* (London, 1998), p. 371.

[12] In 1978, Moray Welsh, who had previously performed the work with the BBC Symphony Orchestra (cond. Andrew Davis) and the BBC Scottish Symphony Orchestra (cond. Christopher Seaman), recorded the work with David Atherton and the Royal Liverpool Philharmonic Orchestra. This recording, for the Unicorn label, has been re-released on NMC D082.

[13] Composer's note to the score.

movement' in bars 138–96 (what Wood designates the 'secondary group'), and treat Wood's 'development' as a kind of scherzo.

Table 5.3   Form of Cello Concerto Op. 12

Section		Bars	Description
Introduction		1–39	Statement and development of opening theme (Example 3.3a)
Exposition	*First subject group*	40–73	Allegro theme (Example 5.3a) and development
		74–87	Secondary theme (Example 5.3b) in orchestra
		88–95	Scherzo interlude
		96–121	Development and climax
		122–37	Codetta based on Example 5.3a
	Second subject group (Slow movement)	138–59	Slow movement theme (Example 5.3c)
		160–70	Secondary theme (Example 5.3d)
		171–96	Cadenza-like passages, with reference to Examples 3.3a, 5.3c and 5.3d
Development	*(Scherzo)*	197–236	Orchestral passage
		236–89	Cadenza for solo cello
Recapitulation	*First subject group*	290–306	Example 5.3a in orchestra
		307–24	Development of Example 5.3a in cello
		325–33	Example 5.3b in cello
	Second subject group	334–41	Example 5.3d in violas
		352–64	Orchestral climax and postlude
		365–71	Peroration of Example 5.3c in cello
		372–86	Development of Ex 5.3c
Coda		387–410	Based on Example 3.3a and Example 5.3c
		411–28	Partial reprise of Example 3.3a; Elgar quotation (Example 5.4)
		429–41	Final chords

The analysis in Chapter 3 (pp. 61–8) of the opening 31 bars of the Cello Concerto revealed a long-breathed sense of phrasing and a rich harmonic language based on octatonic formulations. Both qualities are typical of the concerto as a whole. The first 31 bars function as an introduction to the work as a whole, providing an intervallic motto (the E♭–A tritone and its characteristic rhythm) and

Example 5.3   Cello Concerto Op. 12 (a) bars 40–49; (b) bars 74–80; (c) bars 138–41; (d) bars 160–67

a variety of motifs that inform the sonata-allegro proper. Moreover, the twelve notes of the opening theme (see Example 3.3, p. 61) recur at the most significant formal junctures, and in particular, form the basis of the Coda. Example 5.3 presents material derived from Example 3.3.

From bar 12, as the cello develops the motif of a rising semitone and falling tone (the inversion of motif *x*; see Example 3.3b and c), the manner of expression becomes increasingly romantic, building up to a melodic and harmonic climax in bars 30–31. This is followed by a contrapuntal passage in which the material dissolves, though the use of additive rhythms in the brass (bars 31–2) hints at the scherzo character that becomes increasingly important as the concerto unfolds. Up to this point, the orchestra has been primarily accompanimental, with no 'voice' of its own, serving instead to provide harmonic and contrapuntal support to complement and intensify the emotional trajectory of the solo cello. With the climax and transition, the orchestra assumes briefly the primary role; the subsequent shifting of attention between cello and orchestra becomes another expressive device of the concerto.

The declamatory Example 5.3a is what Wood describes as 'the primary allegro melody', the opening theme of the first subject group. Much of the material is based on three descending semitones, the third of which is transposed into a different register. The resulting contour of a descending semitone and minor ninth (*w*) recurs throughout the concerto, primarily using the same pitch-classes (an instance, perhaps, of the significance Wood seems to place on the association of thematic ideas with distinct pitches). The expansiveness of the gesture stands in contrast to the cramped figuration (based on inversions of motif *x*) that punctuate it. The derivation of the material is unusual for Wood's music: it is based on the retrograde inversion of the first six notes of Example 3.3a, accompanied by its complement in double stops. Scherzo-style interludes, as in the introduction, begin once again to interrupt the argument (bars 57–60, 71–3), and serve to end the section.

The second theme of the first subject group (Example 5.3b) is given to the orchestra alone, the first time in the concerto that the orchestra is consistently asserted as an equal partner in the dialogue. Beginning with a retrograde of the opening pitches of Example 5.3a in the violins, and emphasizing three-note chromatic segments, the theme opens out into a widely spaced version of the theme from Example 3.3, transposed by a major sixth.[14] The significance of this, perhaps, is that the transposition ensures that the outer notes of the latter half of Example 5.3b are the thematically important A and E♭. The harmonization is once again built on octatonic 'dominant' sonorities, so arranged as to suggest a cycle of fifths: a moment in which a traditional gesture suddenly wells up and colours the expressive trajectory of the concerto.

The brief flowering of warmth in the orchestral theme is interrupted with a return to the solo cello in a staunchly scherzo character (bars 88–95), in a neat mirroring of the orchestra's earlier use of scherzo ideas to punctuate the material given to the cello. From bar 96, cello and orchestra alike develop motivic fragments, blending the more romantic element (long pedals in the bass, rich harmonies) with scherzo rhythms in the brass. A stretto trumpet figure in bar 107, based on motif *x*, initiates a build-up to an orchestral climax in bar 113. After a tumultuous gesture, the mood suddenly

---

[14]   The use of this particular transposition at this point is instructive. Because the two hexachords of Example 3.3a are tritone transpositions of each other (see Example 3.3b), the tritone transposition of the theme is closely related to the original. The use of the transposition at the major sixth thus ensures some degree of contrast (recall too the similar emphasis on this transposition in the *Capriccio*).

changes, the textures and timbre recalling opening of the concerto. A reminiscence in bar 122 of Example 5.3a (using the original pitches) closes the first subject group with its opening material. Equally significant, formally and expressively, is the sombre iteration of the E♭–A tritone motif in the tuba and bassoon.

The retrospective air of the passage closing the first subject group strengthens interpretations in which the second group is heard as a separate slow movement. The two thematic ideas of this 'movement' are given in Example 5.3c and d. The first of these grows from an inversion of the first three pitches of the concerto (x); the second is a reworking of the entire twelve-note theme in Example 3.3a. The use of the pitches of Example 3.3a for the final 'new' thematic idea in the concerto is significant, once again establishing a structural close. The general downward turn of the first of these themes hints at the lamenting, inward quality of the material, emphasized by its sparse orchestration. The second theme is somewhat richer, initially accompanied by fragments of a chorale-like harmonization of the inversion of motif x. Its ascending profile complements the more introverted first theme; it relates, too, to Example 5.3a (note the use of motif w at the tritone).

Following Example 5.3d, there is a series of descending single- and double-stops outlining the inversion of motif x (bars 169–71). This leads into a lengthier *alla cadenza* passage in which a series of Bach-like arpeggios spell out a series of mostly octatonic chords. The cadenza opens with a wedge-like figure in the outer voices, filled-out with octatonic-derived harmonies. The cadenza culminates with a recollection of Example 5.3c, not at pitch, but which nevertheless serves texturally as a closing figure.

In terms of expression, the slow movement is notable for its avoidance of the scherzo character that has had such an important discursive role within the concerto. Nor does the orchestra intrude upon the prominent role played by the soloist. This results in an exposition (if we are to return to the sonata model) in which nearly all of the thematic material is initially presented, and mostly developed, by the soloist. The role of the orchestra has been to accompany the cello, following its emotional twists and turns, occasionally providing interruptions and comments upon the material.

This situation changes quite dramatically in the second half of the concerto, from the 'development' onwards (bar 197). The development takes the form of a series of waves in which the descant ascends, with large-scale semitone motion predominating in the bass; in this sense, it is an intensification of the expressive shape of the introduction (see Example 3.4, p. 65). The development opens with driving quavers over which the brass play a 'snarling' version of the first hexachord of Example 3.3a. These alternate with high woodwind and string tremolandi: the textural contrast highlights the E♭–A tritone present in the upper voices at these points. The third, fourth and fifth pitches of Example 3.3a (D–F–E) introduce the next section (bar 213), which is treated sequentially. In bar 220, the style becomes more romantic, with an extensive melodic line containing exaggerated leaps and semitone inflections. The lighter, more sonorous texture contrasts greatly with the heavy woodwind and brass scoring of the preceding material, but the change is short-lived. In bar 229, the woodwind and brass interrupt yet again with scherzo-style rhythms, sweeping the development into the cadenza via a series of climactic chords reminiscent of bars 30–31. The development thus draws extensively from the introduction, in its use of fragments from the theme and certain textures. The opposition between romantically expressive and scherzo styles that informed so much of the drama in the exposition is replicated again here, only this time it is the romantic style acts as the intruder. The expressive characters (scherzo–lyrical–scherzo) impart a ternary shape to the development, and hint at the underlying scherzo form to the section as a whole.

The development marks the first sustained emphasis given to the orchestra; it is counterbalanced by a similarly long focus on the soloist in the cadenza. The cadenza, as one might expect, reworks and juxtaposes a number of key motifs from throughout the concerto, especially the inversion of motif *x*. There is also a hint of the harmonic goal of the concerto: a focal pitch of C♯/D♭ in the bass, and continued reference to E♭–A in the descant. Midway through the cadenza, there are rapid shifts of character between adagio arpeggiations of chords and scurrying *sul ponticello* wisps of an allegro character. This draws together features of the earlier *alla cadenza* passage with scherzo-style material. More significantly, it points to the rapid juxtapositions and bloc-type construction Wood was to explore in his Second Quartet, and which was to become an important feature of his later style. The cadenza closes first with an *estatico* presentation of the E♭–A motto and then a series of trills marked *con grand'intensita*. The climactic use of trills, first explored in the Quintet, is another gesture that was to become significant in Wood's music in later years.

One of the principal features of the recapitulation is that nearly all the themes that had originally been presented initially by the soloist are given to the orchestra, and vice versa. Scherzo interludes once again disrupt the musical flow. Where the musical argument differs from the exposition is in the development of ideas after their presentation: this is given mostly to the solo cello. (One might say that the orchestra is now repeating what the cello said in the exposition, and the cello is developing the idea further.) The cello's expansive and euphoric development of ideas (for instance, *molto lirico* bar 325, *estatico* bar 329) contrasts strongly with the shorter phrases of the scherzo elements. The ecstatic mood prevails through all of the interruptions, and it appears that the concerto is to end at some emotional distance from the opening. Not even a third appearance of the climactic cadence of bars 30–31 in bar 352 can change the overall character of the recapitulation, for it is followed by triumphant peroration of Example 5.3c, marking the emotional high-point of the concerto. This is the only theme that is presented solely by the cello: here at last the soloist's supremacy over the orchestra is finally asserted, after the struggles in the development, cadenza and recapitulation.

It is as a result of this assertion that the turning of tables so as to end with a bleak coda is so telling. Although the 'sonata' that began in bar 39 is formally closed by the recapitulation of the various themes at pitch, the concerto as a whole is not: the return of Example 3.3a with the original pitches is required to achieve this. This occurs, albeit in a fragmentary and partially re-ordered form, in bars 409–13, with only the E♭–A motif omitted. From here, the tension rises again, culminating in the Elgar quotation in bars 427–8 (Example 5.4).[15] Marked *lontano* (distant), the quotation is the expressive climax of the work; its detachment serves to intensify the

---

[15]   The source of the quotation can be found an octave lower, three bars before rehearsal mark 70 in the final movement of Elgar's concerto.

tragedy of what follows. Beginning in bar 429, a final bleak chord, *senza vibrato*, is built over a D♭ pedal (reinforcing its status as a focal pitch-class for the work), whilst the solo cello takes the tritone motto through a number of octaves, returning to the register of the Elgar quotation. This use of the motto 'completes' the opening statement left unfinished in bar 413, and creates the possibility – structurally, at least – for the work to close.

Example 5.4   Cello Concerto Op. 12, bars 427–8

The majority of the harmonic material in the exposition, like that of the introduction, draws on chords from the octatonic sets CI and CIII. Similarly, the thematic material, whilst highly chromatic, gravitates towards the octatonic. With the *alla cadenza* in bars 171–7, there is a shift towards an organization based on sets CII and CIII; in the development, CI and CII provide the underlying harmonic focus. The recapitulation returns to the harmonic 'centres' of CI and CIII. The harmonic argument of the concerto is concluded with the Elgar quotation. The pitches of the quotation all belong to the octatonic set CII; note that the lower and upper pitches are respectively D♯ and A – the source, perhaps, of the tritone motto that dominates the concerto and the pitch level of its most important presentation. The fact that the quotation is drawn from CII might also explain why many of the other themes utilized harmonies and linear progressions based on the other octatonic sets: they required the Elgar quotation to 'restore' the balance.

The fact that the quotation shares harmonic material with the rest of the concerto ensures its 'correctness'.[16] Yet, as ever with Wood, the quotation possesses both musical and biographical associations, not least the connection between Jacqueline du Pré and the Elgar concerto. Another clue to the biographical importance the quotation has for Wood comes from his observation that his own concerto was 'a stranger on the scene of 1970, remote from the preoccupations of my contemporaries in form, content, idiom, style'.[17] Thus it shares with Elgar's Cello Concerto, which was similarly out of place in the post-First World War musical climate, a sense of not belonging, yet of having an intense emotional message to convey. It is inconceivable

---

[16]   Anthony Bye, for one, states that the quote is accommodated 'without incongruity' [Review of UKCD 2043], *Tempo* 178 (1991): 52–3 (p, 53)

[17]   Wood, 'Hugh Wood on his own work': 605.

that Wood did not have this in mind when he used the quotation, and in doing so paying, as he stated, 'more than one homage'.

Expanding the Expressive Range (1969–1971)

With the Second String Quartet Op. 13 (1969–70), Wood sought deliberately to widen his range of expression; his writings of the period suggest that he was beginning to find the intimate link between expression and particular techniques in his music restrictive. The close motivic and twelve-note working of his music was based on an 'ideal' that measured 'compositions only on one particular scale'.[18] For Wood, this could result in 'attending to the details at the expense of the whole' thereby neglecting 'the surface allure and the grand gesture'.[19]

In the Second Quartet, Wood explored alternative means of musical expression through the expansion of his technical resources. To enrich his existing methods, rooted in the modernism of the first half of the twentieth century (Schoenberg, Stravinsky, and so on), Wood turned to more recent European traditions. In particular, the formal and textural innovations of composers such as Lutosławski and Ligeti (as well as those by Gerhard) suggested means by which Wood could learn to loosen his grip on his material, finding a way of achieving 'surface allure' and 'grand gestures' without compromising his earlier aesthetic position.

String Quartet No. 2 (1969–1970)

A superficial glance at the score of the Second String Quartet, or an inattentive hearing, would suggest that, in comparison to the works that preceded it – particularly the First Quartet – it was by a different composer. The work evinces a rethinking of Wood's musical language, in which new levels of importance are assigned to previously secondary phenomena such as texture and sonority, and new means found of relating these to melody, harmony and rhythm. Formally, the work is closely related to the Trio Op. 3, consisting of 39 juxtaposed blocs. The distribution of these blocs in a ternary design (Table 5.4) is characteristic of the balance between Wood's new-found mild avant-garde tendencies and the more traditional leanings evident in much of his music of the 1970s.

The first section of the quartet introduces many of the new ways that Wood was thinking about his music. The first twelve blocs are based on three contrasting ideas. The first of these embodies the type of 'grand gesture' Wood was seeking;[20] a 'cauldron' from which subsequent ideas could be derived.[21] This is announced first by a powerful and visceral twelve-note chord, after which all four instruments launch into a 'free-for-all':[22] unsynchronized and rhythmically approximate flurries of notes guided solely by the spatial arrangement of the notes in the score. The immediate purpose is

---

[18]   Ibid.
[19]   Ibid.
[20]   Ibid.
[21]   Composer's note to the score.
[22]   Wood, 'Hugh Wood on his own work': 605.

Table 5.4   Distribution of related blocs, String Quartet No. 2 Op. 13

	Cauldron	Clusters	Chords	Duets	Climax	Slow	Scherzando
A	1	2					
	3	4					
	5		6				
	7	8					
	9	10	11				
	12						
				13	14 15		
				16			
				17			
B	18	(18)	19				
						20	21
						22	23
(mainly slow)		24	(24)				
					25 'Still Centre'		
						26	
		27	28	29			
				30			
A₁	31	32					
	33	34					
	35	36					
	37	38					
	39						

textural and colouristic: in addition to the predominantly *détaché* manner of delivery, Wood asks for *sul ponticello* and pizzicato effects. The explosive energy of the opening is such that specific details – intervallic relationships, motivic shapes – are obscured; these nevertheless remain available as resources for later (traditional) development.

An eleven-note chord introduces the second bloc. From this emerges a sustained F♯; subsequent notes fan out from this pitch to create material based on chromatic clusters. The third idea, a gentle procession of chords, is introduced in the sixth bloc. The players are instructed to play over the fingerboard for a veiled sound; a light portamento that connects the upper notes of the chord (outlining a three-note chromatic cluster C–B–C♯) suggests a slightly surreal serenade character. The chords are derived from varied arrangements of a six-note chord and its complement.

The ideas presented in blocs 1, 2 and 6 continue to alternate and develop individually: the changing contexts in which they combine and separate serve to throw new interpretive light on the material. The first unambiguous melodic idea is announced in bloc 13: a melodic (but not rhythmic) canon at the fourth between first violin and cello. This leads towards a climax in blocs 14 and 15, and the introduction of a further new concept. Bloc 14 consists of alternating *ppp* and *ff* chords; the former decreases in length by a crotchet on each occurrence, and the latter increases by a quaver. The diminution of one idea is thus balanced by the augmentation of the other (see too p. 56). For all of its mechanical nature, it must be understood in terms of its expressive function: that is, to signify a climax; it is in this capacity that Wood uses this technique in later works. Bloc 15 sustains the resulting tension in a flurry of pizzicato notes that tumble into the transition to the middle section.

What is perhaps most surprising about the first section of the quartet is its harmonic stasis. Example 5.5 shows the chords that divide each bloc (the chords representing the suave chordal idea of blocs 6 and 11 are the opening harmonies). Save for an ascending semitone step in the second half of the section (compare chords 1 and 7, for example), there is little by way of harmonic 'development'.Only at the end of the section (blocs 13–15) is there any decisive harmonic motion. Until then, direction within the music – the sense of tension and release – is provided by means of texture and sonority, rather than through line or harmonic density.

Bloc 16 contains yet another new sonority – scurrying ostinati outlining dense chromatic clusters – that is used in the transition to and from the middle section of the quartet. These provide an indeterminate harmonic background in which the effect is enhanced by the use of cross rhythms, tremolandi and the quiet dynamic. Like the microstructures of Ligeti, Wood's choice of pitches for this background is far from arbitrary, but the overall effect renders these pitches all but inaudible. The resulting 'cloud' is used to underpin a second duet, a delicate canon at the fifth between the second violin and viola in harmonics.

The middle section (blocs 18–26) begins with recollections of the first three ideas, transformed into material of a slow movement character. The furious writing of the first bloc thus becomes a tightly knit dialogue between lower instruments, interspersed with pizzicato figures from the first violin; it is followed by a brief polyphonic working of the second bloc. Bloc 19 is a slow version of bloc 6, against which the second violin holds a long B♮ embellished with short lamenting melodic fragments.

Example 5.5   String Quartet No. 2 Op. 13, opening chords of blocs 1–15

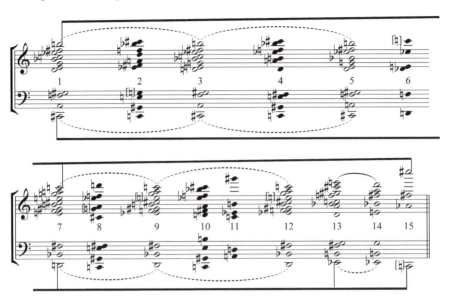

The B♮ falls to a sustained B♭ in bloc 20; calm melodic lines of an adagio character circle around it. This material alternates with nocturnal *scherzando* figures. Bloc 24 develops the cluster idea from bloc 2, again in a slow tempo; fragments of bloc 6 can be heard towards the end. As with bloc 19, another long B♮ emerges, falling again (indirectly) to a B♭ at the beginning of the 'Still Centre'. Here, the rhythmic vitality of the quartet is finally dissipated. The material is based on a whole-tone group (A♭–B♭–C–D); the absence of semitones providing a stark contrast to the chromatic formulations elsewhere in the work. Each instrument is given its own pitch: there is no harmonic development or motion. Wood has never again written anything quite as static. In the context of the Quartet, it provides a calm around which a threatening storm rages; an inverse climax to the tensions of bloc 14.

From this point of maximum remove, the material begins gradually to coalesce. This at first is achieved with a lengthy reworking of the slow material in bloc 26. There is then a string of familiar material: fragments based on chromatic clusters in bloc 27, and an extended reprise of the chordal figure of bloc 6 in bloc 28. There is then a dissolve into the *sul ponticello* ostinati of bloc 16 and, in bloc 30, the final duet pairing of the work (second violin and viola). But where this pairing in bloc 17 was ethereal, in 30 it is aggressively forthright, leading in bloc 31 to a return of the opening material as part of a compressed recapitulation. The suave chordal idea (bloc 6), having had a triumphant apotheosis in bloc 28, does not return; what remains are alternations between 'cauldron' and 'cluster' material. There is a slight stall in the penultimate bloc – one last *molto lirico* fragment in all the parts – before the quartet judders to a halt.

The idea that texture and sonority can be thematic elements as important as melodic and rhythmic themes has dramatic consequences for Wood's use of the instruments in the Second Quartet. In comparison with the First String Quartet, the Second displays a riotous use of colour, such as in the use of *sul ponticello, tremolando, senza vibrato* and strange combinations of registers. The partially aleatoric passages in which the instruments are unsynchronized also opened up hitherto unused textural possibilities. Yet the middle section, in which familiar expressive characters are placed in new contexts, reveals that the Second Quartet is more than just an exploration of alternative expressive and technical resources. Rather, it is a compelling and convincing enrichment of existing habits, which points to new possibilities within Wood's musical language

The Second Quartet was Wood's fourth BBC commission, and was premiered by the Dartington String Quartet at a BBC Invitation Concert in Cardiff on 6 November 1970.[23] The following year, it was selected by the British Jury and performed in June at the International Society for Contemporary Music Festival in London.

Canon in memoriam Igor Stravinsky

Written in July 1971 in memory of Igor Stravinsky, Wood's canon was published along with numerous other composer tributes in a special issue of *Tempo*.[24] The work opens and closes with chords for flute, clarinet and harp; the main body of the work is a double canon for string quartet. Wood thus combines the instrumentation of two little memorials Stravinsky composed in 1959: *Epitaphium* and *Double canon: Raoul Dufy in memoriam*.[25] Although there is no actual quotation of material, Wood's canon evokes the same sad ceremonial atmosphere as Stravinsky's pieces.

Chamber Concerto Op. 15

The Chamber Concerto Op. 15 (1970–71; revised 1978) was commissioned and premiered on 27 November 1971 by the London Sinfonietta. The work explores both conventional and unconventional groupings within the large chamber ensemble for which it is scored, as well as providing opportunities for solo writing. There are similarities with the shifting colours and textures of the Quintet, although the larger forces allow for greater homogeneity as well as heterogeneity. The exploration of sonority and texture in the Second String Quartet is also continued and extended in the Chamber Concerto; the tensions between traditional and non-traditional modes of organization are never more pronounced in Wood's music than in this work.

The Concerto consists of four movements. As with the First String Quartet, the first movement is introductory. The second movement, a series of solos, trios and interludes, functions as a scherzo. The third movement is a memorial to Roberto Gerhard (to whose widow the work is dedicated), quoting Gerhard's music and,

---

[23]   The Dartington Quartet's recording of the Second Quartet accompanied the First in their 1973 Argo recording (Argo ZRG 750). The Chilingirian Quartet have also recorded it (Conifer 75605 51239-2, 1994).

[24]   *Tempo* no. 97, 1971.

[25]   This instrumentation was requested by *Tempo*.

as with the canon in memory of Stravinsky, alluding to his use of harmony and instrumentation. The final movement, a Rondo, has the greatest weight of the four.

Where the Second String Quartet opens with violence, the Chamber Concerto begins with the opposite extreme: a solitary and sustained E♮, coloured by various woodwind instruments and a horn. The rate of attacks on this note steadily accelerates, and the dynamics mirror this increase in energy by growing from *ppp* to *fff*. There is no melodic development: the section is abruptly cut off by a piano chord which initiates a short section for percussion alone. The extreme contrast between pitch and rhythm initiates a series of alternating blocs that increase in length on each occurrence: interludes for percussion are interspersed amongst 'pitched' blocs that unfold material fanning out from the central E. The harmonies that result from this expansion are given in Example 2.7a (p. 45); these are taken up in turn by each of the instrumental 'families' of wind, brass and strings. The first movement of the Concerto, at least, preserves such traditional groupings. Whilst one family sustains the harmonic content, the others supply fragments of melodic material that reflect the intervallic content of the chord. In the wind and brass, this melodic material often consists of a single line built up from short gestures – often a single note – passed from one instrument in the family to the other. The precise rhythmic co-ordination and balance required to achieve this effect is one of the many virtuosic ensemble passages in the Concerto. The strings provide accompaniment figures in which short ideas are repeated independently from each other and from the other families; as with the opening of the Second String Quartet, the result is mild aleatoricism that creates textural variety. The movement culminates firstly in chords of ever-decreasing duration being passed from one family to the next.[26] The process climaxes in a chord sustained by all three families: the chord's 'colour' is made to shift continuously as each instrumental group crescendoes and diminuendoes independently. A flurry of quavers passed through the ensemble from highest to lowest instruments provides an explosive conclusion.

The first movement has certain properties in common with the first section of the Second String Quartet: both focus on sonority, rhythm and texture. Similar, too, is the presentation of intervallic ideas that are taken up later in the work; the first movement of the Concerto is truly introductory in this respect. But the minimal role played by melodic development in the shaping of the movement is unique in Wood's output.

The melodic activity of the Scherzo, by contrast, is prominent, although even here this activity is strongly conditioned by an evolving intervallic expansion (as in the first movement). Each of the three large sections of the movement draws on a different interval: the material of the first section of the Scherzo is characterized by the use of the semitone, the second section by the minor third, and the final section by the 0,1,6 trichord.

The Scherzo follows the first movement without a break. It opens with a cadenza for amplified double bass, played pizzicato: the effect is somewhat jazz-like. The addition of a bass clarinet and harp creates a low-pitched Trio, which combines the jazz quality of the cadenza with that of a rhythmically supple scherzo that moves

---

[26] See Chapter 3, p. 56.

fluidly between simple and compound metre. The low tessitura and uncommon grouping create a dark atmosphere: glissando pizzicati in the double bass are as much mournful as playful. Much of the material of both cadenza and Trio is based on chromatic clusters in which semiquavers are emphasized. A tuba is added to the final four bars of the section for additional weight leading towards a climax. As with the transition between blocs in the first movement, the climax is abruptly cut off: there is tension but no immediate release. The cut off is achieved by a sudden change of texture and timbre: an D♭–E♭ dyad in the horn and trumpet (doubled by xylophone). This initiates a short interlude: a series of three chords in the strings. The chorale-like serenity of the chords stands in contrast to the dark murmurings of the Trio.

The pattern of solo–Trio–interlude is repeated twice more. The second group opens with an alto flute solo over the final chord of the previous string interlude. Oscillations in minor thirds establish the dominant interval of the section; it is joined by flute and clarinet in quicksilver figurations for the second Trio. In comparison with the first Trio, the approach to the ultimately avoided climax is extended: celeste (later piano), strings, piccolo, bassoon, oboe and a second clarinet all contribute to an increasingly dense and detailed textural build-up. The interlude opens with the same same dyad between horn and trumpet; the subsequent string interlude contains highly embellished upbeats to its three chords.

A cadenza for trumpet opens the third section; semitones and tritones are the predominant intervals. A Trio for trumpet, horn and trombone follows, characterized by furious fanfare figuration. Material from the other Trios is superimposed, creating a tumultuous texture; once again, this is interrupted, the final interlude functioning as a postlude. The string chords are drawn out, now consoling after the preceding storm.

The novel colouristic and textural effects notwithstanding, neither the first nor second movement of the Chamber Concerto has the same sort of emotional impact as Wood's earlier music. The over-reliance on intervallic expansion in lieu of thematic development seems to have inhibited expression. No such charge can be made of the memorial to Roberto Gerhard, the emotional core of the concerto. It opens with a low repeated D in the harp and piano. The desolate atmosphere is increased on the entry of the first quoted theme, nearly four octaves higher, in the flute and piccolo. The quotation is from two bars after rehearsal mark 38 in Gerhard's Concerto for Orchestra; it is based on a series of expanding intervals that recalls the content of the first two movements of Wood's Chamber Concerto. The pitches and rhythms might be Gerhard's, but the character is Wood's, for he transforms a theme that is originally of a fugitive scherzo character into a lament. The quotation is subjected to further reworkings throughout the movement; first a string chorale, and then a haunting melody for horn over a murmuring E♭ and F in the wind and harp.

The two basic states suggested by the low funereal D and the slightly faster mid-register aleatoric murmurings frame and provide background to the remainder of the movement. Two further quotations are introduced, the first from Gerhard's First Symphony (four bars before rehearsal mark 6); the second a reprise in the viola of the opening lament. One final quotation, the concluding wind chorale from Gerhard's *Hymnody* (rehearsal mark 540), ends the movement. Yet for all that Wood intended to capture some of Gerhard's compositional mannerisms in the movement, the voice that speaks most clearly is his own. It can be heard in the use of clearly definable emotional states in the slow movement, and in the subsequent evolution of the thematic material. The result, as with the Adagietto of the First String Quartet, is that simple materials and processes are invested with profundity.

The Stravinskian chorale that concludes the third movement also informs the character of the Finale. It opens with a unison B♮ that dissolves into a rapidly rising arpeggio, a dramatic gesture that punctuates the movement in the manner of a rondo. Between these gestures are a series of blocs that develop independently, as in the Second String Quartet. The first of these blocs consists of leaping lines in a scherzo character. The second transforms the energy of these wide leaps into repeated pulsed quavers: the insistence of the figure motivates Wood to describe it as a 'tapping'.[27] One might attribute this to the influence of minimalism, but a more likely source is Gerhard's Concerto for Orchestra.[28] Other material looks back to earlier movements: the pitches of chords 1–3 from the first movement are used as a trope to provide the upper line of a brusque chorale in wind and brass. Later on, this chorale returns spectrally in the strings, accompanied by indeterminate murmurings in the wind and brass recalling the aleatoric textures of the first two movements.

The chorale material intensifies in the final section of the movement. A solo trombone, adopting the role of a cantor, alternates with chorale responses in the wind. The hieratic atmosphere intensifies with the closing chords: solemn and ritualistic reworkings of chords 1, 2 and 3 that lengthen systematically, accruing tension until a chilling cadence onto a widely expanded chord 1.

Much of the Chamber Concerto takes the principles of the Second Quartet to their logical extremities within Wood's style. In particular, the emphasis on the thematic treatment of colour and texture is unparalleled in his output. That Wood did not continue with this line of thought, and reverted to more traditional melodically based methods of thematicism in the final two movements is, I believe, a reflection of his commitment to the human and communicative qualities generated by this tradition. Whilst the Chamber Concerto never abandons Wood's intentions to communicate, and above all, communicate *expressively*, it does at times severely test the boundaries Wood has set himself. It is not a surprise that the direction the Second Quartet and Chamber Concerto were pointing towards was never continued, and that Wood instead sought to draw the technical and conceptual ideas posited by these works into his pre-existing language, in order to maximize their expressive potential. Both the Quartet and Concerto contain some of Wood's most arresting music, such as the uninhibited violence at the opening of the Quartet; the same work's 'Still Centre'; the playful use of colour in the Trio of the Concerto and above the overwhelming conclusion to its Finale. That Wood took a step back from the extremes of these works is not a symptom of any inherent weakness: these are gripping, vital pieces of music, and their influence can be heard in the works that followed.

---

[27] Composer's note to the score.

[28] See, for example, rehearsal mark 8 in Gerhard's Concerto for Orchestra, described by Gerhard in his composer's note to the score as 'static yet pulsating constellation-like patterns'.

Chapter 6

'Wir Wandeln durch des Tones Macht'
1971–1982

In 1971, Wood took up a lecturing post at Liverpool University; in 1973 he converted this to part-time for a further two years. Wood then returned to London in 1975 for freelance work. Following Alexander Goehr's appointment as Professor at Cambridge in 1976, Wood joined the music faculty there, and was appointed lecturer in music and Fellow of Churchill College the next year. He was to hold this position for 22 years.

For all that he would hate to admit it, these appointments reflect Wood's increasing role as an 'establishment figure'; similarly, the music of the 1970s suggests a composer coming into his prime. The compositions of this period are predominantly 'big' works along traditional lines, and among Wood's finest. The first of these, the Violin Concerto (1970–72), was commissioned by the Royal Liverpool Philharmonic Society and performed in Liverpool in September 1972. It was followed by another BBC commission, a Song Cycle to Poems by Pablo Neruda (1973–74).

There then appeared to be a hiatus in Wood's output, as if external pressures were taking a toll. A set of Robert Graves songs were completed in 1976, but the next major work to appear was the Third String Quartet. This was completed in 1978 and premiered by the Lindsay Quartet. The emotional passage of the quartet, from bleak frozen stasis to vernal freshness, coupled with poetic inscriptions above the score that mirror this journey, suggested to many at its premiere the autobiographical depiction of 'the misery of a fallow spell and the joyous relief at the return of creativity'.[1]

Similar themes of struggle over adversity can be found in Wood's Symphony, the most ambitious and important work of this period. The Symphony was the third BBC commission for Wood in the decade. The first ideas towards the Symphony came in 1974; most of the composition took place in 1979–81. It was premiered in 1982, shortly after the composer's fiftieth birthday.

All of Wood's music displays personal emotional involvement, and indeed, this is one of the reasons that it communicates so directly and so humanely. The music of the 1970s, however, wears its heart particularly prominently on its sleeve. This is certainly the case in the ravishing love poetry set in these years, but it is also true for the not-so-hidden programmes that can be found in the concerto, quartet and symphony alike. Paradoxically, then, it transpires that the grand public gestures of the decade simultaneously belong to Wood's most personal, intimate statements.

---

[1]   William Mann, 'Lindsay Quartet', *The Times* (2 June 1978); see also Bayan Northcott, 'Hugh Wood's String Quartet No. 3', *Tempo* 126 (1978): 53.

Vocal Music

The music Wood wrote for solo voice in the 1970s is exclusively about love. His highly charged settings of poems by D.H. Lawrence and Pablo Neruda occupy a different emotional climate to that of his Hughes and Muir collections of the 1960s, reflecting the textural and colouristic resources explored in the Second Quartet and Chamber Concerto. The set of six songs to texts by Robert Graves also explored facets of love, and was the first published fruit of Wood's long-standing artistic identification with Graves's work. The decade also saw the first performance of the Laurie Lee Songs, in a concert in Liverpool Cathedral in May 1971, and the composition of two choruses to words by W.B. Yeats. It is regrettable that in the record catalogues there are fewer vocal works than instrumental ones, for the vocal music represents some of Wood's most compelling music, not just of the decade, but also of his career.[2]

D.H. Lawrence Songs Op.14: 'Dog-Tired', 'Gloire de Dijon', 'Kisses in the Train'

The D.H. Lawrence songs consisted originally of three settings, 'Dog-Tired', 'Gloire de Dijon' and 'Kisses in the Train'. Early catalogues of Wood's music suggest that these were written in 1966,[3] but the dates on the manuscripts point to a far more convoluted genesis: see Table 6.1. In fact, the first three songs were not fully completed until October 1982, and a further revision was made to 'Kisses in the Train' in 1997. In comparison, the composition of two further songs added later to the set was swift. 'River Roses' was written over four days in the summer of 1994, and 'Roses on the Breakfast Table' in five days in August 2001 (see Chapter 9, p. 216).

Wood's setting of 'Dog-Tired' captures the languor of summer nights and the wait for a lover whilst on the verge of sleep. Although the tempo is fast ($\downarrow$=132–144), the melodic line is broad: rapid quaver motion in the accompaniment provides the sort of nervous energy one has when exhausted but excited. Much of the piano writing veers towards registral extremes, as with the opening clangour of the song: a bell-like oscillating minor third E♭–C over a D♭ towards the upper end of the keyboard. Although octatonic in origin, this is unlike the sonorous octatonic harmonies of the Cello Concerto or the frosty stasis of 'The Horses': the sound world of 'Dog-Tired' is leaner, alternately glistening in the treble or rumbling menacingly in the bass. The intervals of the opening bell sound infuse both harmony and melody: the opening vocal motif of a rising minor third and falling semitone is characteristic.

'Gloire de Dijon' is by contrast expansive and sensual, in response to the eroticism of the poem. Lengthy melismas in the vocal line at the end of each stanza, whilst unusual in Wood's vocal writing, capture the narrator's lingering gaze. The accompaniment alternates between a steady quaver tread, often thickening the melody, and opulent chords that are derived from superimposed triads a tritone apart (that hence suggest octatonicism; see Chapter 2, pp. 40–41). A final twelve-note

---

[2]   Recordings of all three instrumental works considered in this chapter have been issued; at the time of writing, none of the vocal music has been released on disc.

[3]   See, for example, Black 'The Music of Hugh Wood', and Payne, 'Hugh Wood'.

chord is built up slowly, the prominent use of thirds resulting in a glowing sonority of Mediterranean warmth.[4]

Table 6.1   Dates of composition of the D.H. Lawrence songs Op. 14

Song	Dates on manuscript
Dog-Tired	3 June – 5 July 1966; July 1968; 1970; 10 March 1974
Gloire de Dijon	February 1967; May 1968
Kisses in the Train	13 April 1970 – 16 October 1982 Drafts: 23 April 1970; 13 April 1971; 1–14 April 1973; 16–17 July 1982; 9 October 1982; 1 December 1997
River Roses	31 July – 3 August 1994
Roses on the Breakfast Table	25–30 August 2001

The varied sequences of 'Kisses in the Train' reflect the rising passion of a couple on a train. Wood's sensitivity to the rhythms of D.H. Lawrence's text have a similar effect. Although 'I saw the Midlands revolve through her hair' and, later, 'And still as ever the world went round' have the same number of syllables, the shorter vowel sounds of the latter give rise to a setting in 3/4 and 6/8, compared to the additive 8/8 of the first line. The changes of metre also result in a compression of harmonic rhythm: without altering the underlying tempo (the protagonists' perspective) the rest of the world appears to pass by at ever changing speeds, just as it does on a moving train. Contrast is created at the end of each verse with a melodic and harmonic stasis representing the narrator's inner calm: as the voice revolves around a central B♭, a softly tolling 0,1,6 trichord gently marks the passage of time.

The first three songs of Op. 14 form an attractive set, clothing Lawrence's passionate texts in contrasting yet complementary styles; the use of octatonic material provides a common musical thread. Unlike the rudiments of a love affair depicted in the Four Logue Songs, there is no underlying narrative in the D.H. Lawrence songs. Rather, they cohere by virtue of the exploration of a shared theme – love – from a variety of different angles. This approach differs from the less obviously motivated collections of Hughes and Muir songs in *The Horses* and *The Rider Victory*, and suggests the model that would become the norm in Wood's sets of Robert Graves songs.

To a Child Dancing in the Wind Op. 16 no. 1

To a Child Dancing in the Wind (1973) is an unaccompanied chorus to words by Yeats. The poem falls into two halves, the first depicting the carefree world of a child, the second the harder, harsher world of adult responsibility. This motivates a musical

---

[4]   Contrast this with twelve-note chord built in fourths and fifths at the end of the Cello Concerto, which is used to create a sombre conclusion.

design in which the second half is an extended reworking of the first.[5] Though there are shared materials between the two halves, the character is sharply contrasted. Sprightly rhythms to the word 'dance' (bars 4–6) and light scherzo-like imitation for the phrase 'and tumble' depict the child; the music for the adult expresses regret ('love lost', bars 29–33) and dread. The dense, dark writing of the latter provides the most memorable effect of the work: a sombre and sonorous melisma to the word 'monstrous' (bars 47–51). To get the required menacing effect, Wood asks that a repeated pitch pattern in the tenors and basses be sung 'progressively out of phase with each other'.[6] This is the last time Wood asks for aleatoricism in any of his works: in future scores, he achieves similar results with precisely notated details. A second Yeats chorus, *To a Friend Whose Work has Come to Nothing* was also written in 1973; it was completely rewritten in 1989 (see Chapter 7, pp. 161–2).

Song Cycle to Poems of Pablo Neruda Op. 19

In late summer 1973, Wood began setting poems from Pablo Neruda's 'Twenty Love Poems and a Song of Despair', using Christopher Logue's translation in *Wand and Quadrant* (1953). Wood was drawn to the manner in which Logue combined the exotic, erotic and passionate character of the original with his own voice. The complete collection presents the rise and fall of a love affair, from which Wood selected seven poems. The first five of songs build towards a climax in the sixth; the desolation of the seventh depicts the end of the affair.

The first song, 'Two humans stand on a promontory' begins, like the Chamber Concerto, with a sustained E♮, here given to the voice and delicately coloured with metallic percussion. The vocal part of the first section can be found in Example 6.1. The use of speech rhythms is highly typical, as is the craftsman-like attention to detail. Note, for instance, the change of dynamics and the use of quarter-tones to inflect the words 'the moon sickens their flesh'; this serves also to initiate a melodic and harmonic motion fanning out from the central E♮. As the text turns from the heavens to the earth, the vocal line drops an octave, the vocal contours imitating the swell of the ocean. The turn to the sea also heralds the introduction of the wind instruments, which provide a carefully wrought murmuring support that reinvents the textural effects of the Second String Quartet and Chamber Concerto. As the passions grow, the tessitura rises in both voice and ensemble, straining for, but not quite returning to, the opening pitch of the work (this is achieved at the start of the next verse).

The glittering sonorities and hazy textures of the opening are treated as thematic elements, resulting in a multifaceted background in which colour and texture, rather than melodic development, are the primary means by which the accompaniment responds to the shifting emotional states of the text. A further source of material, throbbing chords in the strings, appears as the narrator turns to describe the body of his lover. The song climaxes with a top B♭ on the word 'consent', a tritone away from the opening of the work. There then follows a return of the opening, which

---

[5]   Such a binary scheme become increasingly important in Wood's later music.

[6]   Footnote in score.

Example 6.1   Song Cycle to Poems by Pablo Neruda Op. 19/i, bars 1–24 (voice only)

functions as a refrain throughout the song; a largely unaccompanied coda ('Little grasshopper') introduces scherzo-like rhythms in the vocal part.

The scherzo implications of this coda are taken up in the second and fourth songs. The first of these, 'Snared by the dying light', is set at dusk: scurrying and overlapping figures in the strings, pizzicato or *sul ponticello*, and fluttertonguing wind create a fugitive, nocturnal atmosphere. Brief trills and sparkling harp and celesta provide short interludes depicting falling flowers. The voice floats over this background, the emotional intensity mirrored by the frequent use of the lyrical rising major third/falling semitone motif. The vocal writing of the fourth song, 'In the hot depth of this summer', is more passionate, characterized by rising arpeggios. The accompaniment contrasts pulsating quaver figures with more sustained gestures that release their energy in short abrupt notes. The movement conjures up the oppressive heat of a dusty summer; a storm is threatening.

Between the scherzi is a slow processional movement ('Steep gloom among pine trees'), recalling the textures of the memorial to Gerhard in the Chamber Concerto.

As with the first movement, the mention of water in the text gives rise to murmuring figures in the wind. Sonorous dominant chords in the strings and harp provide the accompaniment to a more lyrical middle section; the sombre procession returns at the end.

The glittering summer heat of the fourth song is transformed into the warm autumnal tones of obbligato cor anglais and alto flute in the fifth, 'I remember you from last fall'. Similarly, the passions of the start of a relationship give way here to calmer reflection. In Wood's setting, this is achieved with reminiscences from earlier songs in the cycle. To this end, spacious string chords that recall the start of the coda to the first song alternate with the scurrying sounds of dusk from the second. Emotionally and thematically, the fifth song thus completes an arc begun with the first song, and prepares for the climax in the sixth song, 'Call the sky mine'.

The first three stanzas of the sixth song are an exultation of love. The fourth, however, is a shattering revelation that this love is over: 'the mutual dream is broke'. As with the previous song, there are reminiscences to earlier material. In the context of the first three stanzas, these have an almost celebratory quality; when the truth is revealed, they assume a tragic function.

The texture of the opening of 'Call the sky mine', a series of chords focused on C♮, recalls the first song, and refers back to the beginning of both the cycle and love affair. What follows is in Wood's romantic style, making use of extended dominant chords (of octatonic origin) in the strings and harp, befitting the emotionalism of the text. This culminates in the ecstatic 'your flesh' over a dominant chord on G. A short interlude based around displaced rising semitones in semiquavers delays the second stanza, which has a marked change of mood. Having recalled the first song in the introduction, Wood here looks back to the textures of the scherzi of the second and fourth songs. This is followed by a sudden return to the chordal texture of the opening, marking the start of the third stanza. Beginning in bar 40, there is an even stronger recollection of the opening of the cycle, with the soprano once again declaiming an E♮, and colouring the word 'moon' with quarter-tones.

Following this brief overview of the earlier songs, Wood brings the cycle as a whole to a climax on the word 'Rape' on a top B♭. The melodic motion is similar to that over the dominant G in bar 17, but more tellingly, there is a musical and dramatic parallel with the word 'consent' in the first song. It is harmonized by a root-position C major chord, is then sustained for the rest of the song, effectively eliding the end of the third stanza with the start of the fourth. A repeated F♯ played by the piano, horn and trombone, reminiscent of a tolling bell, adds both bite and octatonic inflections to the chord. The unchanging harmonic background suggests numbness; the loss has yet to be accepted.

The seventh song, 'Tonight, I write sadly' provides such an acceptance, albeit one that is despairing. The focus is on the voice, with the orchestra providing the sparest of accompaniments. If one considers the song cycle to be a concerto for voice,[7] then this is the cadenza, in which the soloist demonstrates virtuosity primarily through the conveyance of a rapid succession of emotional states. The opening, for example, moves from sadness to dispassionate narration (a recollection of the 'little

---

[7]   As Leo Black has done. See Black, 'Hugh Wood', p. 57.

grasshopper' material of the first song) within a matter of bars; only with a description of the night wind does lyricism return. As the narrator kicks through the embers of the ended relationship, warm octatonic chords appear, recalling the passions of earlier movements. As these memories accumulate, the emotions rise, building to one final top B♭ ('I shout, shout her *name*') over a rich extended dominant on A. But the recollections fade, and the climax is followed by a coda for the voice, accompanied only by guide pitches from the celesta. The use of a solo voice dramatically captures the loneliness of the narrator; the brief lyrical flourishes throw the despair of the text into sharp relief.

Although not as static as the conclusion of 'Call the sky mine', 'Tonight, I write sadly' is also characterized by a degree of harmonic immobility. Much of the melodic writing is centred on E♭ and its chromatic auxiliaries. This provides a focus for the shifting emotional states of the song: a still centre around which conflicting passions rage. The dramatic pacing of these states thus become the primary means by which momentum is manipulated. Such is Wood's assured handling of his expressive material, one regrets that he has never written for the operatic stage: the dramatic and emotional force of the song as conclusion to the set is magnificently realized.

The orchestral forces for the Song Cycle to Poems by Pablo Neruda are similar to those in the Chamber Concerto, calling for an additional flautist and clarinettist in lieu of a bassoon and tuba; the emphasis in the percussion is on metallic sounds. The timbral and textural variety of the song cycle reflects the Chamber Concerto, but there is little of the reworking of traditional instrumental groupings that one finds in the earlier work. The vocal writing explores similarly a range of timbral effects and modes of performance for expressive purpose. Within the first song alone, the singer is instructed to sing in turn in a declamatory manner, sweetly, sonorously, distantly, lyrically, warmly, darkly, as if in a recitative, languorously and playfully.[8] The melodic style and choice of register supports these characters. For instance, at bar 40, the line marked *lirico* opens with the lyrical major third and falling semitone figure common to Wood's vocal music; when the figure returns almost immediately in a lower register, the singer is asked to colour it both warmly and darkly. Elsewhere, the declamatory passages are based on repetitions and gradual expansions from a focal pitch, as at the opening, and so on.

The singer is also required to make use of less common techniques, embellishing the declamatory phrases with quarter-tones, and performing certain notes in a semi-voiced manner. In the third song, the singer recites lines over the processional accompaniment in a kind of *Sprechstimme*, delivered in a low forceful manner (*voce basso*). Forming a middleground between this and the sung material elsewhere in the song are some further semi-voiced passages; in the closing bars, there is a fluid motion between the different vocal states as conflicting emotional states pass by in rapid succession. It is telling that, as the cycle builds to its passionate climax, there are fewer non-traditional vocal techniques, suggesting that these are used to signal emotional states other than love/passion. This certainly appears to be the case in the final song, which begins somewhere between song and recitative, and

---

[8]   *Declamato appassionato, dolciss., sonore, lontano, lirico,* warm, *oscuro, quasi recit., languoroso* and *quasi scherzando.*

proceeds to move back and forth between these modes of delivery. Later on, both semi-voiced and *voce basso* passages appear as the poet recalls both love and loss; the closing pages draw together the emotional threads of the work in a gesture of calm resignation rather than transcendence.

Prior to *Wild Cyclamen* Op. 49 (2005–6), no other collection of songs in Wood's output explored the passions of love with such sustained emotional intensity as the Neruda songs. The vivid use of orchestral colour and texture combines with the inspired setting of Logue's passionate texts to create a minor masterpiece of the genre, and one of Wood's finest scores.

Robert Graves Songs Set I Op. 18

Wood's response to the work of Robert Graves forms a significant part of his vocal output.[9] The first collection of Graves songs is typical in its long gestation, for although the majority of the songs were written in September 1976, their initial conception came a decade earlier. The opening song, 'The Rose', acts as an overture. The songs that follow – 'Records', 'The Foreboding', 'Always', 'A Last Poem' and 'The Green Castle' – all possess in varying degrees the exaltation of love combined with doubts, real and imagined, of its longevity. Correspondingly, all these songs are characterized by shifting emotional states that recall to some extent those of the Song Cycle to Poems by Pablo Neruda.

The formal simplicity of 'The Rose' – two verses, the second of which is a calm reworking of the strident first – is reciprocated in the directness of the musical language. Much of the material draws on whole-tone formulations or major triads whose roots are a semitone apart; the vocal lines are predominantly scalic. The simplicity of the setting looks ahead to Wood's late music (for instance, the Erich Fried Songs Op. 43); more pertinently, it embodies the assuredness with which the poet presents his truth ('When was it that we swore to love forever? When did the Universe come at last to be? The two questions are one').

The second song, 'Records', opens broadly and passionately, the extended upbeats in semiquavers to whole-tone harmonies recalling the piano figuration at the start of each half of 'The Rose'. The vocal writing is more lyrical than the first song, as befits the nature of the text – a direct address to the loved one rather than a series of questions. A darker middle section, characterized by a greater emphasis on chromatic motion, builds to a climax. The low piano writing of much of this section contrasts with the emphasis on the treble of the opening; throbbing repeated quavers providing a similar, if more sinister, intensity to that in 'The Confirmation' from *The Rider Victory*. The final section is a varied recapitulation of the first, in which the harmonic progressions are reordered and the emotional ardour cooled: the ending is a hushed whisper.

'The Foreboding' draws on the same literary tradition as Heine's 'Der Döppelganger' (set by Schubert), namely the vision of oneself in torment over a love lost. Wood communicates the anguish and the horror of the situation with a cramped language based on chromatic clusters. The opening melodic statement shares the intervals and contours of motif *y* in Example 2.4 (p. 30); variants of this permeate

---

[9]   See Chapter 7, pp. 153–9 and Chapter 9, pp. 221–5.

both the voice and piano parts. Bursts of dense imitative counterpoint proliferate in the accompaniment – reflections upon reflections – amidst alternately curt clusters of semitones and momentary warm sonorities that are soon snatched away. Rising scales in the voice, doubled in three octaves by the piano, form a grim parody of equivalent figures in 'The Rose'. In this way, the hopeful 'When did this Universe come at last to be?' of the first song becomes, in turn, 'I thought that I had suddenly come to die', 'But the vision was false, this much I knew', and finally, tellingly, 'That the love you cruelly gave me could not last'. Within the set as a whole, 'The foreboding' represents a crucial turning point, an epiphany, set to a music in which emotional directness and technical fluency combine hauntingly.

The entranced opening of 'Always' stands in contrast to the tense violence of 'The Foreboding'. A softly repeated A♮ in the piano conjures up a sense of timelessness in its steadfast refusal to suggest a pulse. Around this, delicate embellishments are used to gently blur the harmonic centre as the text, lyrically and lovingly set, describes the poet lost in the moment with his love. But it is clear that this beautiful vision of eternity is illusory: a passionately angular outburst reveals that it is but a moment prolonged in the mind.

The opening of the fifth song, 'A Last Poem', was given in Example 2.2 (p. 27). After a further series of questions, first frenzied and then more reflective, the material of the opening returns, transformed, as the narrator imagines his love responding positively to the poems. Only the harmonic outline is retained: the chords marked * in Example 2.2, stripped of the upbeat material that ushers them in, become delicate bell-like enrichments of the now lyrical melodic line. As with a similar transformation in 'The Rose', the use of the same material for two contrasting expressive states heightens their differences, but dramatically emphasizes that the two are both intimately related.

The final song, 'The Green Castle' is also the longest. The poem describes the various 'heavens' one can encounter, each of which is given their own characteristic setting. The arrival at the 'seventh heaven' is particularly striking: richly embellished A major and B♭ major chords (the latter combined with an E major triad) provide the basis of the harmonies, the left and right hands of the pianist at opposite ends of the piano keyboard. Over the fluttering of trilled notes within these chords, the singer presents a lyrical, if detached recollection of how he and his love 'once contrived to enter/ By a trance of love'. But as with 'Always', real life is unable to sustain such moments of wonder: the final pages of the setting review and rework elements of the first half of the poem as the protagonists, 'at a loss' try to recount their experiences. Only the vision of the castle remains, but this too fades into the distance.

Although Wood states that the songs can be performed individually, and in any order, he suggests that 'The Rose' is repeated at the end if the entire set is to be sung. Doing so throws the song into new light. When positioned at the beginning of the set, it speaks of an unwavering confidence in love. On its return at the end, after a series of visions of love into which reality has sometimes intruded brutally, the second half of 'The Rose' suggests a degree of doubt: 'Grant me honest sleep/ Sleep, not oblivion'. In doing so, it encapsulates the content of the set as a whole, in which the reworking of material into different emotional states vividly and directly depicts both the euphoric and despairing aspects of love. The use of the same pitch material for different expressive purposes is one of Wood's familiar compositional habits (witness the Quintet and Cello Concerto), but allied to Graves's texts, the result in the song set is even more pronounced and moving.

Musicians Wrestle Everywhere

Musicians Wrestle Everywhere belongs to a series of occasional pieces in Wood's output (for instance, *Lines to Mr Hodgson* and *Comus Quadrilles*) that is written in a light style. It was written for the opening of new Music Rooms at Churchill College on 25 October 1980, and sets for choir and orchestra a text by Emily Dickinson. The work is characterized by shapely and lyrical vocal lines, long diatonic passages, clear tonal centres and a harmonic vocabulary based on common triads with added seconds or sixths. The strident opening section in A major makes use of driving scales and strident chords; contrast is provided by a more lyrical second section in C in which six solo cellists accompany the female voices.[10] There is soon, however, a return to A major, now coloured by the sharpened fourth (D♯); more rapid changes of key follow, still underpinned by boisterous scalic motion in both voice and accompaniment. The final third of the setting begins with a second brief passage for solo cellos, here in A major with a sharpened fourth; this is transformed swiftly into purely diatonic writing for the full ensemble. The sonorous closing passage is enriched by ecstatic trills that culminates on an A major chord with an added sixth; there are parallels with the radiant closes of the Third String Quartet and Symphony.

Concerto – Quartet – Symphony

The Violin Concerto, Third Quartet and Symphony all possess, to varying extents, clearly identifiable programmatic elements. This is not the only feature that these works have in common. Each traces a path from suppressed or tumultuous worlds of expression to conclude emphatically with emotional states that are buoyant, rejuvenated or radiant; bound up with this is the transformation of material based on cramped chromatic clusters into something more expansive. From these shared expressive and technical backgrounds come three very individual foregrounds that find continued riches in the same fundamental sources.

Violin Concerto Op. 17

The Violin Concerto (1970–72) was written for Manoug Parikian.[11] It is in three movements, with a central Scherzo flanked by two slower movements. Ideas for the Scherzo were derived from sketches made in 1968 for an abandoned second

---

[10]   The section for solo cellos was written for the six cellists who happened to be in the orchestra at that time.

[11]   Parikian recorded the concerto in 1978 for Unicorn Records (re-released by NMC in 2001, NMC D082). His performance recalls that of the premiere, which William Mann, writing for *The Times*, found 'marvellously vivid and committed throughout, in rapid as well as ruminative passages' ('Wood Violin Concerto' (20 September 1972)).

movement of the Cello Concerto; further ideas came to Wood on August 31 1970 by the Thames, and exactly a year later in an orchard in Hertfordshire. The bulk of the composition was written in 1972, and the work was finished on 31 August 1972.

The orchestral forces in the Violin Concerto are similar to those of the Cello Concerto, with the addition of a piano (doubling celesta). The percussion section is expanded too, recalling that of the Chamber Concerto: tom-toms, bongos and a tambourine add drive; a crotale, a glockenspiel and a triangle provide glitter. The delicacy with which much of this is handled, and the thinner textures generally, stand in contrast to the fuller treatment of the orchestra in the Cello Concerto. Indeed, the Violin Concerto explores considerably cooler emotional waters than that for the cello, and the large orchestra is used to colour this journey with subtle nuance of timbre rather than the overwhelming sonority of a tutti orchestra in full flight.

The first movement is best thought of in three sections, each with its own thematic material, with hints of the first section recurring in the third. The Scherzo, following *attacca*, occupies the same position as the development in the Cello Concerto. Cutting across its Scherzo-and-Trio design are three varied repetitions of a dramatic idea that serve further to drive the music forward. A cadenza at the start of the third movement precedes a recapitulation of the opening of the first movement; this is followed by a sudden burst of renewed energy in the form of an Allegro that serves as a Coda. Although the concerto is in three discrete movements, the character and function of these movements, together with numerous thematic interconnections, suggests numerous analogies with a single-movement sonata form, thus reversing the situation to be found in the Cello Concerto (see Table 6.2).

The concerto opens with an ethereal high B♮ sustained in the violins, flute and piccolo, coloured by piano and harp, in a similar, although less urgent, manner to the opening of the Chamber Concerto. From this, the solo violin emerges to present a lyrical and lamenting theme that forms the basis of the first section and a source of motifs for subsequent sections (Example 6.2, bars 8–17). The varied treatment of the chromatic figures that decorate this theme, bracketed in Example 6.2, hints at the nature of the material to come. This basic idea initiates an extended paragraph that descends through an octave and back over a sustained augmented triad (E♭–G–B) in the orchestra. Upon completion of the paragraph, orchestral instruments enter to create a polyphonic dialogue, their melodic fragments derived from a transposed inversion of the soloist's opening material. The fragments are taken up again by the orchestra at the start of a short and energetic transition that culminates in a brief section for solo violin, *alla cadenza*.

The initially slower second section that begins in bar 106 draws on many of the more romantic of Wood's characteristic gestures. Opening with a figure closely related to motif *z* of Example 6.2, the lyrical continuation transposes the tightly knit chromatic clusters of the opening melodic paragraph into widely spaced and highly expressive shapes. A gentle trill in the flute's lowest register leads into warmly scored chords based on sevenths. The mood is intensified by a sudden orchestral outburst, *molto animato*: the soloist re-enters with a descending chromatic scale, spread over three octaves, accompanied by yearning appoggiaturas in the trombones. These two elements – the orchestral outburst and the descending chromatic scale – alternate in increasingly impassioned variations that form the climax of the movement.

Table 6.2   Interlocking formal designs in the Violin Concerto Op. 17

Movt	Bars	Material	Sonata Analogy
i	1–105	Section I: bars 1–30 basic idea of concerto (Example 6.2)	Exposition, first subject group
	106–71	Section II: bars 106–24 lyrical theme; bars 124–71 alternations of solo and tutti material	Second subject, first thematic group
	172–226	Section III: sparser textures, some reworking of section I	Second subject, second theme
	227–38	Coda	Codetta
ii	1–25	Basic material of Scherzo presented (A)	Development (Scherzo)
	26–64	Extended passage for soloist and percussion (B)	
	65–104	Reworking of opening; 'sword' motif bars 100–105 (A_1)	
	105–33	Transition to Trio, based on (B)	
	134–244	Trio; bars 239–44 second presentation of 'sword' motif	
	245–76	Truncated reprise of A section of Trio	
	277–339	Scherzo: reprise of opening material; bars 315–22 final presentation of 'sword' motif	
	340–59	Final references to Trio material	
	360–67	Coda	
iii	1–80	Cadenza	Recapitulation
	81–120	bars 81–94: reprise of i/ bars 106 –24; bars 99–120: reprise of i/bars 1–30	Compressed reprise of first and second subject material
	121–51	Allegro; basic material recalls scherzo ideas	Coda
	152–83	Coda	

A second *alla cadenza* for solo violin leads into the third and final section of the movement. After a hesitant start, the soloist and the orchestral violins pass lyrical material between them; there is a serenade-like quality to the music. But the movement ends with a sudden cooling of the emotional climate. The double basses intone the opening of the movement, the solo violin fades into ghostly echoes of

Example 6.2   Violin Concerto Op. 17/i, bars 8–30 (solo violin only)

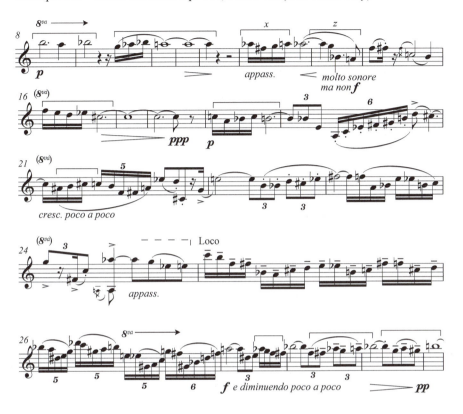

firstly the start of the third section, and then, in harmonics, the motto tritone E♭–A of the Cello Concerto, perhaps a reference to the origins of the subsequent Scherzo in the sketches of the earlier work.

Unlike the extended paragraphs of the first movement, the Scherzo begins with short figures in the orchestra: the soloist remains silent. Yet the use of chromatic clusters as the basis of the material links the movements: the first idea of the Scherzo consists of a ghostly fanfare in the trumpets derived from interlocking whole-tones (the upper line of which is a transposition of motif *y*, Example 2.4; compare also with *x* in Example 6.2). This is followed by a figure in the clarinets that consists of a crescendo through a sustained whole-tone dyad (E♭–F) that plunges down over two octaves to another dyad (D–E). The manner in which the two ideas introduced at the outset of the Scherzo are alternated and developed is reminiscent of the bloc technique of the Second String Quartet. Where it differs is the motivic connection between the two ideas: the clarinet figure is a reworking of the interlocking tones of the trumpet fanfare. The clarinet figure also becomes the basis later on of what Wood has called the 'sword' motif, a thrice-presented figure in the brass that punctuates the Scherzo-and-Trio form of the movement (see Table 6.2). Evidently there is a hidden programme to the music. An epigraph at the head of the movement reads 'flame, sword, flower'. The 'sword' motif forms one of these three; the 'flame' might be hinted at by the instruction for the soloist to play 'urgently, and with great fire' at the opening of the Trio; but the musical role played by the 'flower' remains a mystery.[12]

The introduction of the soloist in bar 26 reveals a similar formal construction to the opening of the Scherzo. Two further ideas are contrasted, the first consisting of rapidly ascending arpeggios in thirds followed by descending octatonic scales, and the second widely spaced leaps. The play between groups of two and three quavers, as well as conjunct and disjunct melodic motion, contributes to the light and limber quality of the material. The accompaniment to both ideas is exclusively percussive, surrounding the pitched material in the violin with metallic washes of sound from the cymbals and insistent tapping from wood blocks and tom-toms.

The reprise of the opening (bar 65) is shared more evenly between soloist and orchestra. The fanfare material dominates, leading to increasingly dense figuration in the strings based on the same interlocking tones: this forms the swirling peak of the Scherzo. Over this, the brass section intones the first of the three climactic 'sword' motifs. There follows then a review and reworking of the soloist's material from bars 24–65, now shared between solo violin and the orchestra, which serves also as a transition into the Trio.

The Trio opens with three broad paragraphs, each consisting of distinct material. The first of these begins with glistening repeated chords in crotchets in the strings and celesta, over which the soloist gradually ascends with successive transpositions of a cramped three-quaver figure. The second paragraph reworks material from earlier in the movement, suggesting that the boundaries between Scherzo and Trio are thus fluid and permeable. Major thirds become increasingly important in the third paragraph, at first unassuming in the accompaniment, and then made prominent in the wind, cellos and piano in a gesture reminiscent of the 'statue theme' in *Scenes from Comus*. These basic elements – ascending solo line, material from the Scherzo and material based on thirds – are repeated a further two times, each time subject to greater development and modification, in what is effectively a modified strophic form. Prior to the final version of the material based in thirds, the 'sword' motif interjects again as the climax of the Trio.

The recapitulation introduces a further reworking of the pitches of the opening fanfare: F–G–A♭–F♯ becoming G–F–A♭–F♯ (bars 280 ff.). Though a comparatively slight change, the melodic contour that this creates, combined with an additive rhythm of 3+3+2, is used to form a distinct new motivic idea. The significance of this idea remains unclear within the Scherzo, for it fulfils a predominantly secondary role; only in the final movement does the full reason for its introduction become clear. Much of what follows is hushed: only with the third and final use of the 'sword' motif do the dynamics rise above *mp*. Yet even this climax is undercut: the swell in the brass is reversed, and the 'sword' motif ends in shadows. From here, there is a swift review of the material of the movement; a concluding harmonic C♮ in the solo violin is cut-off by a low thud from the cellos and basses.

---

[12]   It appears that the epigraph must remain unexplained, for Wood claims that he can no longer remember the significance of it, save that it served as a motivation for the movement as a whole.

Although the surface of the Scherzo is alive with quavers grouped additively, the underlying harmonic motion is comparatively slow, making use of pedal notes and, in particular, ostinati. In essence this is no different to the techniques used in the exuberant scherzi of *Scenes from Comus*. In *Comus*, the sectional construction gives rise to a series of climaxes that have a cumulative effect and shattering release. In the Violin Concerto, where the same techniques are wedded to material of an almost sinister character, the effect is somewhat different, recalling at times the darker moments of the Scherzo in the First String Quartet.

If the Violin Concerto is viewed as a large-scale sonata form, then we find that the cadenza occurs in the same place as in the Cello Concerto, just before the 'recapitulation'. The difference lies in terms of the dramatic impact of the cadenza: in the Cello Concerto, the cadenza occurs at the point of highest tension, after the orchestral 'development', but in the Violin Concerto it creeps in, *esitando*, after the spectral conclusion to the Scherzo. As one might expect, the violin cadenza combines individual virtuosity with a review and reworking of thematic ideas from the concerto. In this light, it is perhaps significant that much of the cadenza is concerned with material from bars 172–226 of the first movement. In addition to the dramatic showcasing of the soloist's ability, the cadenza thus functions as a recapitulation of the 'second thematic group' of the 'second subject area'. Much of what follows has a similarly retrospective air. In bar 81, the orchestra tentatively re-enters, *molto tranquilo e largamente*, with a return of second subject material (i/bars 106 ff.), leading in bar 95 to the texture of the first subject. By bar 120, this has thinned out to a single B♮ held by the leader of the orchestra, and it is as if the work is to end, like the Cello Concerto, on a bleak note. However, a slow C major glissando on the harp leads to a short scherzo-like coda that brings the work to an unexpectedly buoyant close.

The final stages of the Violin Concerto are thus far removed in temperament from the endings of the Cello Concerto, Second String Quartet, Chamber Concerto and Neruda Songs. Leo Black has noted that such a conclusion

> has puzzled well-disposed people, who find such a 'happy ending' hard to credit. They cannot feel it to have been inevitable. Well, indeed (to compare great things with lesser ones), why should Mozart have tagged on that complacent D major coda at the end of his tragic D minor piano concerto, or Beethoven that skittish prestissimo in the major after the grim struggles of his serious String Quartet in F minor? These are mysterious matters, in which it may not be a good idea to claim too much understanding.[13]

The *mood* of the ending might have raised eyebrows (though this is part of the charm of the concerto), but the work nevertheless seems to demand that *something* follow the reprise of the first movement. Taken on its own, the third movement is too slight to balance the sum of the first two movements. To correct this imbalance, the concluding allegro drew on the hitherto secondary idea introduced in the repeat of the Scherzo (bar 280), using it as the basis of the brisk coda to the work. In a sense, the coda elaborates and 'explains' the inclusion of the figure in the Scherzo, and suggests a method of linking movements that was to bear richer fruit in both the Symphony and Piano Concerto.

---

[13]   Black, 'Hugh Wood', p. 57.

String Quartet No. 3 Op. 20

The Third Quartet is dedicated to Alexander Goehr. Like the Second, it is constructed from a series of largely self-contained blocs, but whereas the blocs in the earlier work combine to suggest a ternary form (see Chapter 5, pp. 108–10), the grouping of blocs in the Third Quartet does not display characteristics of any formal archetype. Rather, the material of the blocs articulates stages of an emotional narrative that moves from despair to joy. This much is abundantly clear from the character of the music alone. However, the general expressive journey is made more specific by literary quotations above key passages in the score that describe the passage of winter to spring, from (creative) barrenness to fertility. That these outline a personal journey is suggested by the inclusion of a short transcription of an extract from Wood's setting of Laurie Lee's 'April Rise'. Table 6.3 summarizes the quoted material in the Quartet; Table 6.4 details the form suggested by the musical character and material. Comparison between the two tables reveals that each cluster of quotations is identified with a different musical character.

The quartet opens bleakly: quietly sustained harmonics in the strings, together with an occasional pizzicato upbeat, lead to a swiftly stifled climax that subsides into the lower registers. The material outlines chromatic clusters, organized (in a similar manner to Example 2.4, motif y) to emphasize major seconds: the first four pitches are C♯–E♭–E–D. Much of the melodic motion too is based on (expanded) major seconds; both violins play material that is exclusively whole-tone, yet placed in a chromatic context. The second bloc provides contrast in terms of interval and register, with low sonorous chords following a dense chromatic cluster from G–B♭. The voice-leading between chords is exclusively by semitone step, giving the effect of a sigh. The first of these chords is a permutation of the first four notes of the B♭ major scale (D–E♭–B♭–C); the second (from the cello upwards, C♯–E–A–B) was taken from Goehr's third string quartet.[14] In each case the chord consists of two whole-tone steps plus an additional note; the harmonic implications of this become clearer as the quartet progresses.

These two chords, and to a lesser extent the cluster that precedes them, form the basis of a series of 'chorale-variations',[15] a description that suggests both the character of the chords and the method by which they are developed. In the third bloc, for instance, the progression is extended by repeating the pair of chords in different inversions and with altered spacing. To this is added first a repeated harmonic E in the first violin, reminiscent of Messiaenic birdsong,[16] and second a cadenza-like idea in the bass for pizzicato cello. All of these elements recur in the more animated fourth bloc (the second chorale variation). In some cases, notes are added to or

---

[14] This is second of two specific borrowings from Goehr that can be found in Wood's music. The first was the unison doubling of cor anglais and bass clarinet in Goehr's *Hecuba's Lament* (1961) that made a brief appearance in *Scenes from Comus* (see Wood, 'On Music of Conviction', p. 328).

[15] Composer's note to the score.

[16] This is particularly the case for the stylized birdsong of 'Liturgie de Cristal', the first movement of Messiaen's *Quatuor pour la fin du temps*, which has a similar static quality to that of the opening of Wood's Third Quartet.

Table 6.3   Textual content of String Quartet No. 3 Op. 20

Bloc	Quotation	Source
2	For I am every dead thing ... ... and I am re-begot Of absence, darkness, death; things which are not.	John Donne, 'A Nocturnall upon S. Lucies day' (lines 12, 17–18, 1)
end of 8	Tis the yeares midnight, and it is the dayes, ...	
12	How fresh, O Lord, how sweet and clean Are thy returns! ev'n as the flowers in Spring; To which, besides their own demean, The late-post frost tributes of pleasure bring ...	George Herbert, 'The Flower' (lines 1–9)
13	Grief melts away Like snow in May, As if there were no such cold thing.	
14	Who would have thought my shrivel'd heart Could ever have recover'd greennesse?	
23	If ever I saw blessing in the air I see it now in this still early day Where lemon green the vaporous morning drips wet sunlight on the powder of my eye	Instrumental setting of words from Laurie Lee's 'April Rise' (lines 1–4)
24	And now in age I bud again, After so many deaths I live and write; I once more smell the dew and rain, And relish versing.	George Herbert, 'The Flower' (lines 36–9)

Table 6.4   Form of String Quartet No. 3 Op. 20

Bloc number	1–10	11–16	17–21	22–3	24
Section	A	B_1	B_2	C	B_3

omitted from the chords to vary further the material; the spacings and additions create and emphasize 0,2,6 'dominant' trichords as the basis of the reworked chords that contribute to a gradual increase in the warmth of the quartet.

Slight stirrings of life are combined in the fifth bloc with reminders of the glacial opening. A rising arpeggio rich in major thirds leads to a high, closely spaced and quiet chord, from which a sustained E♭ emerges. This provides a static background to a melodic figure in the violin which begins the pitches of the first four-note clusters in both the first and second bloc, before leaping to a repeated 'birdsong' on F♯. Of note is the descending major second E–D that initiates the melody: this dyad becomes increasingly important in the latter half of the quartet.

The 'coming of spring' is now only a matter of time, but first one must endure late wintry snaps and frosts. Increasingly impassioned versions of bloc 5 are interrupted by *feroce* passages that fragment into the sparer textures of the opening blocs. Finally, in blocs 9 and 10, the 'birdsong' idea is transformed into repeated figures which, like the mechanical durational patterns of the Second Quartet and Chamber Concerto, propel the music into a climax. From here, the texture rapidly dissolves into *pp* tremolando semiquaver murmurings (as at the end of the first section in the Second Quartet): this passes down through the quartet, culminating in an ostinato in the cello based on the opening pitches of the opening of the work in the cello (bloc 12). It is here that the textual programme turns to Spring (see Table 6.3). The cello ostinato transforms into a scurrying ascending line that thickens as it passes into the viola and second violin. Over this, there are melodic fragments based on thirds (contrasting with the major and minor seconds that dominate the first section) and then a longer, more lyrical treatment of melodic whole-tone dyads. Characteristic of this treatment is a dialogue created through the separation of the interlocking tones of the opening into registral extremes: one whole-tone pair is placed at the top of the quartet's texture, and the second pair positioned in the bass.

The dialogue intensifies in the thirteenth bloc, with the addition of the stylized birdsong. This culminates in a *ff* tremolando chord created from the entire whole-tone set built on G. The expectant mood suddenly changes: the dynamic drops, the melody consists of sweet yet insistent iterations of the E–D dyad, and the texture switches to homophony based on the *other* whole-tone set (Example 6.3). With this 'arrival of Spring', the whole-tone implications of the chorale variations at the start of the work are thus realized. The interlocking major seconds of the first violin in bars 176–7 (motif *x*), initiates an ebullient reworking of the more lyrical presentation of this idea in bloc 12. The whole-tone material is coloured increasingly with chromatic additions: the radiant climax develops bars 172–9 of Example 6.3 with richer harmonies and euphoric triplet figuration in the accompanying parts.

The exuberance of bloc 14 is swiftly undercut by a return, for two mysterious bars, to an adagio tempo. Chromatic clusters emphasizing semitones form the basis of the outer voices; the harmonies are derived from a further reworking of the chords of the chorale variation. The turn to material from the opening of the work is completed in the subsequent bloc (16), in which the glacial melodic and harmonic content of bloc 1 is transformed into vigorous and tightly knit contrapuntal fragments.

Blocs 17–21 vary and intensify the material of blocs 12–16: this large-scale repetition of an entire section recalls the Trio of the Violin Concerto (see Table 6.4). The repetition concludes with a series of jubilant trills in the upper instruments, which ushers in the climax of the entire work. Over resonant arpeggiated chords based on C major in the cello, and later whole-tone chords on F♯, the upper instruments combine in an extended contrapuntal reworking of motif *x*. The passion gradually subsides, out of which emerges the transcription of a gentler evocation of spring, the opening of Wood's 'April Rise'.[17] The arrival of the transcription is prepared through the progressive alteration of the intervals of motif *y* (Example 6.3) to something resembling the profile of 'April Rise' (see Example 1.2, bars 42–3; p. 13). Because

---

[17]   See also Chapter 1, pp. 11–13.

Example 6.3   String Quartet No. 3 Op. 20, bars 170–79

the quartet gains much of its intensity from the juxtaposition of contrasting ideas, the slow process of transformation that enables the accommodation of the quotation draws a certain amount of attention to itself, functioning as aurally perceptible inverted commas. Nevertheless, the effect of the transcription remains one of poetic beauty, a moment of wondrous and warm reflection before the jubilant close of the work.

Immediately after the glimpse back to the start of Wood's compositional career comes a reminiscence of the opening of the Third Quartet, with a review of the second bloc and a fragment of bird song. The return of the chords of the chorale enables a return of the mysterious adagio interruptions from bloc 15. From this are spun increasingly lyrical lines over a buoyant quaver accompaniment. This yields to an impassioned version of Example 6.3, punctuated with exultant trills. The work concludes with a chord built over a second-inversion C major triad; the complete chord contains all the notes of the C major scale, but with a sharpened fourth (F♯ instead of F) at the top of the chord. The chord recalls the harmonic language of the lyrical climax in bloc 21; the approach to the top F♯ (via C, B♭ and A♭) links to the whole-tone motion that infuses the entire work.

The Third Quartet embodies a vernal freshness quite different from the energetic dances of *Comus* or the Quintet, and a lyricism that owes little to the expansive paragraphs of the Cello and Violin Concertos and the Song Cycle to Poems by Pablo Neruda. With its taut bloc construction and unusual form, the quartet offers a unique vehicle for its traditional emotional trajectory. The shifting melodic, harmonic and expressive contexts in which the germinal whole-tone step is placed sweeps the listener along through a work that is by turns haunting and beautiful. In a decade of consistently fine scores, the Third Quartet stands out as one of the finest of all.[18]

Symphony Op. 21

The emotional narrative of the Symphony (1974–82), as with the Third Quartet, is communicated unambiguously. The passage depicted in the music from turmoil and tragedy to radiance and triumph is an appropriately traditional symphonic topic for a composer of Wood's predilections. The burden of tradition weighs heavily, and fruitfully, on the Symphony. It would not have escaped Wood that his Symphony shares the same opus number as Beethoven's First and Webern's. Wood's use of a traditional four-movement plan (with slow movement and Scherzo) indicates that it has more in common with the former composer than the latter. Nevertheless, the first movement is not the sonata-allegro one might expect in a 'traditional' symphonic design. Its title, *Tempesta*, reveals its stormy nature: the movement is an extended, almost obsessive, study of turmoil and violence that has an introductory role. Only with the coda to the movement is a contrasting idea (approximating to a lyrical 'second subject') introduced.

The *Tempesta* leads without a break into the slow movement, whose title, *Elegia*, serves also as an indication of character. Taking its cue from the Coda to the *Tempesta*, the *Elegia* in effect provides a large-scale contrast to the first movement. The fruits of this contrast are worked out in the final two movements, a Scherzo with Trio and an extended Brahmsian Passacaglia in which the weight of the work is situated; these are also played without a break. The Symphony ends in a jubilant A major recalling the ebullience of the close of Janáček's *Sinfonietta*.

The recollection of Janáček is not, however, a direct quotation. Rather, it belongs to a network of allusions and quotations (not all of them musical) that situate the Symphony within a historical (traditional) and emotional context, imbuing the tragic to triumphant narrative of the music with more specific meanings. In the preface to the score, Wood details the genesis of the Symphony and the nature of the ideas that gradually crystallized into the finished work. Having first mentioned the work in a Projects notebook dated 30 March 1974, a further note made two months later, confirmed that the Symphony was to be 'a commentary on the Magic Flute ... still a *Quest* with darkness & estrangement and ordeals & Valkyrie Act I will be there'.[19] Quotations from both of these operas appear in the first half of work. To this was

---

[18]   To date, the quartet has been recorded twice, firstly by the Lindsay Quartet, who premiered the work (ASV CDDCA825, 1980), and more recently by the Chilingirian Quartet (Conifer 75605 51239-2, 1994).

[19]   Composer's note to the score.

added a further layer of programmatic inspiration, Cavafy's poem *The God Abandons Antony*; which, although literary in origin, had potential musical corollaries: 'The God Abandons Antony – why it's essentially a *musical* idea in itself – the half-heard bacchic revel – the elegiac looking-back (Lulu adagio) between the recognition of *all that we have been* (find the Eliot)'.[20] As with the text and quotations of the Third String Quartet, such connections are wrought into the design of the Symphony: they are no mere intrusion, but part of the warp and weft of the material.[21]

Tempesta   Turning the elegiac and frigid openings of the Violin Concerto and Third String Quartet on their heads, the Symphony opens with barely controlled fury that surpasses even the untrammelled onset of the Second String Quartet. A tumultuous outburst from the timpani leads to a low pedal E in the timpani, piano and double basses. This E functions as a focal pitch: the presence of chromatic auxiliary notes around it creates menacing noise rather than ambiguity. Over this, the basic motivic material of the work is presented in the brass: long dramatic held notes interrupted by short stabbing gestures (Example 6.4), in the manner of the 'sword' motif of the Violin Concerto. The emphasis is on chromatic motion: much of the material progresses by (expanded) semitone step, and each half of the theme is based on a chromatic hexachord, as in the Cello Concerto (see Example 6.4 and also 3.3b, p. 62). Between thematic statements the strings and woodwind provide increasingly long snatches of a rapid figuration based on thirds that contrasts dramatically with the elongated brass statements. The theme traces an ascending line from the G in bar 2 through to the octave above in bar 15: though fragmented, it nevertheless possesses a certain familial resemblance to the melodic material discussed in Chapter 2 (pp. 24–32). The section ends with a longer timpani solo (bars 15–18) against which the strings sustain a twelve-note chord clustered into the space of a single octave. The effect, enhanced by the orchestration of snarling brass, thunderous timpani and fugitive strings, is one of turmoil, of powerful and elemental forces violently taking shape.

The first paragraph is then subject to two varied repeats, each of its constituent parts developed independently, as with Wood's use of bloc form. The increasingly prolonged returns of the twelve-note clustered, for instance, are embellished with surging and dramatic arpeggios and trills. The brass theme that these chords punctuate is transformed into first two-, then three-part counterpoint. The introduction of counterpoint as a means of sustaining and intensifying the musical argument is common in Wood's music: consider the soaring string and brass inventions that appear early on in *Scenes from Comus*. What is significant in the Symphony, however, is that the intertwining brass lines occur in the bass, and not in the higher, brighter registers that characterize those in *Comus*; the resulting energy is correspondingly dark and oppressive, not buoyant and liberating.

The counterpoint hints also at technical features that become increasingly important as the Symphony progresses. The material draws upon the characteristic melodic shape of alternately rising and falling tones and semitones that recurs throughout Wood's oeuvre (for instance, Example 6.4, motif *x*). From reiterations of

---

[20]   Ibid.

[21]   See also Chapter 1, n. 47, p. 21.

Example 6.4   Symphony, Op. 21/i, bars 1–19 (brass and timpani only)

this motif, a 'new' twelve-note line is created,[22] against which is counterpointed its inversion at the tritone. This is the first of a number of instances in the Symphony in which thematic material is derived from the application of basic serial operations to

---

[22]   Compare this with the derivation of a second twelve-note line from the opening theme in the Cello Concerto (Examples 3.3a and c, pp. 61–2), in which the motif of a semitone and a tone is also prevalent.

a melodic idea, though it should be stressed that the harmonic material remains non-serial. In fact, the harmonic centre of gravity within the repetitions of the opening paragraph remains firmly rooted on E, interspersed with dense twelve-note clusters. Unlike the evolving harmonic contexts of the repetitions in the Trio of the Violin Concerto and in the Third Quartet, the Symphony remains harmonically inert, the violence of the beginning unable to find a significant release or outlet.

An attempt to wrench the music free from this inertia heralds the start of the second section. The violas, divided into four, initiate a busy accompaniment in semiquavers, making use of the intervals of motif *x*, that is taken up firstly by the cellos and then the violins. The overlapping and layering of this accompaniment at different pitch levels creates a shifting and unstable version of the chromatic cluster that had opposed the pedal E in the first section. Over this, wind, brass and percussion instruments present brief fanfare ideas derived from Example 6.4, motif *w*. Subsequent reiterations of these ideas are transposed ever higher, before settling into quasi-ostinato figures that decrease steadily in duration on repetition. The result is an unsynchronized tumult of sound, steadily accelerating in frequency of attacks. In contrast to the sophisticated treatment of ideas elsewhere in the Symphony, the mechanistic treatment of material here has the air of passagework, building steadily, if prosaically, to the heart of the second section, an extended brass chorale. Rather than the traditional expressive functions (such as meditative, noble) one might expect from such a chorale, the context renders it here almost oppressive. However, the use of the lyrical rising major third and falling semitone figure (outlined in Example 6.4, motif *y*) hints at a more conciliatory role for the chorale in the movements to come. The scurrying figuration of the wind and string accompaniment to the chorale echoes its motivic and intervallic details. As the intensity of this accompaniment grows, borne on the wash of metallic percussion, contrapuntal fragments are tossed between wind and brass, building to a climactic reprise of the first section.[23]

The recapitulation follows the primary thematic material of the exposition closely. The bass has returned, stubbornly, to the embellished E♮ upon which the first half of the movement was built; the accompaniment, however, is more intricate, drawing on figures from the second section to create greater density. Over the twelve-note cluster is layered a series of motivic fragments, passed up from the lower registers to the higher ones. This leads to repetitions of a climactic twelve-note chord, a thrice-struck hammer-blow. Behind these chords, the back two desks of the cello sustain a chord (F–C–E♭–B♭) that creeps out, *ppp*, from the resonance of the orchestral chords. This leads into the first quotation of the work, taken from the moment at which Siegmund realizes his love for Sieglinde in the first scene of *Die Walküre*. Just as flowers can grow in the rubble of a city devastated by violence, the quotation appears amidst the ruins of the first movement. Initially performed without expression, the cellos grow in volume and intensity in a moment of great poignancy and beauty.

It was part of Wood's original conception of the Symphony to have this quotation 'release memories, bring them to the surface, and thus make possible the retrospective slow movement'.[24] It achieves this by irrevocably disrupting the *Tempesta*, by virtue

---

[23]   Compare with Example 2.6, p. 36.

[24]   Composer's note to the score

Example 6.5   Symphony Op. 21/i, bars 141–9

of its unrelated expressive state and motivic shape. Just as the introduction of an unexplained idea in the recapitulation of the Scherzo in Wood's Violin Concerto necessitated the Coda at the end of the final movement, so too does the rupture created by the *Walküre* quotation require musical explanation. But this cannot happen without psychological cost. The quotation is interrupted by five bars marked 'Wild', in which the entire orchestra erupts in apparent protest at the intrusion; layers upon layers of material, full volume, compete for our attention, but nothing concrete can penetrate the noise. There is a collapse, as if exhausted, into a trilling chromatic cluster in the wind, from which a Coda emerges.

The start of the Coda is given in Example 6.5. The pedal E in the bass that rooted much of the movement now supports a warm extended A major chord.

Example 6.5 (continued)

Fragments of melodic material based on the continuation of the *Walküre* quotation are passed around the orchestra; an arching melody in the violin suggests a motto (motif *z*) that is taken up in later movements. It is plausible to suggest that the romantic rhetoric of this passage is one of the 'memories' released by the quotation and the image of love that it embodies. The movement closes in a dramatic inversion of how it began, with the timpani quietly outlining expanded semitones, no longer urgent and threatening, but uncertain and inconclusive.

The emotional gulf between the violence of the opening and the ecstatic Coda is far too wide, far too significant, to be left unresolved. Similarly, the tantalizing fragments of thematic material and harmonic argument hint at a more sustained development to come. Unlike the *Introduzione* of the First String Quartet, therefore, the *Tempesta* really does feel like an extended upbeat to what follows, functioning as a compelling, and at times overwhelming, curtain raiser.

Elegia   The second movement is subtitled Ἀπολείπειν ὁ θεὸς Ἀντώνιον (*The God Abandons Antony*), after Cavafy's poem. Cavafy describes Antony, the night before defeat in battle, hearing the sound of a ghostly procession that symbolizes the God Hercules leaving him; the underlying message is that one should courageously accept one's fate. Spectres of a march haunt the movement, becoming eventually the first of two quotations from the trials in *The Magic Flute*. As with the quotation from *Die Walküre*, the extramusical influences in the *Elegia* are used for retrospective purpose, hinting at a drama that preceded the Symphony, and which created the turmoil of the *Tempesta*. The emotional strain created through the combination of evocations of the past and the experiences of the present can be detected in the numerous and sharp contrasts of moods and textures of the *Elegia*, realized musically with contrasting technical and tonal procedures.

The movement opens with a statement of motif z transposed by a tritone (D♭–B♭–A–A♭) in the cellos; from this emerges a broad and brooding theme (hereafter 'cello theme'). More so than the fragmented material of the *Tempesta*, this theme is subject to traditional developmental processes: the idea is stated, then developed, and the second half of the theme begins with an inversion of motif z. Low-lying wind instruments and harp offset the timbre of the cellos and provide a sparse contrapuntal accompaniment that echoes the main material. There are obvious affinities with the similarly expansive openings of the Violin and, particularly, the Cello Concertos; the opening of the *Elegia* thus suggests that the movement is going to be in Wood's most eloquent, romantic vein. However, whereas the concertos build to a climax, the *Elegia* gradually sinks down, quietly returning to the D♭ with which it began, harmonized by a major third B♭–D in the bassoons.

The cello's D♭ is followed by an octave C in the piano, initiating the second section; it leads to a quiet passage for snare drum, gongs and hourglass drums. This is the first hint of the procession that later assumes concrete form: the rhythms and, in the hourglass drums, the approximate pitch contours, are those of the march in C major from the Act 2 Finale of *The Magic Flute* that is quoted at the end of the *Elegia*. In his programme note to the score, Wood suggests that this is the first stage in the reproduction of a patrol 'approaching and withdrawing' (from Antony's perspective);[25] in the light of the Wagner quotation, it can be heard equally as belonging to the summoning and crystallization of distant memories.

A version of the opening cello theme in the upper strings returns after the procession, as if the memories evoked by the procession had disturbed an otherwise continuous musical argument. Yet the theme has been transposed by a tritone, as if it were impossible to pick up the train of thought exactly where it had been left off. Formally, the transposition by a tritone is used as a substitute dominant:[26] a means of preparing the return of the opening material at pitch at the close of the work. Without perfect pitch, it is impossible for a listener to follow the transpositions of an idea through a work, and so these transpositions are combined with other processes that clarify their formal function. The return of the theme after the procession, for

---

[25]   Ibid..

[26]   Schoenberg would sometimes use transpositions of his rows at the tritone as a substitute dominant; see for example his Piano Suite Op. 25

example, opens out into an energetic two-part counterpoint that suggests development and expansion, rather than recapitulation and conclusion. This is the vigorous sort of counterpoint typified by *Comus*, not the sombre brass lines of the *Tempesta*. Perhaps to emphasize the contrast in mood between movements, the counterpoint in the strings becomes increasingly impassioned and the brass enter for the first time in the *Elegia*, warmly intoning a chorale evoking the climax, though not the mood, of the *Tempesta*'s central section. Leaps of a fifth in the upper line of the chorale also foreshadow the Passacaglia theme of the Finale (Example 2.3, p. 29). The chorale and counterpoint die away; the second half of the cello theme (beginning with the inversion of *z*) appears in the unaccompanied first violins.

The passage rapidly regains momentum. Recollections of the *Walküre* quotation proliferate in even quavers in the wind and viola as counterpoint to the violins, and the harmonic language becomes increasingly radiant. The music surges towards a climax over a dominant chord build on G, ostensibly returning to the C major implied by the piano at the opening of the section. However, this musical (and emotional) release is denied. Instead, there is an immediate cooling of the mood: a mechanical toy march of piccolo, flutes, clarinets and celesta, accompanied by brittle, intricately intertwined lines in the marimba and xylophone, ends the section.

Romantic tendencies that had been suppressed in the first two sections are given greater prominence in the third. It opens with a lyrical twelve-note melody in the violas (hereafter 'viola theme'), harmonized by warm dominant chords. The bass line is derived from the retrograde of the theme, stretched out to support the entirety of the first paragraph. Much of the material is based on whole-tone segments; scalic accompaniment figures in the inner voices gradually thicken to become series of whole-tone chords. The paragraph is then reworked a tritone higher, as with the cello theme in the first two sections, with the whole-tone material becoming increasingly prominent. There is no immediate return of the viola theme back at the original pitch. Instead, a lengthy viola line rich in whole-tone fragments is the basis of the closing paragraph, dwindling away into gently rocking minor sevenths, recalling the pastoral close of the Adagietto in the First Quartet, and far removed from the tensions and dissonances of the *Tempesta*.

The tranquillity is short-lived, for it is interrupted by a return of the mechanical rhythms and military timbres of the second section. The winds present a grotesque parody of the Mozartian march, in tight imitative counterpoint: the soothing whole-tones of the previous section are transformed into restless descending scales. Underneath, the marimba and xylophone continue to provide a hollow tattoo, and muted horns and trumpets recreate the toy march as a sinister parade. As the different elements jostle, Ives-like, they continue to thicken and expand, culminating in a nightmarish descent into the climax of the movement.

With the climax, the romantic impulses implicit in much of the lyrical material are finally unleashed. A version of the cello theme begins the section, accompanied by glowing dominant harmonies and countermelodies derived from the inversion of the *Walküre* reminiscences from earlier in the movement. This is followed by a *fff* peroration of the viola theme using the original pitches, thereby picking up the thread of the 'tonal' argument left hanging at the end of the third section, and 'resolving' it.

A sudden forceful interjection of the *Walküre* quotation by the brass leads to a gentler figure in the double basses and harp. The even rhythms of this figure recall the contrapuntal manipulations of the *Walküre* quotation earlier in the movement; the listener becomes aware that the one has evolved from transformations of the other. Yet the origins of the 'new' figure are in fact external to the Symphony: as the figure passes up through the orchestra in close imitation, it takes its place in part of a transcription in F♯ of the vocal quartet (originally in F) from the Finale of Act 2 of *The Magic Flute* scored for solo string quartet, *pp lontano*. The argument of the *Elegia* has therefore served to make transparent the musical and emotional connections between the quotations from Mozart and Wagner. The original text of the quoted material is significant: 'Wir Wandeln durch des Tones Macht / Froh durch des Todes düst're Nacht'.[27] This hymn to music prefigures Pamina and Tamino's trials by fire and water, symbolizing (in part) their love and commitment to one another. But Wood's transcription is stifled midway through, on what would have been the word 'Todes' (death), interrupted by the brass with another suitably darkly hued version of the *Walküre* quotation.

The passionate outburst swiftly dissolves, out of which comes a low-lying C major chord scored for piano and divided double basses – shades, perhaps, of the writing for basses in Berlioz's 'March to the Scaffold' (*Symphonie Fantastique*),[28] another work suffused with memories of times past. But it is another march that emerges, a second quotation from *The Magic Flute*, that of the march in C major depicting the passage of Tamino and Pamina through their trial. Wood thins Mozart's scoring to its bare essentials: flute and timpani. It is also the final appearance of the procession that has evolved throughout the movement, in its most simple and direct form. It is significant that this is reserved for (in Wood's terms) the procession as it recedes: as with that from *Die Walküre*, the quoted material seems to belong to an irretrievable past. In the context of the Symphony's programme, these quotations, voiced in the musical language of the past, speak of a love that has been lost (and again, the reference to the *Symphonie Fantastique* is appropriate here); this is the human drama that precedes the *Tempesta* and which causes its turmoil. The conciliatory and elegiac character of the *Elegia* suggests that the fictive protagonist of the Symphony, like Antony, must endure this loss with fortitude.[29] In doing so, it prepares the way emotionally for the resolution of the turmoil of the *Tempesta* in the concluding Passacaglia.

Shortly after the march begins, the violas creep in with a D♭; to this a B♭ is added. These were the first two pitches of the movement, and these grow to overwhelm the *Magic Flute* quotation; from this emerges a final statement of the opening cello

---

[27]   'Through the power of music we step / Lightly through the dark night of death'; English translation by Lionel Salter for the recording by Archiv Produktion 449 166–2 (1996), p. 196.

[28]   See, for instance, the G minor chords with which the movement opens, which Berlioz scores for double basses (divided in four), cellos and timpani.

[29]   Malcolm MacDonald offers a different analysis of these quotations, informed by Wood's writings on tradition: 'What Wood's use of Mozart and Wagner seems to say is that these composers are *gone*; we can still profit from their example, but there is no going back to them. [...] We acknowledge that something infinitely precious has been lost, but then move on.' [Review of NMC D070] *Tempo* 221 (2002): 61–4 (p. 64).

theme. It is followed by the briefest of codas, a series of quiet timpani strokes that mirror the ending of the *Tempesta*.

The *Elegia* thus contains two formal procedures. The first is a kind of arch form: radiating out from the central viola theme are the mechanical marches and, on the flanks, variants of the cello theme. Cutting across this form, and interacting with the themes, are the three processionals that culminate in the *Magic Flute* quotation. There is a parallel with the formal fluidity of the Scherzo in the Violin Concerto and the climactic use of the 'sword' motif. These formal processes are also articulated by two different tonal arguments. The first of these is the transposition of thematic material by a tritone to represent a substitute dominant, to be followed by a recapitulation back at the original pitch level. There are also hints of more traditional tonal functions, in which C as a tonal centre was hinted at not only in the quoted material, but in the emphasis given to the dominant chord on G in the second section.[30] Elements of both arguments can be found in the two *Magic Flute* quotations: the transposition of the vocal quartet into F♯ 'prepared' the eventual appearance of the march in C.

Above all, the *Elegia* can be considered the dramatic reverse of the *Tempesta*. Taking its cue from the memories unleashed by the *Walküre* quotation (Example 6.5), the *Elegia* was dominated by lyrical material in the strings and (less so) the wind; the writing for brass, so forceful in the *Tempesta*, was by turns calm and romantic in the second movement. Only towards the end of the movement, surrounding the transcription of the vocal quartet, does the brass hint at the thunderous passions of the *Tempesta*, with low and menacing references to the *Walküre* quotation (the exact opposite of the end of the first movement). The suggestion is that the darker emotions of the *Tempesta*, and much of its material, have yet to be fully worked out, and this indeed is the task of the final two movements.

Scherzo   Whereas the *Elegia* drew on the coda of the *Tempesta* for some of its musical content, the Scherzo turns to the main body of the first movement for its material. In this respect at least, it is analogous to the Scherzo in the Chamber Concerto. Similar too, is the playful use of colour, but where the Chamber Concerto explores unusual and darker instrumental groupings, the Scherzo of the Symphony blazes with primary colours. The Scherzo begins comparatively lightly, but following an impassioned Trio, the Scherzo material returns with explosive gestures recalling the *Tempesta*. These gestures return shortly before a brief reprise of the Trio; this leads to a climax that melts into the Finale.

The opening bars reveal the extent to which the Scherzo has transformed the material and content of the *Tempesta*. It opens with a short prelude for timpani, developing the expanded semitones with which the *Elegia* ended. The horns build a chord centred on G, embellished by throbbing quavers in the harps and quicksilver arpeggios in the wind: the mood is expectant. Two of the features of the snarling brass theme that opens the *Tempesta* (Example 6.4) – the expanded semitone leaps and the linear ascent through an octave – are here given new form. As the horn chord takes shape, its upper voice traces out a similar ascent from G to G (and beyond to B♭). The

---

[30]   A similar tonal argument can be found in the sixth song of the Song Cycle to Poems by Pablo Neruda; see p. 122.

semitone leaps return in a skittish semiquaver figure in the strings that transform the once tense leaps into playful secondary material. In this way the Scherzo not only finds new expressive contexts for the material, but also changes its significance, shifting our perspective, as if viewing some of the *Tempesta*'s material through a microscope, and certain other ideas through the wrong end of a telescope.

The material that follows the opening bars of the Scherzo engages in similar play. Wind arpeggios and trills recalling those over the twelve-note cluster in the *Tempesta* float above driving passages in major thirds in the brass. Unlike the portentous thirds of *Comus* or the Trio of the Violin Concerto, the effect here is to intensify the forward momentum, rather than hold it in check. This is followed by an airier texture in which oscillating semitones in the strings underpin a brittle figure in quavers for xylophone and oboes (C–D–C; C♯–E–C♯). Out of this emerges a long sustained note in the piccolo and violins that plummets down through two octaves and a semitone; though derived from bars 2–5 of Example 6.4, it is also a version of the 'sword' motif of the Violin Concerto. As it ends, a motif consisting of alternating rising tones and falling semitones appears in the wind and percussion, recalling motif x and some of the accompaniment figures in the *Tempesta*; from this come a further statements of the brittle oboe/xylophone figure. Finally, the fanfare figure from the central section of the first movement (motif w) returns amidst insistent figures in the wind and strings.

Virtually the entire opening of the Scherzo, from the horn chord focused on G to the fanfare figure, is then subject to a varied repeat involving changes to harmonic context, phrase length, orchestration, and ordering of material. After the repeat comes one further reference back to the opening, which functions as a sort of refrain. Ringing crotchet Gs, alluding to the horn chord, arrest the motion (there is some parallel here with the start of the Trio in the Violin Concerto), out of which comes a final flurry of the wind arpeggios and driving thirds in the brass. These lead without a break into the Trio.

The character of the Scherzo comes from the ways in which this material is treated. Much of the harmonic language is based on octatonic fragments and varied sequences; the use of numerous ostinati serves less to suspend the harmony, but rather position it within a dynamic rhythmic framework. The swift succession of ostinati and thematic ideas stands in contrast to the weighty unfolding of material over the pedal E in the *Tempesta*; by contrast, the Scherzo is quicksilver and kaleidoscopic.

The Trio opens with a fiery and chromatic melody for violins that consists of long sustained notes punctuated by bursts of shorter notes that function as ornate upbeats. It can be thought of as an extension and intensification of the fanfares (motif w) that occurred in the Scherzo. The accompaniment consists of busily chattering wind in a dense imitative texture. The combined effect creates a shimmering whole-tone background; as different instruments rise up and down, their colours briefly capture our attention before receding into the background. This is replaced by a more straightforward ostinato in the horns, and later, wind for the second half of the Trio. Again, the harmonic language leans towards whole-tone formulations; above this, the soaring violin melody flares into a two-part invention between upper and lower strings. Whilst a common gesture in Wood's music, it is no less effective here, intensifying the argument and leading to a reprise of the Scherzo.

The beginning of the reprise opens with the quaver figure originally given to oboes and xylophone returns, now scored for timpani, piano, brass and wind. No longer brittle, the fuller scoring of this figure gives it a savagery akin to the opening of the *Tempesta*; it too is built upon an embellished pedal E in the bass. This dramatic, percussive gesture alternates with statements of the fanfare (motif *w*), and leads to denser textures (based on *x*) and storm-tossed accompanimental figures that also look back to the first movement. A reappearance of the crotchet Gs suggests a return to the lighter expressive states of the beginning of the Scherzo; a fragment of the Trio melody, the skittish string semiquavers, and the surging wind arpeggios follow in succession. But the moment is short-lived: the percussive gesture returns with renewed energy. The outbursts become increasingly insistent and frequent, yet ultimately impotent: there is no climactic release to dispel the tension.

Instead, there is a sudden change of emotional climate, and a return to the whole-tone harmonies and chromatic melody of the Trio. Now on the trumpet, this melody makes timbral reference to the fanfares that it is related to, but also steps back from the emotionalism of the original violin presentation. A return to the high-voltage expressive language of the Trio straight after the aggression of the percussive gestures would detract from the eventual climax of the movement. This comes soon after, and once again, it is the fanfare figure (motif *x*) in the trumpets that is of most importance. Around it the wind, harps and piano provide cascades of quavers over an extended B♭ chord in the strings. As this subsides, the glockenspiel and xylophone enter with a measured flow of semiquavers, providing a quasi-ostinato figure that transforms the hollow mechanical figuration of the marimba and xylophone in the *Elegia* into something glittering and magical.

Finale   The model for the lengthy Passacaglia which concludes the Symphony, as Wood points out in the score, is the 'great exemplar' of Brahms's Fourth Symphony,[31] not least in the way that the variations are grouped into a three-part structure with a slow central section. But, as Brahms said of the resemblance between the principal themes of the last movements of his First Symphony and Beethoven's Ninth, 'any fool can see that'. What is of more importance is the way in which Wood's Finale fulfils its function as a counter-balance to, and means of reconciling, the 'anxieties and nightmares' of the *Tempesta*;[32] accordingly, one must take into account its expressive language, and the technical means by which this is realized. Nevertheless, the genres of a multi-movement symphony and of a Brahmsian Passacaglia, combined with the quotations and allusions to tradition that appear in the work, promote certain expectations. The listener who approaches Wood's music with these expectations in mind is no fool; rather, he or she is best prepared for responding to the music as Wood conceived it.

The first variation on the Passacaglia theme is given to the brass (Example 2.3) accompanied by the quasi-ostinato of the percussion (to which wind instruments are added). The effect is noble and spacious, announcing from the outset that the Finale is conceived on a grand scale.

---

[31]   Composer's note to the score.
[32]   Ibid.

There is a sudden change of character for the second variation. The tempo slackens, and the texture is reduced to a single line – the theme – distributed between timpani (again!), harps and double basses. Over the next three variations, the theme remains in the double basses, over which there are increasingly elaborate contrapuntal dialogues between the upper strings. At first elegiac, the music increases in tempo, energy and passion as sections are added; the texture thickens gradually from three- to five-part counterpoint.

A whip crack and a brisk punctuating arpeggio in the wind section announce the start of the *vivo* variation six. Snarling trombone fanfares and, later, vigorous string figuration, return the Symphony briefly to the nightmarish world of the *Tempesta*. Something of this character remains in the seventh variation which, through increasingly urgent wind counterpoint and the steady build up of brass chords, creates a further increase in tension.

A partial release occurs at the start of variation eight. The Passacaglia theme returns, augmented, to the bass, providing support for rich harmonies and textures that recall the more lyrical passages of both the *Tempesta* and *Elegia*. The cello theme of the *Elegia* appears in the violins, opening with motif *z* back at the original pitch level of Example 6.5. Though the violins are marked *molto cantabile*, the mood is not the dreamy ecstasy of Example 6.5, the brooding of the opening of the *Elegia*, nor the rapture of the *Elegia*'s climax. The tempo has remained that of variations six and seven, now marked *urgente*, thereby suppressing the expansive implications of the theme and preventing a full, radiant release.

Variation nine inverts the cello theme; the Passacaglia theme remaining in the bass. There is a sudden change in sonority at the start of the tenth variation, with the Passacaglia theme appearing in the lower voice of high chords in the harp, and fragments of the inverted cello theme passed between solo wind. A rapid thickening of the texture results in the theme returning to the double basses on the low E, a note that has been marked as structurally significant in both of the preceding variations. Its arrival in the tenth variation ushers in with chattering triplets and soaring violin and brass melodies. From here there is a steady acceleration to the *vivacissimo* of the eleventh variation, the Passacaglia theme, now in retrograde, transformed into a powerful and widely spaced violin melody.

Variations eight through to eleven thus form another small grouping within the Passacaglia, characterized by lyrical contrapuntal explorations of the Passacaglia theme, mostly in combination with variations of the cello theme of the *Elegia*. The energy accumulated by this counterpoint, heightened by the numerous shifts in colour and dynamic, is finally released in the twelfth variation. Here, the Passacaglia theme is passed through the brass section in the form of a series of strident figures that collapse downwards. Circling this is a precipitously busy wind figuration that descends through the variation from the top of the piccolo register through to the lowest notes of the contrabassoon. As if exhausted, the thirteenth variation progressively slows down, the orchestration thinning out. The first half of the Passacaglia theme is only alluded to in the bass; the second half (beginning with the D upbeat to a low E) is given in full. Against this, the cellos have their theme for one last time, before the music sinks into silence.

With the close of the thirteenth variation, the first dramatic arc of the Finale is concluded. Although grounded on the Passacaglia theme, this arc is shaped by the control of contrapuntal energy, which creates dynamic motion between and across variations; references to earlier movements provide emotional and expressive orientation. In the middle section of the Finale, a 'slow movement' consisting of variations fourteen to eighteen, links to the first three movements of the work are veiled, but nevertheless present. The most immediate of these is the continuous presence of a chorale in brass and then wind that binds together the five variations of the middle section; one is reminded not only of the opening of the Finale, but of the chorales that punctuate all of the movements. The chorale in the middle section is derived from the division of the Passacaglia theme into chords, in a manner reminiscent of Wood's method of troping.

Variation fourteen opens with muted trombones and tuba softly intoning the Passacaglia in the form of four slow trichords. Over it, wind and solo violin add soft fragments of melodic material which at first consists of descending semitones in fleeting semiquaver pairs, a distant relative, perhaps, of the stormy opening to the Symphony (Example 6.4). A hesitant four-part imitative counterpoint in the wind barely disturbs the slow solemnity of the chorale. Indeed, the pace slackens for the fifteenth variation, in which the stately tread of chords, now in the horns with altered spacing, underpins a counterpoint that is more sustained but still lightly scored for solo strings and wind. It is with the return of motif z in the second horn at the outset of the sixteenth variation, sharing with a tuba a final statement of the cello theme, that the contrapuntal argument of the middle section begins to accumulate energy.

There is a sudden halt to the proceedings with variation seventeen. The tempo slows again, to *Adagio molto*, and the harmonic sequence of the previous variations is terminated. In its wake comes a six-part chorale in the wind, each chord formed from one of the hexachords of the Passacaglia theme. Over this, celeste, pizzicato violin and harps tentatively try to reinstate the quasi-ostinato of the first variation. In the eighteenth variation, they try again, with greater success: glockenspiel and xylophone are added, preparing the return of the theme.

Variations nineteen to twenty-one consist of repetitions of the Passacaglia theme, in its full brass-chorale version (Example 2.3), in ever-broader terms; the ostinato background becomes increasingly fully and intricately scored. In the twentieth variation, the two hexachords of the row are reversed, and internally permuted; the upper line of the chorale in the final variation is based on an inexact retrograde of the theme.

From here, the Symphony approaches its final apotheosis. Example 6.6 gives a reduction of the brass in the closing thirty-three bars, with some salient features of the rest of the orchestra sketched in. In this final paragraph, the component chords of the brass chorale are separated and freely re-ordered, interspersed with jubilant flurries of notes that dimly recall the 'Wild' passage of the *Tempesta* in their multi-layered textures. These interjections become more insistent, culminating in a thrice-repeated sequence of trills over a second-inversion A major chord (beginning in bar 214; Example 6.6). Out of this emerges the final, climactic chord of the work, a radiant root-position A major, that brings the work to an affirmative close.

Example 6.6   Symphony Op. 21/iv, bars 190–223 (reduction)

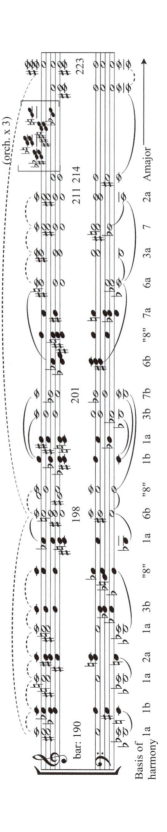

This ending puzzled some commentators – not least Hans Keller, who asked in a letter to Wood: 'Is the A maj. end prepared for from the outset? No doubt it is – but I missed it'.[33] To answer this question, one must understand how a densely chromatic work of some forty minutes can find resolution in a major triad; only then can we begin to approach the issue of why this should be A major rather than any other major triad.

For the first point, we can note that quotations of tonal material in the first half of the Symphony can be interpreted as tokens of distant memories that predate the violent anxieties of the *Tempesta*. The material of the first pair of movements is then transformed in the final pair; correspondingly the darker emotions of the *Tempesta* and *Elegia* are balanced by less tragic emotional states. By concluding on a major triad, the end of the Symphony suggests that anxieties have finally been resolved, allowing the distant memories to be accepted positively: the language of the quotations is thus integrated into that of the Finale, rather than held at a distance, as in the first two movements.

A programmatic reading of the final chord such as this might explain the significance of the ending, but scarcely justifies it in terms of absolute music. For this, we must turn to the nature of Wood's language. As was shown in Chapters 2 and 3, chromatic musical surfaces common to much of Wood's music are underpinned frequently by structures based on octatonic, whole-tone or even tonal models. The allusive nature of this language allows such models to drift in and out of focus as demanded by the expressive argument of a given work; witness, for example, the C minor conclusion of Wood's Variations for Viola for which the welling-up of tonal model provides an emotional outlet (see Chapter 1, p. 16).

With the Variations for Viola, one is able to say that, although the tonal release is prepared for expressively, there is not an equivalent structural justification: there is little or no sense across the variations that C minor is a goal that is being striven for. In the Symphony, on the other hand, the close in A major is planned from the very beginning. There are hints in the *Tempesta*, not least in the way that the pedal E that underpins most of the movement is transformed into the bass of an A major chord in the Coda (Example 6.5). At this point, the A major occurs within a largely octatonic context (note in Example 6.5 how motif *z* leans heavily on the tritone E♭). In the *Elegia*, the harmonic centres of gravity shift to C and F♯; the major chords on both of these roots belong to the same octatonic collection as A and E♭. The Scherzo leads into more remote harmonic waters, but the language continues to draw on octatonic material. With the reprise of the Scherzo, the bass returns to a pedal E, although there is no subsequent motion to A major (as in the *Tempesta*). With the opening of the Finale, the tonal implications of the previous movements begin to find more concrete expression. The brass chorale (Example 2.3) progresses from A major to E major, all in an octatonic context (see Chapter 2, pp. 40–42). As the variations unfold, these tonal relationships become even clearer: in variation thirteen, which closes the first section of the Finale, the underlying chords are dominant sevenths on A (with an added sharpened fourth) and E (with an added sixth). And, as has been noted, the E

33   Wood, [Contribution to Hans Keller Memorial Symposium]: 400.

of the theme is often the cue for a significant event when it occurs in the bass (for instance, variation ten).

None of the above can be said to create the sort of implications that can be found in classical tonal structures, and nor are they intended to. Rather, it is the fact that such features occur often enough, and in conjunction with moments of expressive significance, that they are asserted as important points of harmonic orientation. The eventual close on A major results from the cumulative force of these assertions, both structural and expressive. And it is for this reason that the close speaks with such eloquence, grandeur and a satisfying feeling of inevitability.

Chapter 7

After the Symphony
1982–1989

In contrast to the big public statements of the 1970s, Wood's output in the years following the Symphony was predominantly for chamber forces. Much of this was for voice, including further collections of Robert Graves songs for voice and piano, two choral works, and a setting of a T.S. Eliot poem (*Marina* Op. 31). Punctuating the stream of vocal pieces are three major instrumental works, the Trios for Piano (1982–84) and Horn (1987–89), and a *Paraphrase* for clarinet and piano of Wood's setting of Graves's 'Bird of Paradise'. Only two pieces call on orchestral forces: an orchestration of the 1959 Laurie Lee Songs, and the Cantata Op. 30, to words by D.H. Lawrence.

The last of these works, along with *Marina*, was dedicated to Wood's daughter Jenny, who was murdered in September 1988.[1] Both the Cantata and *Marina* transcend the unspeakable horror of this event with painfully intense and yet at times serenely beautiful music. Intimate and passionate, loving and mournful, these works summarize tragically the themes that connect Wood's compositions in the 1980s.

Vocal Music

Robert Graves Songs Sets II–IV Opp. 22, 23 and 36

In the years immediately following the Symphony, Wood collated and completed two sets of songs to poems by Robert Graves; to these we can add a fourth set, compiled in the mid-1990s from songs composed between 1966 and 1984. As with the Logue, D.H. Lawrence and Neruda collections of the 1960s and 70s, the topic of the Graves songs is love. For Graves, the question of 'how to restore the lost age of love-innocence between men and women' is 'the main poetic problem' he faced;[2] elsewhere, he has stated that his 'main theme was always the practical impossibility, transcended only by a belief in miracle, of absolute love continuing between man and woman'.[3]

This fact alone is insufficient to explain why Wood has over many decades been drawn to Graves's work. An additional reason, I would suggest, is that in Graves's lyrics Wood finds not only the type of passionate verse that he evidently favours, but a consummate technique that is at one with the manner of expression. There

---

[1] Serenade and Elegy, composed in 1999, was dedicated to the rest of Wood's family, in memoriam Jenny.

[2] Robert Graves, *Robert Graves' Poems About Love* (London, 1969), p. 5.

[3] Robert Graves, *Collected Poems 1965* (London, 1965), p. ii.

is an obvious parallel with Wood's approach to his own art, not just in the mutual dependence of form and content, but in the painstaking drafting and crafting that is required for the two to fuse. The following quotation was written about Graves: one need only change the name and art form to have it apply to Wood:

> Technique, as used here, suggests a more mechanical process than the craftsmanship Graves favors. It is partly timing and emphasis that makes the difference. The master of technique may be more concerned with showing off his rhetorical skills than conveying a poetic message – like an orator who sounds impressive, but makes no sense. For Graves, a poem must make sense; deliberate obscurity is an affectation. [...] But the poem must begin 'beyond reason' in inspiration, welling up from the poetic trance. After the initial rush of expression comes critical appraisal and meticulous rewriting, where all the poet's craft is put to the service of the unique requirements of this particular poem. Graves says he writes approximately ten drafts of a poem.[4]

Both poet and composer thus display meticulous attention to detail in their mutual harnessing of technique to meet the demands of intense expression; in this sense, one understands completely what Michael Kennedy means when he describes Wood's settings of Graves as 'an ideal meeting of minds'.[5]

An overview of the sets II–IV of Graves songs and dates of composition of individual songs can be found in Table 7.1. As can be seen, there are overlaps between the composition of songs in each set (and indeed that of set I; see Chapter 6, pp. 124–6). Some of the songs appear to have been composed as a set, as with three of the four songs in Op. 36 that were composed in a short burst over the summer of 1984. Other songs seem to have been composed independently, often over many years; only later were they brought together into collections.

As with the first set of Graves songs, the later sets do not outline a narrative as such. Rather, they explore the 'practical impossibility' of love, combined with the 'belief in miracle, of absolute love continuing between man and woman' from a variety of perspectives. It is this underlying thematic unity that enables each set to present a range of styles, tempi and modes of expression as a coherent group.

The second set of Graves songs (Op. 22) begins with the terse 'Symptoms of Love'. The song opens with repeated quavers in the bass register. The same technique was used to signal intensity of feeling in 'The Confirmation' (Op. 11/iv) and 'Records' (Op. 18/ii); here the repetitions combine with the words, at first bitter and later resigned towards love, to create nervous energy. The contrasting emotional states conveyed by the words motivate a setting in which the second half is a transformation of the first; Example 7.1 shows the opening of each half. In both extracts, a whole-tone cluster played in the middle register of the piano provides the basis of the harmony. To this is added initially an A and B♭ in the piano and voice (Example 7.1a); in the Example 7.1b the roles are reversed. The difference in effect is startling: whereas the A in the bass results in a rather dissonant effect (a 'migraine ... blotting out reason'), the bass B♭ in the second half suggests a warmer dominant

---

4   Katherine Snipes, *Robert Graves* (New York, 1979), pp. 14–15.
5   Kennedy, [Hugh Wood: Chester Music Promotional brochure]. See also n. 3, Chapter 2, p. 23, for further parallels between Wood's and Graves's artistic approaches.

sonority (note the prominent B♭–D–G♯ in this chord, an 0,2,6 trichord). The leap of a tritone in the bass (bar 30) then creates another dominant type chord (note the prominent E–D–G♯) which functions as a dominant to the following A in the bass (overall, the progression is ♭II–V–I; compare with Example 2.2, p. 27). The sudden flowering of functional harmonic relations allows the lyrical material above it to glow with passionate sincerity.

Table 7.1   Dates of composition of Robert Graves Songs Sets II–IV

Set	Song	Date of Composition
II	Symptoms of Love	19–23 October 1982; fair copy 8 Dec 82
Op. 22	The Visitation	17–18 July: 1–16 October 1982
	Fragment	5–13 September 1977
	Ouzo Unclouded	11–14 September 1977
	Seldom yet now	[no date given]
III	Mid-winter Waking	6–9 April 1979; revised 14–16 October 1982; fair copy 28 Jan 1983
Op. 23	The Hazel Grove	8 March 1974 – 8 March 1978 for 11 March 1978
	To Tell and be Told	[no date]
	Bird of Paradise	30 January – 10 February 1983
IV	The Door	1966: Christmas 1972; 4 April 1973; 10 March 1974
Op. 36	The Three-faced	26–30 July 1984 (different draft from 1966)
	A Lost Jewel	28–9 July 1984
	On Giving	June: then 12 July 1984

The continuation of each extract is also telling: whereas the former is cramped and strained, the second, making use of similar chromatic patterns, is lyrical and expansive. The contrast between the 'practical impossibility' of love and 'a belief in miracles' is immediately audible, as is the difference between the pounding quavers of the first extract and the throbbing hairpins of the second. The reworking of the same material for contrasting expressive purposes, as here, becomes an increasingly regular and important model in Wood's later music.

'The Visitation', like 'Symptoms of Love', offers another portrait of a lover captured and captivated in a relationship; here, the wondrous disbelief that the other partner can feel the same way forms the object of study. A rapt, trance-like atmosphere is created by a steady crotchet tread in the piano accompaniment; shimmering acciaccaturas and semiquavers provide musical analogies to the description of wind and moonlight in the text. The vocal line begins on a repeated F; as the song continues it builds in lyricism and energy through to a passionate climax at the end of the song.

Example 7.1   Robert Graves Songs Set II Op. 22/i, 'Symptoms of Love'

(a) bars 1–6

(b) bars 27–34

The two earliest songs of the set are both scherzo-like. The first of these, 'Fragment' asks a series of questions about love. The word setting, as one would expect, closely follows the nuances of the text, moving from short, insistent questions at the opening to wonderfully expansive, arcing lines: 'Does Time cease to move/ Till her calm grey eye/ Expands to a sky'. Underneath these passionate declarations is a whispering figuration of oscillating major thirds in quintuplets. Whilst this to an extent recalls the ethereal grace of a Mendelssohn scherzo, the performance indication of 'hushed, urgent' suggests that the narrator is not as self-possessed as the lyrical vocal lines imply: there is an insistence here that borders on obsession.

'Ouzo Unclouded' provides a contrast to this. The ouzo of the title functions as a metaphor for love: it is to be taken as it is, not watered down nor consumed in too measured or too excessive a quantity. Marked 'debonair', Wood's setting passes through a variety of moods as it depicts the different ways in which ouzo can be drunk; these moods are framed by effervescent scherzo rhythms that give the song its character. A moment of sincerity towards the end ('But keep your eyes on mine') is offset by a throwaway staccato ending that encapsulates the sparkling wit of this wonderful song.

The miniature 'Seldom Yet Now' provides a moving end to the collection. The brief poem describes the fierce and passionate ardour of a deeply felt moment, set with typical intensity. The semitones and major thirds of the vocal line contribute to the characteristic lyricism (cf. motif y, Example 2.5, p. 32); the harmonic language is rich and sonorous. The accompaniment at the start of the song suggests a chorale, taken up more fully in the setting of the second line, which heightens the solemnity and seriousness of the song. Murmuring triplets and fluttering trills create contrast in the third line, delicately picturing the reference to birds in the text, before a passionate outburst brings the song to a climax at the start of the fourth and final line. At the close, the opening melodic notes return; the accompaniment reworks the opening chords. But here, in a moment of heightened poeticism, a major seventh in rocking triplets in the right hand of the piano fades to nothing: one is reminded of the close of the Adagietto in the First String Quartet, and the precious fragility of the loving moment is made clear.

The third Graves set (Op. 23) contains four songs. The first of these, 'Mid-winter Waking' opens with a recitative-like passage ('Stirring suddenly from long hibernation'). This first hint of spring described in the text is followed by an allusion in the piano to the harmonies of the second bloc of Wood's Third String Quartet Op. 20, and indeed the spirit of joyous self-renewal that infused this earlier work can be felt throughout the song. The whole-tone motion central to the argument of the quartet finds new expression in 'Mid-winter Waking', for much of the material in both voice and piano is generated from rising and overlapping whole-tone scales that convey the rising excitement of the text (which correlates with increased self-awareness, and the coming of spring). A faster middle section, based on falling tones in the voice (and falling sevenths in the piano) recalls the ebullience of Example 6.3 (p. 135); the left hand of the piano provides broken chords in quintuplets that have the textural plenitude of the climax of the Third String Quartet as well as outlining an A major tonality. A second reworking of the second bloc of the quartet leads to a shortened recapitulation, opening with descending whole-tones, as the poet's attention turns from the stirrings of nature to the presence of his beloved. In a rapt coda, the scales turn once more upwards, whilst the piano accompaniment quietly harmonizes a twelve-note line derived from successive transposition of chromatic fragments (for example, D–C♯–B–C) that remind us, via their association with the clusters of the Third Quartet, of the distant winter.

The rolled chords and luxuriant arpeggios in the accompaniment for 'The Hazel Grove' take their cue from a mention of a harp towards the end of the poem, a symbol of the enduring and all-encompassing love described by the poet. The rich harmonic language, which makes use of extended chords built on major triads (but not always octatonic), provides a sonorous backing to the increasingly passionate melody in the voice based on carefully controlled upward linear motion.

The sinewy textures (which at times recall a three-part invention) and playful mood of 'To Tell and be Told' stand in contrast to the expansive 'Mid-winter waking' and 'The Hazel Grove'. The opening piano figure gives rise to a series of repetitions in both piano and voice, each time a semitone lower, conveying restlessness. As thoughts turn to the beloved ('To be with you') the rhythms of the voice shift from compound to duple, creating the effect of time suddenly halting as thoughts turn inward. Each verse ends with the line 'to tell and be told', which recurs with the same pitches in the voice, but with different harmonic support. At the end of the song, each of the different harmonizations appears in rapid succession, as if the protagonist were collecting together all his thoughts.

The final song of Op. 23, 'Bird of Paradise', is a wonderful example of how technical rigour, expressive power and an intuitive response to the poem fuse in Wood's songs. Graves's opulent text suggests a musical setting of tremulous chords and rippling arpeggios, against which two passages of strident and exultant chords capture the proud strutting of the male bird on display. The emphasis is on immediacy of expression: from a calm, mysterious opening the music, carried by the expanding intervals and registers of the voice, becomes increasingly impassioned, providing a sonorous analogue to the unfolding of the bird's wings described in the text. The harmonic language encompasses chromatic clusters (to which one might add the opening twelve-note melody in the voice), whole-tone and octatonic formulations and glissandi on first the black notes, and then the white notes of the piano keyboard. Whilst we might note technically that it is the presence of shared intervallic figures that enables the materials to be brought together without incongruity (see Chapter 2, pp. 41–3), what intrigues the ear most is the kaleidoscopic shifting from one type of material to another, just as the eye is entranced by the bright hues of the bird of paradise.

The Op. 36 collection, like Op. 23, consists of four songs that include one that is characterized by scherzo rhythms. It opens with 'The Door', the earliest song to be included in sets II–IV. The short poem describes the entrance and exit of a loved one through the door of the title; through the door the sea could be seen. The marine imagery suggests one of Wood's seascapes: murmuring and closely scored chromatic clusters rich in triplet motion in the piano (cf. 'Two humans stand on a promontory', Op. 19/i and *Marina* Op. 31). Against this constricted accompaniment, the voice moves in widely spaced arcs, suggesting the power of the sea 'which no door could restrain'. Against this is the apparent immobility of the narrator, held fast by his vision: the harmonies are rooted on F and A♭, only wrenching themselves free, momentarily, from these focal pitches when the beloved takes 'her leave'. These contrasts – static accompaniment and harmonic language and mobile vocal line – give rise to a powerful expressive effect that is intensified by the brevity of the song.

A dramatic outburst announces the start of 'The Three-faced'; what follows is a gentler meditation on three qualities of a female object of desire. Each of these qualities is set to a varied sequence that concludes on a characteristic chord: first a dominant seventh on D, then an combination of major thirds on B♭ and E (a relative of the combined major triads a tritone apart prevalent in much of Wood's music) and finally a chord built from major thirds on A♭ and B♭. Only the A♮ in the first chord disturbs the 'background' whole-tone scale to which all these chords belong; the musical surface, which at times alludes to chromatic and octatonic formulations, pulls against this. One might interpret this harmonic language as representing the tension between the different 'faces' presented by the object of desire and the underlying unity that results from them being one and the same person. The song ends with an extended melisma ('endless moment'); echoes of the final vocal phrase in the accompaniment serve further to freeze experienced time.

'A Lost Jewel' is the scherzo of the set. The text is directed towards a lost love who still dreams of previous happiness. Wood's setting differentiates between the images of past and present loves through the contrast of lyrical vocal lines, often in duple time, and more declamatory phrases, mostly in compound time. Both the opening and closing passages of the song feature lines predominantly doubled in octaves between voice and piano, as if to suggest that, despite the intervening memories of happiness, the present state of affairs is to remain unaltered, the former love never to be recaptured. Wood rewrote this song in 2006 for the song cycle *Wild Cyclamen* Op. 49 to poems by Graves, superseding this earlier version.

'On Giving' is a meditation in the same order as (for example) 'The Confirmation' Op. 11/iv and 'Seldom Yet Now' Op. 22/v. A one-bar introductory motif in the piano suggests a melodic shape that dominates the vocal line; the accompaniment that follows is derived from discrete units: a rising diminished or augmented octave, plaintive 0,1,6 trichords, warm extended dominant chords, and delicate echoes of falling triplets in the voice. The second verse slightly modifies these basic materials, but they remain recognizable. In its brevity, economy and directness of expression, 'On Giving' looks ahead to Wood's later songs (and particularly the Erich Fried Songs Op. 43)

Wood's music engages with Graves's words as an equal partner in a dialogue. In maintaining this delicate balance, Wood's settings demonstrate his continually keen response to the demands of the text, sensitively highlighting obscure poetic connections and intensifying their emotional ardour. Above all, the ways in which Wood confronts and embodies in his music the tensions present in Graves's poetry between hope and resignation, idealism and realism, ensure that these collections form a significant contribution to both Wood's oeuvre and English art-song.

Other Songs: Songs Op. 25, Laurie Lee Songs Op. 28, Lines to Mr Hodgson

Not all of Wood's songs from this period were to texts by Graves. In his collection of Songs Op. 25,[6] Wood returned to poems by Logue ('How am I Poor Tonight') and Laurie Lee ('Home from Abroad'). To these were added settings of Yevgeny Yevtoshenko ('The Blue Coat', original English title 'Waiting') and Stephen Spender ('Ice'). As with the Graves collections, these songs were written over a number of years and collated at a later date; there is not, however, a linking theme.

The first song of the set, 'Ice', was begun in January 1969 and completed on 29 March 1973. Much of the piano writing ventures no lower than the B below middle C; it glistens and swirls like the snow and ice of the poem. As the text turns to 'fire', 'warmth' and 'brilliance', the accompaniment suddenly plunges into deep, warm chords: a simple device, but brilliantly effective.

'Home from Abroad' (2–12 September 1982) shares with the early Laurie Lee songs a warm pastoral atmosphere, here created by emphasis on 'flat' tonal regions in comparison to the eventual tonic G. A motif of rising fourths and falling minor thirds pervades the vocal part and accompaniment, alluding to folk-like penatonicism but clothed in a tonal language that is considerably more sophisticated and subtle than can be found in the 1958–59 Laurie Lee songs.

'The Blue Coat' was completed on 8 March 1975; like 'Ice', it dates from Wood's time in Liverpool. A fiery description of the excitement felt when waiting for a loved one, the song opens both passionately and powerfully, the singer straining to leap a major seventh, fall an augmented octave and then leap a major tenth, accompanied by clangourous chords rich in whole-tones. Scherzo-like quaver motion pulls the tessitura down to the bottom of the piano keyboard in a rumbling depiction of night; the return of the opening vocal gesture leads via sinewy lines to a lyrical climax that swiftly dissolves. The final third of the song suddenly clears the textures, the voice and piano now alternating in dialogue. The music becomes increasingly serene, far removed from the explosive opening, before the music dissolving into a peaceful silence.

Early drafts of 'How am I Poor Tonight' date from 1959 (therefore contemporaneous with the Four Logue Songs Op. 2) although it was written mostly in winter 1982–83. One would be hard-pressed though to find traces of Wood's early style here: the harmonic language is certainly post-*Comus* with its blend of warm sonorities, ringing major third dyads and chromatic melodic motion. The musical surface, whilst responding to the nuances of the text, remains coherent through the recurrence of clearly defined and recurring motifs and textures.

Between April 1986 and April 1987, Wood orchestrated his 1959 Laurie Lee songs for soprano and chamber orchestra (Op. 28). These are conventional transcriptions, orchestrated with an endearing transparency that enhances the freshness of the settings. There are a few alterations: the latter half of 'April Rise' is made more radiantly expectant through fluttering horn, string and wind additions, and 'The Easter Green' opens with two extra bars for orchestra. More extensive changes are

---

[6]   Originally Op. 23; see the 1991 Chester Music Promotional Catalogue of Wood's works which lists 'Amor' (later Op. 37) instead of 'How am I Poor Tonight'.

made to the latter half of 'Town Owl', a scena describing the bird of the title. Wood's changes occur with the phrase 'candelabra swung', set in a rather strait-laced fashion in the 1959 version, but here transformed into a dark waltz. This seemingly simple modification breathes new life into the setting, preventing the flagging of tension that weakened slightly the original.

Lines to Mr Hodgson is an occasional piece, written for the bicentennial celebrations of Lord Byron in 1988, and commissioned by Trinity College, Cambridge. The poem conveys vividly the crowded conditions and colourful characters on board the Lisbon packet, the *Princess Elizabeth*, on which Byron once sailed. Accordingly, Wood's setting opens with a cheerful allusion to a hornpipe and rushing scales. Byron's lavish descriptions of the passengers's vomiting motivate similarly tongue-in-cheek seasick musical responses. Nevertheless, the frivolity is underpinned by a tightly knit tonal structure based upon large-scale symmetrical partitioning of the octave. Beginning and closing in C major, four of the five stanzas close in (respectively) A, F♯, E♭ and C major (all a minor third apart). The remaining stanza, the fourth, does eventually land on a C major chord but not one prepared (as elsewhere) by a dominant. The blurring of the tonal waters at this point captures succinctly the narrator's uneasiness: 'Zounds! My liver's coming up;/ I shall not survive the racket/ Of this brutal Lisbon packet'. This blend of structural control and riotous musical expression is typical of the song, a minor work, but great fun nevertheless.

Choral Music: A Christmas Poem Op. 27; To a Friend Whose Work has Come to Nothing Op. 16 No. 2

A Christmas Poem Op. 27 (1984) was Wood's first published chorus in over a decade. Written for the Chester Book of Carols, it was first performed by the Cambridge University Chamber Choir in Trinity College Chapel on 27 November 1986; it was later selected for the nine lessons and carols for the King's College service on Christmas Eve 1990. The text, written by Dick Davis in 1982, describes over four stanzas the different ways in which those present at the Nativity relate to the infant Christ: the oxen recognizes Jesus as a fellow carrier of burdens, the shepherd sees a watcher and guardian, the wise man a king, and Mary his selfless heart. Wood's setting is reverential without being sentimental; the use of false relations, derived from octatonicism, provides an archaic air.

On a larger scale, a tonal structure based in root motion by major thirds offers similarities to the minor thirds of *Lines to Mr Hodgson*. The opening of the work, as well as the cadences of the first and fourth stanzas, is in an extended B♭; the second and third stanzas cadence in D and F♯ major respectively. As with *Lines to Mr Hodgson*, these points of tonal stability serve to orient the more chromatic passages that separate them. The fluctuating textures of the chorus are also used structurally, the choice of texture determined very much by the nature of the text being set. Narrative passages describing the course of action are normally set with polyphonic and predominantly imitative textures; it is in such sections that word-painting occurs most frequently, such as the low repeated tenuto F in the tenor for 'a toiler' (bars 8–9), and increasingly florid melismas for 'drifted snow' (bars 23–4) and 'golden' (bar 41). In contrast to the narrative passages are those passages for solo voices that precede the imitative writing (for example, bars 1–2: 'one of the oxen said …'), and homophonic passages at the end of stanzas that describe the emotional responses to the infant Jesus. The key emotional phrases are thus given most weight and expressive immediacy; the chorus as a whole speaks with directness and elegance.

The terse *a cappella* setting of Yeats's *To Friend Whose Work has Come to Nothing* for SATB chorus occupied Wood between 25 September and 3 October 1989; the score states that it is a 'complete re-working of [a] draft of 17–18 July 1973'. The poem describes the nobility and difficulty of coping with apparent failure, and attacks too those who would provide criticism – themes that are echoed in Wood's writing about music. The musical language is acerbic, with harmonic and melodic material rich in semitones and their transpositions. Although the presence of recurring harmonic and melodic figures helps orient the singers, this remains difficult to sing and later choral settings by Wood employ a less astringent syntax. The setting falls into two halves (as with the first Yeats chorus, *To a Child Dancing in the Wind*), the second half a compressed and modified recapitulation of the first. After a homophonic opening, the first half dissolves into imitative counterpoint for Yeats's depiction of those who dishonourably dispense criticism. In the reworked second half, different imitative figures are used for a more positive appraisal of what the friend of the title might achieve. Suggestions of whole-tone linear motion in the outer voices of the homophonic passages that open and close the work provide a characteristic means of generating motion; the final chord, which has the widest interval between outer voices of the whole work, ends with an unresolved strain that mirrors the constant struggle to be found in all worthy artistic enterprise.

Chamber Music

Piano Trio Op. 24

The Piano Trio stands as an example of what has been described as Wood's 'absolute commitment to the expressive value of pure music'.[7] The working-out of the structural and contrapuntal possibilities of the material is inextricable from the compelling expressive argument that unfolds over its three movements. The first idea for the work occurred to Wood 'near the bus station at Bergamo' on an Italian holiday.[8] But this was no extramusical idea: it was instead a powerful gesture characterized by a chromatic cluster of four notes, presented by the violin and cello two octaves apart with harmonic support and dramatic fusillades of semiquaver and sextuplet semiquaver upbeats in the piano. The idea became eventually the principal theme of the first movement, the seed out of which everything else grew. Wood appears, as is his practice, to have conceived of the idea initially in terms of its presentation rather than as an abstract figure. From its rhythms and contour is drawn motif *y* (see

---

[7]   Jeremy Thurlow, 'Hugh Wood', p. 549.
[8]   Composer's note to the score.

Example 2.4, p. 30; subsequent references to motifs also relate to this example), which takes on a variety of forms and manner of presentation within the unfolding musical argument. Recurrences of the principal theme *as* a theme, however, are made clear by the spacing of a double octave between cello and violin.

The expressive argument of the first movement involves progressive transformations of the nature of the principal theme, from its powerful and triumphant first appearance through increasingly soft and spectral variations to the final halting, gasping and tragic version. The subsidiary material responds to this emotional passage, at times contrasting, and at others, such as leading into the coda, offering weary acceptance of the inevitable outcome. Table 7.2 gives an overview of the form of the first movement of the Piano Trio; the distribution of material implies a binary form with a compressed recapitulation. The outbursts of the opening yield to equally passionate but more lyrical and reflective solos given in turn to violin (Example 2.4) and cello, both accompanied by piano. The lyrical strain continues in a series of duets between the stringed instruments, punctuated by forceful piano chords built from sixths and sevenths that recall the opening bars of the movement. In this way, at least two oppositions present in the presentation of the principal motif are developed: those between the dramatic and the lyric, and between the piano and the strings.

The forceful piano figuration that divides the duets is taken up and extended in the third section of the movement by the whole ensemble. This builds through a series of waves to the climax of the first half of the work, a soaring reworking of the lyrical solo material over typically sonorous chords outlined in the piano. From here, there is a gradual subsidence as the textures thin and the emotional ardour cools. The effect resembles the dissolution of the emotional crux of the Cello Concerto (see Chapter 5, pp. 106–7), but in the Piano Trio, the ramifications of the changes in emotional climate are worked out at greater length, in the modified recapitulation.

Table 7.2   Form of Piano Trio Op. 24/i

Section	Bars	Details
A	1–23	Dramatic opening; bars 5–15 introduction and extension of principal theme; bars 16–23 more lyrical piano idea disrupted by brief string outbursts
B_1	24–42	Solos: violin (bars 24–31, see Example 2.4) and cello (bars 32–41)
B_2	43–76	Duets; motif *y* returns bars 75–6.
C	77–93	Climax I
A	94–104	Truncated reprise of bars 5–23
B_1	105–120	Solos: cello (bars 105–110) and violin (bars 111–19); motif *y* returns bars 119–20
B_2	121–32	Duets
C	133–9	Climax II
Coda	140–51	Reiterations of principal theme

The effects of this cooling are immediately palpable, for the reprise of the principal theme is hushed and delicate, rather than strident, the strings playing *sul tasto*. From this emerges a brief passage for violin and cello and a sonorous reworking of motif *x*. This is no direct recapitulation, but part of a permutation of various motifs from the first half of the movement: it leads to three calm chorale-like bars in the piano (bars 102–4), a compressed reprise of bars 16–23 that brings motif *w* to the foreground. Solos for cello and violin follow, with mostly chordal accompaniment from the piano (compare this with the contrapuntal textures of Example 2.4).

The series of duets (bars 121–32) begin with a ghostly version of the principal theme, the cello playing high pizzicato notes, the violin artificial harmonics. Driven by increasingly intricate piano accompaniments, the duets surge twice towards an eventual climax beginning in bar 133, which is based on the dramatic outburst that opened the movement. This fragments into the punctuating and percussive sixths and sevenths of the first main climax; as these lose impetus the dramatic outburst is heard once more, now drained of energy. Out of this come haunted, obsessive repetitions of motif *y*, tossed from cello to violin in close imitation. To end, there are three final statements of motif *y* as the 'principal theme', in double octaves between violin and cello, the rhythms continually stretching as the movement grinds to a sombre close.

Following the tragic first movement, the slow second movement is an extended, mournful and elegant lament.[9] A high opening violin melody transforms the percussive double-stopped sixths of the first movement into a sighing figure. Accompanied by glacial tintinnabulations from the piano and sustained harmonics in the cello, the theme occupies a similar emotional territory to the start of the Violin Concerto.[10] As the violin becomes increasingly impassioned, the cello joins it in a duet; sonorous harmonies in the piano, directed by a slow-moving bass rising by step, lead to a temporary close over a dominant chord on C. A middle section, initiated by a lyrical piano gesture, transforms the opening violin theme into graceful dance-like figures. The piano gesture returns to the foreground, and is taken up by the cello and then the violin, *sul ponticello*, in busy figuration that spirals upwards into a scurrying quasi-ostinato in a high register. Out of this emerges the recapitulation, the theme in the piano. The strings once again take up the lyrical and lamenting character of the first section, but there is to be no affirmative resolution. After an abortive attempt from the piano to recapitulate the second section, the strings lead into a coda that concludes in the same icy register with which the work began.

It is the task of the energetic third movement, a lively scherzo that looks back to the *moto perpetuo* finales of Haydn, particularly those of his Op. 20 quartets, to dispel the tragedy of the first movement and the lament of the second. The violin announces the main theme, a recasting of motif *y* into a hushed yet teasing gesture, echoed shortly after by the cello. Out of this grow more extended developments that toy with quavers grouped in twos and threes; all the while the piano adds fleeting arpeggios that quickly traverse its entire range. What follows expands and develops

---

[9]   Wood's description of this movement can be found in Chapter 3, p. 57.

[10]   The Piano Trio was commissioned and premiered by the Parikian-Fleming-Roberts Trio to whom it was dedicated; Manoug Parikian was also the dedicatee and first performer of the Violin Concerto.

this basic material, rarely rising above *sotto voce*, and never letting the momentum flag. Lyrical subsections recalling passages in both the first and second movements provide contrast and draw together the thematic strands of the work. A series of dynamic surges allows the music to emerge from capricious whispering into a full-blooded conclusion; trills in the cello and violin that incorporate all four pitches of the opening motif usher in the jubilant close.

Paraphrase on Bird of Paradise Op. 26

Paraphrase was commissioned by and written for the clarinettist Nicholas Cox, who premiered the work in March 1985 with the pianist Vanessa Latarche.[11] The work consists of a series of variations, commentaries and expansions on Wood's 'Bird of Paradise', from early 1983 (see Table 7.1).

There are in total five linked sections. The first of these is introductory in nature, presenting characteristic harmonic and textural ideas. From nebulous beginnings – the clarinet opens with major third tremolandos in a variety of registers that outline whole-tone groups – recognizable melodic fragments begin to emerge amidst rich trills. Yet as soon as these fragments begin to coalesce into extended melodic structures, the section concludes. In its wake comes a murmuring piano texture (cf. 'Always' Op. 18/iv and 'The Door' Op. 36/i) that, under the influence of arabesques and trills in the clarinet part, transforms into further trills outlining whole-tones. A series of dramatic upward swoops in the clarinet are answered by downward flurries in the piano; driven by an accelerando, these lead into the third section. This is a miniature scherzo based on tremulous minor thirds passed between instruments and through rapid changes of register. (In this respect, it is similar to the accompaniment of 'Fragment' Op. 22/iv, and looks ahead to the eighth variation of the orchestral Variations Op. 39.)

The extended fourth section balances the succession of contrasting characters within the first three sections. The first half of this section closely follows the original song, albeit with modifications to the rhythms and register of the vocal part: here, notes are displaced by octaves to intensify the expressive effect of the original line. The piano accompaniment is also stretched rhythmically to accommodate these changes, but the underlying harmonic patterns are subject to only minor alterations. Omitted from this varied transcription are the opening and closing bars of the song. In place of the latter comes a virtuosic extension based initially on the exultant chords of the song's climax and a florid passage that recalls in its dialogue between clarinet and piano the close of the first two sections.

The final section opens with a reworking of the opening melody of the song as a chorale in the piano, over which the clarinet provides rising lines in even quavers that sketch out important motivic shapes of the work. This builds into a transcription of the final bars of the song, which, as with the opening melody, were 'missing' from the fourth section. With these recollections, the paraphrase (as such) is complete. Then something unexpected happens: as the final chord of the song fades away, the opening

---

[11]   The work has been recorded by Kate Romano and Alan Hicks for Metier Sound and Vision (MSVCD2013, 2000).

bars of Hugo Wolf's song 'Phänomen' can be heard in the piano, over which the clarinet once again softly intones rising lines in quavers. The notes of the quoted melody are a whole-tone set (A–B–C♯–E♯–A–D♯); their link with the whole-tone material of 'Bird of Paradise' is clear. Further extracts from 'Phänomen' are elided to this quotation, over which the clarinet adds fragments of melodic material from Schubert's 'Der greise Kopf'. (The latter half of this material, densely chromatic, also provides intervallic links with 'Bird of Paradise'.) A final appearance of the 'Bird of Paradise' melody follows, high up in the clarinet, in a final vision of ecstasy.

The white hairs of old age described in both the Schubert and Wolf songs form a vivid contrast with the colours of the bird of paradise. Both settings in their original forms imply that the ecstasies of love offered by 'Bird of Paradise' are not denied to the elderly, and offer positive acceptance of ageing. But Wood does not seem to share this optimism, and stifles the quotations before their conclusion. One is left wondering if the high register of the final presentation of the 'Bird of Paradise' melody is to emphasize how unobtainable this ecstatic love is, or whether it is a transcendent image of love; once again, Wood's music represents tellingly the confrontation between belief in miracle and practical impossibility to be found in Graves's poetry.

Comus Quadrilles

The quadrille as a genre had, in the late nineteenth and early twentieth centuries, become a source of fun: 'the plundering of all sorts of musical sources for themes for new dances and the musical distortions that often had to be made to satisfy the restricted musical form of the quadrille made it a target and vehicle for musical jokes through the arrangement of themes from particularly incongruous sources'.[12] A sense of exuberence pervades too Wood's *Comus Quadrilles*, commissioned by the BBC for William Glock's eightieth birthday. Wood describes the quadrilles as 'a small bouquet of tunes from pieces written to [Glock's] commission between 1962 and 1969'.[13] Although none of the quadrille's original dance forms are preserved in *Comus Quadrilles*, the use of distinct sections based on material from *Scenes from Comus* create the sense of multiple dances appropriate for the genre. Into these sections are woven quotations from the First String Quartet (*Introduzione* and Scherzo), 'September', 'Pennines in April' and 'The Horses' (from *The Horses*), and the Cello Concerto, often revealing motivic connections between these works. Scored for a small chamber ensemble of string trio, piano, percussion, flute, clarinet, horn and trumpet, *Comus Quadrilles* is a vibrant acknowledgement to a man who did so much for Wood's early career, and an enjoyable reminder of the music that he enabled.

Horn Trio Op. 29

The Horn Trio was composed between March 1987 and April 1989 in fulfilment of a Koussevitsky Music Foundation Award. The first movement returns to the technique

---

[12]   Andrew Lamb, 'Quadrille', in Stanley Sadie (ed.), *The New Grove Dictionary of Music and Musicians II* (London, 1991) vol. 20, pp. 653–4 (p. 654).

[13]   From the dedication at the start of the score.

whereby contrasting blocs of material are juxtaposed to build an extended formal structure, drawing on material of a first movement and slow movement character. The second and final movement is considerably shorter and, like the Finale of the Piano Trio, is able to counterbalance what precedes it by virtue of the sustained energy of its material.

The form of the first movement as originally published is given in Table 7.3. For a performance given as part of his sixty-fifth birthday concert, Wood cut most of bloc 9 and all of bloc 13; these cuts are to be considered permanent and this is the form the work took in a recording of the Trio made in 2000.[14] As can be seen, the first blocs to be juxtaposed embody Wood's favoured contrast of a vigorous allegro figure and a lyrical melodic idea (Example 7.2). The first of these ideas is characterized by fanfare-like material in the horn (first based on fourths/fifths and then thirds); the violin and piano outline harmonic material. The second idea, initially a lyrical solo for violin accompanied by piano, contains the rising major third/falling semitone melodic figure characteristic of such material in Wood's music.

Table 7.3   Form of Horn Trio Op. 29/i

Bloc	Content
1	*Molto energico*: fanfare in horn, (see Example 7.2)
2	*Poco meno mosso*: lyrical violin solo, light piano accompaniment
3	*Tempo primo*: reworking of bloc 1; introduction of 'tapping'
4	Piano solo: soft chords
5	Expansion of 'tapping' idea
6	*Poco meno mosso*: horn takes up violin solo of bloc 2
7	*Tempo*: fanfare and tapping material
8	*Lirico*: development of lyrical material as duet for violin and horn
(9)	*Tempo*: based on bloc 1 (cut from final version)
10	Expansion of material (I): Reworking of bloc 4 for full ensemble
11	Expansion of material (II): extension of 'tapping' idea
12	Expansion of material (III): *Tempo primo (di 2, 6, 8)* 'Slow movement'; first expansion of horn and violin duet, then lyrical passage for full ensemble
(13)	*Agitato*: spectral, scherzo-like combination of themes (cut from final version)
14	*Vivacissimo*: continuation of spectral character, emergence of fanfares
15	*Maestoso*: climax of 'slow movement'/lyrical material; transformation of *energico* material
16	*Largamente*: tranquil restatement of chord idea from bloc 4; reminiscences of other themes

---

[14]   Erato 8573-80217-2. The Trio was recorded by David Pyatt (horn), Levon Chilingirian (violin) and Peter Donohoe (piano); Pyatt was also the horn player at the 65th birthday concert.

Example 7.2   Horn Trio Op. 29/i, bars 1–9

Blocs 3 through to 7 continue to exploit the basic contrast between energetic and calm. To this, two further ideas are introduced. In bloc 3, a 'tapping' motif based on repeated pitches combines with the fanfare; the ancestry of the tapping can be traced to the Finale of the Chamber Concerto (see Chapter 5, p. 115). The fourth bloc, which consists of soft chords in the piano, is also distantly related to the tapping idea by virtue of gently repeated notes at the top of each chord, coloured by the shifting harmonies beneath them. These ideas, along with those from the opening blocs, are circulated in blocs 5–7; bloc 8 is a lyrical duet between horn and violin that expands the material from the second bloc.

Blocs 10 through 12 function in the manner of a development. Each focuses on a particular thematic idea presented in the first half of the work, exploring it at length. Wood draws particular attention to the 'slow movement' character of the twelfth bloc which, after an extended reworking of the horn and violin duet, opens out into a sustained lyrical paragraph for the full ensemble.[15]

If the first eight blocs are an exploration of the tensions that result from the juxtaposition of ideas, and blocs 10–12 a detailed examination of the constituent parts, then the final section of the work serves to draw together the separate ideas into some sort of dramatic resolution. Bloc 14 opens with scurrying figures in the violin and horn from which recollections of the fanfare can be discerned. In bloc 15, the lyrical material returns to the fore in a majestic climax; towards the end, the opening horn fanfare makes a lyrical and rhythmically augmented reappearance. The final bloc further eradicates the differences between ideas. The suave repeated chords of bloc 4 return to underpin slow reminiscences of the energetic and lyrical ideas, the latter enhanced by radiant trills in the violin. In the closing bars, all the ideas return, as if a distant memory, their juxtaposition no longer able to generate the dramatic tensions of the opening as if their energy has been drained.

The Finale consists of three small and related fugatos interspersed with rhythmic interludes. Although the duration of the movement is only around a third of the length of the first movement, the vigorous counterpoint generates sufficient weight to conclude the work satisfactorily. In a radio talk given in 1997, Wood describes the influences on the Finale:

I hope they're not the sort of academic [...] fugatos. I think of a Tippett quartet [No. 3] which runs three fugues, one on top of another [...] and they're not academic there [...]. I think of the fugue, when in the hands of somebody like Beethoven (in the *Hammerklavier*) or Messiaen (in *Vingt Regards* with its marvellous big fugal movement) as a source of great energy, and that was my ideal.[16]

The three fugato themes were given in Example 3.2 (p. 55), each presented initially by a different instrument of the trio. The first (Example 3.2a) divides the chromatic scale into a hexachord of 'white notes' and a hexachord of 'black notes', to which F has been added. The 'white note' half in particular emphasizes falling fourths, linking the theme to the fanfare of Example 7.2. By dividing the twelve-note theme in this way, it is possible to suggest motion from one harmonic region to

---

15 Composer's note to the score.
16 BBC Radio 3, 19 December 1997.

another, intensifying the forward momentum inherent in the rhythm and contour of the theme. The second fugato theme is a near-inversion of the first; the third flowers into the first.

The relationship between the fugato themes and the opening fanfare of the first movement enables a return of this fanfare at the close of the work. As with the end of the first movement, it appears in a rhythmically augmented version that transforms the virile energy of Example 7.2 into a noble summation of all that has gone before. Against it, the violin supplies flurries of quavers that reflect the contours of the fanfare; the piano adds sonorous and slow-moving chords. But there is one final trick to be played: the quavers of the violin seem to motivate a sudden change of character from the horn, which lets loose a sudden quick-fire burst of the fanfare in quavers, imitated in a stretto by the violin and piano. There is a short pause, then a loud cadence as the work comes to an explosive and spirited end.

Later Vocal Music

In mid-August 1988, Wood began work on a setting of T.S. Eliot's 'Marina', a meditation on the scene from Shakespeare's *Pericles* in which an ageing father encounters his daughter whom he believed had died. In his preface to the score, Wood cites the words of the English literary critic Helen Gardner, who describes the poem as 'the prelude to a moment of ecstatic recognition [...] Its theme is not the immortality of the soul, but resurrection'.[17] The text of Wood's Cantata, D.H. Lawrence's posthumously published 'Bavarian Gentians', explores related themes. The blue trumpet-shaped flowers of the Bavarian Gentian open in autumn, which Lawrence associates with the myth of Persephone, who is guided into Hades by the light of the flowers. Persephone, like Marina, is a lost daughter: she too is destined to return. But Lawrence's text is darker than Eliot's; by focusing solely on Persephone's descent into Hades, he is preparing for his own imminent death.

Wood's youngest daughter, Jenny, was murdered in Bavaria on 10 September 1988, one week before her twenty-seventh birthday. The Cantata, dedicated to her memory, was composed between 18 April and 26 July 1989. After its completion, Wood returned to his draft of *Marina*, which he finished on 10 September 1989; it too is dedicated to his daughter.

Cantata Op. 30

The Cantata, for mixed chorus and orchestra without percussion, opens with a delicate and shimmering texture within which flute, viola and trumpet introduce the main motivic material of the work (Example 7.3). Although each instrument outlines an undulating contour of alternating ascending and descending intervals, their material is nevertheless clearly individuated. Motif x, for instance, is Wood's characteristic lyrical figure, its affective qualities heightened by its gentle triplets and soft scoring in the flute's lowest register. The wide leaps of motif y allude to the

---

[17]   Composer's note to the score.

greater tensions to come; the measured augmented triad of *z* suggests that there will be whole-tone colouring in the harmonic language as well as octatonicism derived from *x*. The chords that follow (bars 5–7) together employ all twelve notes; each chord incorporates something in turn of motifs *x*, *z* and *y*. Wood does not treat the chords systematically as a twelve-note trope, but they can be heard to influence much of the harmonic argument of the work. The contrasting timbres of the chords, dividing the orchestra into broad instrumental families of brass, wind and strings, remains the norm throughout the work; one is reminded of passages in the Chamber Concerto (see Example 2.7a, p. 45, and p. 113). The emphasis on low and mid-range scoring is typical for the work: compared with the similarly scored Laurie Lee Songs Op. 28, the sound world is of the Cantata is much darker, often with dense chords for divided lower strings.

Example 7.3 Cantata Op. 30, bars 1–7

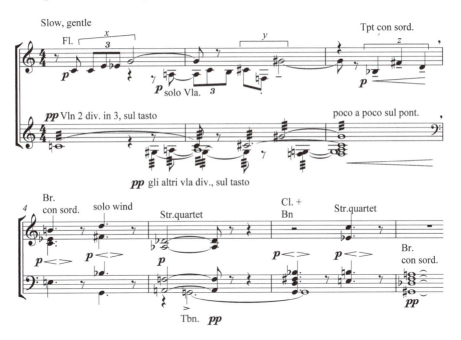

After this evocative opening, the weight of the subsequent argument can be found in the material given to the choir. The first choral entry is hushed and compact, the sopranos in their lowest register. This leads towards two harmonized statements of motif *x*, the first to the words 'in soft September', the second transposed up by a major third for 'at slow, sad, Michaelmas' (bars 8–15). Underneath, harp, bass clarinet and double basses provide a soft and low accompaniment, with gently rocking leaps that recall the tranquil moments of the First String Quartet and Symphony (see Chapter 4, p. 77 and Chapter 6, p. 143). Here, however, the text and scoring infuse the rocking with an autumnal pastoralism, an elegiac commemoration of the passing of the seasons.

The words 'Bavarian gentians, big and dark' mark the start of the first extended stanza. Gently unfolding vocal counterpoint in which motifs *x* and *y* are prominent, sustains and intensifies the emotional intensity. The words 'torch-like with the smoking blueness' introduce an important melodic figure (*w*) that opens with an inversion of *x* (Example 7.4). This figure pushes the choir upwards; concurrently, over a warm 0,2,6 dominant trichord on F♯, a chord in fifths occurs in the upper strings, played with harmonics. This is echoed by the choir at the end of the phrase, with sopranos and altos sustaining the bare fifth F♯–C♯ for the word 'gloom' (bar 27). The cadential property of these fifths becomes increasingly important as the work progresses.

Densely harmonized versions of motif *w* in the strings alternate with impassioned choral statements to reach a climax in bars 39–40, in which unaccompanied chords in fourths and fifths to the words 'spread blue' are followed immediately by a weighty chord from the full orchestra. Out of this comes a sudden and unexpected calm with the return of the low-pitched pastoralism of bars 8–15, the low instruments sighing delicately underneath gentle homophonic chords in the choir that once again conclude with superimposed fifths ('day', bar 44).

The second half of the first stanza (bars 45–85) beings with oscillating triplets in the strings, working up from the double basses through to the second violins. The text develops the earlier imagery, and Wood's setting correspondingly reworks the material based on motif *w*, and in particular the dialogue between choir and orchestra. Bars 66–70 are an extended version of bars 39–40, with massed chords in the orchestra culminating with the central climax of the work in bars 78–85. Here the 'frustrated passion' of the piece is given its first outlet:[18] a ferocious series of widely spaced chords and dense clusters that contract and expand respectively in the manner of a grotesque ritualistic dance.[19]

Emotional release is provided at the start of the second stanza with a return of the chorus ('reach me a gentian', bar 86) and a radiant chord in fifths in the strings. From here, the texture thins to return once again to the sparse autumnal sound world of bars 8–15. Over soft declamations in the choir, a solo soprano sings of Persephone. The prevailing tranquillity is disturbed for a return of motif *w* in first the strings and then the full orchestra (bars 128–41), which provides a final burst of light ('the splendour of torches of darkness'). This functions as a catharsis, for all the profound serenity of what follows: a return of the pastoral leaps in the bass instruments, over which a twelve-note chord in fifths for choir and orchestra is built slowly to bring the work to a luminous close.

The Cantata stands as a powerful example of how simple compositional devices can be used to create overwhelming emotional effect. The trajectory of the first half of the work, from the soft opening of Example 7.3 to the almost impotent rage of bars 78–85 is balanced by an increasing calmness in the second half. Central to the musical depiction of this emotional transformation is the role played by perfect fifths, used at first to harmonize key words such as 'gloom' (bar 27), 'blue' (bar 39)

---

[18]   Kennedy, [Hugh Wood: Chester Music promotional brochure].

[19]   The technique is identical to similarly climactic passages in the Second String Quartet and Chamber Concerto (see Chapter 3, p. 56).

Example 7.4   Cantata Op. 30, bars 21–4

and 'day' (bar 44). Following the climactic chords of bars 78–85, the text asks for the gentian to light the protagonist's path into the underworld (bar 86). The use of fifths in the harmony at this point suggests that the fate foretold in the first half of the work has thus been accepted and, by the time the final chord unfolds, this acceptance has become transcendent. Yet for all of this, the recurrent timbres of bass clarinet, harp and double bass tinge the work with a dark-hued melancholy. There might be an acceptance of the passing 'one soft September' of the 'lost bride and her groom', but the pain that this causes remains hauntingly audible.

Marina Op. 31

Wood's setting of *Marina* (1988–89) is scored for high voice and a small instrumental ensemble of alto flute, horn, harp and viola. As with the Cantata, these mid-register instruments provide an autumnal character, but they offer too the potential for bright, biting and forceful attacks in the treble and bass registers where necessary.

The work opens with a delicately coloured E♮, around which chromatic pitches lap delicately to create a sonorous but hazy texture.[20] As the vocal line gains in intensity (see Example 2.5, p. 32), fragments of word-painting come to the surface: a sudden bird-call in the alto flute at the words 'woodthrush singing', and increased textural density for the word 'fog'. At the word 'images', the texture simplifies abruptly, reduced to a solitary sustained E♭ in the horn. To this, the viola and alto flute add a G♭ and F to produce a softly held chord that is derived from the final three notes of motif x (Example 2.5). This chord accompanies the return of motif x_1 in the voice to the words 'oh my daughter' (bars 13–16). The simplification of both texture and material heightens the profound effect of the images that jostle together in the mind of the father suddenly clearing with a moment of clarity at the recollection of his daughter.

Alternations between forceful declamations and moments of calm follow. The juxtaposition of contrasting expressive states is common to Wood's music, and its use in *Marina* to depict the emotional turmoil of the father is deeply affecting. A brittle figure in flute and harp (bars 16–17) first disturbs the lucid calm of 'my daughter'; this leads to a hollow four-note chord spread over four and a half octaves. Against this, the voice adds a forceful contemplation of death, coloured by furious double stops in fourths and fifths, tremolando and accented, in the viola. The sequence of upbeat figure, chord and declamation is repeated a further three times. Each ends with a loud, sustained harmony to which the horn adds a low foghorn-like bass note. This foghorn, perhaps, has two functions: to steer travellers away from the fog and the images of death that permeate the poem, and to act also as a signal that beckons to the absent daughter.

The words 'are become unsubstantial' (bar 35) motivate a further change, as echoes of the voice proliferate in the alto flute and viola. There is a similarity here with the clouded textures of the opening paragraph. Indeed, this is one of numerous reminiscences that begin to permeate both text and music: one senses that the father is losing the ability to differentiate clearly between the past and present, the real and imaginary. As the flute and viola spiral upwards, the music dissolves into a wide-spaced C major triad, coloured by a high D–A harmonics in the viola. There is a turn

---

[20]   There are similarities here with both the Chamber Concerto and the seascapes of the Pablo Neruda songs.

Example 7.5　*Marina* Op. 31, bars 47–52

in the text once again (bar 42) from marine imagery to more concrete reflections of the daughter, and with this a return to the calm and sorrowful atmosphere of bars 13–16. The vocal line is haunted increasingly by allusions to and repetitions of previous melodic figures, beginning with an entranced extension of motif *y* (Example 2.5), here transposed by a tritone to begin on C. It is significant that motif *y*, here and elsewhere, tends to be associated with physical sensation: in bar 9 it is 'scent', bar 37 'breath' and at 42 the image of a face and later a pulse. The rising minor third and falling semitone D–E–F, first heard with the word 'image' (Example 2.5, bar 13) returns, extended, with the words '[more] distant than [stars]' (Example 7.5). Against this, alto flute and harp are in canon at the distance of a quaver, their lines rich in fourths and fifths. Both lines are in harmonics that suggest the cold twinkling of the stars. The images that have already been revealed as insubstantial thus slip further out of the father's reach.

From here there is a whirlwind of fleeting impressions and memories. The fugitive rustlings of bar 35 return in bar 57, punctuated by a brief return to C major in bar 60. Out of this the viola and flute once again ascend upwards (as in bars 39–41). There is then a series of rapid alterations between the forceful death-laden declamations of bar 17 and the calmer C major of bar 42. The declamatory phrases become increasingly contrapuntal as the father recounts the building of ships (perhaps the craftsmanship of one is reflected in the other). In the C major sections, it is the creation of life, not of ships, that forms the basis of the father's reflections. A short vigorous passage for instruments alone leads to an extended return of the C major material. The canon between harp and flute harmonics returns once again to depict distance ('Living to live in a world of time beyond me').

This final meditation appears to make possible a visionary moment: swirling arpeggios in fifths (largely on the black notes, in contrast to the underlying C major of the preceding section) surround the voice (bars 112–14). But then all is stilled, with only a held E in the horn remaining. This leads to a short reprise of the opening section. As before, when the fog clears, only one thing remains: the haunting vision of 'my daughter', set to a simple rising major third D–F♯ that is achingly tender.

As with the Graves songs, musical technique and poetic insight are fused in the Cantata and *Marina* to the extent that one cannot talk meaningfully of one without mention of the other. Similarly, the instrumental contexts of these works intensify the sensitivity to colour and texture one finds in Wood's piano accompaniments. Above all, it is the eloquent transformation and transcendence of bitter personal experience into universal statements that characterizes the most profound and significant aspects of Wood's art.

Chapter 8

'Many-splendoured Things'
1991–1997

After the intimate music that dominated the years following the Symphony, Wood's music of the 1990s suggested a return to the public statements that characterized the 1970s. Two large orchestral works bookend this period. The first of these, the Piano Concerto (1989–91), was a Proms commission. The second, the Variations for Orchestra (1994–97; revised 1998) was commissioned for a BBC Symphony Orchestra tour of the Far East; in 1998 a revised version was given its European premiere at the Last Night of the Proms.[1] Conducting both of these concerts was Andrew Davis, who was also responsible in this period for revivals of *Scenes from Comus* and, more importantly, the Symphony, of which recordings were finally released in 2001.[2]

Between the Piano Concerto and Variations for Orchestra was a further BBC commission, which gave rise to a Fourth String Quartet (1994). This, perhaps Wood's finest chamber work, is a passionate and beautiful summation of his achievements to date in the genre. Yet it, along with smaller works such as *Funeral Music* for brass (1992) and *Poem* for violin (1993), also contains seeds of technical and expressive devices that become increasingly prominent in Wood's more recent music.

Two anniversaries were celebrated belatedly by the BBC in this period. In 1992, shortly after his sixtieth birthday, Wood was BBC Radio 3's 'Composer of the Week', when five one-hour programmes were dedicated to his music. Five months after his sixty-fifth birthday, the Birmingham Contemporary Music Group gave a concert that was broadcast on BBC Radio 3 the following month. Alongside new and reissued recordings of Wood's music that appeared in these years,[3] these events served to reinforce his significant artistic reputation.

---

[1]   Wood's inclusion in the programme of the Last Night of the Proms, that bastion of pomp, circumstance and jubilant flag-waving, reflected his status as 'one of this country's senior composers', as the radio announcer would have it (BBC Radio 3, 12 September 1998). Wood's reaction was typically enthusiastic. 'You wouldn't believe the amount of snobbery I encountered from friends and colleagues, who thought it would embarrass me. But I was delighted to be performed there – and the Proms audience always really listens, even on the Last Night' (Wigmore, 'Hugh Wood': 40).

[2]   See Preface, p. xi.

[3]   Between 1991 and 1994, recordings of all three of Wood's concertos were (re)released, along with new recordings of all four of the numbered string quartets (at that time).

Orchestral Music I

Piano Concerto Op. 32

The Piano Concerto, like the Symphony nine years before it, was a BBC commission. Wood was asked originally for a Viola Concerto, but soon decided to write instead for his former Cambridge pupil Joanna MacGregor, who premiered the work on 10 September 1991 at the Proms. The work attracted a greater amount of pre-publicity than was typical for Wood's music, and both the first performance and MacGregor's subsequent recording were lauded.[4] Much of the critical focus was on Wood's successful integration of multiple styles and techniques within the concerto. One of the inspirations for this eclecticism was Wood's intention to capture something of MacGregor's personality and musicality in his music, just as his Cello and Violin Concertos were written with the playing of Jacqueline du Pré and Manoug Parikian in mind.[5]

More so than Wood's two earlier concertos, the Piano Concerto is composed against the background of traditional classical forms. The first movement is a sonata-allegro with a double exposition and the slow second movement a set of variations. As with works such as the Violin Concerto, Piano Trio and Horn Trio, the Finale is relatively short: a buoyant quasi-rondo in which rhythmic impetus obviates the need for a lengthy counterbalance to the previous movements.

The first movement opens with a sequence of bell-like chords for piano alone (Example 8.1a), invoking comparison to the start of Beethoven's Fourth and Rachmaninoff's Second Piano Concerto;[6] there are textural similarities between the latter and Wood's opening. For all of the memorability of this rhetorical gesture, it is typical that Wood does not treat it as a source of motivic material or a motto in the way that he did with, say, the theme of the Cello Concerto or Piano Trio. Rather, it offers a concise summary of the harmonic language of the movement, out of which the ensuing material grows. The series of chords in the upper system thus reflect the chromaticism of the music that follows, given direction through rising fourths in the treble voice and the circle of fifths in the bass register (A–D–G–C).

The opening chords serve to emphasize dramatically the prominent role of the solo piano, so that its absence is felt during the subsequent exposition for orchestra alone. The angular melodic motifs and astringent harmonies of the orchestral theme provide immediate contrast; the material is derived from a twelve-note trope that consists of four three-note chromatic cells (see annotations to Example 8.1a). The similarity between cells, which might lead to harmonic greyness, is offset by insistent quaver motion, dance-like interjections (for example, bars 6 and 8) and rapid changes of orchestral colour that together provide considerable forward momentum. Pulsing chords in the lower strings, based on the same material, follow at rehearsal mark 2;

---

[4]   MacGregor's recording of the work was issued by Collins Classics 20072 (1993).

[5]   These are just the most prominent examples: as an eminently practical composer, Wood has always, when possible, written music tailored towards the particular qualities of his performers.

[6]   See, for instance, Walsh, [Sleeve notes to Collins Classics 20072].

Example 8.1(a)   Piano Concerto Op. 32/i, bars 1–8

wind and brass re-enter with an energetic reprise of the angular melody to close the thematic group. The entire group is then repeated (rehearsal marks 3–5), given further energetic impetus through contrapuntal workings.

The second thematic group begins with a melodic idea in the wind, accompanied by playful descending chords in the violins and surging arpeggios in the lower

Example 8.1(b)   Piano Concerto Op. 32/i, bars 41–7

strings (Example 8.1b). The wind melody is a new twelve-note theme that opens with Wood's characteristic lyrical figure of a rising major third and falling semitone (motif *y*). The violin chords that harmonize this melody are derived for the most part from the cells of Example 8.1a; note too that the extract opens with a chord in the wind taken from the piano introduction. Such recollections and derivations act as a constant reminder that the varied musical surface of the movement, rich in contrasts, is nevertheless tightly organized.

An immediate development of Example 8.1b is characterized by greater contrapuntal complexity, as with the first thematic group. This segues into the darker

Example 8.1(c)   Piano Concerto Op. 32/i, bars 61–4

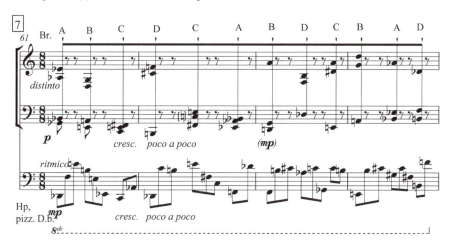

hues of brass, harp and double basses in the third thematic group (Example 8.1c). Whereas the second thematic group was melodic in character, the third group is dominated by an insistent scherzo-like rhythm in groups of 3+3+2 quavers. The harmonies draw on another twelve-note trope, which consists of two cells built in fifths (A and B) and two from 0,2,6 dominant trichords (C and D). A short codetta, based on the cells of Example 8.1a, brings the orchestral exposition to a close with a riotous unaccompanied melodic line coloured by orchestral whoops and glissandi, as if summoning the soloist back into the fray.

The second exposition opens with a variation of the opening bars, now based on the harmonies of Example 8.1c, which leads to an extended version of the third thematic group itself (rehearsal marks 9–11). This is followed by material from the first thematic group, in which the emphasis is thrown onto the pulsing chordal figure, which is given an expansive reworking by the solo piano between rehearsal marks 12 and 13. Instead of the second thematic group, there is a graceful new idea of a repeated chord in fifths introduced by piano (rehearsal mark 14); from here, fifths feature ever more prominently in the material. Orchestral outbursts derived from the first and third thematic groups lead to a vigorous codetta of trumpet fanfares based on motif *y*. The exultant quality of these fanfares recalls the calls to dance in *Scenes from Comus* (see Chapter 4, p. 85), though in the Piano Concerto one is required to wait for the revels.

As if deaf to the orchestra's summons, the solo piano begins the development with *cantabile* musings on the material of the second thematic group (rehearsal mark 18).[7] It is answered by an increasingly important variant of this melody that begins with a motif of a falling fourth and rising semitone. From this emerges a

---

[7]   In his 'A Photograph of Brahms', Wood describes the 'tantalising omission of the second subject proper from the orchestral exposition', in Brahms's Violin Concerto that 'makes its eventual appearance in the hands of the soloist all the more ravishing' (p. 286). One wonders if he had this in mind when composing the Piano Concerto.

hushed theme for piano characterized by oscillating fifths in the treble (motif *z*) that is transposed upwards through successive semitones, accompanied by soft sustained string chords. To statements of motif *z*, the piano adds dreamy passagework that recalls jazz improvisation; wind instruments add gentle countermelodies.[8]

At rehearsal mark 20, the violins creep in on a high B with an inversion of the melody of Example 8.1b, followed by ever more impassioned workings of the second thematic group material, including the variant motif introduced at the start of the development. The contours of motif *y* also inform the material in the second half of the development (beginning at rehearsal mark 25), which balances the lyrical first half with vigorous reworkings of Example 8.1c and the fanfares of the codetta to the second exposition.

A compressed recapitulation begins with a return of the first thematic group at rehearsal mark 30. The tendency of the second exposition to give emphasis to the pulsed chords within this group is developed further to reach a climax around rehearsal mark 32. Out of this comes the second thematic group, now transposed by a tritone. Following a short recollection of the codetta to the first exposition, the second group returns at the original pitch (that is, beginning on C) to lead into a reprise of the hushed theme from the development. A solo horn now takes motif *z*, giving the piano freedom to decorate more elaborately the rich harmonies. A short cadenza leads to the final reprise of the third subject group for orchestra alone (rehearsal marks 39–41). The piano returns for the final nine bars, providing a bustling accompaniment to trumpet fanfares based on motif *y* that bring the movement to an energetic close.

The first movement, then, can be characterized as a continuous shuffling of the thematic material of Example 8.1, given dramatic impetus through the contrast of piano and orchestra. The play of formal associations, and in particular the function of the lyrical material of Example 8.1b, is also crucial in determining the expressive character of the movement. This is most clearly demonstrated with respect to the fifths that inform the material of the development, and in particular motif *z*. The open sound world created by this material blurs the distinction between what is developmental, and what is expository. Yet it would be erroneous to say that with these fifths 'comes a harmonic expectancy not present at the start of the work, though the harmonic material is not strictly new'.[9] In fact, these fifths are present in the outer voice of the piano chords at the start of the work, becoming increasingly prominent in the animated third subject group (Example 8.1c), and determining the harmonic orientation of the second exposition and development. Just as the seeds of the triumphant A major conclusion to the Symphony were planted in the instability of the *Tempesta* that opens that work, so too do we find in the Piano Concerto a carefully planned and executed harmonic design.

If the appearance of the fifths of motif *z* can be accounted for harmonically, its character, which is a distant remove from the terse orchestral theme of Example 8.1a, cannot be anticipated so readily. Its mode of expression and its rhapsodic treatment stand apart from the main argument in the manner of an episode, or as if in inverted

------

8   This theme is equivalent to the 'new themes' one finds in the second exposition of (say) a Mozartian piano concerto, displaced here into the development.

9   Walsh, [Sleeve notes to Collins Classics 20072].

commas. There is a precedent, once again, in the Symphony, in which the coda to the *Tempesta* (Example 6.5, pp. 140–41) necessitates a more extended treatment in the subsequent *Elegia* and Passacaglia. In the Piano Concerto, the second movement elevates the intimate 'light night jazz' style of these episodes to centre stage.[10]

The second movement opens with a delicate reworking of the first four bars of the first movement, again with rising fourths in the treble, and again for piano alone. Now a reverie in the upper registers, the motto is stripped of the dramatic confrontation between treble and bass that initiated the dramatic first movement. This leads into a series of mournful chords (Example 8.2). Their slow tread and sonorous scoring for strings recall as a distant memory the accompaniment to motif *z* in the first movement.

Example 8.2   Piano Concerto Op. 32/ii, bars 6–15 (strings only)

The sequence of chords is the basis of five further variations (Wood labels the chords as variation one); a piano cadenza and coda follow. The second variation presents the chords in diminution, effectively doubling the perceived tempo: it becomes almost a slow sarabande. Over this is laid delicate figuration in the woodwind, with repeated notes in the oboe being particularly prominent. Unlike the pulsations of the first movement, the repeated notes have no urgency; the variation is reminiscent of Bartókian night pieces. In the third variation, the material in the wind is far more intricate, tracing delicate arabesques in predominantly treble registers. The fourth variation is one of charming simplicity: there are just four sustained chords, over which the piano adds a single line in steady crotchets that slowly descends from glistening treble into sonorous bass.

In variation five, the sequence of Example 8.2 is used to harmonize the first trombone, in a 'very slightly swung' version of 'Sweet Lorraine', the 1928 Cliff Burwell song popularized by Nat King Cole.[11] Upon hearing it, one realizes that certain characteristics of the previous variations, such as the repeated pitches and

---

[10]   Jazz was a shared passion between MacGregor and Wood. In the programme booklet to *Goehrfest*, a celebration held in 1999 of the composers working at Cambridge in the twenty-five years after Goehr's appointment, MacGregor describes how Wood 'came round early to give me a hand in preparing a dinner party. As he hovered over a chopping board, I put on some Ella Fitzgerald. "Oh *come on*", he sighed, "you can't expect me to concentrate on chopping carrots to *that*."' (pp. 19–20)

[11]   Recall that Wood's family were avid collectors of gramophone records (see Chapter 1, p. 3); it is perhaps less of a surprise that a popular song should appear in Wood's music than that it took so long for one to appear at all.

melodic contours were pre-echoes of this theme. A stream of semiquaver chords in the piano provides a scintillating accompaniment in which perfect fifths are prominent both vertically and, in the accompaniment's sequential patterning, horizontally. Out of this comes a short interlude for piano that at first echoes the conclusion to the trombone line, becoming increasingly dense with augmented triads in each hand.

This leads to the sixth and most extended variation of the movement, the material of 'Sweet Lorraine' dispersed throughout the orchestra, to which the piano adds a swinging counter melody. A warm *cantabile* line given first to the cellos and then repeated in other sections brings the variation to a glowing climax. Yet, as is so typical in Wood's music, there is no emotional release. Rather, a heavy chord stifles the argument, and brilliant semiquaver chords in the piano spiral down from the top to the bottom of its register.

To this point the weight of the musical argument has been given to the orchestra. The substantial piano cadenza that follows the sixth variation opens with wide-spaced and arpeggiated chords that span the entire keyboard, which suggests initially a return to the dramatic opposition between piano and orchestra that was found in the first movement. However, the rhetoric of the first movement is alien to the gentler second. The cadenza swiftly subsides into a reprise of the 'Sweet Lorraine' material, here labelled 'Theme' to indicate that its hushed sound world had been the goal of the movement all along. A singing fantasy on this theme concludes the cadenza, which delicately tiptoes its way into a coda: a final reprise of the chord sequence of Example 8.2, and a return to the lightly fluttering decoration in the upper voices.

Driving quavers in the brass dispel the magic cast by the end of the slow movement: the Finale bursts to life with the additive scherzo rhythms of Example 8.1c. At last the summons to revelry in the first movement has been answered, and it appears that everyone is keen to enjoy the dance. Varied repetitions of this summons punctuate the movement in the manner of a rondo refrain; successive transpositions through thirds structure the harmonic progression of the movement in a manner akin to *Lines to Mr Hodgson* and *A Christmas Poem*.

Woven in between statements of this refrain are thematic ideas that refer back to the previous movements. Unlike the first movement, in which the lyrical passages seemed to become detached from their surroundings, resulting in the second movement, the Finale offers a clearer balance between contrasting characters. It would be inaccurate to describe the conclusion as a dialectic resolution between strident and lyrical material, but one senses that a balance has nevertheless been reached.

The piano introduces in the third bar the first of the themes relating to the first movement, a spiky, chromatic figure in buoyant additive rhythms. Underneath it, a sustained chord in the wind and strings harks back to the language of the slow movement. A flurry of descending quavers in perfect fifths leads to pulsing chords passed from strings to wind; against this, strings add angular melodic fragments that recall the leaps of Example 8.1a, bars 5–7. A reprise of the spiky theme makes clear the connection with these bars, for it employs the same twelve-note trope. Another burst of busy figuration, here sequentially falling through fifths, leads to an extended development of the pulsing chords. Though such mechanical repetitions have been explored before in Wood's music,[12] their insistence and orchestration here bring to mind minimalist composers such as John Adams. This side-effect can be attributed to the fact that the repetitions do not sustain the energetic thrust of the movement sufficiently: the effect is closer to hypnotic stasis rather than dynamic impetus.

Regardless of the relative success of the pulsed chords, the appearance of the lyrical material from their remnants is a calculated surprise that is brilliantly effective. The piano, in a *dolcissimo* A♭ major that is a close relation to Example 8.2 (see the first chord), introduces a theme in which singing whole-tone lines provide strong echoes of 'Sweet Lorraine'. A solo cor anglais takes over the tune; later in the movement, this flowers into duets between piano and muted trumpet, and then later between piano and horn.

As is common in Wood's scherzo-like movements, the various elements are subject to continuous juxtaposition and permutations. This shuffling of ideas creates a significant dynamism that propels the work towards its conclusion: an orchestral reworking of the opening bars of the work (Example 8.1a, bars 1–4). The piano adds a whimsical sign-off, an unaccompanied rising whole-tone scale that provides a last, capricious glance back to 'Sweet Lorraine', answered by a single crash from the orchestra, built on the foundations of an A♭ major chord.

Though the Piano Concerto ends with high jinks, its tongue planted firmly in cheek, there is nevertheless an underlying seriousness to the work as a whole. The spirit of the work belongs to the pluralism of the 1960s rather than that of the 1990s. Similarly, the mixture of styles and techniques in the concerto are motivated by expressive necessity rather than the toying with (ransacking of?) the past that characterizes some of the younger generation of composers. Thus, whatever the influence MacGregor may have had on the exuberant character of the work, it nevertheless remains unmistakably and compellingly Wood's voice that we hear.

Chamber Music

Funeral Music Op. 33

Begun in late March 1992, *Funeral Music* for brass quintet was completed on 27 July that summer. Wood's father had died on 27 July 1966; the work was intended as a memorial to 'him and other members of [Wood's] family, as well as several friends who have died'.[13] The specific inscription is however to Stefan Pal, a son of friends in Bavaria, who had died in 1990. The work was commissioned by the Three Choirs Festival for the London Gabrieli Brass consort, who gave the first performance on 24 August 1992.

The work begins with the dark-hued colours of the tuba, which gives a sombre air to the opening motif of long sustained notes divided by a short upbeat. It is soon joined in duet by the horn in its lower registers. From this flowers a polyphonic dialogue: the addition in turn of the trombone, trumpet II and trumpet I causes the

---

[12]   Recall, for instance, the 'tapping' figures of the Chamber Concerto and Horn Trio.

[13]   Composer's note to the score.

upper line of the ensemble to rise and the overall timbre brighten. As the line climbs up to a climax, the bass descends chromatically; this contrary motion culminates in wide-spaced and dramatic chord (bar 23). A series of chords characterized by abrupt dynamic changes and urgent surges follows, functioning as an extended and dramatic upbeat to the funeral march that follows.

The march consists of lyrical and lamenting melodies that are given in turn to trombone, first trumpet and horn, and which climax with a duet between second trumpet and horn. The accompanying chords are in crisp martial rhythms, the most characteristic of which is a figure that consists of three quavers, the first slurred to the second; both the second and third notes are staccato. Much of the outer voice-leading of these chords is by (expanded) whole-tone step. After the horn and trumpet duet, the accompaniment thins and the tuba picks up the melodic thread. As the energy of the music dissipates, the character of the music becomes increasingly mournful as the tuba sinks into silence.

To this point, there is a clearly defined arc leading from dark colours and low registers to brighter, higher tessituras and back. In the next section, however, timbre and register are more sharply contrasted. It opens with overlapping whole-tone fanfares in the trumpets, marked *lontano* (distant). These alternate with sustained phrases of the Lutheran chorale 'Mit Fried und Freud ich fahr dahin' ['With peace and joy I go there'; Luther's version of the Nunc dimittis], delivered slowly and at first softly by the lower brass instruments with Wood's own harmonization. Only at the radiant climax do the fanfares and chorale combine ('Wie Gott mir verheißen hat, Der Tod ist mein Schlaf worden [As God promised me, Death has become my sleep]).

This leads to a repeat of the chords of bars 25–33, transposed up by a semitone and more stable dynamically. The context provided by the preceding chorale and a simplification of the phrasing lends to these chords a sense of stability lacking from their first appearance. From here, there is a repetition of the opening polyphonic passage, now in a slightly varied retrograde that progresses from full ensemble down to the quiet, sombre timbres of tuba alone which concludes the work.

Fifty Chords for David Matthews

Fifty Chords for David Matthews, along with tributes by six other composers, was written for a concert celebrating David Matthew's fiftieth birthday (1993). Wood's contribution was simple: fifty piano chords, to which a string trio provides contrast. Employing the German system of naming pitches, in which B♮=H and E♭=(e)S, the pitch content of the first seven chords gradually spells out the dedicatee's name (DAviD mAttHEwS). Subsequent chords harmonize warmly successive statements of falling semitones and rising major thirds (for example, B–B♭–D–D♭). Though this melodic figure is octatonic, the harmonies do not belong to any particular mode for any significant length of time: succession seems to have been determined by ear, empirically assessing the relationship between chords to build up extended phrases. There is a continual crescendo through chords 12–23, the latter marking the first climax of the work. As the resonance of this climactic chord fades, the cello enters, almost imperceptibly. There is a then another slow build-up in the piano towards a climax, underneath which the string trio, entering one note at a time, build up a chord using the 'David Matthews' pitches. A second climax occurs on chord 48, from which emerges a precipitous flurry of quavers from the strings. This concludes with a sustained C♯ that is cut off by a cheerful two-chord cadence in the piano to close the work.

Poem Op. 35

Poem for violin and piano was composed in June and July 1993. The title provides a clue to the character of the work, but not its form: Wood notes in the score that there were 'no attempts at imitation of sonnet structure or any arcane rhyming scheme: it just seemed like a nice name for a piece which was intended to be straightforwardly lyrical'.[14] The piece was commissioned by the Park Lane Group Young Artists Concerts New Year Series 1994, and first performed by the work's dedicatee Clio Gould on 10 January 1994. Since then, it has been taken up and performed by Alexandra Wood (no relation) and Huw Watkins, also Park Lane Group artists, who recorded the work in 2005.[15]

Poem opens with an exultant theme in the violin, mostly in multiple stops, accompanied by sonorous chords in the piano. The material is exclusively white-note, the descending violin line an embellishment of a slowly unfolding C major triad (with emphasis on the added sixth A♮), and the piano bass an inexorable diatonic rise from F through to C. Although instances of diatonicism (and specifically white-note passages) can be found in Wood's earlier music, only the occasional *Musicians Wrestle Everywhere* is comparable with the opening of *Poem*. Its function is to offer an open, clangorous and immediately memorable sound world to be contrasted with extended passages of more chromatic music.

Such a passage emerges out of the final chord of the diatonic opening in the form of a lyrical, sustained twelve-note melody for the violin, characterized by numerous descending whole-tones (bar 11). The piano provides a light accompaniment rich in major sevenths; certain notes are sustained in order to create warm harmonies. A sequential passage based on a cramped motif of a descending semitone and a rising tone leads to a local climax at bar 25 (*poco più mosso*) in which the whole-tones of the start of the melody are expanded into highly expressive leaps of sevenths and ninths.

The whole-tone leanings of the material become more prominent from bar 28, in which the cramped motif, now extended by an additional rising tone, returns. A sequential development of this motif from bar 31 creates a twelve-note line that is harmonized by four three-note chords, themselves a twelve-note trope. This chord sequence is developed in a series of repetitions characterized by flowing triplet motion, which gets increasingly impassioned. As the intensity grows, the first three chords of the work return in the piano part, accompanying dramatic chains of double stops in the violin. Finally, at bar 50, a flurry of double stops surge upward, accompanied by a heavy black-note chord in the piano. This leads to a return of the

---

[14]   Composer's note to the score.
[15]   Wood and Watkins' recording can be found on Chimera Usk 1226CD (2005).

opening diatonic material, made more emphatic by the juxtaposition of black- and white-note material.

The reprise of the declamatory opening theme is extended and made more elaborate with exuberant rushing scales in both violin and piano. At the peak of the final scale there is a sudden pianissimo with the return of the chromatic melody, now predominantly in the violin's upper register (bar 66). The piano accompaniment of rippling upward scales, the sustaining pedal blurring them into gentle washes of sound, also begins in the treble. Each successive bar begins in a lower register, with contrasting harmonic materials: the opening black-note scale is followed by white-note and then whole-tone material; as with 'Bird of Paradise', the effect is of iridescent collisions of different colours.

The cramped motif returns in bar 76, but in keeping with the general character of the second half of the work the material moves swiftly towards expansiveness, climbing once again into the upper register of the violin. There is a reworking beginning in bar 95 of the sequential passage of bars 31–4 which leads, via a further black- to white-note cadence, to a final reprise of the diatonic material in bar 101. Ghostly harmonics in the violin and high chords on the piano rob the theme of its swagger; what is left sounds like a distant, nostalgic memory. Chiming thirds in the accompaniment, reminiscent of the tranquil ending of *Scenes from Comus*, bring the work to a close.

As its name suggests, *Poem* does not aspire to overtly virtuosic fireworks or symphonic rigour, though nor it is easy to perform or simplistic in its working. Rather, it is an elegant work unsullied by formal complication or harmonic opaqueness, immediately appealing but by no means superficial. And in this, *Poem* is representative of a series of lighter lyrical works that can be found in Wood's music of the 1990s and twenty-first century that balance his more weighty utterances, just as the playful scherzo-like works such as the *Capriccio* and Quintet did in the 1960s.

String Quartet No. 4 Op. 34

The Fourth String Quartet, like the First and Second, was a BBC commission. It was written for, and dedicated to, the Chilingirian Quartet, who Wood had known since his days in Liverpool, when the quartet was resident at the University. The work was first performed on 19 May 1993, and the Chilingirians recorded it together with the three earlier numbered quartets soon after.[16]

After the use of bloc forms in the single-movement Second and Third Quartets, the Fourth is a deliberate return to a four-movement design. The First Quartet, and indeed the Chamber Concerto and Symphony, provides the model here. The first movement of the Fourth Quartet is thus an *Introduzione*, a Scherzo and Adagio constitute the middle movements, and the work concludes with a weighty Finale.

The *Introduzione* consists of a series of highly differentiated ideas, separated and punctuated by vigorous chords that together outline a strongly defined harmonic progression (the beginning of this progression is summarized in Example 2.7b, p. 46). The character of these chords, and the whole-tone motion in their outer voices,

---

[16]   Conifer 75605 51239-2 (1994).

recalls the opening of Michael Tippett's First String Quartet, which similarly interrupts the unfolding of melodic material with an evolving chord sequence. In Wood's quartet, there is no continuity between melodic statements, which heightens the dramatic juxtaposition of contrasting ideas.

The first group of ideas (bars 1–18) are presented by the second violin and viola, against sustained chords held in the first violin and cello. The first of these ideas consists of a vigorous two-part counterpoint characterized by large leaps that successively push the music upwards; a written out accelerando culminates in a sudden dissolution. The second idea is also imitative, embellished with numerous trills and busy semiquaver figuration. A lyrical twelve-note melody in the second violin, based around Wood's characteristic motif of falling semitones and rising major thirds is the basis for the third idea, harmonized by the viola. This ends in a tight chromatic cluster, the two instruments grinding against each other. Finally, another two-part invention flourishes briefly, distinguished by rapid reiterations and tremolandi at the outset.

From bar 18, the motion of the underlying harmonic argument becomes more complex: the outbursts between melodic ideas are embellished and extended. Between these outbursts, the melodic material continues to explore contrasting emotional characters. A tight-knit two-part invention on the lyrical motif initiates the section; this rapidly dissolves into tremolandi and then reappears, transformed by harmonics into a tiny clockwork figure (bars 21–2). Repeated pizzicato notes in registral extremes form the basis of the next idea; these suddenly become irregular and dwindle away, as if a metronome had suddenly run down. Triplet rhythms in the chords that follow are echoed by the melodic instruments for the next idea. There is then a spectral *sul ponticello* figure for the whole quartet, reminiscent of the cloud-like textures within the Second and Third Quartets. The four instruments converge in a dense cluster around middle C, before opening up in bar 36 into a soft and slowly moving chord progression rich in whole-tone formulations, an extension of whole-tone fragments in the melodic material and the major sixths of the chords.

From bar 42, the chords harmonize an unfolding melodic line of falling semitones and rising major thirds that is eventually taken over by the first violin alone. This flowers into a cadenza, the early placing of which was an idea 'lifted from Elliott Carter's First Quartet',[17] that develops some of the lyrical material of the movement. Wood's friendship with the members of the Chilingirian Quartet, and the desire to highlight their individual strengths, is doubtless also behind his decision. The cadenza allows the spotlight to fall dramatically onto the first violin, which had spent much of the *Introduzione* in an accompanying role to the second violin and viola; the cello must wait until the third movement before it is given a prominent solo role.

The *Introduzione* differs markedly from its precedents in Wood's output. Unlike the First Quartet and Symphony, there is no recapitulation or repetition of material, save for the continued presence of the framing chords. There are some similarities with the harmonic progression that structures the Chamber Concerto (see Example 2.7a, p. 45), but the most striking resemblance is to the opening of the Second Quartet, for both quartets present a series of ideas that are left undeveloped, ripe for treatment

---

[17]   Composer's note to the score.

that is more expansive later in the piece. In this way, the *Introduzione* to the Fourth Quartet presents a fascinating hybrid of the long-range planning associated with the use of an introductory first-movement model with the bloc-working expounded elsewhere in Wood's output.

The violin cadenza closes with a series of upbeat gestures to a high-pitched rising line; the Scherzo follows *attacca* once the peak of the line has been reached. There are obvious similarities with the First Quartet, Chamber Concerto and Symphony, in which the first two movements were played without a break. In each of these cases, the join heightens the introductory nature of the first movement, in contrast to the discrete movements of works such as the Piano and Horn Trios: the parallel is with the link between slow introductions and the material that follows in Classical and Romantic symphonies.[18]

Much of the material of the Scherzo is concentrated in the treble register: only rarely does the cello venture into the bass in order to initiate swiftly rising arpeggios in thirds. The movement opens with *sul ponticello* ostinati scurrying in the violins and viola that create a harmonically static yet texturally unstable chromatic cluster (Example 8.3). Against this, the cello announces the first idea, a variant on the 'Sword' motif from the Violin Concerto (see Chapter 6, pp. 129–30). Placed high in its register, the cello provides an intense counterbalance to the spectral whisperings in the other instruments to create a nightmarish melange.

The imitative counterpoint of bar 18 in the first movement is used as the basis of a short contrasting section, yet the accompaniment, sustained harmonics in the first violin and viola, refuses to ground the material with a harmonic bass: all remains airy and insubstantial. The reprise of Example 8.3 is transformed into an intense contrapuntal dialogue based on the 'sword' motif, no longer accompanied by the nocturnal shimmer of the chromatic cluster. Instead, the cluster is displaced to bar 27: beginning in the cello, the pattern of alternating major thirds and falling semitones that was part of the contrasting section builds up through the quartet to create a dense and highly chromatic texture. Yet as swiftly as it appears, the texture dissipates, leaving behind (from bar 32) ostinati based on chromatic clusters in the extreme bass and treble registers, *ppp*. The change of texture provides a dramatic point of articulation, though what follows was not intended as a discrete formal unit in the manner of a Trio,[19] for it continues to draw on material from the primary 'Scherzo' section.

Whereas the ostinati at the outset of the movement were made more dynamic by virtue of crescendi, the beginning of the second section is motionless. The wide space between treble and bass creates the expectation of it being filled. Into this gap comes a fanfare figure from the viola, the upper line a further version of the falling semitone/rising major third, harmonized in perfect fifths and major thirds. It is answered by a bustling line in the second violin that also recalls a distorted trumpet call. This second idea is subject to a certain amount of development with

---

[18]   The *attacca* between movements in the Violin Concerto, and the recapitulation of material in the Finale, makes this a special case. It is at once a multi-movement form like the Piano Concerto and a single-movement sonata form like the Cello Concerto: all of which can be considered a most Schoenbergian aspiration.

[19]   Composer's note to the score.

Example 8.3   String Quartet No. 4/ii, bars 1–4

imitative counterpoint between viola and first violin in bars 38–40, and it is inverted in bar 43. The fanfare is presented four times in total, and is extended on the second and fourth occurrences. On each appearance, it is to be played *lontano* (distantly); one is reminded of the ghostly processions that haunt the Elegia of the Symphony, never able to dispel the sense of menace that surrounds them.

There is a brief reminiscence of the contrasting idea of the Scherzo (bars 50–52) before the texture rapidly thickens in the manner of the transition to the second section. A pizzicato chord, *subito piano*, announces the reprise of the fanfare figure, now accompanied by insistent pizzicato (compare with bars 23–5 of the *Introduzione*) and increasingly prominent. The pizzicato erupts into a ferocious swarm of arpeggios in all the instruments, based around augmented triads but sufficiently dense to create chromatic saturation (bars 65–8). There is then a further recollection of the contrasting idea from the Scherzo, which mutates into the mechanical ostinato of the first movement, bars 21–2. Against this, second violin and viola (and later first violin and cello) have a two-part counterpoint based on slowly descending chromatic lines, the high register and tremolandi imparting a sickly surrealism to the proceedings.

The reprise of Example 8.3 begins in bar 85 with a return of the scurrying *sul ponticello* figures. These climb upwards to settle once more in the treble register, against which the cello reinitiates the first idea. The contrasting idea, which made two appearances in the second section, does not recur in the recapitulation. The final nineteen bars are a deathly hush based on the material of the second section: the fanfares return, *lontano*. Fragments of the pizzicato figure from bars 65–8 return, now drained of their ferocity but nevertheless macabre, before the movement chokes to a close.

The extreme instability of the Scherzo, typified by its unnatural string colours, its stratified textures and its relentless drive, is balanced by an extended and weighty Adagio. The movement opens with profoundly calm polyphony, the upper voices interweaving unhurried lyrical lines over a slow-moving sustained bass line in the cello. Unlike the strained harmonies and sinewy textures of the Scherzo, the Adagio is rich and warm, the upper lines at first concentrated in the tenor registers over the sonorous bass before overlapping lines carry the music upwards. A closing passage, beginning in bar 16, suggests a serenade, with strummed pizzicato chords in the viola and softly repeated notes in the second violin.

The harmonic language is rich in tonal allusions, enabled by a bass line that moves in descending semitones or rising tritones. The numerous sevenths above this bass are characteristic for Wood, but the chords are given a bitter-sweet flavour by virtue of chromatic decoration that gives simultaneous major and minor thirds to the chords (see for instance the start of Example 8.4 which recapitulates the opening of the movement). The result is one of searing intensity; coming after the Scherzo, it is profoundly moving.

A ticking pizzicato figure in the violin begins the second section (bar 26). This is swiftly transformed into an accompaniment to a lyrical solo for cello, the character of both theme and accompaniment reminiscent of the funeral march of Op. 33. The upper instruments combine contrapuntally with the cello to bring the section to a climax; as this recedes, the melodic line is transferred to the viola. Eventually, the viola is left unaccompanied, with sighing figures reminiscent of the first section.

A violent contrast occurs with the return of the opening chords of the work in bar 65, here in dialogue with similar chords in the inner voices. There is a second outburst, now homophonic but with more insistent rhythmic figures, in bars 76–9. The disruption to the eloquent unfolding of melodic material in the movement is short-lived, however, and the lyrical impulse is soon reasserted. This is firstly achieved with an extended and radiant reworking of the opening melodic line (given to the cello) that bears the traces of the textures and material of the second section. There then follows a tranquil coda which follows the character and textures of the opening far more closely, until successive overlapping motivic fragments (beginning in bar 132) cause the upper line to ascend into the ether (Example 8.4).

Nevertheless, for all of this rich outpouring of melody, the spectre of the chords at the centre of the Adagio remains. This is taken up and developed in the Finale, which begins with a reprise of the chords, complete with imitation in the inner voice. Subsequent material develops the lyrical idea from bars 8–9 of the *Introduzione*, accompanied by quicksilver arpeggios. Denser, gruffer imitative writing breaks up this material and provides contrast.

Example 8.4   String Quartet No. 4 Op. 34/iii, bars 129–46

The middle section is organized around a slowly moving bass line in the cello, above which polyphonic lines in the upper instruments recall the intensity and textures of the slow movement. Similar, too, is the fact that although the material draws on motivic and intervallic properties of the *Introduzione*, it does not directly recall any of the ideas presented there: the spaciousness of this section is unsuited for the brief melodic ideas of the first movement.

Example 8.5 is a summary of the bass motion in the middle section; the upper lines reveals a sequential pattern in the upper voice. The motion between G and D♭ in the bass (and also in the treble, bars 61–3) belongs to a large-scale harmonic argument that, as with the Symphony, is revealed most clearly at important structural and thematic junctures throughout the work. The first hint of this argument, unsurprisingly, occurred with the opening chords (see Example 2.7b); here, the upper voice moved through an octave from G to G, and the bass ascended from C to C. The perfect fifth C–G initiated the *lontato* fanfare figure in the Scherzo; on its repetition the fanfare was presented against driving pizzicati on first G and then D♭. Traces of C, D♭ and G as focal pitches permeate the Adagio, but are most prominent in the coda to the movement (Example 8.4). Here, the harmonic centre of the passage is C, approached first by semitone step (bars 129–30) and then by fifth (bars 143–4); the stable fifths with which the Adagio ends are can be heard as a development of the fifths within the fanfare in the Scherzo. In Example 8.4, the prominence of G and D♭ in the bass has the quality of a dominant pedal.[20] This temporarily comes to rest on a C with the recapitulation of the first section (bar 109), but more conclusively at the end of the recapitulation (via a D♭) in bar 139.

Example 8.5   String Quartet No. 4 Op. 34/iv, summary of bass line, bars 51–106

The Coda that follows opens with the fanfare figure; this is answered by exhilarating flurries of semiquavers. The semiquavers continue in the passage that follows, a chorale based on the violin cadenza that closed the *Introduzione*. The chorale is unlike the Stravinskian close to the Chamber Concerto, or the Lutheran majesty of *Funeral Music*; rather, the flowing semiquavers and, later, extended trills, suggest the ebullience of the Third String Quartet and the Symphony. At the height of the chorale, the fanfare interjects again, its continuation transformed into a further reworking of the opening chords of the work. Then, finally, the minor sixths of these chords contract into the perfect fifths that had become increasingly important over

---

[20]   Recall how the expositions of the String Quartet in B♭ and Cello Concerto treat tritone poles as equivalent (see in particular Chapter 3, pp. 64–5).

the course of the four movements, and which dominate the closing passage. The final cadence, a black-note chord built on D♭, leading ultimately to a white-note chord on C, ends the work with a luminous blaze of colour that provides an exciting and satisfying conclusion to the expressive, harmonic, and intervallic arguments that span the quartet.

The breadth of the Fourth Quartet's conception, its emotional range and the technical means by which these were achieved, marks it as one of Wood's most significant works. Not least amongst the piece's considerable merits is its mastery of the string quartet idiom, developed in Wood's earlier essays in this genre, but here raised to new heights. With it, Wood's ongoing cycle of quartets must be counted as one of the foremost in twentieth-century British music.

Vocal Music

Two sets of songs were collated in the first half of the 1990s: the fourth collection of Graves songs Op. 36 (see Chapter 7, pp. 155 and 158–9) and a second set of Songs, Op. 37. There was also a return to the ongoing D.H. Lawrence collection with the composition of 'River Roses' in 1994; a fifth Lawrence song was added in 2001 (see Chapter 6, pp. 118–19). An anthem for unaccompanied choir, *The Kingdom of God*, was composed in 1994 in response to a commission from the City of London Festival; it was premiered by the St Paul's Cathedral Choir for whom it was written.

Songs Op. 37

Songs Op. 37 (1984–93), as with the earlier Op. 25 collection, draws together settings composed over a number of years. The theme of love, and particularly that of seizing the moment provides a connective thread through the collection, as does Wood's characteristic use of instrumental archetypes in the ordering of the movements: the second and third songs are slow and scherzo-like respectively.

With Edmund Waller's 'Goe Lovely Rose', Wood set the poetry of the seventeenth century for the first time since *Scenes from Comus*. As with Wood's interpretation of *Comus*, the emphasis is on the sensual elements of Waller's poem. In Wood's setting, Waller's elegant coaxing of an object of desire to 'suffer herself to be desired' is given a light and fragmentary accompaniment, which flowers warmly and passionately only as the lyrics move from the 'lovely Rose' to the lady herself. In this way, the mannered, gallant and understated language that Waller uses to constrain and suppress the erotic sentiments is made to speak anew; the physical implications of the moral to make the most of oneself before death are conveyed clearly.

Wood's setting of 'White Heliotrope' marries Arthur Symons's poem with a musical language that in its heady sensualism recalls Messiaen. The vast majority of the song's rich harmonies are built from the superimposition of two triads (mostly major, minor or augmented). These are combined with a persistent rhythmic figure of three quavers leading to a minim that can be found in all but seven of the fifty-six bars. The result is languidly obsessive, complementing wonderfully the late-Victorian decadence of Symons's text.

'Blue Girls' (John Crowe Ransom) is, like 'Goe Lovely Rose', about the transience of beauty. Wood's buoyant setting captures the playfulness of the schoolgirls of the title, embodied by the soaring G major melody of the opening (with sharpened fourth that is typical of Wood's tonal writing) and driving arpeggios in the accompaniment.

The final song of the collection is Pablo Neruda's 'Amor', in Alastair Reid's translation.[21] Formally, Wood sets it as a recurring refrain separated by varied episodes. The refrain is characterized by a passionate vocal line accompanied by arpeggiated chords rich in fourths, reminiscent of a guitar. These fourths permeate the harmony of the episodes, be it in dark low-pitched rumblings in the bass of the piano, or sonorous chords in fourths reordered to emphasize a minor seventh in the bass (for example, E♭–D♭–A♭). In this way, the fourths unify the otherwise contrasting sections of the song.

The Kingdom of God Op. 38

The text of Francis Thompson's 'The Kingdom of God' is in some ways a mystical complement to the secular concerns of the Songs Op. 37, though no connection was intended. The poem belongs to late-Victorian traditions that sought to locate Christ in the present day:[22] James Ensor's painting *Christ's Entry into Brussels* (1889) depicts Christ as a visionary largely ignored by the throngs of modern society. In Thompson's submission, our 'estrangèd faces ... miss the many-splendoured thing'; one is encouraged to attend to the present and the miracles that one finds all around: 'And lo, Christ walking on the water / Not of Gennesareth, but Thames'.

From the opening bars of Wood's setting, the sense of wide-eyed wonder of the text is conveyed by means of overlapping triads that mimic and intensify the sound of a choir in a resonant building such as St Paul's Cathedral (Example 8.6). The immediate inspiration for this device was Holst's *The Hymn of Jesus*, but one can find also continuity with Wood's habit of constructing harmonies from superimposed triads. At the beginning of the work, many of these chords are white-note, with chords that are predominantly black-note colouring verbs such as 'view', 'touch' and 'know'. As the texture thickens (around the word 'inapprehensible'), a greater number of triads are brought into play, and the distinction between white-and black-note harmonies lessens; one becomes more aware instead of the focal role of chords that are derived from the notes of the G major scale (often with sharpened fourth).

From bar 30, the slow massed chords give way to lithe melodic figures that arpeggiate through a triad plus a perfect fifth; these set images of the natural world ('does the fish soar'; 'the eagle plunges'). Given at first to a quartet of solo voices, these lines are treated imitatively. Contrast of harmonic colour comes in later presentations involving fuller choral textures by the juxtaposition of white-note and black-note material. The climax of the section is with the setting of 'many-

---

[21]   Pablo Neruda, *Extravagaria* trans. Alastair Reid (Jonathan Cape Ltd., 1972).

[22]   There are parallels here with the late-Medieval and Renaissance habit of painting Crucifixions in contemporary dress.

Example 8.6   *The Kingdom of God* Op. 38, bars 1–10

splendoured things' in which the sliding chords of the first section are transformed into fast-moving melismas. To Thompson's account of modern life's blindness to the mystical, Wood adds fragments of the opening chords of the work, which function in the manner of a ritornello that reminds us that the mystical remains a 'world invisible'.

The final section, beginning in bar 67 with the words 'But (when so sad thou canst not sadder)', offers the consolation that the mystical world can be experienced through our encounters with tangible things. There is a return to the G major of the opening section; greater emphasis on the sharpened fourth C♯ enables passages focused on D to function in the manner of a dominant. Reference in the text to Jacob's Ladder ('pitched betwixt Heav'n and Charing Cross') motivates rising scales, often in thirds. In bar 86 there is a passionate reworking of the material from bar 67 to the words 'Yea in the night, my Soul, my daughter'. From here, the top sopranos' line remains on a D for some eighteen bars, rising up through a triad only at the very end of the work to reach top A for the final chord, a complete diatonic collection in G major.

The sumptuous choral textures and sonorous triadic writing of *The Kingdom of God* are only in part responses to the acoustics of St Paul's Cathedral. The nature of the musical material reflects a growing trend in Wood's vocal music to turn away from the angular melodic contours and terse harmonies of, say, *To a Friend Whose Work has Come to Nothing*, or, 'A Last Poem' (Example 2.2, p. 27). Some of the effect of such works comes from the writing that is *against* the voice, which creates palpable effort and tension from the singer(s) in order for them to negotiate awkward registers and wide leaps. In *The Kingdom of God*, which is by no means easy to achieve in performance, the vocal writing nevertheless employs a greater number of smaller intervals in more grateful registers, a characteristic that becomes increasingly the norm in Wood's later works for voice. The emphasis is thus thrown back onto the melody and to the line, and in this we find parallels with the mellifluous writing of instrumental works such as *Poem*.

Orchestral Music II

Variations for Orchestra Op. 39

The Variations for Orchestra was written for the BBC Symphony Orchestra. Impetus came from Wood's familiarity with and affection for the performers, for whom he wrote a sort of mini-Concerto for Orchestra. This is readily apparent in the continual reshuffling and highlighting of different groups and sections within the orchestra over the course of the work.[23] The juggling of the orchestral resources in this manner, coupled with the fact that strings do not become prominent until the last two variations points to the influence of Stravinsky. Indeed, the spirit of Stravinsky's late works in particular hovers over Wood's Variations, not least in the two fugato variations (five and seven). Of these, the latter is subtitled 'Hommage I.S.', and is an affectionate

---

[23]   There are significant parallels between the use of the orchestra in the Variations Op. 39 and that of the ensemble in the Chamber Concerto.

allusion to the fugal writing in Stravinsky's *Agon*.[24] References such as these (and others not discussed) provide clues to the general character of the work, which must be counted as one of Wood's most neo-classical scores in recent years.

The work consists of an original theme and ten variations, framed by an Introduction and Fugue. The theme falls into two distinct halves, the first of which is presented by the oboe and cor anglais, with counter melodies in the wind and horns. The first half of the theme is given in Example 8.7; it can be seen that a twelve-note trope of three tetrachords governs both theme and accompaniment. Indeed, the Variations constitute one of Wood's most concentrated uses of a twelve-note trope in many years; there are similarities, therefore, with the variations of the Op. 3 Trio.

Though the organization of pitch material is redolent of Wood's earliest works, the play of expressive states and characters that are fashioned from this material bespeaks an older, wiser and more experienced composer. The ten variations are, in general, short and fast, in which the motivic and tetrachordal components of the theme are subject to constant permutation, fragmentation and the interlockings. In the first variation ('Più mosso'), the opening six bars thus preserve the pacing of events (in the wind, one tetrachord cell every two bars), but ordering of pitches and most crucially, their musical character, differs. The switch from 2/2 to 8/8 (often 3+3+2/8) transforms the drooping melancholy of the theme into something more dance-like. The same restless spirit imbues the scurrying *sul ponticello* figure passed between string sections and, later in the variation, the ebullient rhythms of the brass. The result belongs to the series of orchestral scherzi initiated by the dances of *Scenes from Comus* Op. 6, here in one of Wood's nocturnal formulations.

The accumulated rhythmic tension of the first variation is partly dissipated by the second ('Feroce'), which functions as a downbeat to the first's extended upbeat. Here, phrases built from precipitous eight-note figures alternate with melodic dyads (displaced as ninths or sevenths) that preface abrasive chords. The diversity of material is reflected in the varied means of its derivation. Thus the eight-note figures are constructed from the interlocking of two tetrachords, the linear dyads are derived from the permutation of each tetrachordal cell into two pairs of whole-tones, and the chords are vertical arrangements of the tetrachords. But the listener is probably going to be unaware of such technical details. Instead, their focus will be the carefully delineated contour of the eight-note figure that ensures comprehensibility amid the considerable violence of the writing. The resulting intensity, both technically and emotionally, is characteristic of the work as a whole.

The third variation ('minaccioso') draws on march topics for sinister and threatening effect; strings and percussion provide harmonic support in martial rhythms, punctuated by fluid wind arpeggios, over which the brass intone a variation of the theme in largely dotted rhythms. As with the first two variations, the third is linked *attacca* into the fourth. The longest variation to this point, the fourth begins as a *molto più mosso* intensification of the preceding thematic material, with a transformation of the brass theme into 12/8. Chorale-like harmonizations of four-note chromatic figures related to the tetrachords provide contrast (specifically, the

---

[24] This is Wood's second explicit homage to Stravinsky involving contrapuntal procedures, the first being his 1971 memorial in *Tempo* (see Chapter 5, p. 112).

Example 8.7   Variations for Orchestra Op. 39, bars 22–7

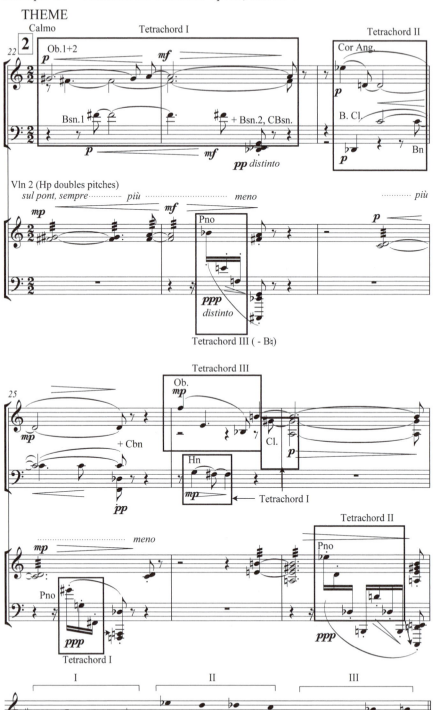

contour of the figure is the retrograde of Example 8.7, tetrachord I). Unlike variations one to three, the fourth ends quietly, bringing the opening group of variations to a close.

A broad fugato for brass provides textural contrast in the fifth variation, expanding out from the middle registers of trombone and horn to a sonorous climax. One of the properties of the twelve-note trope, namely that the first two tetrachords are tritone transpositions of each other and the third cell is replicated at the tritone, is exploited so that the fugal answer, presented at the tritone, ensures chromatic and motivic saturation. The restricted orchestration and leaner textures of the variation distinguish it from the variations that surround it, so that it functions as a buoyant interlude providing a clear point of articulation within the passage of the work as a whole.

Variation six continues and intensifies the rhythmic impetus of the brass fugato, playfully juxtaposing repeated chords (built from the tetrachordal cells) in groups of four staccato semiquavers with more lithe passages in which the semiquavers are grouped in threes and twos. These juxtapositions recall, in a much more lively and direct manner, the differing metrical organizations of the theme and first variation. The fleeting scherzo mood is interrupted two bars before the end by an enigmatic passage, marked *lontano*, in which the repeated semiquavers are followed by a sustained note, before being brusquely cut off by a *sffz* chord.

The mystery of this ending is not immediately explained by the opening of the seventh variation. The subject of the opening three-part fugato (violas, second violins, cellos) is once again twelve-note, constructed from (at first) the three tetrachords. Unlike variation five, the successive entries are not positioned at the tritone, but rather at successive downward transpositions of a tone. Complementing this descent is a carefully controlled linear ascent in the second violin. The fugato is abruptly cut off by chordal fanfares that recall (and therefore reveal to be pre-echoes) the last two bars of variation six. The fanfare is used to frame and divide two lyrical (and imitative) wind episodes that look ahead to variation eight. But one is not allowed to dwell on these episodes, for the fugato returns in five parts and inverted, as an extended close to the seventh variation. Once again, a fanfare is used to interrupt a climax; here, it also serves to end the variation. Nevertheless, by following it with the tiny variation eight, eight bars of fugitive arpeggios orchestrated for wind and cymbals alone, there is an allusion to the central section of variation VII. The result is a blurring of the boundaries between variations: all is transitory, in flux.

The formal instability and uncertainty of variations six to eight prepare by way of contrast the expansive lyricism of variations nine and ten. Characterized by their generosity of spirit as well as their duration, these final two variations together constitute the emotional core of the work. The harmony of both of these variations makes frequent use of sonorities based on seventh chords, which, coupled with the predominant string tone, signifies a change of mood. Of particular note is the tune for the cellos that forms the tenth variation, in which Wood's romantic impulse is finally, unreservedly, unleashed.[25]

---

[25]   The solo for the cello section reflects Wood's admiration for the cellists of the BBC Symphony Orchestra. Yet the cello has long been an instrument for which Wood writes

The fugue follows straight on from the final variation, with the scoring at first continuing to emphasize the strings; wind and brass add weight to entries. The opening subject demonstrates the rhythmic suppleness of much of Wood's writing, the inherent energy of the lines coming from a further permutation of the tetrachords, making use of wide expressive leaps that marks Wood at his most insistent (Example 3.2d, p. 55). In total, there are four complete entries of the fugue subject, each transposed to begin on a note of a diminished seventh chord (the entries are, in turn, on G♯, D, B and F), followed by a short 'codetta' focusing on the original transposition and then at the tritone. After this 'exposition', there follows a sort of jazzy brass chorale, superimposed over further fugal entries (on F, G♯ and D) in the strings. These entries are now restricted to the first six notes of the subject, and, indeed, the full fugal theme does not recur in the work. However, motivic fragments from both subject and counter-subject continue to be heard and elaborated in free counterpoint, or, following the brass chorale, in pre-cadential wind and brass gestures that precede the coda. The coda draws together the various gestures of the fugue, and ends with a reference to the opening flourish of the Introduction.

By ending the Variations with material from the opening, Wood makes use of a formal device that appears in much of his music. On a larger scale, the various groupings that emerge in Op. 39, such as the macrorhythmic 'upbeat' and 'downbeat' effect within the first four variations, the interpenetrations of the middle variations and the shared emotional world of the final variations, suggest innovative solutions to formal problems that go beyond, but are intimately concerned with, surface events. Such compositional responses are reflections of Wood's enduring concern of balancing the demands of local detail within the global architecture of a work, a concern that typically results, as here, in coherent end-weighted structures that are both intellectually and emotionally satisfying.

---

sympathetically for, with the Cello Concerto and the long cello melody in the Adagio of the Fourth String Quartet being but two of the many prominent examples.

Chapter 9

Recent Years

The Cheltenham Festival provided for Wood a number of important premieres at the start of his career: the String Quartet in B♭, String Quartet No. 1 and the Quintet all received their first performances under the Festival's auspices. In the late 1990s, under the directorship of the composer Michael Berkeley, the Festival was the location of two further premieres: the Clarinet Trio (1997) and Serenade and Elegy (1999), a Festival commission. Other pieces by Wood have been performed at Cheltenham over the years, including all of the String Quartets: a Fifth (2001) was performed there in 2002. For Berkeley's retirement from the Festival (2004), Wood wrote a short tribute for solo viola 'in memory of (and with thanks for) many happy occasions at Cheltenham'.

Berkeley's departure was not the only one commemorated by Wood's music in this period. *This is the Record of John* (2001) and the Erich Fried Songs (2000–2001) were written respectively for the Reverend Prebendary John Slater and Alexander Goehr, the latter a belated retirement gift: both Wood and Goehr left Cambridge in 1999. Familiar festivals and friends provide the impetus for other works of the period. *Cantilena and Fugue* for trumpet and organ (2004), like *The Kingdom of God* before it, was premiered at the City of London Festival. The aforementioned Fifth String Quartet was written for the Lindsay Quartet; after the Lindsays retired in 2005, their leader, Peter Cropper, commissioned Wood's *Overture* for the newly formed Cropper–Welsh–Roscoe Piano Trio.

Since Wood's retirement, there have been two events offering mini-retrospectives of his work: an early celebration of his seventieth birthday at the Royal College of Music (7 March 2002) and two study days at Lancaster University (29–30 April 2002). The poet Geoffrey Hill delivered a more substantial birthday tribute in the form of a book of poems, *Scenes from Comus*, which took its title from Wood's Op. 6 and is dedicated to the composer.[1] The two men have been friends for many years and are exact contemporaries: for the poet's seventieth birthday Wood wrote a vocal-instrumental setting of Hill's *Tenebrae* (Op. 46). In July 2006 Wood was awarded an honorary doctorate from Liverpool University in recognition of his contribution to music and, during his tenure at the University in the early 1970s, to the city of Liverpool.

Wood's music has ever been concerned with human relationships and his recent compositions, a succession of works written for or dedicated to friends and family, reflects this. Above all, however, is Wood's commitment to love, and in his

---

[1]   Geoffrey Hill, *Scenes from Comus* (London, 2005). The first twenty of these poems were published, along with a short article by Martin Anderson about Wood, in *The Stand* 172 Vol. 3(4) & 4(1) (2002): 3–23 and 25–6.

magisterial *Wild Cyclamen* (2005–6), his first BBC commission in nearly a decade, he once again explores this theme through Graves's words.

Instrumental Music

Although Wood has not consciously pursued a 'late style' (see Chapter 2, p. 23) in which there is a deliberate change in technique or aesthetic, one can nevertheless detect in his recent music certain shared characteristics that might constitute, if not a late style, then certainly a 'late sensibility'. These characteristics include, but are not limited to, a paring-down of material; the increased use of recognizable pitch formulations in both melody and harmony (such as augmented triads and white-note material); a generally autumnal sound world; a greater emphasis on melodicism; and nocturnal rather than dancing scherzi. It is impossible to pinpoint precisely when this sensibility emerges in Wood's oeuvre, for all of these qualities can be detected to varying degrees in numerous pieces in the preceding decades, yet it is also true that the works considered in this chapter manifest the above characteristics consistently in a manner that his earlier music does not. Perhaps it is most accurate to say that in Wood's later music one can hear most clearly echoes of Brahms, a composer with whom he has identified increasingly.[2]

Clarinet Trio Op. 40

The Clarinet Trio Op. 40 was commissioned by the Trio Gemelli, who gave the first performance at the Cheltenham Festival in July 1997.[3] Wood notes in the score that the opening movement 'concentrates on the members of the trio as solo instrumentalists'.[4] In addition to the character of the material, the players seem to have inspired the character of the material; for the Clarinet Trio, this can be said too for the musical procedures and structures that shape the movement. Although the nature of the extended canonic writing, internal symmetries and interaction between the two melody instruments is firmly rooted within Wood's style, the particularly

---

[2]   Wood's 1970 article on Beethoven and his later 1999 'A Photograph of Brahms' make for interesting comparison in this light, for both argue in similar terms for the continued relevance of the composer in the light of contemporary reactions to tradition. Yet the qualities of each composer that Wood focuses on demonstrates the degree to which Wood's own artistic priorities change in the intervening years. With Beethoven, Wood admired with 'his mastery of the full statement' and the heroic way by which Beethoven reminded Wood of the 'marvellous things human beings can do' (p. 328). At the turn of the millennium, Wood's responses were directed to the 'quality of seriousness – springing, in Brahms's case, from acute personal misery' (p. 270). Of Brahms's First Piano Concerto, Wood asked 'what music could better give a sense of the melancholy with which we wander through the world, dazed and questing, scarcely able to believe in the beautiful and terrible things that we encounter, that sometimes happen to us and that we sometimes make happen?' (p. 286).

[3]   A recording of the Clarinet Trio by the Trio Gemelli has been released on CD (Divine Art 25009).

[4]   Composer's note to the score.

intense manner in which it is realized is mirrored by the fact that the original players (John and Adrian Bradbury) are identical twins.

The first movement opens with a lyrical twelve-note melody in the cello, followed in canon by the clarinet a bar later and a tritone higher (Example 9.1). Wood follows this melody with the first five pitches of its inversion, not for serial purposes, but as a means to generate further motivic relationships. The opening augmented triad – an increasingly common melodic figure in Wood's music – is thus re-ordered in bars 4–5 (to become C–E–G♯), with the climatic G♯–A figure referring back to the same appoggiatura-like motivic shape in bars 2 and 3. A distant D major/minor tonal background is suggested by the first piano chord, and is intensified by the descent to the dominant in the bass (the opening chord returns as the final chord of the movement).

The canonic introduction to the movement is mirrored by a coda. Together, these canonic passages frame the main discourse, which consists of two extended solos, the first for clarinet, the second for cello, each of which is followed by a duet between the two. In the middle of all of this is a section for solo piano. Although Wood's Piano Trio similarly had passages for solo instruments accompanied by piano (see Chapter 7, pp. 162–5 and Example 2.4, p. 30), these solos belonged to a larger scheme in which textures, themes and, above all, characters were in dramatic opposition. In the Clarinet Trio, the emphasis is on lyricism rather than drama; in this respect there are parallels with *Poem* for violin.

The character and construction of the clarinet melody (bars 23–40) can be taken as representative. The melody consists of two broad phrases, accompanied by delicate semiquaver arpeggios in the piano, separated by a very brief middle section that creates a gentle hemiola across the underlying harmonic rhythm. The first phrase is derived (unusually, for Wood) from the retrograde of the twelve-note canon that opens the work, beginning on the sixth note. The head of the melodic line thus becomes a D–C♯ dyad, and these pitches return at the close of the phrase. For the final phrase, Wood uses a transposed inversion of the opening line so that this dyad is reversed, now recalling the cello in bar 2 of Example 9.1; the final cadence is extended to initiate a duet with the cello. Although predicated on serial operations, the aural emphasis of the melodic line is on the leading note–tonic relationship implied by the semitone dyad, providing further allusion to the background 'tonic' D. As ever, Wood is far more concerned with the aural properties of his material and its expressive significance, than with abstract theoretical notions.

Wood describes the middle movement as a scherzo-march. There is certainly a processional element to it, for, within the first couple of pages, five different 'characters of material' swiftly pass by, once again 'to be identified with particular instruments'.[5] A sixth, more lyrical, character is soon added (bar 17). The playful way in which these jostle with one another marks Wood at his most impish: at one point (bar 71), the pianist is instructed to play 'like Chico'![6] Despite the fluid shifting between blocs, not to mention the continued development of the ideas as they pass between instruments, a loose ternary structure can be detected. The middle section

---

[5]   Ibid.

[6]   Chico Marx, that is.

Example 9.1   Clarinet Trio Op. 40/i, bars 1–7

takes the lyrical sixth character as a basis for another canon between cello and clarinet: one wonders again the degree to which the personal qualities of the Trio Gemelli have shaped the work. Whatever the specific impetus might be, the youthful vigour of the writing is recognizably Wood's.

The lively interplay of different characters and general high spirits of the Scherzo is starkly juxtaposed with the slow elegiac mourning of the Finale, which pursues its emotional topic with remarkable intensity. A sonorous passage concentrated in the lower registers of the instruments and rich in (vertical) thirds and fifths opens the movement. These ever-shifting harmonies result from the interaction of polyphonic lines built from short fragments that consist of chromatic clusters; the resulting tension between the melodic chromaticism and warm harmonies is deeply expressive. The subsequent section is projected against the background of a funeral march. As with *Funeral Music* and the Adagio of the Fourth String Quartet, this background is sometimes explicit, such as with the 'funeral drum-beat on the piano' that accompanies two extended solos,[7] first for cello (bar 15), then for clarinet (bar 45). More often, though, it is indirectly alluded to through the use of stark textures and a continued focus on the instruments' lower registers.

A respite is found in a warmer, *cantabile più mosso* section, in which the melodic chromatic clusters open out lyrically. Wood describes this as 'the climax of the movement', but the references to the first movement (amongst others, the prominent use of augmented triads and canonic writing) suggest that it is also the climax of the entire work.[8] Yet the respite is short-lived: the return of the 'drum-beat' signals the start of a drastically compressed recollection of material, in which the extended cello and clarinet solos are stripped down to just three notes each. A longer version of the opening polyphonic passage concludes the movement; against the background of the funeral march, the chromaticism is imbued with a greater sense of loss, concluding one of Wood's most affecting tributes.[9]

Serenade and Elegy Op. 42

The Serenade and Elegy for string quartet and string orchestra (1998–99), written in memory of his daughter Jenny and dedicated to Wood's family, was first performed by the London Mozart Players with the Chilingirian String Quartet – their second Wood premiere in six years. The basic pitch material of the first movement (Serenade), a twelve-note trope, is given in Example 9.2a. At first Wood emphasizes the linear qualities of this material, so that the first eight notes in particular function as a 'motto theme' for the movement as a whole. This motto, which opens the work, is a quotation from Kurtág's *Játékok*, bearing the words 'Virág, virág az ember' ('Flowers we are but flowers'), both words and music pointing to the character of the work as a whole. Wood gives this motto to the solo first violin: the remaining four notes of the chromatic scale (cells E and F) are introduced in the opening notes of a two-part dialogue that follows in the orchestral violins. A second dialogue follows in the lower strings, presenting the motto theme once again, now integrated into the prevailing 6/8 of the serenade.

The motto theme remains recognizable in all of its appearances in the Serenade, though there is greater variety of contrasting material based on the remaining cells. Thus the two orchestral dialogues mentioned above are interrupted by a chord in the solo quartet built from cells E and F, in contrast to their previous linear appearance. A similar thing happens at rehearsal mark 2, when the quartet interrupts with a further twelve-note idea, derived from vertical rearrangements of the original dyads (Example 9.2b). This melody remains dormant for the rest of the movement, to

---

[7] Composer's note to the score.

[8] Ibid.

[9] The Finale was written as a memorial tribute to a friend of the composer who died in 1997.

Example 9.2   Serenade and Elegy Op. 42/i

(a) pitch material

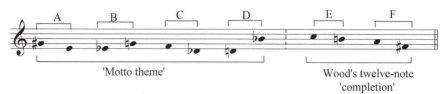

(b) bars 13–23

return in the next in the manner of the Symphony and Piano Concerto. Nevertheless, passages that involve the quartet, juxtaposed with serenade-like ideas in the orchestra, retain the elegiac mood. In this way, the intrusions into the serenade atmosphere cast a shadow over the first movement; a shadow that deepens into the second.

The opening of the Serenade therefore presents fragments of material that are developed in the course of both movements. For the first movement, the most important of these are the two main serenade ideas that derive ultimately from the orchestral two-part dialogues at the start; it is to the orchestra that the first extended section, and climax, is entrusted (rehearsal marks 5–7). The solo quartet emerges from this climax with 'concerto-like' entrances, which lead to a stylized birdsong passage. This passage, and its subsequent return at rehearsal mark 16, frames a central section in which quartet and orchestra, individually and together, develop the serenade themes. The heightened lyrical expression of the central section is accompanied by rich chords derived from triads and seventh chords in Wood's romantic vein. The movement concludes with a compressed section that ends with a recollection of the opening motif; another instance of Wood using pitch and theme to articulate form.

The expansive Elegy that concludes the work is formally and thematically unusual. It consists of three independent sections that are loosely connected by a shared E–D melodic dyad, but more closely, by a shared emotional world.[10] The first of these sections draws on the pitch material of the first movement in order to provide its harmonic resources; the melodic material comes chiefly from the hitherto undeveloped elegiac theme given to the solo quartet in Example 9.2b. After an orchestral introduction, the emphasis is firmly on the string quartet, which at rehearsal mark 2 begins to engage in a series of tightly wrought imitative duet pairings.[11] By rehearsal mark 5, this becomes four-part counterpoint, which alternates with orchestral passages based on six-part chords that derive from free combinations of the cells in Example 9.2a. Underneath increasingly elaborate writing in the quartet, the harmonic argument presented in the orchestra intensifies, reaching the first climax of the movement at rehearsal mark 11. At this point, the E–D dyad first appears, as the top voice in *pesante* complementary chords (the first built from cells A–C, the second D–F). Further repetitions of the E–D dyad are harmonized by increasingly thin and softly scored chords, until only a gently oscillating E–D in the solo violin remains, acting as a transition to the second section.

The second section of the Elegy draws on material first heard in the duet pairing at rehearsal mark 2. This tune, 'very much in slow movement character',[12] as with that of Example 9.2b (with which it has motivic connections), was accompanied originally by chords derived from the cells of Example 9.2a, but in the second section

---

[10] The sequence of intervallically related but otherwise contrasting series of ideas in the *Introduzione* to the Fourth Quartet is the only comparable movement in Wood's output. However, whereas the ideas in the quartet are linked by virtue of the underlying harmonic progression, in the Elegy is expressive character that binds the material together.

[11] There is a further connection with the Fourth Quartet here, which similarly makes extended use of duos within the quartet.

[12] Composer's note to the score.

it receives a new, unrelated harmonization. The shift away from material based on Example 9.2a to something else, though related, carries with it the expectation of the return of this material in some form.

The E–D dyad crucial in the transition between first and second sections returns in the string quartet at the start of the third, a 'virtual transcription' of Pfitzner's setting of Eichendorff's 'Zum Abschied meiner Tochter'. Both the subject of the poem, in which 'a father is bidding farewell to his departing daughter', and its original setting prompted Wood to state that these 'expressed what I wanted so very much better than anything I could write'.[13] To this there is a final heart-rending stroke, in which Wood layers over the transcription recollections of the pitch material, and particularly the motto theme, from the first movement (see, for example, the solo orchestral violin two bars before rehearsal mark 29). Against the C major of Pfitzner's setting, the chromaticism of the motto assumes an achingly poignant bitter-sweet quality, before it is eventually absorbed once again into pure diatonicism. The recall of this material fulfils the 'tonal' expectations established by the second section, and provides coherence across the work as a whole.

By bringing together allusions to the motto theme with the delicate Pfitzner transcription, Wood highlights the different functions of the quotations. Although both have deep personal resonance, Kurtág's motto is used as a means of generating further material, whereas the Pfitzner is used for 'conclusive emotional reference'.[14] As with all of Wood's quotations, they thus serve a direct communicative purpose (comprehensibility, emotion), intensifying and casting new light on the existing musical and emotional argument provided by Wood's own music.

String Quartet No. 5 Op. 45

Wood's Fifth String Quartet was commissioned by Yorkshire ArtSpace and Music in the Round to celebrate the opening of a purpose-built visual artist's studio named 'Persistence Works': a name which could well be a motto for Wood's approach to composition. It was first performed in October 2001 by its dedicatees, the Lindsay Quartet. With Bartók's Fourth Quartet as an obvious model, Wood's quartet is in five movements, arranged symmetrically around the slow movement, a *Romanza*. Two *Nocturne-Scherzi* are placed either side of the *Romanze*. Of the outer movements, the first corresponds to a sonata-allegro, the last to a rondo: these are roughly equal in weight, and give greater emphasis to the symmetrical construction of the work.[15]

The first movement of the Fifth Quartet provides a concise example of the sort of synthesis and refinement of technical, aesthetic and expressive aspects of Wood's language that is typical of his later music. The energetic descent through an augmented triad at the beginning of the work (Example 9.3), accompanied by the remaining nine notes of the chromatic scale, demonstrates how a familiar musical object can be made to yield strongly contrasting expressive states: compare with

---

[13]   Ibid.

[14]   Ibid.

[15]   In this, the Fifth Quartet is strikingly dissimilar to the goal-oriented schemes of the First and Fourth Quartets.

Example 9.1, which opens with the same pitches. A series of dramatic chords lead to brief pairings of instruments, accompanied by surging arpeggios: the augmented triad remains a point of harmonic reference throughout.

Example 9.3   String Quartet No. 5 Op. 45/i, bars 1–7

The juxtaposition of contrasting ideas, one visceral and gestural, the other lyrical and contrapuntal, reminds one of the agglutinative forms that typify Wood's Second and Third quartets, and the opening movement of the Fourth. The skeleton of a three-part form can be detected; the final section is a compressed recapitulation in which the lyrical idea is omitted. Evidence of a suppressed (or distorted) sonata background can be detected in the second section, which contains also elements that signify traditional developmental procedures. The first idea thus becomes an energetic fugue; the lyrical idea evolves into a 'new' theme, which is also treated contrapuntally. The tensions between the suppressed background and energetic, dramatic and fragmented foreground contribute to the exhilaration of the movement. It is entirely typical of the composer that the fundamental formal questions that arise – namely, how to generate coherence in a work that is characterized by discontinuity – are dealt with intuitively, rather than through systematic means.

The scherzo-writing of the second and fourth movements must count among Wood's most macabre. For the most part, they present material in hushed whispers, with scurrying lines constructed from chromatic clusters, often in imitation or even canon, and dynamic climaxes that are stifled swiftly. Contributing to the fugitive atmosphere is an evasion of lyricism, coupled with a general avoidance of normal string tone. This latter tendency is particularly marked in the second Scherzo, in which all the material is played either as harmonics (or *flautando*), pizzicato, or *col legno*. The emotional world occupied by these movements is far removed from the high spirits of the Scherzo in the Clarinet Trio, or the barely restrained impulse to dance of the scherzo variations in the Variations for Orchestra. Instead, they have more in common with the scherzi in Wood's Song Cycle to Poems by Pablo Neruda, but rather than evoke the haziness of summer and the hum of the bees (as in the Neruda songs), the quartet movements conjure up something far more sinister and spectral. These are *Nocturnes* in which the moon, if present at all, is closer to *Pierrot Lunaire* than *Clair de lune*.

In naming the central movement *Romanza*, Wood draws our attention to the fact that he has composed a relatively light slow movement, more in the recent tradition of *Poem* than the deep and intense Adagios of works such as the Fourth String Quartet and the Symphony. Such a designation captures the mood of the movement, as well as the nature of the material. The movement can be divided into two 'stanzas', of which the second is a reworking of the first, followed by a brief coda. The two stanzas can each be divided into a further three sections. The first of these sections is introductory. The second consists of a lyrical melody: in the first stanza this is given to violin I (bars 12–20); in the second, a decorated version is given to the cello (bars 55–68). As with the first movement of the Clarinet Trio, tunefulness is the central concern of this section, rather than contrapuntal complexity. It is in the third section of each stanza (respectively, bars 21–42 and 69–79) that the texture becomes more intricate. At the end of the first stanza, contrapuntal working leads to a climax; at the end of the second, it ushers in a warm coda in which violin I dominates once more. By positioning a movement with such a direct manner of communication after the densely organized and suffocating sound world of the first Nocturne-scherzo, the effect is dramatically and affectively powerful.

The material of the *Romanza* is as straightforward as its overall form. Nowhere is this more apparent than in the introductory sections to each stanza. The lyricism and delicacy of the opening of the movement is in no small part due to its *faux-naiveté*. The main materials are deceptively simple: the upper line largely based on descending whole-tone scales, and contrapuntal lower voices that are also whole-tone in origin. There is also a seemingly unsophisticated use of sequence, each of the three phrases being based on successive upward transitions by a tone. Subtleties such as the rhythmic transformation of motifs and the placing and combination of material reveal that the nature of the introduction is that of a calculated artlessness.

The final movement, 'a sort of rondo',[16] opens with a direct reference to the first theme of Example 9.3. But this proves to be playfully misleading, for it is not this theme, but rather a homorhythmic figure in the second violin, that provides the basis not just for the rondo theme, but the first episode too. The inventiveness resulting from the extended focus on a single idea, coupled with the buoyant rhythmic impetus, reminds one of Haydn finales. As is common in Wood's music, the recapitulation of material is compressed, often through elision or juxtaposition of material. The resulting shifting of textures and moods brings the quartet to a lively dramatic close, rather than the weighty solutions offered in many of Wood's previous works.

Cantilena and Fugue Op. 47

The *Cantilena and Fugue* for trumpet and organ (2004) was commissioned by Deborah Calland and premiered by her and the organist William Whitehead at the City of London Festival. The basis of the *Cantilena* is a broad twelve-note theme first announced by unaccompanied trumpet. The theme's leisurely unfolding of an ascent from A to G over nine bars is reminiscent of the opening of *Scenes from Comus* (Example 2.1, p. 25). Both themes, too, are constructed from a series of variations upon a single motivic shape: in the case of the *Cantilena*, this shape consists of a rising major second followed by a leap of a fourth or more.

The climax of the trumpet solo coincides with the entry of the organ. The lower manual of the organ repeats the material given to the trumpet, the pitch-classes transposed down by a tone, each motif positioned in an increasingly low register. The gradual ascent that characterizes the trumpet phrase is thus replaced by a staggered descent that, at its extremes, encompasses nearly three octaves. In the upper manual, staccato descending chords derived initially from a trope of the trumpet line provide contrast. The upper voice of these chords is taken and developed freely as a counter-melody. Continually underpinning this free development, the slower-moving theme in the organ left hand functions almost in the manner of a cantus firmus. The final note of the theme is not given to the organ, but rather is reached by a widely spaced melodic idea in the trumpet that traces out lines that converge on the end of the theme. From here, there is a rhythmically contrasted 'second subject' based on the same pitch material as the opening melody; the organ pedals add a further twelve-note countermelody. Although the emphasis is on the melodic material and motivic concentration rather than colour, the careful selection of organ stops nevertheless articulate clearly the thematic material and structure.

What follows is formally simple, but crucial in determining the character of the music: a mini-development and climax, a varied recapitulation and a final statement of the opening theme, at original pitch, for solo trumpet. This can be understood as a sonatina, a view supported by the generally lyrical character of the material, and by the absence of dramatic oppositions. The initial theme frequently recurs to either provide, or underpin, the musical argument; more often than not the end of one

---

[16]   Composer's note to the score

statement is elided with the start of the next. Such economy makes the *Cantilena* one of Wood's most concentrated works since the Quintet Op. 9. That this concentration should occur in a work of lyric fantasy, whose surface charm belies the rigour of its working, is typical of Wood.

The lyricism of the *Cantilena* stands in contrast to the brashness of the subsequent Fugue. The widespread twelve-note working of the first movement is also notably absent in the latter: after a chromatic three-note incipit, the fugue subject spirals off into strings of ascending fifths and descending fourths.[17] Before the exposition finishes, the theme is presented in regular crotchets that cut across the underlying 6/8. This points to two of the most endearing characteristics of the movement: a cheerful rhythmic vitality and a staunchly non-academic treatment of fugal procedures. The first episode begins with a motif derived from the subject's incipit, and there is a stretto in the middle entries. Two greatly augmented versions of the theme in dotted minims follow, first on the organ pedals (bar 30) and then in bar 32 in the trumpet. After a second episode the subject appears in inversion in another stretto. Suddenly, the fugue is abruptly cut off to make way for a coda, announced by rumbling quavers in the organ pedals and making use of dramatic discourse between sprightly organ chords and driving trumpet arpeggios. The subject appears briefly just before the end, shared between organ and trumpet, by way of closure. Such are the facts, but dry description cannot convey the energy of the movement: this is Wood at his contrapuntal best.

Tribute to Michael Berkeley

The *Tribute to Michael Berkeley* for solo viola (2004) represents Wood at his most romantic and eloquent. It opens with arcing melodic lines that are based on rising whole-tone fragments. A flurry of semiquavers leads into a passionate and lyrical central section which colours the whole-tone material with chromatic auxiliaries. Gradually the emotions subside, signalling a return to the opening material. But before this appears, there is a quotation of the opening three chords of Beethoven's Sonata Op. 81a ("*Das Lebewohl*"). The descending whole-tone melody of this quotation reflects the harmonic language of the work, but, as with the use of Pfitzner in Serenade and Elegy, the quotation provides a convincing emotional climax to the work, bidding fond farewell to Michael Berkeley, whose tenure at the Cheltenham Festival brought about so many performances of Wood's music.

Overture Op. 48

The retirement of the Lindsay Quartet in 2005 marked the end of a long association between the quartet and Wood; the Lindsays had premiered both Wood's Third and Fifth String Quartets. However, Peter Cropper, the indefatigable leader of the Lindsays, commissioned from Wood a work for his next venture, the Cropper–

---

[17]   There are similarities with the fourth-dominated fugal themes of the Horn Trio (Examples 3.2a–c, p. 55).

Welsh–Roscoe Piano Trio. The result was *Overture* Op. 48, which was premiered in the trio's inaugural concert in Shrewsbury's Maidment Hall on 29 September 2005.

As the work's no-nonsense title suggests, Wood's response to the commission was to provide a straightforward concert opener, its cheerful verve reminiscent of Classical overtures. It opens with a series of fanfare-like gestures in the strings, punctuated by sonorous chords and driving semiquaver figuration from the piano. This swiftly gives way to a lyrical duet between violin and cello, the piano now supplying the accompaniment. An extended middle section begins with just violin and cello, and ends with piano alone. The fanfares return twice more, at first spectrally, to announce the start of an altered recapitulation, and then again at the outset of a vigorous coda (see also Chapter 3, pp. 58–9).

The contrasting characters within the *Overture* are familiar topics in Wood's music; so too is the nature of their material. The opening fanfare, for instance, is derived from a four-note cell of rising whole-tones from G.[18] Accompanying the fanfare is a chord in the piano that consists of another whole-tone tetrachord, this time beginning on B♭. Both of these tetrachord cells, along with a third that is their complement, are treated as a twelve-note trope that, in various combinations, permutations and vertical arrangements, underpin much of the musical development. The lyrical material is contrasted from the fanfares in both character and harmonic language. Rising major thirds and falling semitones once again imbue the material with an octatonic flavour, though whole-tone material is never far from the musical surface.

In many ways the *Overture* is a review and reworking of certain stylistic and technical characteristics of Wood's. In a musical climate in which there remains an obsession with the new and with originality, such an observation can be a damning indictment of the work. But if one were to look beyond superficial appraisals of what the work is, and focus instead on what the work *does*, the *Overture* strikes one as a sparkling and energetic work that nevertheless, by virtue of its detailed working, possesses seriousness and gravitas.

Vocal Music

As with Wood's instrumental music of recent years, his vocal music is also suggestive of a late sensibility. The concern for writing for rather than against the voice noted with *The Kingdom of God*, and the preference for lyrical meditation over expressionistic drama, is pronounced in all of the works considered here. Some of these pieces return to familiar poets, as with the D.H. Lawrence and Robert Graves songs, but there are some novelties too: settings of Erich Fried in the original German, and a turn to Biblical texts for the choral *This is the Record of John*.[19] A set of Greek Songs begun in 1993 (originally Op. 41) were eventually re-conceived and re-written as *The Isles of Greece* Op. 52 (2007): the songs are representative of Wood's enduring passion for the country. Wood's setting of Geoffrey Hill's *Tenebrae* for chorus and

---

[18]   There are similarities here with the whole-tone trumpet-calls of 'The Rider Victory'.

[19]   An unpublished choral setting of 'Rise up, my Love' from the Song of Solomon dates from 1957 (see Chapter 1, p. 9).

orchestra (Op. 46, 2002–03) was given its first performance in 2007. Unpublished songs from this period include settings of Thomas Hardy and Jacques Prévert, which may well appear in collections in later years.

D.H. Lawrence Songs Op. 14: 'River Roses', 'Roses at the Breakfast Table'

Thirty-five years separate the start and completion of the collection of D.H. Lawrence songs (see Table 6.1, p. 119). The vibrant settings of the 1970s convey the experiences of love at the height of passion, both vivid and extreme (see Chapter 6, pp. 118–19). With the songs added later, the first flush of love has given way to a calm intensity.

The opening bars of 'River Roses' (1994), for instance, are in a radiant G mixolydian (that is, using only white notes); the melodic motion, delicately echoed in the accompaniment, is largely by step or small leaps. The harmony, rich in minor sevenths, ninths and thirteenths, remains rooted on G, which suggests spaciousness and tranquillity, but not inertia: warmly expressive descending whole-tone appoggiaturas generate motion. The appoggiatura motif permeates the song, linking the diatonicism of the opening to contrasting passages that employ whole-tone clusters. Unlike Wood's earlier music in which motivic saturation of this nature had an obsessive quality (for instance, 'The Foreboding' or the Cello Concerto), in 'River Roses' it has the quality of rapt meditation. This can be felt in, for example, the way in which the harmony melts into A♭ major (with sharpened fourth) and back in bars 16–21. Yet by the end of the song, the whole-tone clusters (that first appeared in bar 12 to the word 'marsh') become increasingly prominent, clouding, but not overwhelming, the intense nostalgia of the song.

'Roses on the Breakfast Table' (2001) is a companion piece in which the roses 'gathered from the Isar' in the earlier song have aged. The beginning makes this connection clear: a falling figure of intertwined fifths (G–D) and a D♭ major chord melts into a direct allusion of the opening harmony and melodic figures of 'River Roses'. In its evocation of faded beauty, 'Roses on the Breakfast Table' draws on a wider range of sonorities and textures than its predecessor, bound together by a harmonic language rich in octatonic formulations that allow sharp dissonances to coexist with glowing chords. The closing bars allude to another D.H. Lawrence song: a leap from a top B♭ to a low F♯ on the last two syllables of the word 'discloses' recalls a similar fall from B♭ to A on the word 'roses' in 'Gloire de Dijon'. In this way, it is possible to hear 'Roses on the Breakfast Table' not just as a counterpart to 'River Roses', but as a tranced reflection on the complete set of Lawrence songs.

Erich Fried Songs Op. 43

On their retirement from Cambridge, Alexander Goehr and Wood exchanged musical presents. Wood's gift was to set seven songs contemplating themes of art, creativity and old age, which he drew from Erich Fried's *Love Poems*, a collection given to Wood by Goehr some years before.[20] Dedicated to Goehr, the songs received their first performance on 7 March 2001, at the Austrian Cultural Institute.

---

[20]   Erich Fried, *Love Poems* trans. Stuart Hood (New York and London, 1991).

The poems are characterized by their brevity and intensity, which in turn motivate musical settings in which Wood's already concise and expressive style is concentrated further. Music and verse combine to create seemingly straightforward songs, but just beneath the surface can be found a multitude of conflicting and complex undercurrents – tenderness, irony, introspection, hope, bitterness and so on. Directness of communication is not to be confused with simplicity of message, however.

The opening poem, 'Gedichte Lesen', consists of just two sentences, and characterizes the concentrated writing style of the set in general. The first sentence claims that those seeking salvation from a poem ought to learn how to read poems. Conversely, the second sentence, which differs from the first only by one letter (changing 'seine Rettung' (his salvation) to 'keine Rettung' (no salvation) suggests that those expecting no salvation from a poem also ought to learn how to read poems. The underlying message is that poems are worth reading in themselves, even if they don't change your life.

Wood's setting is equally compressed, its two stanzas spanning a mere eighteen bars. Much of the second stanza (bars 10–18) is a reworking of the first, transposed up by a tone. But there are also crucial differences. Thus in the first stanza, the word 'seine' occurs as an upbeat figure; in the second, the equivalent 'keine' is given greater emphasis by being placed on the beat. The melodic profile of the phrase is also altered: instead of a diatonic fanfare-like figure for 'seine Rettung' we have instead for 'keine Rettung' an angular line rich in tritones (bars 12–3). The crucial verbal change on which the meaning of the poem hinges is therefore highlighted by significant rhythmic and melodic changes from one stanza to the next.

Even when repetitions from one stanza to the next are taken into account, the shifting musical contexts within the second stanza signal a sensitive, as well as extreme, musical response to the demands of the text. The rapidity with which the contexts change suggests a somewhat expressionist rhetoric, in which each of the four two-bar units (the last extended by a further bar) contain contrasting textures, melodic contours, harmonic density, dissonance and, significantly, motivic content. Nevertheless, there exists a sense of continuity within the passage beyond that conferred by the text. In particular, characteristic melodic and intervallic motion in the vocal line (semitones, as well as leaps of fourths/fifths) imparts a certain sense of coherence across the otherwise fractured musical surface.

In 'Gedichte Lesen', the directness of expression of the musical setting is strongly determined by the nuances of the poem: the resulting absence of strongly defined motivic coherence represents something of an extreme in Wood's song writing. In the second song of the set, 'Grabschrift' ('Epitaph'), the opposite pole is encountered. Here, the entire vocal line is explicitly derived from a three-note whole-tone motif (B♭–C–A♭); everything that follows relates to this motivic shape. Furthermore, of the thirteen motivic repetitions that constitute the vocal line, eleven are direct transpositions of the opening figure to begin on B♭, C♯, G or E. The transposition of the motif onto these four pitches alone ensures all the notes of the chromatic scale are brought into play.[21]

Wood instructs the singer to deliver his/her line in an 'ironic' fashion, and we can assume that the motivic saturation, lacking Wood's characteristic subtlety, is a musical corollary to the required mode of performance. Although the motivic repetitions act as a pitch constraint, they nevertheless enable the freeing-up of other aspects of the music. For instance, in responding to the micro-rhythms demanded by the poetic text, Wood does not repeat the rhythm of a single bar in the vocal part. The dynamic interaction between musical structure and textual demands is intensified midway through the song, when, speaking of the hunger of the poem's protagonist (who chose his art before bread), the poem mentions 'no cook at all, for there was no broth to spoil'. At this crucial point of the poem, the motif is transposed to begin on first E♭, then A, with the fall of the major third between the final two notes of the motif contracted to a minor third. These are the only transpositions of the motif not to begin on the underlying diminished seventh. This slight change – a considerable deformation in the context of the song – initiates a series of imitations in the piano that releases the piano from a purely accompanimental role, thus emphasizing the content of the text. In this way, what appears at first to be 'ironic' and uncharacteristic motivic repetitions are revealed to be an intimate and intrinsic part of the musical response to the poem.

The tiny 'Altersschwäche?' ('Weakness of old Age?') is a cheerful depiction of an old man being teased by his daughter. Wide and vigorous leaps in the voice at the start of the song contrast with sentimental descending semitones for the daughter's comment of 'altes Schwein' ('old swine'). The opening melodic line is octatonic in nature; later, widely spaced augmented triads become increasingly prominent. The harmonic language reflects the delicate poise between the minor thirds that underpin the octatonic material and the major thirds of the (whole-tone) augmented triad: many of the chords can be understood as combinations of triads a third apart, and root motion is also often by thirds.

The text of 'Der Einzige Ausweg' presents a succession of objects contained within objects, which, like Russian dolls, are ultimately empty. Wood responds to this with a setting dense in motivic working. Accelerandos in each line lead to pregnant pauses that are left unfulfilled: the final line dissolves into nothing.

The carnivalesque atmosphere of the fifth song, 'Homeros Eros', is achieved through the simplest of means: an extended prolongation of a B♭ major chord and the superimposition of a 5/8 metre in the right hand of the piano over 3/4 in the voice and piano left hand. Combined with a throwaway ending, which punctures the mood with what seems to be an exaggerated raising of the eyebrows, the song reveals a type of humour that rarely finds a place in Wood's music, but is all the more telling when it does so.

Rippling fifths in the accompaniment characterize 'Abschied', a fleet-footed setting in which the rise and fall of the music depicts that of the sun.

---

[21]   The initial ordering of these transpositions – beginning on B♭, E, C♯ and G respectively – divides the twelve chromatic notes into two whole-tone sets, as in the Passacaglia theme of the Symphony (Example 2.3, p. 29).

The final song, 'Vielleicht', is the longest and finest of the seven Fried songs. In its clarity of texture, material and means of expression, it embodies the general remain long after its creator's death, motivating one of Wood's most contemplative settings. The opening stanza is given in Example 9.4. The harmonic motion of the passage as a whole, which gently shifts from a diminished triad on D towards B♭ is best thought of as a slowly evolving harmonic field around a focal D. Combined with the motivic echoes and pre-echoes of the voice in the piano part, and the softly stumbling rhythms, the impression in bars 1–6 is one of expansiveness, and of reflection. The

Example 9.4   Erich Fried Songs Op. 43/vii, 'Vielleicht', bars 1–15

second half of the example (bars 7–13) employs Wood's characteristically lyrical series of alternating rising major thirds and falling semitones. This shape appears twice, each time forming a complete octatonic set. A second octatonic set (CI) on 'überdauern', contains a diminished triad on D as well as a B♭ major chord: this collection thus contains and summarizes the harmonic motion of the stanza. Once again, we are confronted with simplicity of means, but, as with all the songs in the set, the end results are both subtle and sophisticated.

This is the Record of John Op. 44

This is the Record of John, a setting of John 1, 19ff, was written for unaccompanied SATB to mark the Reverend Prebendary John Slater's departure from St John's Church, St John's Wood in 2001. An occasional work written for a church choir, the piece nevertheless demonstrates Wood's fluency in creating well-balanced musico-dramatic structures.

In keeping with the nature of the text, the work falls into three sections. The first is a short introduction, setting the words 'This is the Record of John, when the Jews sent priests and Levites from Jerusalem to ask him, Who art thou?' The musical language is initially diatonic (C major), and largely triadic, with frequent added notes (particularly sevenths and ninths). Only with the question at the end of the section, a *fortissimo* statement in octaves, is the first non-diatonic note introduced (a C♯). This question, and the corresponding ruptures to the musical language, set in motion a series of dramatic interchanges that form the second section of the work. Here, the musical language changes to a more chromatic idiom; the textures also become more fragmented as the textual dialogue intensifies. John is represented initially by a solo bass voice. The choir ask him three questions. Each of his three answers ends a semitone lower than the one before (descending from F♯ down to E); these bass notes function as points of reference within the section as a whole.

The second section ends with the fourth question of the chorus, 'What sayest thou of thyself?' John's answer is first given to a solo tenor ('I am the voice of one crying in the wilderness'); its continuation is swiftly taken up and developed polyphonically by the whole choir ('Make straight the way of the Lord/ Amen'). The musical language of this third and final section returns to the diatonicism of the first, albeit greatly extended. In total, the final section accounts for roughly half the work's length, and acts as a musical and emotional counter-balance to the drama of the second section.

Comparison with the final section of Serenade and Elegy, one of Wood's few other works to make use of such extended diatonicism, illuminates the relationship between diatonicism and tonal function in *This is the Record of John*. In Serenade and Elegy, the unambiguously C major context of the Pfitzner quotation is marked by regular perfect cadences. The use of diatonicism enhances the affective qualities of tenderness and innocence, and it is into this diatonicism that Wood's bitter-sweet chromatic superimpositions are gradually absorbed. In contrast, although the rhythmic and textural foreground of the final section of *This is the Record of John* evokes traditional cadential patterns, it is not supported with comparably unambiguous tonal references: it is 'on' rather than 'in' C. Thus, unlike much of

Wood's music, tonal allusions are not given their force through being fleeting, fugitive or momentarily beguiling. Rather, through being situated in an extended diatonic context, such events are rendered significant through their distance or proximity to traditional tonal models. For instance, the closing section (bars 33–51) can be characterized by an avoidance of a strong leading note: the one instance of a B rising directly or indirectly to a C is not supported by a dominant-tonic harmonic progression (bars 37–8; tenor voice). As the passage progresses, linear motion in the bass begins to assert a clearer tonal background, moving towards a dominant pedal (bars 43–7). But this ends with an ambiguous sixth over the pedal (suggesting a 6/4 chord) that does not 'resolve' to the expected dominant chord. Instead, there is an implied plagal cadence (bars 48–51; to the word 'Amen'), in which the concluding 'C major' chord is in second inversion with added sixth and ninth. The result is a musical language that is delicately balanced between meandering diatonicism and directed tonal motion: by achieving this balance, the work achieves expansiveness and familiarity of expression but without direct recourse to traditional gestures.

Wild Cyclamen Op. 49

This book began with mention of Wood's attendance at the Manchester group's London concert in 1956; it ends with the premiere of Wood's Op. 49 Robert Graves songs, given in Manchester, just over half a century later. It is perhaps fitting that this survey of Wood's music should stop here, for his response to English poetry, and above all that of Robert Graves, is one of Wood's most significant artistic achievements.

Commissioned jointly by the BBC and the Royal Philharmonic Society, *Wild Cyclamen*, a setting of Graves's poetry for voice and piano, was composed between August 2005 and January 2006. As with Wood's other songs to Graves's poems, the underlying theme is that of love. However, Op. 49 differs from the earlier sets in that the chosen poems allude to the dramatic arc of a love affair from its inception through to its dissolution, as with the Song Cycle to Pablo Neruda. Although Graves wrote no cycle, Wood's selection nevertheless compensates for the lack of a strong narrative thread by virtue of shared images between songs. What emerges is a series of poetic reflections on the stages of a love affair, rather than a direct account of the experience itself.

The first song of the cycle, 'A Dream of Frances Speedwell', opens with unaccompanied voice (Example 9.5), gently reminiscing on the first experience of love. Though lyrical, the mood is generally restrained: the song is a prelude to the highs and lows that are to follow. As with the Erich Fried songs and 'River Roses', the setting is motivically dense: the opening figure of a falling semitone and rising third (motif x; a variant of the lyrical motif that permeates Wood's output) dominates. Balancing the octatonic implications of this figure are fragments of whole-tone material, embodied initially by a descending augmented triad (motif y). The major thirds of both motifs provide a link between them; only at the end of the declamation, when a shadow passes over the memory ('Until last night') does a minor third become prominent (motif z).

Example 9.5   *Wild Cyclamen* Op. 49/i, 'A Dream of Frances Speedwell', bars 1–11

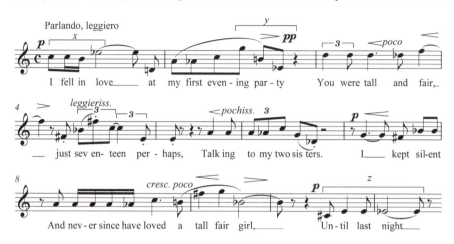

The effect of the change from major to minor is magical, capturing dramatically the shift from the narration of a distant event ('my first evening party') to something in the very near past ('last night'). Under this, the piano creeps in, first with a low major seventh, and then with material based on perfect fifths. The warm open harmony that this produces creates a sense of expectation and of excitement: a fitting accompaniment to the description of an encounter with a 'tall fair girl' who wore the 'white dress' of the beloved. But this was not the loved one from that first party; rather, the poem recounts the start of a new relationship. The final bars of the song rework the material from the first two bars against dry chords in the piano: the narrator recognizes that this is somebody new, but finds in her aspects of the former love.

The second song, 'Wild Cyclamen', depicts the growing closeness of the lovers. It is set as a quicksilver scherzo, mostly hushed but punctuated by sudden outbursts of emotion. The opening figure belongs to the same family as the whole-tone fanfares of 'The Rider Victory' and *Overture*, though here it has a coquettish playfulness rather than a function as a brash call to attention. The vocal line alternates between light scherzo-like passages that tend to narrate the scene, and more sustained lyrical lines, often in a 3/4 that cuts across the underlying 6/8 for the depiction of passion.

Though there is not a direct narrative between the first two songs, they nevertheless present situations and emotions that listeners can identify as belonging to the early stages of a relationship. For the third and fourth songs, however, Wood has selected poems that 'universalize the experience first from the poet's, and then from the woman's point of view'.[22] The first of these, 'Beatrice and Dante' is a poetic reflection on Beatrice, Dante's love and muse. It opens with a low-pitched sustained three-part polyphony between voice and piano in which motif *x* is prominent. The use of a relatively severe contrapuntal texture suggests both the medieval subject of the poem (though the music is far from antique) as well as the craftsmanship of the

---

[22]   Composer's note to the score.

artist. The mention of Beatrice releases a series of imitative figures based again on motif *x*; combined with a crescendo, these lead to a radiant climax. The second half of the song traces a similar motion from quiet intensity to exultation, characterized by a greater emphasis on fourths and fifths: one is reminded of the stirring love in the first song.

'The Garden', a portrayal of love from a female perspective, is a soft lyrical song set in a limpid G major. The accompaniment consists for the most part of gently rocking chords in which the left and right hands of the pianist are over two octaves apart, for sonorous effect. There is a general avoidance in the piano of the metrically strong beats, which combines with the chords to create a timeless, spacious quality well suited to the imagery of being 'Entranced in a tower'. The textures change at mention of birds that 'grumble in dreamy dissonance', a phrase which encapsulates the nature of the song, and which Wood sets with his characteristic major triads a tritone apart. There are certain similarities in tonality and character with the meditative 'River Roses', but the sensuousness and ravishing beauty of 'The Garden', of time and place held frozen in rapture, is unparalleled in Wood's song output.

The fifth and sixth songs form another pair, and initiate a sequence of four songs that focus on the passions of a love affair. 'The Leap' opens with an exultant declamation of love against a series of chords built from notes of the E♭ major scale (with sharpened fourth). There is a change of harmonic organization at the end of a rising scale that sets 'And in its waking thought of you'. The scale is reminiscent of similar reflections on sleep and awakening in both 'The Rose' (Graves Songs Set I Op. 18) and 'Mid-winter Waking' (Set III Op. 23).

Sleeplessness, in the form of staying up all night 'for pure joy', is the subject of the sixth song. The energetic vocal line, often based on major or minor triads, stands in contrast to the mostly conjunct motion of 'The Leap', from which 'Not to Sleep' follows *attacca*. The accompaniment is similarly vigorous, alternating between surging scales and arpeggios and dry punctuating chords. There are numerous textual and musical references to the first five songs. Thus underneath the opening G major triad of the song, the left hand descends through fifths, recalling the first and third songs. The birds of 'The Garden' return in bars 6 and 36 against a cascade of octatonically related triads, 'grumbling gently', and the white clothes of the beloved make a reappearance in bar 11 over a white-note chord based on C. The presence of such connections suggest that 'Not to Sleep' is the culmination of their growing intimacy within the cycle to this point; it also reflects the care with which Wood selected complementary poems when assembling the text for the work.

Rushing octatonic scales in semiquavers against a descending octatonic line in the voice announce the ardent 'The Crab-Tree'. In the final stanza, the octatonic colour is transformed briefly into diatonic white-note harmonies of radiant tranquillity that captures magically the sense of profound calm at the heart of tumultuous passion.

'Bites and Kisses' opens with a distant fanfare that recalls the Prelude of *Scenes from Comus*. Out of this comes an accompaniment figure in the piano, the upper voice of which consists a series of rising fourths in sequence; here there is a connection to the pastoral fourths of 'Home from Abroad', and indeed the text is dominated by nature imagery. Against such a mobile accompaniment, the voice is increasingly expansive, exploring in a different way to 'The Crab-Tree' the coexistence of exultation and serenity at the heart of a relationship. At the song's climax (bar 49), the material becomes wholly white-note, connoting a similar blend of contrasting emotional states. Only at the end of the song, with 'jewelled pebbles' (bar 67) and 'dragonflies' (bar 72), does the iridescent chromaticism of the opening return.

'Horizon' opens with the rhythms of a Habanera in the accompaniment, which continue for much of the song, a sensuous depiction of betrayal. The first three notes of 'Horizon' recall the opening of 'The Garden', and the octatonic descent of 'And after sunset' (bar 7, and again to 'lovers long past in bar 20) is reminiscent of 'The Crab-Tree'. Above all, however, the rising fourths of 'Bites and Kisses' remain to colour the melodic and harmonic content of 'Horizon'. Such allusions to figures from earlier songs in the vocal line suggest that the singer is oblivious to the consequences of his actions. However, the rhythms of the Habanera, evoking Carmen and her claim that 'l'amour est un oiseau rebelle que nul ne peut apprivoiser',[23] would indicate that the betrayal within the song is at least on some level a decision taken willingly.

If 'Horizon' is thus poised between states of knowing and not knowing, 'The Window Sill' confirms in a dream the end of the relationship. An obsessive syncopated rhythm in the accompaniment underpins much of the song, related distantly to the Habanera of 'Horizon'; a figure in the left hand distorts the fourths and fifths of the earlier songs into tritones. Much of the song is hushed, but at the climax, 'Then a wild sobbing spread from door to door', there is a dramatic outburst; rocking triplets in the accompaniment recall as a nightmare the sonorous textures of 'A Dream of Frances Speedwell'. At the end of the song, the text refers back to 'The Garden' and the line 'The twin buds of her breasts opening like flowers'. In the dream of 'The Window Sill', these have withered to 'a white and cankered rose'.

The penultimate song in the cycle is 'A Lost Jewel'; its opening line of 'Who on your breast pillows his head now' makes an effective link from the previous song. This is a recomposition of the setting in the Op. 36 set (see Chapter 7, p. 159). Certain features of the original are retained. For instance, the vocal lines at the opening of both settings have the same contours; a later contrasting idea ('At dawn will hear you') is based on repeated tappings and dark, obscure chords. The most significant musical difference lies in the metric emphasis: the later setting tends towards more rapid motion in the dramatic passages (for instance, the opening phrase changed from 8/8 to 6/8) and greater expansiveness given to lyrical material. Emotionally, the later setting benefits from a more reserved use of the accompaniment at key moments. Whereas the 1984 setting follows the line 'you were sworn to keep' with imitation in the piano, the 2005 version set the line over a sustained chord. The same device recurs with the words 'Light on my finger, fortune in my head' (bars 43–6). In each case, the effect of sudden motionlessness in the accompaniment heightens the sense of loss described in the text.

Allusions to earlier songs in the cycle also serve to invest 'A Lost Jewel' with poignant reminders of the past. The opening vocal line recapitulates a semitone lower the whole-tone fanfare from 'Wild Cyclamen', and the fourths and fifths that coloured much of the harmony of the cycle recur in despairing exclamations at the end of the song. The setting of 'fortune in my head' contains a direct repetition of

---

[23]   'Love is a rebellious bird that none can tame'; Act I aria from Bizet's *Carmen*.

the first four pitches of Example 9.5, bar 2. This reference to the opening of the cycle prefigures a more extended recollection in the final song, 'Hedges Freaked with Snow'. Here, there is at first a return to the unaccompanied voice of 'A Dream of Frances Speedwell'; later, the piano duets with the voice using the melody of Example 9.5. The recurrence of material from the beginning of a work at its end is a familiar enough device in Wood's output, but never has it been used so baldly, or so tellingly. The counterpoint of the bleak vocal line with the memory of a lost love is hauntingly expressive, and must be considered amongst Wood's most masterly musical responses to 'the practical impossibility, transcended only by a belief in miracle, of absolute love continuing between man and woman' that defines both his and Graves's enterprise.[24]

Envoi

Surveying the twentieth century, Wood has written:

> A new and terrible world was lining up outside, ready to take over, at the moment of [Brahms's] death. The Habsburgs fell and Lenin rose; there was the Jazz Age and the Weimar Republic and the Bauhaus and the Wall Street Crash. Then came dictatorships all over Europe, another world war, the death camps and the holocaust: Sartre, abstract expressionism, the hydrogen bomb, the cold war: international terrorism: at last the fall of the Berlin Wall: the computer revolution. And here we are, standing on the further side of all this.[25]

Faced with such events, what is the individual – the divided, alienated modern subject – to do? What can an artist offer a society or another human being? For Wood, the answer is not to be found in a music that reflects uncritically the times in which it is composed. In such cases, all that can result is

> that welter, that helter-skelter succession of revivals and renewals and betrayals; of re-assessments and re-creations and returns and completely new starts; that sequence of immediately trumped extremes and immediately discredited theories to support those extremes; all that ill-judged co-option of ill-digested mathematics and politics and drama and philosophy and sociology and technology; that retreat into a myriad of private worlds, at first that of the coterie and the true believer, but later, more ominously, into the infantile solipsism of the nursery; finally, irresponsible, irrational pre-natal regression to the womb itself, with no past – therefore no future. Latterly we have experienced all the commercial horrors of cross-over, the voluntary espousal of all that is most ephemeral and idiotically mechanical in modern life; and, (reaction against a reaction) the resort to a cut-price religiosity which will heal all wounds, a pocket mysticism breathing some divine muzak adjusted to the attention-span of the middle-brow purchaser of a compact disc: essential easy listening, feel-good religion without dogma, without tradition, without sense. Maybe we are passing though a bad patch: but every society gets the sort of music it deserves.[26]

---

[24] Graves, *Collected Poems 1965*, p. ii.

[25] Wood, 'A Photograph of Brahms', p. 275.

[26] Ibid., pp. 275–6.

Wood's modernism – the way in which he responds to his times – belongs very much to the tradition of humanism embodied by Beethoven and Tippett. Take, for example, Wood's description of Beethoven's 'immense moral power', which stems from

> having seen the worst. In his huge, laughing, bludgeoning scherzos you're aware of the good conscience of the fighter, the same grimly smiling spirit that produced the death-bed remark: *Plaudite, amici, comoedia finita est.* There are worst responses to disaster than to shake one's fist at it, whether in the age of Goethe or the age of Beckett.[27]

Wood's music offers too an assertively defiant code of behaviour that results from his confrontation with the modern world; in this lies his authority.[28] Leo Black has written of Wood's predilection for scherzos in terms remarkably similar to Wood's appreciation of Beethoven: 'lightness of heart is not what seems to lie behind this impulse to dance. What, then? An assertion of vitality against some unspecified odds? A vigorous gesture of protest? Didn't Stevie Smith's most famous poem have the title "Not Waving but Drowning"?'[29]

We find here distant echoes of Nietzsche's tragic artist, who 'is not a pessimist – it is precisely because he who *affirms* all that is questionable and terrible in existence, he is *Dionysian*'.[30] And yet for all of the bacchanalian revels of *Scenes from Comus*, Nietzsche's image of a '*Dionysian* world of the eternally self-creating, the eternally self-destroying' is alien to Wood. A world caught in a ritual of doing and undoing is one in which all is in flux is one in which communication is impossible, for there is no basis for understanding. Such a world has more in common with the artistic upheavals decried by Wood above than with the relationship with tradition that informs his music.[31] Wood is able to offer in his music affirmation of the modern condition, be it defiant or conciliatory in tone, but it is precisely *because* of this that his need to communicate is so strong.

Allied to this is the pronounced expressive content of Wood's music. Against the abstractions or ironic detachment of some of his peers, the intense emotionalism to be found in much of Wood's music might strike some as naïve romanticism. There may be some grain of truth in this, but it is also true that the emotionalism is a vital part of the resistance against the mechanical, artificial and dehumanized world in which we live. The evocations of love and loss and the elevation of individual over collective experience to be found throughout Wood's oeuvre speak eloquently of the

---

[27]   Wood, 'Beethoven': 328.

[28]   Recall that important figures in Wood's early years provided examples of conduct that fed into Wood's musical understanding (see Chapter 1, pp. 6–7). It is telling, too, that Wood concluded his reflection on Brahms with 'the Parthian shot of "if there is anybody in this room that I have not insulted – I apologise". Another good motto from the Beard in the Middle Distance – and an admirable guide to behaviour'. Wood, 'A Photograph of Brahms', p. 287.

[29]   Black, 'Hugh Wood', p. 56.

[30]   Friedrich Nietzsche, *Twilight of the Idols*, cited in David Clarke, *The Music and Thought of Michael Tippett: Modern Times and Metaphysics* (Cambridge, 2001), p. 91.

[31]   Friedrich Nietzsche, *The Will to Power*, cited in Clarke, *The Music and Thought of Michael Tippett*, p. 92.

importance of holding on to that which makes us human. And every now and again, such as in the Violin and Piano Concerti, the Third and Fourth Quartets and the Symphony, we are reminded that there is room too for a cautious optimism. 'Art', Wood once wrote,

> is not the more or less successful realization of a theory, and nor is it to be judged by the degree of such success or lack of it. Art is the individual act of creation, it is the unique human decision, it is (Clausewitzianly) the continuation of the personality by other means, and this lovely, irreplaceable flower of the spirit may burgeon upon any old dunghill of rhetorical contradiction.[32]

---

[32] Wood, 'Following the row'.

Generic List of Works

ORCHESTRAL WORKS

Symphony Op. 21
for large orchestra (1974–82)

4 fl. (3. d. picc.; 4. d. picc. and a.fl.) * 3 ob. (3. d. cor ang.) * 3 cl. in A (2. d. cl.in E♭; 3. d. b.cl.) * 3 bn (3. d. cbn) / 6 hn * 4 tpt * 4 tbn.* 2 tba / timp. / perc. (4 players: mar., 3 timb., 4 susp.cymb., 3 bong., ant.cymb. (C♯, G), tr., s.dr., cl.cymb., glsp., b.dr., 3 small gongs, xyl., 3 large gongs, African drum (or tabla), whip, low pitched s.dr) / 2 hp. / pno (cel.) / str.

Commissioned by the BBC
First performance by the BBC Symphony Orchestra conducted by Gennadi Rozhdestvensky, Henry Wood Promenade Concert, Royal Albert Hall, London, 23 July 1982

40 mins
Chester Music CH60895

Variations for Orchestra Op. 39
(1994–97; rev. 1998)

3 fl. (3. d. picc.) * 3 ob. (3. d. cor ang.) * 3 cl. in A (3. d. b.cl.) * 3 bn (3. cbn) / 4 hn * 3 tpt in C * 3 tbn. * 1 tba / timp. / perc. (3 players: susp.cymb., s.dr., cl cymb., b.dr., cymb., large tam tam, cast., tr., t.drum, tamb.) / hp. / pno / str.

Commissioned by the BBC
First performance by the BBC Symphony Orchestra conducted by Andrew Davis, Suntory Hall, Tokyo, Japan, 20 May 1997

12 mins
Chester Music CH61837

Divertimento Op. 51
(2007)

String Orchestra (6.5.4.3.2)
Commissioned jointly by the Hampstead and Highgate Festival and Presteigne Festival
First performance by the Hampstead and Highgate Festival Orchestra conducted by George Vass, St. John-at-Hampstead Church, London, 9 May 2007

10 mins
Published by Chester Music Ltd

CHAMBER ENSEMBLE

Chamber Concerto Op. 15
for chamber ensemble (1970–71; rev. 1978)

2 fl. (1. d. picc.; 2. d. picc. and a.fl.) * 1 ob. * 2 cl. in A (2. d. b.cl.) * 1 bn / 1 hn * 1 tpt *
1 tbn. * 1 tba / perc. (3 players: xyl., a.cymb., 2 timb., 4 t.bl., 3 gongs, tamb., b.dr., s.dr.,
3 susp.cymb., cl.cymb., small t.t., whip) / hp / pno (d. cel.) / str. (1 * 1 * 1 * 1 * 1)

Commissioned by the London Sinfonietta
*First performance by London Sinfonietta conducted by Andrew Davis, Queen
Elizabeth Hall, London, 27 November 1971*

28 mins
Chester Music CH55316

Comus Quadrilles
for small chamber ensemble (1988)
1 fl. * 1 ob. / 1 hn * 1 tpt / perc. (s.dr., cymb., glsp.) / pno / vln * vla * vc.

Commissioned by the BBC for Sir William Glock's 80th birthday
*First performance by the London Sinfonietta conducted by Elgar Howarth, BBC
Radio Broadcast, 3 May 1988*

3 mins
Published by Chester Music

WORKS FOR SOLOIST(S) AND ORCHESTRA/CHAMBER ENSEMBLE

Scenes from Comus Op. 6
for soprano, tenor and orchestra (1962–65)
Text: John Milton

3 fl. (2. d. picc., 3. d. a.fl.) * 3 ob. (3. d. cor ang.) * 3 cl. (1. and 2. in B♭; 3. in A, d.
b.cl.) * 3 bn (3. d. cbn) / 4 hn * 3 tpt * 3 tbn. * 1 tba / timp. / perc. (4 players: s.dr.,
b.dr., gong, tamb., tr., cymb., 2 susp.cymb., 3 t.t., xyl., glsp.) / 2 hp / pno / cel. / str.

Commissioned by the BBC
*First performance by Jeannette Sinclair, Kenneth Bowen and the BBC Symphony
Orchestra conducted by Norman Del Mar, Henry Wood Promenade Concert, Royal
Albert Hall, London, 2 August 1965*

28 mins
Published by Chester Music

Cello Concerto Op. 12
for solo cello and orchestra (1965–69)

3 fl. (2. d. a.fl.; 3. d. picc.) * 3 ob. (3. d. cor ang.) * 3 cl. in A (3. d b.cl.) * 3 bn (3. d.

cbn) / 4 hn * 3 tpt * 3 tbn. * 1 tba / timp. / perc. (4 players: xyl., 2 susp.cymb., whip, tam-tam, 2 cymb., b.dr.) / 2 hp / str.

Commissioned by the BBC
First performance by Zara Nelsova and the BBC Symphony Orchestra conducted by Colin Davis, Henry Wood Promenade Concert, Royal Albert Hall, London, 26 August 1969

20 minutes
Chester Music CH55142
Arranged for Cello and Piano: CH55402

Violin Concerto Op. 17
for solo violin and orchestra (1970–72)

3 fl. (1. d. picc.; 2. and 3. d. a.fl. and picc.) * 3 ob. * 3 cl. in A (3. d. b.cl.) * 3 bn / 4 hn * 3 tpt * 3 tbn. * 1 tba / perc. (3 players: s.dr., b.dr., susp.cymb. (high, medium and low), cl.cymb., crot., xyl., glsp., small gong, large tam-tam, bong. (high and low), t.t., tamb., w.bl., tr.) / hp / pno (d. cel.) / str.

Commissioned by the Royal Liverpool Philharmonic Society and the Gulbenkian Foundation
First performance by Manoug Parikian and the Royal Liverpool Philharmonic Orchestra conducted by Sir Charles Groves, Philharmonic Hall, Liverpool, 19 September 1972

29 minutes
Chester Music CH55051
Reduced score: CT55152

Song Cycle to Poems of Pablo Neruda Op. 19
for high voice and chamber orchestra (1973–74)
Text: Pablo Neruda, in the English version by Christopher Logue

3 fl. (2. d. picc.; 3. d. a.fl.) * 1 ob. (d. cor ang.) * 3 cl. (3. d. b.cl.) * 0 / 1 hn * 1 tpt * 1 tbn. * 0 / perc. (3 players: s.dr., b.dr., 3 susp.cymb., 3 tam-tams, 2 cymb., tr., xyl., glsp., a.cymb.) / hp / pno (cel.) / str. (1 * 1 * 1 * 1 *1)

Commissioned by the BBC
First performance by Morag Noble and members of the BBC Symphony Orchestra conducted by Elgar Howarth, The Roundhouse, London, 18 February 1974

25 minutes
Chester Music SOS11749
Reduced Score: SOS01749

Laurie Lee Songs Op. 28
for solo soprano and orchestra (1986–87)
Texts by Laurie Lee: 'Boy in Ice', 'The Edge of Day', 'The Easter Green', 'Town

Owl', 'April Rise'

2 fl. (2. d. picc.) * 2 ob. (2. d. cor ang.) * 2 cl. (in B♭; 2. d. cl. in A and b.cl. in B♭) * 2 bn / 2 hn * 1 tpt * 1 tbn. * 0 / perc. (1 player: susp.cymb., cl.cymb., tr.)/ hp / str.

Arrangement of 1959 version for piano and voice

20 minutes
Published by Chester Music

Piano Concerto Op. 32
for solo piano and orchestra (1989–91)

2 fl. (2. d. picc.) * 2 ob. (2. d. cor ang.) * 3 cl. (1. in A, 2. in A d. b.cl., 3. in E♭) * 2 bn (2. d. cbn) / 2 hn * 2 tpt * 1 tbn.* 1 tba / timp. / perc. (3 players: xyl., tamb., cl.cymb., whip, tr., 4 bong., 5 t.t., b.dr., medium susp.cymb., tam-tam, s.dr., 3 susp. cymb., w.bl.) / cel. / hp / str.

Commissioned by the BBC
First performance by Joanna MacGregor with the BBC Symphony Orchestra conducted by Andrew Davis, Henry Wood Promenade Concert, Royal Albert Hall, London, 10 September 1991

25 minutes
Chester Music CH60963

Serenade and Elegy Op. 42
for solo string quartet and string orchestra (1998–99)

Commissioned by the Cheltenham Festival
First performance by the Chilingirian String Quartet with the London Mozart Players conducted by Matthias Bamert, Cheltenham Festival, 15 July 1999

20 mins
Chester Music CH61619

Violin Concerto No. 2 Op. 50
for solo violin and orchestra (2003–04)

(ms.)

CHORUS AND ORCHESTRA

Musicians Wrestle Everywhere
For SATB chorus and orchestra (1980)
Text: Emily Dickinson

2 fl. * 2 ob. * 2 cl. in A * 2 bsn / 2 hn * 1 tpt * 1 tbn.
* 0 / timp. / perc. (cymb., tamb.) / str.

(ms.)

Cantata Op. 30
for SATB chorus and orchestra (1989)
Text: D.H. Lawrence

2 fl. (2. d. picc.) * 2 ob. * 2 cl. in B♭ (2. d. b.cl.) * 2
bn / 2 hn * 1 tpt * 1 tbn. * 0 / hp / str.

Commissioned by the 5th European Conference on Clinical Oncology (ECCO5)
First performance by the Richard Hickox Singers and the City of London Sinfonia
conducted by Richard Hickox, private concert, Royal Festival Hall, London, 4
September 1989

12 mins
Published by Chester Music

Tenebrae Op. 46
for solo soprano, alto, tenor and baritone, SATB chorus and orchestra (2002–03)
Text: Geoffrey Hill

fl. * ob. * cl. * bsn. / vn. * vla. * vc.

First performance by Kokoro and Canticum conducted by Mark Kirkgen, St Stephen's
Church, Bournemouth, 3 November 2007

15 mins
Published by Chester Music

CHORUS A CAPPELLA

Three Choruses Op. 7
for SATB chorus (1966)
Texts: Ted Hughes, 'The Hawk in the Rain'; James Joyce, 'Sirens' (arr. Wood);
Edwin Muir, 'All we'

First performance by the John Alldis Choir, Wigmore Hall, London, 6 May 1966
c 11 mins
Chester Music SOS02259 (published originally by Universal Edition)

To a Child Dancing in the Wind Op. 16 no. 1
for SATB chorus (1973)

To a Friend Whose Work has Come to Nothing Op. 16 No. 2
for SATB chorus (1973; completely rewritten in 1989)
Text: W.B. Yeats

First performance by the English Chamber Choir conducted by Guy Protheroe, 29
October 1989, Royal Court Theatre
Chester Music CH55571 (Op. 16 No. 1), SOS03724 (Op. 16 No. 2)

A Christmas Poem Op. 27
for SATB chorus (1984)
Text: Dick Davis

First performance by the Cambridge University Chamber Choir conducted by Richard Marlow, Trinity College Chapel, Cambridge, 27 November 1986

6 mins
Chester Music CH59220

The Kingdom of God Op. 38
Anthem for SATB chorus (1994)
Text: Francis Thompson

Commissioned by the City of London Festival
First performance by the St. Paul's Cathedral Choir conducted by John Scott, St Paul's Cathedral, 3 July 1994

8 mins
Chester Music CH61093

This is the Record of John Op. 44
for SATB chorus (2001)
Text: John 1, 19ff.

First performance by the Choir of St John's Church conducted by Robert Greenhill, St John's Church, St John's Wood, London, 24 June 2001

c 5 mins
Chester Music CH67166

Preces and Responses
for SATB chorus (2007)

First performance by the Choir of The Queen's College conducted by Owen Rees, The Queen's College, Oxford, 24 January 2007

(ms.)

VOCAL

Laurie Lee Songs
for high voice and piano (1956–59)
Texts by Laurie Lee: 'Boy in Ice', 'The Edge of Day', 'The Easter Green', 'Town Owl', 'April Rise'

First performance by Naomi Hoyland and Susan McGaw, Liverpool Cathedral, 23 May 1971

20 mins
Chester Music SOS01707

Four Logue Songs Op. 2
for contralto, clarinet, violin and cello (1960–61; rev. 1963)
Texts from *Wand and Quadrant* by Christopher Logue: 'The Image of Love Grows',
'Bargain my Love', 'In the Beloved's Face', 'Love, do not Believe'

First performance by Rosemary Johnson and the Melos Ensemble, ICA concert,
Wigmore Hall, London, 7 March 1961

12 mins
Chester Music CH55491

The Horses Op. 10
for high voice and piano (1963–67; rev. 1968)
Texts by Ted Hughes: 'The Horses', 'Pennines in April', 'September'

Commissioned by the Dartington Summer School of Music for the 1967 Summer
School, and offered to William Glock on the occasion of his sixtieth birthday
First performance of the complete set by Jane Manning and Susan Bradshaw,
Macnaghten Concert, Wigmore Hall, London, 13 November 1967

12 minutes
Chester Music SOS01699

The Rider Victory Op. 11
for high voice and piano (1968)
Texts by Edwin Muir: 'The Rider Victory', 'Sorrow', 'The Bird', 'The
Confirmation'

First performance by Josephine MacQueen and Julian Dawson, Fore Hall, Glasgow
University, 28 November 1968

10 minutes
Chester Music SOS01723

D.H. Lawrence Songs Op. 14
for high voice and piano (1966–2001)
Texts by D.H. Lawrence: 'Dog Tired', 'Gloire de Dijon', 'Kisses in the Train', 'River
Roses', 'Roses on the Breakfast Table'

c 16 minutes
Chester Music SOS01780

Robert Graves Songs Set I Op. 18
for high voice and piano (1966–76)
Texts by Robert Graves: 'The Rose', 'Records', 'The Foreboding', 'Always', 'A
Last Poem', 'The Green Castle'

First performance by Brian Burrows and Oliver Davies, Dartington International
Summer School, 30 July 1977

c 15 minutes
Chester Music CH55848

Robert Graves Songs Set II Op. 22
for high voice and piano (1977–82)
Texts by Robert Graves: 'Symptoms of Love', 'The Visitation', 'Fragment', 'Ouzo Unclouded', 'Seldom yet now'

First performance by Lorna Anderson and Malcolm Martineau, Canterbury Festival, 29 September 1987

c 15 minutes
Chester Music SOS01731

Robert Graves Songs Set III Op. 23
for high voice and piano (1974–83)
Texts by Robert Graves: 'Mid-winter Waking', 'The Hazel Grove', 'To Tell and be Told', 'Bird of Paradise'

Chester Music SOS03790

Songs Op. 25
for high voice and piano (1959–85)
Texts: Stephen Spender, 'Ice'; Laurie Lee, 'Home From Abroad'; Yevgeny Yevtushenko, 'The Blue Coat'; Christopher Logue, 'How am I Poor Tonight'

Published by Chester Music

Lines to Mr Hodgson
for soprano and piano (1988)
Text: Lord Byron

Commissioned by Trinity College, Cambridge, for Lord Byron's Bicentenary
First performance by Lorna Anderson and Malcolm Martineau, private concert, Trinity College, Cambridge, 24 April 1988

4 mins
Chester Music SOS01715

Marina Op. 31
for high voice, alto flute, horn, harp and viola (1988–89)
Text: T.S. Eliot

First performance by Alison Gough and the Jeux Ensemble, BBC Lunchtime Concert, BBC Concert Hall, London, 4 April 1990

6 mins
Chester Music CH60933

Robert Graves Songs Set IV Op. 36
for high voice and piano (1966–84)
Texts by Robert Graves: 'The Door', 'The Three-faced', 'A Lost Jewel', 'On Giving'
(ms.)

Songs Op. 37
for high voice and piano (1984–93)

Texts: Edmund Waller, 'Goe Lovely Rose'; Arthur Symons, 'White Heliotrope'; John Crowe Ransom, 'Blue Girls'; Pablo Neruda, 'Amor'

(ms.)

Erich Fried Songs Op. 43
for high voice and piano (2000)
Texts by Erich Fried: 'Gedichte Lesen', 'Grabschrift', 'Altersschwäche?', 'Der Einzige Ausweg', 'Homeros Eros', 'Abschied', 'Vielleicht'

First performed at the Austrian Cultural Institute, London, 7 March 2001

(ms.)

Wild Cyclamen Op. 49
for high voice and piano (2005–06)
Texts by Robert Graves: 'A Dream of Frances Speedwell', 'Wild Cyclamen', 'Beatrice and Dante', 'The Garden', 'The Leap', 'Not to Sleep', 'The Crab-Tree', 'Bites and Kisses', 'Horizon', 'The Window Sill', 'A Lost Jewel', 'Hedges Freaked with Snow'

Commissioned jointly by the BBC and the Royal Philharmonic Society as part of BBC Radio 3's New Generation Artists Scheme.
First performance by Andrew Kennedy and Simon Lepper, Bridgewater Hall, Manchester, 1 February 2006

Chester Music CH71291

'The Isles of Greece' Op. 52
for baritone and piano (2007)
Texts by Lawrence Durrell, 'Delos' and 'Nemea'; Robert Graves, 'Ouzo Unclouded'; Seferis, "In the sea caves..."; Demetrios Capetanakis, 'The Isles of Greece'; Lawrence Durrell, 'Bitter Lemons'

First Performed by Roderick Williams and Iain Burnside, Ludlow Parish Church, Ludlow, 1 June 2007

10 mins
Published by Chester Music

CHAMBER WORKS

String Quartet in B♭
(1956–57)

First performance by the Amici String Quartet, SPNM Concert, Cheltenham Festival, Cheltenham, 11 July 1959

18 mins
Published by Chester Music

Variations Op. 1
for viola and piano (1957–58)

*First performance by Cecil Aronowitz and Margaret Kitchen, Wigmore Hall, London,
7 July 1959*

12 mins
Chester Music CH55924 (published originally by Universal Edition)

Trio Op. 3
for flute, viola and piano (1961)

Commissioned by the John Lewis Partnership
*First performance by William Bennett, Patrick Ireland and Susan Bradshaw, John
Lewis Partnership, London, 5 December 1961*

12 mins
Chester Music SOS00865 (published originally by Universal Edition)

String Quartet No. 1 Op. 4
(1962)

Commissioned by the BBC
First performance by the Dartington Quartet, Cheltenham Festival, 5 July 1962

19 mins
Chester Music SOS03808 (published originally by Universal Edition)

Quintet Op. 9
for clarinet, horn, violin, cello and piano (1967)

Commissioned by the Music Group of London
*First performance by the Music Group of London, Cheltenham Festival, 11 July
1967*

6 mins
Chester Music CH61359

String Quartet No. 2 Op. 13
(1969–70)

Commissioned by the BBC
*First performance by the Dartington Quartet, BBC Radio 3 Invitation Concert,
University College, Cardiff, 2 November 1970*

13 mins
Chester Music CH55141

Canon in memoriam Igor Stravinsky
for flute, clarinet, harp and string quartet (1971)

Tempo 97 (1971)

String Quartet No. 3 Op. 20
(1976–78)

First performance by the Lindsay Quartet, Bath Festival, 31 May 1978

17 mins
Chester Music CH55247

Piano Trio Op. 24
for violin, cello and piano (1982–84)

Commissioned by the Parikian-Fleming-Roberts Trio
First performance by the Parikian-Fleming-Roberts Trio, Brighton Festival, 10 May
1984

18 mins
Chester Music SOS10840

Paraphrase on 'Bird of Paradise' Op. 26
for clarinet and piano (1984–85)

Commissioned by Nicholas Cox with funds made available from the Arts Council of
Great Britain
First performance by Nicholas Cox and Vanessa Latarche, Wigmore Hall, London,
4 March 1985

11 mins
Chester Music CH55690

Horn Trio Op. 29
for horn, violin and piano (1987–89)

Written in fulfilment of a Koussevitzky Music Foundation Award and dedicated to the
memory of Serge and Natalie Koussevitzky
First performance by Frank Lloyd, Marcia Crayford and Ian Brown, BBC Lunchtime
Concert, St. John's, Smith Square, London, 27 November 1989

18 mins
Chester Music CH55919

Funeral Music Op. 33
for brass quintet (1992)

Commissioned by the Three Choirs Festival, written for the London Gabrieli Brass
Consort
First performance by the London Gabrieli Brass Consort, Three Choirs Festival, 24
August 1992

10 mins
Chester Music CH60856

Fifty Chords for David Matthews
for piano and string trio (1993)

First performed at the Purcell Room, London, 8 April 1993

2 mins
Published by Chester Music

String Quartet No. 4 Op. 34
(1993)

Commissioned by the BBC, written for the Chilingirian String Quartet
First performance by the Chilingirian String Quartet, BBC Birmingham, Pebble
Mill Studios, Birmingham, 19 May 1993

25 mins
Chester Music CH60931

Poem Op. 35
for violin and piano (1993)

Commissioned by the PLG Young Artists Concerts New Year Series 1994
First performance by Clio Gould and Sophia Rahman, Purcell Room, London, 10
January 1994

8 mins
Chester Music CH61140

Clarinet Trio Op. 40
for clarinet, cello and piano (1997)

Commissioned by the Gemelli Trio with funds from the Britten-Pears Foundation,
the Po-Shung Woo Foundation and the Arts Council of England
First performance by the Gemelli Trio, Cheltenham Festival, 7 July 1997

21 mins
Chester Music CH61401

String Quartet No. 5 Op. 45
(2000–01)

Commissioned by Yorkshire ArtSpace and Music in the Round
First performance by the Lindsay Quartet, Crucible Studio Theatre, Sheffield, 5
October 2001

c 20 mins
Chester Music CH63745

Cantilena and Fugue Op. 47
for trumpet and organ (2004)

Commissioned by the City of London Festival

First performance by Deborah Calland and William Whitehead, Temple Church, London, 7 July 2004

Published by Chester Music

Overture Op. 48
for violin, cello and piano (2005)

Commissioned by Music in the Round for the Cropper-Welsh-Roscoe Trio, with funds from Arts Council England.
First performance by the Cropper–Welsh–Roscoe Trio, Maidment Hall, Shrewsbury, 29 September 2005

c 7 mins
Published by Chester Music

Clarinet Quintet Op. 53
(2007)

First performance by Nicholas Cox and the Chilingirian Quartet, St George's Hall, Liverpool, 20 November 2007

14 mins
Published by Chester Music

SOLO INSTRUMENTAL

Three Piano Pieces Op. 5
(1960–63)

First performance by Susan McGaw, Cheltenham Festival, 2 July 1963

9 mins
Chester Music CH55903 (published originally by Universal Edition)

Capriccio Op. 8
for organ (1966–67; rev. 1968)

First performance by Gillian Weir, Westminster Cathedral, 17 May 1967

8 mins
Novello & Co NOV101135

Tribute to Michael Berkeley
for solo viola (2004)

First performance by Roger Tapping, Cheltenham Festival, 9 July 2004

3 mins
Published by Chester Music

Chronological List of Works

Op.

–   **String Quartet in B♭** (1956–57)

1   **Variations** for viola and piano (1957–58)

–   **Laurie Lee Songs** for high voice and piano (1956–59)

2   **Four Logue Songs** for contralto, clarinet, violin and cello (1960–61; rev. 1963)

3   **Trio** for flute, viola and piano (1961)

4   **String Quartet No. 1** (1962)

5   **Three Piano Pieces** (1960–63)

6   **Scenes from Comus** for soprano, tenor and orchestra (1962–65)

7   **Three Choruses** for mixed chorus *a cappella* (1966)

8   **Capriccio** for organ (1966–67; rev. 1968)

9   **Quintet** for clarinet, horn, violin, cello and piano (1967)

10   **The Horses** for high voice and piano (1963–67, rev. 1968)

11   **The Rider Victory** for high voice and piano (1968)

12   **Cello Concerto** for solo cello and orchestra (1965–69)

13   **String Quartet No. 2** (1969–70)

–   **Canon in memoriam Igor Stravinsky** for chamber ensemble (1971)

15   **Chamber Concerto** for chamber ensemble (1970–71; rev. 1978)

17   **Violin Concerto** for solo violin and orchestra (1970–72)

16/1   **To a Child Dancing in the Wind** for mixed chorus *a cappella* (1973)

19   **Song Cycle to Poems of Pablo Neruda** for high voice and chamber orchestra (1973–74)

18   **Robert Graves Songs Set I** for high voice and piano (1966–76)

20   **String Quartet No. 3** (1976–78)

–   **Musicians Wrestle Everywhere** for SATB chorus and orchestra (1980)

21   **Symphony** for large orchestra (1974–82)

22   **Robert Graves Songs Set II** for high voice and piano (1977–82)

23   **Robert Graves Songs Set III** for high voice and piano (1974–83)

24   **Piano Trio** (1982–84)

36   **Robert Graves Songs Set IV** for high voice and piano (1966–84)

25   **Songs** for high voice and piano (1959–85)

26   **Paraphrase on 'Bird of Paradise'** for clarinet and piano (1984–85)

27   **A Christmas Poem** for mixed chorus *a cappella* (1986)

28   **Laurie Lee Songs** for solo soprano and orchestra (1986–87)

–   **Lines to Mr Hodgson** for soprano and piano (1988)

–   **Comus Quadrilles** for small chamber ensemble (1988)

29   **Horn Trio** for horn, violin and piano (1987–89)

30   **Cantata** for SATB chorus and orchestra (1989)

31   **Marina** for high voice, alto flute, horn, harp and viola (1988–89)

16/2   **To a Friend Whose Work has Come to Nothing** for mixed chorus *a cappella* (1973; completely rewritten in 1989)

32   **Piano Concerto** for solo piano and orchestra (1989–91)

33   **Funeral Music** for brass quintet (1992)

–   **Fifty Chords for David Matthews** for two pianos (1993)

34   **String Quartet No. 4** (1993)

35   **Poem** for violin and piano (1993)

37   **Songs** for high voice and piano (1984–93)

38   **The Kingdom of God** for mixed chorus *a cappella* (1994)

39   **Variations for orchestra** (1994–97; rev. 1998)

40   **Clarinet Trio** for clarinet, cello and piano (1997)

42   **Serenade and Elegy** for solo string quartet and string orchestra (1998–99)

43   **Erich Fried Songs** for high voice and piano (2000)

14   **D.H. Lawrence Songs** for high voice and piano (1966–2001)

44   **This is the Record of John** for mixed chorus *a cappella* (2001)

45   **String Quartet No. 5** (2000–01)

46   **Tenebrae** for SATB chorus and orchestra (2002–03)

47   **Cantilena and Fugue** for trumpet and organ (2004)

–   **Tribute to Michael Berkeley** for solo viola (2004)

48   **Overture** for violin, cello and piano (2005)

49   **Wild Cyclamen** for high voice and piano (2005–06)

50   **Violin Concerto No. 2** (2003-04)

–   **Preces and Responses for Evensong** for mixed chorus *a cappella* (2007)

51   **Divertimento** for string orchestra (2007)

52   **'The Isles of Greece'** for baritone and piano (2007)

53   **Clarinet Quintet** (2007)

Discography

Cello Concerto, Op. 12
Moray Welsh; Royal Liverpool Philharmonic Orchestra; David Atherton, *conductor*
   NMC D082 (originally released on UKCD 2043)

Clarinet Trio, Op. 40
Trio Gemelli
   Divine Art 25009

Horn Trio, Op. 29
David Pyatt, Levon Chilingirian, Peter Donohoe
   Erato 8573-80217-2

The Horses, **Op. 10**
April Cantelo, Paul Hamburger
   Argo ZRG 750

The Kingdom of God, **Op. 38**
St Paul's Cathedral Choir; Andrew Lucas; John Scott, *conductor*
   Hyperion CDA66758

Paraphrase on 'Bird of Paradise', **Op. 26**
Kate Romano, Alan Hicks
   Metier Sound & Vision MSVCD92013

Piano Concerto, Op. 32
Joanna MacGregor; BBC Symphony Orchestra; Sir Andrew Davis, *conductor*
   Collins Classics 2007-2

Poem, **Op. 35**
Alexandra Wood, Huw Watkins
   Chimera Usk 1226CD

The Rider Victory, **Op. 11**
April Cantelo, Paul Hamburger
   ARGO ZRG 750

Scenes from Comus, **Op. 6**
Geraldine McGreevy, Daniel Norman; BBC Symphony Orchestra; Sir Andrew Davis, *conductor*
   NMC D070

String Quartet No. 1, Op. 4
Aeolian Quartet
  Argo ZRG 575
Chilingirian String Quartet
  Conifer 75605 51239-2
Dartington String Quartet
  Argo ZRG 750

String Quartet No. 2, Op. 13
Chilingirian String Quartet
  Conifer 75605 51239-2
Dartington String Quartet
  Argo ZRG 750

String Quartet No. 3, Op. 20
Chilingirian String Quartet
  Conifer 75605 51239-2
Lindsay Quartet
  ASV CDDCA825

String Quartet No. 4, Op. 34
Chilingirian String Quartet
  Conifer 75605 51239-2

Symphony, Op. 21
BBC Symphony Orchestra; Sir Andrew Davis, *conductor*
  NMC D070

Three Piano Pieces, Op. 5
Susan McGaw
  HMV ASD 2333

Violin Concerto, Op. 17
Manoug Parikian; Royal Liverpool Philharmonic Orchestra; David Atherton, *conductor*
  NMC D082 (originally released on UKCD 2043)

Personalia

Alldis, John (b. 1929), British conductor. Founded John Alldis choir 1962, which gave many distinguished performances of contemporary music. Ran the choir at the Wardour Summer School in 1965. Founded and conducted the London Symphony Chorus (1966–69). Professor at Guildhall School of Music 1966–77. Conducted premiere of Wood's Three Choruses Op. 7.

Andrews, H(erbert) K(ennedy) (1904–65). Appointed organist and choirmaster at New College in 1938; later became lecturer and Fellow. His publications include books on Byrd and Palestrina, and a volume in the *Oxford Harmony* on chromatic harmony in the standard repertory, as well as its compositional applications.

Armstrong, Sir Thomas (1898–1994). Appointed organist at Christ Church, Oxford in 1933, Armstrong went on to tutor and lecture within the Music Faculty at the University. Between 1955 and 1968 Armstrong was Principal of the Royal Academy of Music.

Auden, W(ystan) H(ugh) (1907–73). British poet and critic; later American citizen. Wood set Auden's 'Warm are the Still and Lucky Miles' in the 1954 version of *Songs for Springtime* for chorus and piano, later orchestrating it in the 1958 version.

Bartók, Béla (1881–1945), Hungarian composer and pianist; his output includes opera (*Bluebeard's Castle*), orchestral works, concerti, piano music and six string quartets. His music is influenced by Hungarian nationalism, including folksong (of which he was a collector and scholar), and makes use of dense motivic working.

Berg, Alban (1885–1935). Austrian composer. A pupil of Schoenberg from 1904–10, Berg's music encompasses opera (*Wozzeck, Lulu*), song, orchestral music (including a Violin Concerto) and chamber music (such as the *Lyric Suite* for string quartet).

Berkeley, Michael (b. 1948), British composer and broadcaster; Director of Cheltenham Festival 1995–2004. Wood's *Tribute to Michael Berkeley* was composed to mark the end of Berkeley's tenure at Cheltenham.

Birtwistle, Sir Harrison (b. 1934), British composer. Studied at Royal Manchester College of Music with Richard Hall; later studied at Princeton and University of Colorado. Along with Maxwell Davies and Goehr, ran the Wardour Castle Summer School 1964–65; Musical Director of Royal National Theatre 1975–83; Henry Purcell Professor of Composition, King's College London, 1994–2001. Birtwistle's output includes numerous operas, orchestral works and chamber music.

Black, Leo (b. 1932) read music at Oxford, going on to work for Universal Edition in Vienna and London. He later spent many years working for the BBC, and translated (amongst other things) Schoenberg's *Style and Idea* and Webern's *The Path to the New Music* into English. He has been an articulate supporter of Wood's music, about which he wrote two important articles in the 1970s. Wood's Second String Quartet is dedicated to him.

Britten, Benjamin (Baron Benjamin of Aldeburgh) (1913–76), British composer and pianist. Founder of Aldeburgh Festival and English Opera Group. Britten's music, characterized by its technical fluency, sophistication and awareness of international trends, came to prominence at a time when the British musical mainstream could be said to be mistrustful of such qualities. Big public works such as a series of operas and the *War Requiem*, alongside more intimate songs and chamber music, established Britten as one of the leading British composers of the twentieth century.

Bush, Alan (1900–95), British composer. Writing of Bush's *Dialectic* in 1961, Wood drew attention to the 'mastery of contrapuntal technique and concentration of musical thought unparalleled in English music of the period' – compositional concerns close to his own heart (Wood, 'English Contemporary Music', p. 148).

Byron, Lord (George) (1788–1824). British poet. Wood set Byron's 'Lines to Mr Hodgson, Written on Board the Lisbon Packet' for voice and piano in 1988 as part of the bicentennial celebrations of Byron's birth.

Carter, Elliot (b. 1908); American composer. A composer much admired by Wood; the idea of placing of the cadenza for solo violin early on in the Fourth String Quartet came from Carter's example.

Cropper, Peter (b. 1940), British violinist. Founder member of the acclaimed Lindsay Quartet; the Lindsays premiered Wood's Third and Fifth String Quartets (Opp. 20 and 45), the latter of which is dedicated to them. After the Lindsays retired in 2005, Cropper formed a Piano Trio with Moray Welsh and Martin Roscoe; Wood's *Overture* Op. 48 was written for their inaugural concert.

Dalton, James (b. 1930), British organist; appointed organist of Queen's College Oxford in 1957 and helped design the Frobenius organ built there (1965). Wood first visited Darmstadt with Dalton (1957), and later wrote his *Capriccio* for organ Op. 8 for him.

Davies, Sir Peter Maxwell (b. 1934), British composer. Studied with Richard Hall at Manchester; later studied with Petrassi (1957) and at Princeton (1962–64); along with Birtwistle and Goehr ran the Wardour Castle Summer Schools in 1964–65. A series of music theatre works in the late 1960s established Davies's reputation. Settled in the Orkney Islands in 1971 (where he later established the St Magnus Festival). Since then, his prolific output has included eight symphonies, ten concertos written for members of the Scottish Chamber Orchestra and a series of ten string quartets written for the *Naxos* record label. In 2004 he was appointed Master of the Queen's Music.

Davis, Sir Andrew (b. 1944), British conductor. Organ scholar at King's College; made debut with BBC Symphony Orchestra 1970, appointed its Chief Conductor in 1989 and in 2000 became the orchestra's Conductor Laureate. Davies has been a long-time supporter of Wood's music, and has conducted recordings of the Piano Concerto, Symphony and *Scenes from Comus*.

Davis, Dick (b. 1945); British poet. In 1984, Wood set Davis's 'A Christmas Poem' for unaccompanied choir (Op. 27); it was included in the Chester Book of Carols.

Day Lewis, Cecil (1904–72); British poet. Wood set a number of Lewis's poems in his youth; 'Now the Full-throated Daffodils', first set by Wood in 1949, became the final movement of *Songs for Springtime* (1954; orch. 1958). 'Live you by Love Confined' was also included in the first version of *Songs for Springtime*, set for unaccompanied choir.

de la Mare, Walter (1873–1956). British poet; Wood's early Cantata (1944) set some of his texts.

Donne, John (1572–1631); English poet. Whilst at school, Wood set Donne's 'Busie Olde Foole'; a version can also be found in the choir and piano version of *Songs for Springtime* (1954). A 1955 setting of 'The Good Morrow' was considered by Wood at the time to be his best work. Lines from 'A Nocturnall upon S. Lucies day' were quoted in the score of the Third String Quartet Op. 20.

du Pré, Jacqueline, (1945–87), British cellist famous for passionate performances. Du Pré's first public performance of the Elgar Cello Concerto was in 1959; her recital debut at Wigmore Hall was in 1961. In 1968 she premiered Goehr's *Romanze* for cello and orchestra; Wood wrote his own Cello Concerto with du Pré's playing in mind. Her playing career was cut short through illness.

Eliot, T(homas) S(tearns) (1888–1965). American poet; became British subject in 1927. In 1988–89, Wood set Eliot's 'Marina' for voice and chamber ensemble (Op. 31).

Fried, Erich (1921–88). Austrian poet; emigrated to Britain after the Anschluss, where he adopted British nationality in 1949. In 2000–01, Wood set seven of Fried's *Love Poems* for voice and piano (Op. 43).

Gerhard, Roberto (1896–1970). Spanish (Catalan) composer; emigrated to Britain in 1939 and adopted British nationality in 1960. Studied with Granados and Pedrell; later became pupil of Schoenberg. Worked at BBC; taught also at Dartington. Compositions include the opera *La Duenna*, four symphonies, chamber music and electronic music. Wood's Chamber Concerto Op. 15 is dedicated to Gerhard's widow, and the third movement, a memorial to the composer, quotes from a number of Gerhard's works .

Gilbert, Anthony (b. 1934), British composer. Studied with Milner, Seiber, Goehr and Schuller; on teaching staff of Wardour Castle Summer School 1964. From 1973–99 Gilbert was Head of Composition at the Royal Northern College of Music.

Glock, Sir William (1908–2000), British administrator, pianist and critic. Studied piano with Artur Schnabel at a time (1930–33) when study abroad was frowned upon by the British music establishment. Through his directorship of the Bryanston Summer School (1948–52) and Dartington (1953–79), Glock was responsible for broadening the experience of generations of composers and performers. He was also Controller of Music at the BBC from 1959 to 1973, doing much to promote both contemporary and early music. During this time, the BBC commissioned Wood's First and Second String Quartets, *Scenes from Comus*, and the Cello Concerto; on Glock's sixtieth birthday, Wood offered him *The Horses* Op. 10 (commissioned by Dartington), and on his eightieth the *Comus Quadrilles*.

Goehr, Alexander (b. 1932), British composer. Son of the conductor Walter Goehr, who had studied with Schoenberg. Alexander Goehr studied with Richard Hall and Olivier Messiaen. Along with Birtwistle and Maxwell Davies, ran the Wardour Castle Summer School (1964–65). In 1968–69 he was composer in residence at the New England Conservatoire, Boston, and the following year was assistant professor of Music at Yale. In 1970–71 Goehr worked at Southampton University; in 1971 he was appointed West Riding Professor of Music at Leeds, and in 1976 was appointed Professor of Music at Cambridge University, a post he held until 1999. Goehr's compositions include operas, symphonies, concertos, cantatas and string quartets; he is also an influential teacher and writer. Wood dedicated his Third String Quartet Op. 20 to Goehr.

Graves, Robert (1895–1985), British poet. Graves's poetry has been the inspiration for a significant series of song collections in Wood's output (1966–84); Wood also has created a substantial song cycle (2005–06) from Graves's poems.

Haas, Monique (1909–87). French pianist; her wide repertory was concentrated on modern music.

Hall, Richard, (1903–82) British composer and teacher. Taught at the Royal Manchester College of Music from 1938 to 1956; and at Dartington from 1956 to 1967.

Hamilton, Iain (1922–2000), British composer. Studied composition with William Alwyn at Royal Academy of Music. Early works achieved notable success, including Symphony No. 2 (Koussevitsky Foundation Award) and Clarinet Concerto (Royal Philharmonic Society Prize). Later music investigated serial techniques. Wood studied with Hamilton from 1956 to 1958, and dedicated his Variations for Viola Op. 1 to him.

Herbert, George (1593–1633); English poet. Lines from 'The Flower' were quoted in the score of Wood's Third String Quartet Op. 20.

Hill, Geoffrey (b. 1932), British poet. Professor of English Literature, University of Leeds (1976–80); from 1981 University Lecturer in English and Fellow of Emmanuel College, University of Cambridge. Hill's tribute to Wood's seventieth birthday, *Scenes from Comus* (2005), took its title from Wood's Op. 6; for Hill's seventieth birthday, Wood set for choir and orchestra the poet's *Tenebrae* (Op. 46).

Hindemith, Paul (1895–1963), German composer; became American citizen in 1946. Hindemith's output includes eleven operas, orchestral music and much chamber music. Certain Hindemithian influences can be found in Wood's juvenilia.

Hopkins, Gerard Manley (1844–89), British poet and Jesuit priest. Wood set Hopkins's 'At the Wedding March' for choir in 1956.

Horovitz, Joseph (b. 1926), British composer, conductor and pianist of Austrian birth (emigrated 1935); studied at Oxford, the Royal College of Music and with Nadia Boulanger. Works include the ballet *Alice in Wonderland* and light music.

Housman, A(lfred) E(dward) (1859–1936), British poet. Whilst at school, Wood set Housman's 'With Seed the Sowers Scatter'. In 1954, Wood set 'The Sun at Noon' (from *A Shropshire Lad*) in *Songs for Springtime* for chorus and piano, later orchestrating it in the 1958 version.

Howells, Herbert (1892–1983), British composer. Protégé of Stanford and Charles Wood, Howells taught at the Royal College of Music for many years. Although he rose to fame as a composer of songs, chamber music and orchestral pieces, Howells's posthumous reputation is largely founded on his significant contribution to church music.

Hughes, Ted (1930–98). British poet. In the 1960s, Wood set four of Hughes's poems: three in the song collection *The Horses* Op. 10, and 'The Hawk in the Rain' as the first of his Three Choruses Op. 7.

Joyce, James (1882–1941), Irish writer and poet. In 1966 Wood arranged text from the 'Sirens' chapter of Joyce's *Ulysses* (1922) for unaccompanied chorus (Op. 7).

Keller, Hans (1919–85), Viennese critic and teacher. Emigrated to London in 1938, became British citizen ten years later. Worked for the BBC from 1949 to 1979. Through his work at the BBC, his writings and his teaching (including at Dartington), Keller was a stimulating and provocative figure, and a significant influence on Wood's musical and intellectual development.

Kurtág, György (b. 1926), Hungarian composer. The motto theme of Wood's Serenade and Elegy Op. 42 is taken from Kurtág's *Játékok*.

Lawrence, D(avid) H(erbert) (1885–1930), British writer and poet. Between 1966 and 2001 Wood wrote five songs to his poems (Op. 14); in 1989 he set 'Bavarian Gentians' in his Cantata Op. 30.

Lee, Laurie (1914–97), British poet. In 1956, Wood set Lee's 'April Rise', to which four further songs were added in 1958–59. All five songs were orchestrated in 1986–87 (Op. 28); Wood's setting of 'April Rise' was also quoted in the Third String Quartet Op. 20. In 1982, Wood set 'Home from Abroad', and included it in his Songs Op. 25.

Lloyd Webber, William (1914–1982), British composer and organist. Wood studied with Lloyd Webber between 1954 and 1956, and dedicated his early Piano Suite (1956) to him.

Logue, Christopher (b. 1926), British poet. Wood set four of Logue's poems from *Wand and Quadrant* in his Four Logue Songs Op. 2; a setting of 'How am I Poor Tonight' dates from this time but was not completed until 1983. Wood also set seven of Logue's translations from Neruda in Song Cycle to Poems by Pablo Neruda Op. 19.

Lutosławski, Witold (1913–94), Polish composer; compositions include four symphonies. Initially influenced by folk music, Lutosławski's later works demonstrated non-serial twelve-note writing and, beginning with the orchestral *Jeux Vénitiens* (1960–61), the use of carefully-controlled aleatoric passages for textural purposes.

MacGregor, Joanne (b. 1959), British pianist. Studied at Cambridge with Wood; known for her innovative programming and championing of contemporary music. Wood wrote his Piano Concerto Op. 32 for MacGregor.

Matthews, David (b. 1943). British composer; works include five symphonies and ten string quartets. Wood wrote *Fifty Chords for David Matthews* for a concert celebrating Matthews's fiftieth birthday.

Merrick, Frank (1886–1981), British pianist and composer. An advocate of contemporary music of his day (including Debussy, Prokofiev, Bax, Ireland and Field), Merrick taught at the Royal Manchester College of Music from 1911 to 1929. Taught piano to Wood's mother.

Messiaen, Olivier (1908–92), French composer, organist and teacher. Messiaen's compositions include much piano and organ music, the *Quatuor pour la fin du temps* written whilst in a German prisoner of war camp, orchestral music (including the *Turangalîla-Symphonie*) and an opera, *Saint François d'Assise*. His music is characterized by its rich harmonic language and innovative rhythmic techniques. Organist of the Église de la Sainte-Trinité in Paris (1931–92); taught at Paris Conservatoire from 1941 to 1978 where his pupils included Boulez, Stockhausen, Goehr and Benjamin.

Milner, Anthony (1925–2002), British composer. Studied at the Royal College of Music and later with Mátyás Seiber. Writing in 1961, Wood drew attention to Milner's choral music – of which he wrote a great deal – which 'succeeded in bringing an enlightened and refreshing breath of life to the English choral tradition' (Wood, 'English Contemporary Music', p. 168). Wood studied with Milner in 1958.

Milton, John (1608–74), English poet. Wood's *Scenes from Comus* Op. 6 was based on extracts from Milton's *A Masque Presented at Ludlow Castle, 1634* [*Comus*].

Muir, Edwin (1887–1959), British poet born in Orkney. Wood set Muir's 'All We' in the Three Choruses Op. 7. Whilst Cramb Research Fellow in Composition at Glasgow University, Wood set four of Muir's poems in *The Rider Victory* Op. 11.

Musgrave, Thea (b. 1928), British composer. On leaving Edinburgh University in 1949, Musgrave studied for five years with Nadia Boulanger; in 1970 she became Guest Professor at the University of California, Santa Barbara, and from 1972 settled in the USA permanently. Her music has a strong dramatic element, not only in her ten operas, but also her instrumental music.

Neruda, Pablo (1904–73), Chilean writer and poet. In 1973–74, Wood set seven of Neruda's 'Twenty Love Poems and a Song of Despair', in Christopher Logue's translation, in his Song Cycle to Poems of Pablo Neruda Op. 19. Wood also set 'Amor' for voice and piano (1984), and included it in his Op. 37 Songs collection.

Parikian, Manoug (1920–87), British violinist of Armenian descent. Made solo debut in 1947 in Liverpool. In 1976 formed a Piano Trio with Bernard Roberts and Amaryllis Fleming for the 75th anniversary of the Wigmore Hall. Gave the first performances of numerous violin concertos including those by Crosse, Goehr and Wood's Op. 17; Wood also wrote his Piano Trio Op. 24 for the Parikian-Roberts-Fleming Trio.

Pfitzner, Hans (1869–1949), German composer best known for his opera *Palestrina*. The concluding section of Wood's Serenade and Elegy Op. 42 is based on a transcription of Pfitzner's 'Zum Abschied meiner Tochter'.

Ransom, John Crowe (1888–1974), American poet and critic. Ransom's poem 'Blue Girls' was set by Wood and included in his Op. 37 Songs collection.

Rose, Bernard (1916–96), organist, musicologist and composer. In 1939 appointed organist of The Queen's College, Oxford, becoming a university lecturer in 1955. Principal area of research English music of the 16th–18th centuries, and particularly the choral music of Tomkins.

Sandford, Jeremy (1930–2003). British writer who came to prominence through the TV drama *Cathy Come Home* (1966). Whilst at Oxford, Wood had contributed to Sandford's entertainment *Flagrant Flowers*; in 1957 Wood wrote a choral prelude for organ and a choral setting of 'Rise up, my Love' for Sandford's wedding.

Schoenberg, Arnold (1874–1951), Austrian composer and teacher; American citizen from 1941. Schoenberg's music developed from a late-Romantic style (influenced by Mahler) to a post-tonal expressionist language (such as in *Pierrot Lunaire*); later he formalized his language through the development of a twelve-note technique. His output includes operas (such as *Moses und Aron* and *Erwartung*), four string quartets, two chamber symphonies, two concertos and songs. Together with his pupils Alban Berg and Anton Webern, a member of the so-called 'Second Viennese School'.

Seiber, Mátyás (1905–60), British composer. Emigrated to Britain from Hungary in 1935. After the Second World War, he became 'the most widely known and respected teacher of composition in Britain', counting amongst his pupils Fricker, Milner and Gilbert as well as Wood. His music 'reflects both the breadth of sympathy and the insistence on craftsmanship that marked his teaching'; a particular characteristic was 'the absorption and successful synthesis of the music of Bartók and Schoenberg'. (Quotations from Hugh Wood and Mervyn Cooke, 'Mátyás Seiber', in Stanley Sadie (ed.), *The New Grove Dictionary of Music and Musicians II* (London, 2001), Vol. 23, pp. 46–7, atp. 46.) Wood studied with Seiber in 1959.

Spender, Sir Stephen (1909–95) British poet. Wood completed his setting of Spender's 'Ice' in 1973, and later included it in his Op. 25 Song collection.

Stein, Erwin (1885–1958), Viennese composer. Studied with Schoenberg 1906–10, friend of Berg and Webern. Champion of the twelve-note school, Stein emigrated to England in 1938.

Stravinsky, Igor (1882–1971), Russian composer; naturalized French (1934) and American (1945). Came to prominence with ballets for Diaghilev's Ballets Russes including *The Firebird* and *The Rite of Spring*. Later music displayed neoclassical tendencies and, from the *Canticum sacrum* of 1955, serialism. Wood's juvenilia reflects an interest in and awareness of Stravinsky's neo-classical music; Wood's mature rhythmic language and use of bloc forms owe much to Stravinsky. Wood's memorials to Stravinsky, the *Canon in memoriam Igor Stravinsky* (1971) and sections within the Variations Op. 39 evoke Stravinsky's later serial music.

Symons, Arthur (1865–1945), British poet and critic. Wood's setting of Symons's 'White Heliotrope' was included in his Op. 37 Song collection.

Thomas, Dylan (1914–53), British poet. In 1956, Wood set Thomas's 'Why East Wind Chills' for voice and string orchestra.

Thompson, Francis (1858–1907), British poet. In 1994, Wood set Thompson's 'The Kingdom of God' for unaccompanied choir (Op. 38).

Tippett, Sir Michael (1905–98). British composer whose output includes five operas, four symphonies, two oratorios, and five string quartets. President of Wardour Castle Summer School 1964–65, where he was also on the teaching staff. Tippett was a significant influence on Wood's early music.

Waller, Edmund (1606–87), English poet. Wood included his setting of Waller's 'Goe Lovely Rose' in his Op. 37 Song collection.

Webern, Anton (1883–1945). Austrian composer; pupil of Schoenberg from 1904–08. Webern's music, much of which is post-tonal or twelve-note, is characterized by its textural and timbral clarity as well as a tendency towards brevity.

Wellesz, Egon (1885–1974), Viennese composer, musicologist and teacher. Studied with Schoenberg from 1905; emigrated to England 1938. Became fellow of Lincoln College, Oxford in 1939, a lecturer in 1943 and Reader in Byzantine Music in 1947.

Welsh, Moray (b. 1947), British cellist. Welsh recorded Wood's Cello Concerto in 1978; in 2005, as part of the Cropper–Welsh–Roscoe Piano Trio, he premiered Wood's *Overture* Op. 48.

Yeats, W(illiam) B(utler) (1865–1939), Irish poet. Whilst at school, Wood set Yeats's 'Sailing to Byzantium'; he later showed this song to Bush at Dartington. In 1973, Wood wrote two unaccompanied choruses on texts by Yeats: *To a Child Dancing in the Wind* and *To a Friend Whose Work has Come to Nothing* (Op. 16 nos. 1 and 2). This latter piece was rewritten in 1989.

Yevtoshenko, Yevgeny (b. 1933), Russian poet. Wood set his 'The Blue Coat' (original English title 'Waiting') in 1975, and later included it in his Op. 25 Song collection.

Glossary

Additive Rhythms that are constructed from chains of small rhythmic units are termed additive, to differentiate them from *multiplicative* (or *divisive*) methods of rhythmic construction.

Aleatory Used to refer to passages of music that leave some aspect of the composition or performance to chance, for instance through the use of indeterminate rhythmic notation.

Appoggiatura An unprepared dissonance note that resolves by step (upwards or downwards).

Atonal See *post-tonal.*

Augmentation Rhythmic augmentation is the process of lengthening the time value of notes within a particular passage. Augmentation can be exact, in which case all of the notes are lengthened by the same proportion (for instance, doubled), or inexact. See also *diminution.*

Augmented triad A *trichord* that is built from the superimposition of two intervals of a major third (for instance, C–E–G♯). The addition of a further major third leads to an *enharmonic* return to the first pitch (C–E–G♯–B♯/C); the three equal intervals between notes of the chord is an example of a *symmetrical* division of the octave.

Auxiliary note An embellishment to a melodic line or chord that adds to the underlying harmony a note a semitone or tone (for example the addition of an A♭ or an A to a C major arpeggio or chord). Melodic auxiliary notes frequently return back to the 'harmony' note (for instance, over a C major chord, the melodic motion G–A–G).

Background The term 'background' is often used to refer to the underlying musical processes that govern the immediately perceptible musical material (the *foreground*). In Hans Keller's 'two-dimensional theory of art', the background refers to the expectations aroused by, for example, historical and biographical knowledge of a work, stylistic awareness and understanding of the genre. A given work of art (in Keller's terms, the *foreground*) will to a greater or lesser extent conform to or contradict with this background, from which meaning arises.

Bitonal The simultaneous use of two different keys or *modes.*

Black-note Black-note material is that formed from the pitches on the piano keyboard played by the black keys (C♯, D♯, F♯, G♯ and A♯ and their *enharmonic* equivalents). Twentieth-century composers such as Berg and Bartók have used chords made from these 'black notes', not necessarily in a pianistic context, contrasting them with their *white-note complement.*

Bloc A musical unit that develops independently from those around it.

Canon A contrapuntal musical technique in which one line is imitated by others that enter at regular intervals of time and pitch. Not every aspect of a line needs to be imitated: there can be canons which are imitative in terms of pitch but not rhythm (and vice versa).

Cell   See *trope*.

Chromatic   See *diatonic*.

Chromatic saturation   The consistent use of all twelve pitches of the *chromatic* scale within a given passage.

Cluster   A group of three or more consecutive notes from within a *mode*, used harmonically. For instance, the pitches C–C♯–D–E♭ form a *chromatic* cluster, C–D–E–F♯ a *whole-tone* cluster, and B–C–D–E–F–G a *diatonic* cluster (within a C major context). Composers sometimes derive melodic figures from clusters.

Coherence   See *comprehensibility*

Collection   See *set*.

Complement   The complement of a *set* of pitches consists of all the pitches not contained within that set; thus the complement of the '*white-note*' C major scale is all the '*black notes*' on the piano keyboard and the complement of one *whole-tone* scale is another whole-tone scale a semitone higher.

Compound melody   A type of melody that implies two or more contrapuntal voices.

Comprehensibility   The interrelated principles of comprehensibility and coherence are crucial to Schoenberg's theory of *form*, as evidenced by his *The Musical Idea and the Logic, Technique and Art of Its Presentation*, ed. and trans. Patricia Carpenter and Severine Neff (New York, 1995). Thus, in their commentary on this theory, Carpenter and Neff note that 'coherence' denotes 'relationships that justify connection' (p. 24) of which the most important relationship is *motivic*. In a draft of 19 June 1934, Schoenberg wrote: 'In this way, the smallest musical gestalt fulfils the laws of coherence: the motive, the greatest common denominator of all musical phenomena. Musical art, after all, consists of producing large and small images, which cohere by means of this motive, which in their individual contents likewise cohere with it, and which are assembled so that the logic of the total image is as apparent as that of its single parts and of their combination. This logic rests on the meaningful and purposeful exploitation of musical coherence' (p. 149, original emphasis). 'Comprehension' refers to the degree to which the listener can grasp the similarities generated by coherences: that is, to the extent that they can follow the development of the material. On 11 June 1937, Schoenberg noted that 'in the interests of comprehensibility it will be necessary to have the components that create coherence make their appearance with sufficient clarity' (p. 139, original emphasis).

Diatonic   Using pitches contained within major or minor scales. *Chromatic* music refers to music that draws on pitches from outside of these scales.

Diminished seventh chord   A *tetrachord* that is built from the superimposition of three intervals of a minor third (for instance, F♯–A–C–E♭). The addition of a further minor third leads to an *enharmonic* return to the first pitch (F♯–A–C–E♭–G♭/F♯); the four equal intervals between notes of the chord is an example of a *symmetrical* division of the octave.

Diminution   When applied to rhythms, this refers to the process of shortening the durations of notes in a particular passage. As with *augmentation* this can be exact (for instance, halving all of the note values) or inexact. Diminution can also refer to the embellishment of a melodic line with notes of smaller duration.

Divisive   See *multiplicative*.

Downbeat   The first beat of a bar is conventionally known as the downbeat. However, in a more abstract sense, the term can be used to refer to a musical event that has the same sense of musical release or metrical weight as a downbeat, irrespective of where it falls in the bar. See also *upbeat*.

Dyad   A melodic or harmonic unit of two different pitches.

Enharmonic   The term used to describe pitches that are notated differently, but sound the same. C♯ and D♭ are enharmonically the same note (on the piano keyboard, for instance), but are 'spelt' differently.

Extramusical   A term used to refer to the interpretation of music that takes into account factors external to the score, such as philosophical, historical, biographical, cultural or literary ideas or influences. Often contrasted with *formalism*.

Foreground   See *background*.

Form (binary, ternary)   A term used to describe the relationship between sections within a piece of music. A work in binary form consists of two large sections (AB); a work in ternary form consists of three sections, the third of which is a repeat or variant of the first (ABA).

Formalism   A style of criticism that focuses on musical techniques in themselves rather than external factors, such as historical or biographical context.

Fugue   A contrapuntal composition, or section of a composition. The defining characteristic of a fugue is that a melodic idea (the subject) appears in turn in each of the voices in imitation; the continuation of the subject is known as the 'countersubject'. In an extended fugue, passages in which there are fugal entries alternate with 'episodes' of related material.

Hexachord   Used in this study to refer to a melodic and/or harmonic unit of six different pitches.

Heterophony   A compositional technique in which a melody is presented simultaneously with a variant (usually embellished) of itself; it can also refer to the presentation of two or more statements of the same or similar lines either together or in close proximity.

Hierarchy (tonal hierarchy)   Tonal hierarchy refers to the degree of attraction of a pitch or chord to the tonic in tonal music. The unequal division in tonal music of the octave into an irregular series of tones and semitones (for instance, the major scale) and the propensity of harmonic roots to move by fourths and fifths (which also irregularly divide the octave into unequal intervals) results in certain pitches/chords being more likely to move to other pitches/chords. For instance, the dominant seventh chord of C major (G–B–D–F) is most likely, all other things being equal, to resolve onto a tonic triad. In this case, the bass will fall by a perfect fifth (G–C; the effect is the same if the bass rises by a perfect fourth), the B will rise by a semitone to a C, and the F falling by a semitone to an E (the irregular distribution of semitones in the major scale making such motion more likely). The hierarchies present within melodic and harmonic motion in this way also governed large-scale tonal structures. In the nineteenth century, certain composers enriched and/or undermined tonal hierarchies through the use of chords and progressions, often *symmetric*, that did not imply particular keys or continuations; for some composers at the start of the twentieth century, the avoidance of tonal implications (and thus tonal hierarchies) lead to *post-tonal* musical languages.

Homophony; homophonic   Homophony refers to a texture in which one part is melodic, and the other parts accompanimental (or chordal). The term has also been applied to chorale-like textures in which all the parts move with the same rhythm, though strictly speaking this is an instance of homorhythm.

Horizontal   The term horizontal is used in music to refer to the melodic (or *linear*) aspects of a composition; its converse is the *vertical* dimension, which refers to simultaneous events (for instance, chords or the momentary combination of contrapuntal voices).

Invention, two-part (three-part)   The term invention, in its broadest usage, has come to apply to a short piece or section of a work with no specified characteristics. However, the most famous inventions, Bach's fifteen two-part inventions, and his fifteen Sinfonias (later called three-part inventions due to the similarity of style with the two-part works), are characterized by the contrapuntal and often imitative development of a short *motif*. It is in this Bachian sense that the terms two- and three-part invention has been used in this study.

Inversion   (a) An interval is inverted when the top note becomes the bottom note (such as by being transposed by an octave) and vice versa. In this way, for example, a major third G–B would become a minor sixth B–G. (b) 'Harmonic inversion' applies this principle to chords of three or more notes. A 'root-position' major *triad* is one in which the bass of the triad is also the lowest note (the root; as in a C major triad C–E–G). A 'first inversion' triad is one in which the third of the chord is in the bass (E–G–C); a 'second inversion' triad has the fifth of the chord in the bass (G–C–E), which forms a characteristic interval of a perfect fourth between the bass of the chord and the tonic. (c) The 'melodic inversion' of a motif or melody inverts each ascending interval into its corresponding descending interval. For instance, the inversion of a motif that consists of a rising minor third and a falling semitone (such as A–C–B) would be a falling minor third and a rising semitone (A–F♯–G). In *serial* working, melodic inversion is one of the means to generate different row-forms from the original *series*.

Klangfarbenmelodie   A term introduced by Schoenberg to describe the use of changing instrumental timbre to enhance a melodic line.

Linear motion   Linear motion refers to the directed progression of a melodic line, be it by step (conjunct motion) or leap (disjunct motion); a series of steps and leaps can combine to create an extended line.

Melisma   A vocal setting of a single syllable to a succession of notes.

Mode   A mode is a *collection* of pitches that have a particular *intervallic* relationship with one another (and, sometimes, with a given tonic); modes are commonly represented by a particular scale but they equally imply particular melodic and/or harmonic formulations. Major and minor scales are representations of types of *diatonic* modes centred around a tonic; the *octatonic* and *whole-tone* scales are examples of non-diatonic modes.

Motif; Motivic   A motif is the shortest intelligible fragment of a theme or idea which can be used as the basis for subsequent material (through repetition, transposition and development; see *comprehensibility*). The adjective motivic refers to methods of working or thinking that focus on the manipulation of motifs for developmental or generative purposes.

Multiplicative   Multiplicative (or divisive) rhythms are those that are based on the subdivision of larger metrical units into smaller rhythmic figures. See also *additive.*

Octatonic   The octatonic scale is formed from a series of alternate major and minor seconds (e.g. D–E♭–F–F♯–G♯–A–B–C); its internal *symmetries* mean that there exist only three different versions of the scale. (These are conventionally designated as CI, CII and CIII, beginning on C♯, D and E respectively).

Ostinato   A short musical idea that is repeated continuously through a section for structural or thematic purpose.

Pentachord   A melodic or harmonic unit of five different pitches.

Post-tonal   In this study, the term post-tonal is used to refer to music that does not adhere to any system of key or *mode.*

Retrograde, Retrograde Inversion   A musical idea is retrograded when it is reversed (for instance, the retrograde of C–F–E is E–F–C); this usually applies to pitch and/or duration, but can also apply to (for instance) dynamics and timbre. In *serial* music the retrograde of the pitches of the original *series* is used to generate new row forms. The retrograde inversion of an idea is the melodic *inversion* of the retrograde.

Sequence   The exact or varied repetition of an idea at another pitch level, either higher or lower.

Series, Serial, Serialism   A pitch series is an (abstract) ordered *set* of pitches that, repeated over and over, is used as the basis for material. The ordering of the pitches is not normally altered, but the series can appear in *retrograde, retrograde inversion* and in *inversion*, and all of these forms can be transposed. Although any dimension of music (for instance, duration, timbre, dynamics) can be treated serially (as was the practice for certain composers in the latter half of the twentieth century), the term 'serialism' is most commonly used in reference to the twelve-note working of Schoenberg and his followers. (This is the case in this study.) In Schoenberg's music, the series takes the form of a *twelve-note row.*

Set   A pitch set is an abstract collection of unordered pitches that can be used to form melodic or harmonic ideas; one can also have sets relating to other musical dimensions (such as duration). Sets are considered analytically equivalent if they have the same intervallic structure: the sets {C, D, A♭} and {C, D, F♯} both contain the intervals of a tone, a major third and a *tritone* and can thus be thought of as meaningfully related. Whilst (pitch) set theory can be helpful in identifying recurring intervallic patterns within Wood's music (for instance, the 0,2,6 trichord of which the above sets are both examples), Wood does not think in terms of sets in his compositional practice.

Symmetry   A symmetrical *mode* is one in which the intervallic structure divides the octave into equal steps. For instance, the series of semitone (ST) and tone (T) steps in the *octatonic* scale gives rise to the pattern ST T ST T ST T ST T, dividing the octave into four minor thirds (a semitone plus a tone), whereas the non-symmetrical major scale can be represented as T T ST T T T ST (a fourth and a fifth). Similarly, an *augmented triad* consists of regular intervals of a major third, whereas a major triad consists of irregular intervals of a major then minor third (and then a perfect fourth to complete the octave). See also *hierarchy*.

Tessitura   The general register of a part.

Tetrachord   A melodic or harmonic unit of four different pitches.

Theme   A theme is a musical idea that, by virtue of repetition and development, assumes a significant role within the unfolding of a piece. Themes often contain one or more *motifs*.

Topic   A topic is a generalized kind of music (for instance, march, lament, fanfare, pastoral) that has, by virtue of cultural convention, accrued a particular expressive significance.

Triad   See *trichord*.

Trichord   A trichord is a melodic or harmonic unit of three different pitches. In this study, the term 'triad' refers to trichords built in thirds such as a major or minor chord (for instance, a G major triad) or an *augmented* triad.

Tritone   The interval of an augmented fourth (for instance, C–F♯) is called the *tritone* as it encompasses three *whole-tone* steps (C–D–E–F♯); the term is sometimes applied to its *enharmonic* equivalent, the diminished fifth (for instance, C–G♭).

Trope; Twelve-note trope   A trope is formed through the division of a *twelve-note row* into two or more mutually exclusive 'cells'. The pitches within these cells, and the order of the cells, can be freely permuted to create variety whilst maintaining *chromatic saturation*. This differs from 'classical' *serialism* in which the order of notes within a *series* cannot be altered.

Twelve-note row   A *series* made up of all twelve notes of the *chromatic* scale.

Upbeat   Conventionally, the beat that precedes a *downbeat*. However, upbeat figures and anacruses can last for more than one beat, characterized by rhythmic instability that generates forward momentum to the following downbeat. This principle can be extended further: entire passages can be considered as extended upbeats to what follows.

Vertical   See *horizontal*.

White-note   White-note material is that which is derived solely from the pitches on the piano keyboard played by the white keys (C, D, E, F, G, A and B). See also *black-note*.

Whole-tone   The whole-tone scale, as its name implies, consists of a series of major seconds (for instance, F–G–A–B–C♯–D♯/E♭). There are only two whole-tone *hexachords*; together, they exhaust the entire *chromatic* scale. As with the *octatonic* scale, the whole-tone scale is *symmetric*.

Bibliography

Selected Writings of Hugh Wood

Just before this book went to press, selected writings by Wood were published in *Staking Out the Territory and other Writings on Music*, ed. Christopher Wintle (London: Plumbago Books and Arts, 2007). The volume contains a number of the articles and reviews listed below, as well as a series of concert essays that are not otherwise available.

'English Contemporary Music', in Howard Hartog (ed.) *European Music in the Twentieth Century* rev. edn (London: Penguin Books, 1961), pp. 145–70.

'Hugh Wood on his own Work', *The Listener* (29 October 1970): 605.

'Beethoven', in *The Listener* (10 September 1970): 325–8.

'Stravinsky (1882–1971): A composer's memorial', *Perspectives of New Music* IX/2 (1971): 137–9.

'Tribute to Dallapiccola', *Tempo* 108 (1974): 17–18.

'Thoughts on a Modern Quartet', *Tempo* 111 (1974): 23–6.

[Review of recording of Andrew Imbie: Symphony No. 3], *Tempo* 112 (1975): 48–50.

[Review of John Foulds' Cello Sonata], *Tempo* 115 (1975): 50–51.

'Frank Bridge and the Land Without Music', *Tempo* 121 (1977): 7–11.

'Following the Row', *Times Literary Supplement* (10 June 1977).

[Contribution to Hans Keller Memorial Symposium], *Music Analysis* vol. 5/2–3 (1986): 397–401.

'A Photograph of Brahms', in Michael Musgrave (ed.), *The Cambridge Companion to Brahms* (Cambridge: Cambridge University Press, 1999), pp. 268–87.

'Intimate Letters, Overgrown Paths', *The Times Literary Supplement* (19 November 1999).

'Obituary: Iain Hamilton', *The Guardian* (3 August 2000).

'On Music of Conviction … and an Enduring Friendship', in Alison Latham (ed.), *Sing, Ariel: Essays and Thoughts for Alexander Goehr's Seventieth Birthday* (Aldershot: Ashgate, 2003), pp. 327–30.

with Mervyn Cooke, 'Mátyás Seiber', in Stanley Sadie (ed.), *The New Grove Dictionary of Music and Musicians II* (London, 2001), Vol. 23, pp. 46–7.

Writings of Others

[Anon.], *The Times* (13 July 1959).

[Anon.], 'Lively Young Composers', *The Times* (27 February 1963).

[Anon.], 'Climax let Down by the Dance', *The Times* (13 April 1967).

[Anon.], 'Quintet is Brief but Vital', *The Times* (12 July 1967).

Anderson, Martin, [Article about Wood], *The Stand* 172 Vol. 3(4) & 4(1) (2002): 25–6.

Benjamin, George, *George Benjamin* (London: Faber Paperback Original, 1997).

Black, Leo, 'The Music of Hugh Wood', *Musical Times* vol. cxv (1974): 115–17.

———, 'Hugh Wood', in Lewis Foreman (ed.), *British Music Now: A Guide to the Work of Younger Composers* (London: Elek, 1975), pp. 53–9.

Brown, Geoff, 'Thorns on the Lark', *The Times* (10 February 1999).

Bye, Anthony, [Review of UKCD 2043], *Tempo* 178 (1991): 52–3.

Clarke, David, *The Music and Thought of Michael Tippett: Modern Times and Metaphysics* (Cambridge: Cambridge University Press, 2001).

Cross, Jonathan, *Harrison Birtwistle*: *Man, Mind, Music* (London: Faber and Faber, 2000).

DeVoto, Mark, 'Berg the Composer of Songs', in Douglas Jarman (ed.), *The Berg Companion* (Basingstoke and London: Macmillan, 1989), pp. 35–66.

———, 'Alban Berg and Creeping Chromaticism', in David Gable and Robert Morgan (eds), *Alban Berg: Historical and Analytical Perspectives* (Oxford: Clarendon Press, 1991), pp. 57–78.

Doran, Mark (ed.), 'Hans Keller in Interview with Anton Weinberg', *Tempo* 195 (1996): 6–13.

Driver, Paul, 'Uncool, Britannia', *Sunday Times* (20 September 1998).

———, 'On Record', *Sunday Times* (21 October 2001).

Dunnett, Roderic, 'Sir Peter Maxwell Davies: On Her Majesty's Service', *The Independent* (15 March 2004).

Evans, Peter, [Wood's Variations for Viola], *Music and Letters* 42 (1961): 190–91.

Fanning, David, 'Such Distant Memories', *The Independent* (6 March 1993).

Forte, Allen, *The Atonal Music of Anton Webern* (New Haven, 1998).

Fried, Erich, *Love Poems*, trans. Stuart Hood (New York and London: Calder Publications, 1991).

Glock, William, *Notes in Advance – an Autobiography in Music* (Oxford: Oxford University Press, 1991).

Goehr, Alexander, *Finding the Key: Selected Writings of Alexander Goehr*, ed. D. Puffett (London and Boston: Faber and Faber, 1998).

———, 'What's Left to be Done?', *Musical Times* vol. 40, no. 1867 (1999): 19–28.

Goehr, Alexander, in conversation with Julian Anderson, 'The Way to the New', in Alison Latham (ed.), *Sing, Ariel: Essays and Thoughts for Alexander Goehr's Seventieth Birthday* (Aldershot: Ashgate, 2003), pp. 33–41.

Graves, Robert, *Collected Poems 1965* (London: Cassell and Company, 1965).

———, *Robert Graves' Poems About Love* (London: Cassell and Company, 1969).

Hatten., Robert S., *Musical Meaning in Beethoven: Markedness, Correlation, and Interpretation* (Bloomington: Indiana University Press, 1994).

———, *Interpreting Musical Gestures, Topics, and Tropes: Mozart, Beethoven, Schubert* (Bloomington: Indiana University Press, 2004).

Hill, Geoffrey, *Scenes from Comus* (London: Penguin, 2005).

Howes, Frank, *The English Musical Renaissance* (London: Secker & Warburg, 1966).

Johnson, Robert Sherlaw, *Messiaen* (Berkeley and Los Angeles: University of California Press, 1975).

Keller, Hans, *Hans Keller: Essays on Music*, ed. Christopher Wintle (Cambridge: Cambridge University Press, 1994).

Kemp, Ian, *Tippett: the Composer and his Music* (Oxford: Oxford University Press, 1987).

Kennedy, Michael, [Hugh Wood: Chester Music promotional brochure], 1991.

————, 'Classical CDs', *Sunday Telegraph* (28 October 2001).

Kenyon, Nicholas, 'Scourge of the Nigel Tendency', *The Observer* (8 September 1991).

Kurowski, Andrew, 'Sea, Sun and Shadow', *The Listener* (16 August 1984): 30–31.

Lamb, Andrew, 'Quadrille', in Stanley Sadie (ed.), *The New Grove Dictionary of Music and Musicians II* (London: MacMillan, 1991) vol. 20, pp. 653–4.

Lansky, Paul and Perle, George, 'Twelve-note composition' in Stanley Sadie (ed.), *The New Grove Dictionary of Music and Musicians II* (London: Macmillan, 2001) vol. 26, pp. 1–11.

Larner, Gerald, 'Reviews', *The Times* (20 July 1999).

London, Justin, 'Rhythm', in Stanley Sadie (ed.), *The New Grove Dictionary of Music and Musicians II* (London: Macmillan, 2001) vol. 21, pp. 277–309.

MacDonald, Malcolm, [Review of NMC D070] *Tempo* 221 (2002): 61–4.

MacGregor, Joanne, [Article on Wood], in *Goehrfest Commemorative Programme* (Cambridge: Cambridge University Press, 1999), pp. 19–20.

Mann, William, 'Lindsay Quartet', *The Times* (2 June 1978).

————, 'Wood Violin Concerto', *The Times* (20 September 1972).

Messiaen, Olivier, *Technique of my Musical Language*, trans. John Satterfield (Paris: Leduc, 1956).

Meyer, Leonard B., *Style and Music: Theory, History, and Ideology* (Chicago and London: The University of Chicago Press, 1989).

Neruda, Pablo, *Extravagaria* trans. Alastair Reid (Jonathan Cape Ltd., 1972).

Northcott, Bayan, 'Hugh Wood's String Quartet No. 3', *Tempo* 126 (1978): 53.

Parks, Richard S., *The Music of Claude Debussy* (New Haven: Yale University Press, 1989).

Payne, Anthony, 'Hugh Wood', in Stanley Sadie (ed.), *The New Grove Dictionary of Music and Musicians* (London: Macmillan, 1980) vol. 20, pp. 518–19.

Pettitt, Stephen, 'Thrills from the Punch and Judy man', *The Times* (26 June 1993).

Reich, Willi, *The Life and Work of Alban Berg*, trans. Cornelius Cardew (London: Thames and Hudson, 1965).

Rosen, Charles, *Schoenberg* (London: Fontana/Collins, 1976).

Salter, Lionel, [English translation of the libretto to Mozart, *The Magic Flute*, Archiv Produktion 449 166–2] (1996).

Samson, Jim, 'Instrumental Music II', in Stephen Banfield (ed.), *The Blackwell History of Music in Britain vol. 6: The Twentieth Century* (Oxford: Blackwell, 1995), pp. 278–342.

Schoenberg, Arnold, *Fundamentals of Music Composition*, ed. Gerald Strand (London: Faber and Faber, 1967).

————, *Style and Idea: Selected Writings*, ed. Leonard Stein and trans. Leo Black (London and Boston: Faber and Faber, 1975).

————, *Theory of Harmony*, trans. Roy E. Carter (London: Faber and Faber, 1978).

————, *The Musical Idea and the Logic, Technique and Art of Its Presentation*, ed. and trans. Patricia Carpenter and Severine Neff (New York: Columbia University Press, 1995).

Seymour Smith, Martin, 'Robert Graves' in James Vinson and D. L. Kirkpatrick (eds) *Contemporary Poets* 4th edn (London and Chicago: St James Press, 1985), pp. 317–21.

Simms, Bryan R., *The Atonal Music of Arnold Schoenberg 1908–1923* (Oxford and New York: Oxford University Press, 2000).

Snipes, Katherine, *Robert Graves* (New York: Frederick Ungar Publishing, 1979).

Stein, Erwin, *Orpheus in New Guises* (London: Rockliff, 1953).

Thurlow, Jeremy, 'Hugh Wood', in Stanley Sadie (ed.), *The New Grove Dictionary of Music and Musicians II* (London: Macmillan 2001) vol. 27, pp. 548–50.

van den Toorn, Pieter, *The Music of Igor Stravinsky* (New Haven: Yale University Press, 1983).

Walsh, Stephen, [Sleeve notes to Collins Classics 20072], (1993).

Webern, Anton, *The Path to the New Music*, ed. Willi Reich, trans. Leo Black (Bryn Mawr: Theodore Presser, 1963).

Weissman, John S., [Wood's Variations for Viola], *The Music Review* vol. XXIII (1962): 337.

White, Michael, 'In from the cold', *The Independent* (8 September 1991).

Wigmore, Richard, 'Hugh Wood', *Cambridge Alumni Magazine* (Lent Term 1999): 40–41.

Wilson, Elizabeth, *Jacqueline du Pré* (London: Faber and Faber, 1998).

Wright, David, 'London (i): Musical Life since 1945', in Stanley Sadie (ed.), *The New Grove Dictionary of Music and Musicians II* (London, 2001) vol. 15, pp. 148–54.

Index of Works

The main discussions of each piece are indicated in bold type. Numbers in brackets refer to the Generic and Chronological lists of works.

General Index

Adams, John, 185
Adès, Thomas, 17
Aeolian Quartet, 76, 246
Alldis, John, 90, 247
    John Alldis Choir, 90, 233, 247
Amici String Quartet, 237
Anderson, Lorna, 236
Andrews, H.K., 4, 247
Armstrong, Sir Thomas, 4, 247
Aronwitz, Cecil, 238
Atherton, David, 101, 245, 246
Auden, W.H., 8, 247

Bach, Johann Sebastian, 3, 8, 20, 21, 35, 105
    B Minor Mass, 3
    Inventions, 6, 258
Bamert, Matthias, 232
Bartók, Bela, 2, 4, 6, 10, 12, 19, 33, 34, 44,
    51, 183, 247, 253, 255
    Bluebeard's Castle, 247
    String Quartet No. 4, 210
BBC see British Broadcasting Corporation
Beethoven, Ludwig van, 14, 20, 21, 35, 49,
    54,
    32 Variations in C minor (WoO 80), 16
    late works, 15, 59, 60, 77
    'Rasumovsky' Quartets (Op. 59), 2
    Piano Concerto No. 4 (Op. 58), 178
    Piano Sonata (Op. 81a), 214
    Piano Sonata (Op. 106), 169
    String Quartet in F minor (Op. 95), 131
    Symphony No. 1 (Op. 21), 136
    Symphony No. 9 (Op. 125), 74, 147
Benjamin, George, 45, 252
Bennett, William, 238
Berg, Alban, 2, 12, 17–8, 20, 23, 37, 44, 54,
    56, 64, 69, 247, 253, 255
    Altenberg Lieder, 18, 83
    Lulu, 247
    Lyric Suite, 5, 47, 247
    Violin Concerto, 22, 47, 247

'Why is Schoenberg's Music so Difficult
    to Understand'?, 17–8
    Wozzeck, 247
Berkeley, Michael, 203, 214, 247
Berlioz, Hector, 144
    Symphonie Fantastique, 144
Birmingham Contemporary Music Group,
    177
Birtwistle, Sir Harrison, 1, 69, 247, 248, 249
    Nomos, 87
    Refrains and Choruses, 2
Bizet, Georges, 224
    Carmen, 224
Black, Leo, 5, 56, 122, 247
    on Hugh Wood's music, 8, 39, 49–50,
    51, 89, 131, 226
Boulanger, Nadia, 250, 252
Boulez, Pierre, 101, 252
Bowen, Kenneth, 230
Bradshaw, Susan, 97, 235, 238
Brahms, Johannes, 20, 21, 35, 49, 96, 136,
    147, 204, 225
    Alto Rhapsody, 2
    Horn Trio, 3
    Piano Concerto No. 1, 204
    Symphony No. 1, 147
    Symphony No. 4, 147
    Violin Concerto, 4, 181
Bridge, Frank, xiii, 18–9, 21
    String Quartet No. 4, 18
British Broadcasting Corporation (BBC),
    69, 76, 80, 89, 112, 117, 166, 177,
    178, 188, 204, 221, 229, 230, 231,
    232, 236, 237, 238, 239, 240, 247,
    249, 251
    BBC Henry Wood Promenade Concerts,
    xi, 23, 70, 80, 87, 89, 101, 177, 178,
    229, 230, 231, 232
    Last Night of the Proms, xi, 177
    BBC Philharmonic, xi
    BBC Radio 3, 54, 169, 177, 237, 239